Introduction to
International Relations

Introduction to
International
Relations

Theories and approaches

Robert Jackson • Georg Sørensen

UNIVERSITY PRESS

OXFORD
UNIVERSITY PRESS

Great Clarendon Street, Oxford OX2 6DP

Oxford University Press is a department of the University of Oxford.
It furthers the University's objective of excellence in research, scholarship,
and education by publishing worldwide in

Oxford New York

Auckland Bangkok Buenos Aires Cape Town Chennai
Dar es Salaam Delhi Hong Kong Istanbul Karachi Kolkata
Kuala Lumpur Madrid Melbourne Mexico City Mumbai Nairobi
São Paulo Shanghai Taipei Tokyo Toronto

Oxford is a registered trade mark of Oxford University Press
in the UK and in certain other countries

Published in the United States
by Oxford University Press Inc., New York

British Library Cataloguing in Publication Data
Data available

Library of Congress Cataloging in Publication Data
Data available

ISBN 0–19–926058–3

10 9 8 7 6 5 4 3 2 1

Typeset in Meridien and Congress Sans
by RefineCatch Limited, Bungay, Suffolk
Printed in Great Britain by
T.J. International Ltd, Padstow, Cornwall

To our students

Acknowledgements

The idea for this book took shape in early 1995. We wanted to write a comprehensive introduction to the most important theories, concepts, and debates within the discipline of International Relations. This is what we firmly believe that we have done. We can thus make no excuses for the text; it has come out according to plan. The experience of working on it has even been both delightful and rewarding; we have been able to draw on our individual areas of expertise in a productive and fruitful way. And we have thoroughly enjoyed each other's company in the process.

This second revised and expanded edition of the book has benefited from very helpful comments made by readers of the first edition. Some comments were sent to us directly, some were solicited by our publisher. We were encouraged to stay with the basic aim and format of the book: a succinct and readable introduction to the major IR-theories and approaches. This second edition retains those features. We also received suggestions for expanded coverage. This second edition has a new chapter on post-positivist approaches with a more in-depth treatment of constructivism. There is also a greatly expanded discussion of theories and debates in International Political Economy. The final chapter on 'new issues' has been further developed. The entire text is brought up to date and there are additional study questions and more suggestions for further reading. A website (at www.oup.com) now supports the text with further study questions, useful web addresses, and suggestions for case studies relating to the book.

We are grateful for support and encouragement from a large number of people. Tim Barton of Oxford University Press warmly supported the project from the very start. Several anonymous readers made helpful suggestions for revisions and clarifications. Colleagues in Vancouver and Aarhus provided advice or encouragement: Will Bain, Kenneth Glarbo, Hans Henrik Holm, Kal Holsti, Peter Viggo Jakobsen, Brian Job, Knud Erik Jørgensen, Anne Mette Kjær, Tonny Brems Knudsen, Mehdi Mozaffari, Liselotte Odgaard, Jørgen Dige Pedersen, Thomas Pedersen, Nikolaj Petersen, Jennifer Jackson Preece, Mette Skak, Sasson Sofer, Mark Zacher, and Clemens Stubbe Østergaard.

Svend and Kirsten Stidsen provided the perfect environment for the final work on the manuscript at Løgumkloster Refugium. Jonna Kjær worked hard on a very large number of manuscript revisions and set up the pretty boxes in the text while also supporting the communication between Aarhus and Vancouver and, in the final stage, between Aarhus, Vancouver, and Oxford: thank you Jonna! Angela Griffin took good care of the manuscript as OUP Assistant Editor. Sarah Barrett was a very efficient copy-editor.

We owe special thanks to those readers who provided us with useful comments on the first edition, including the six anonymous referees. We have tried to deal with their many excellent suggestions for improvement without sacrificing the existing qualities of the book which most of them commented on very favourably. We are confident that both instructors and students will find that this second expanded edition has managed to achieve that goal.

Sue Dempsey was a great help as commissioning editor for this second edition. Jonna Kjær again handled the paperwork with her usual efficiency and punctuality. Eva Dyrberg Pedersen did an excellent job collecting and systematizing the links for the book's web site. Finally, we owe special thanks to our wives and children for their support in our continuing endeavour to produce an IR textbook that can communicate to readers not only in North America or in Europe but everywhere that international relations is taught and studied as an academic discipline.

Risskov, Denmark
June 2002

Contents

Detailed Contents

About This Book

Today virtually the entire population of the world lives within the borders of those separate territorial communities we call states—about six billion people are citizens or subjects of one state or another. For more than half a billion people living in the developed countries of Western Europe, North America, Australia, New Zealand, and Japan, basic security and welfare are often taken more or less for granted, because it is guaranteed and sometimes directly provided by the state. But for several billions of people who live in the developing countries of Asia, Africa, and the former Soviet Union, basic security and welfare is not something that can be taken for granted. Protection, policing, law enforcement, and other civil conditions of minimal safety for all cannot be guaranteed. For many people it is a daily challenge to provide adequate food, clean water, housing, and similar socioeconomic necessities. The academic subject of international relations (IR) seeks to understand how people are provided, or not provided, with the basic values of security, freedom, order, justice, and welfare.

What is in the Book?

First and foremost this book is an introduction to the academic *discipline* of IR. What is a 'discipline'? It is a branch of knowledge, aimed at the systematic understanding of a subject. As is often the case in the social sciences, in IR there is no one best way to master the subject. Instead, what we have are several significant theories and theoretical traditions: Realism, Liberalism, International Society, International Political Economy. They interact and overlap in interesting and important ways that we investigate in the chapters which follow. However, each one explores the subject of IR in its own distinctive way. Realism, for example, is focused on the basic value of security, because according to realists war is always a possibility in a system of sovereign states. Liberals, on the other hand, argue that international relations can be cooperative rather than conflictual. That belief is based on the idea that the modern, liberal state can bring progress and opportunities to the greatest number of people around the world.

All the most important theories and theoretical traditions of IR are presented in the chapters which follow. There is no need to give a detailed account of each chapter here. But a brief consumer guide may be helpful. What is it that this book has to offer? The main elements can be summarized as follows:

- The book provides an introduction to the analytical tools that the discipline has on its shelves: IR theories. Some theories have proved to be of more enduring importance than others. In the central chapters of this book we focus on those theories, which we call 'established' or 'main theoretical' traditions. They are Realism, Liberalism, and International Society. We also introduce the three most important theories in the field of International Political Economy (IPE). Finally, we review the leading 'post-positivist' theories which have gained prominence in recent years.

- Theories are presented faithfully, emphasizing their strong sides, and critically, focusing on their weaknesses and limitations. The main points of contention between theories are thoroughly discussed and it is made clear how the theoretical debates link up with each other.

- The book places particular emphasis on the relationship between 'IR theory' or academic knowledge of international relations and 'IR practice' or the real world happenings and conduct of world politics. Important theoretical points are accompanied by empirical illustrations which demonstrate the connection between theory and actual events, both historical and contemporary.

- We also carefully explain how a particular theory organizes and sharpens our view of the world. Ideas and theories matter. We often assume that the sword is mightier than the pen, but it is really the pen, our guiding theories and ideas, which shape the ways in which swords are put to use. Theories matter, not merely for their own sake, but also significantly as a guide to practice.

Learning Aids

To facilitate a rapid entry into the discipline of IR, the chapters have the following features:

- Summary: each chapter begins with a brief summary of the main points.

- Key Points: each chapter ends with a list of the key points brought forward in the chapter.

- Study Questions: each chapter provides a number of study questions that can be used for discussions or as topics for essays.

- Guide to Further Reading: each chapter provides a brief guide to further reading on the subject of the chapter.

The book thus enables students to gain knowledge of IR as an evolving academic discipline rather than merely study current events. The focus throughout is on the most significant theories and theorists. In that way, it is our hope and belief that students who read our book will acquire a basic knowledge of the core of the discipline of IR. While our book is written with introductory level courses in mind, it contains materials and debates that should prove helpful for higher level courses as well. The basic and overriding aim is to make it possible for students to move swiftly from introductory to higher levels of study.

. . . .

For additional material and resources see the companion web site at:
www.oup.co.uk/best.textbooks/politics/jacksonsorensen2e/

List of Abbreviations

EBRD	European Bank for Reconstruction and Development
G-8	Group of Eight (the United States, Canada, Britain, Germany, France, Italy, Russia, and Japan)
GATT	General Agreement on Tariffs and Trade
IGO	intergovernmental organization
IMF	International Monetary Fund
IPE	international political economy
IR	international relations
NATO	North Atlantic Treaty Organization
NGO	non-governmental organization
OECD	Organization for Economic Cooperation and Development
OPEC	Organization of Petroleum Exporting Countries
OSCE	Organization on Security Cooperation in Europe
TNC	transnational corporation
UN	United Nations
UNDP	United Nations Development Programme
US	United States
WTO	World Trade Organization

1 Why Study IR?

SUMMARY

This chapter introduces the historical and social basis of international relations or IR. The aim of the chapter is to emphasize the practical reality of international relations in our everyday lives and to connect that practical reality with the academic study of international relations. The chapter makes that connection by focusing on the core historical subject-matter of IR: modern sovereign states and the international relations of the state system. Three main topics are discussed: the significance of international relations in everyday life and the main values that states exist to foster, the historical evolution of the state system and world economy in brief outline, and the changing contemporary world of states.

....

International Relations in Everyday Life

IR is the shorthand name for the academic subject of international relations. The main reason why we should study IR is the fact that the entire population of the world is divided into separate territorial political communities, or independent states, which profoundly affect the way people live. Together those states form an international system that is global in extent. At the present time there are almost 200 independent states. Everybody on earth with very few exceptions not only lives in one of those countries but is also a citizen of one of them and very rarely of more than one. So virtually every man, woman, and child on earth is connected to a particular state, and via that state to the state system which affects their lives in important ways that they may not be fully aware of.

States are independent of each other, at least legally: they have sovereignty. But that does not mean they are isolated or insulated from each other. On the contrary, they adjoin each other and affect each other and must therefore somehow find ways to coexist and to deal with each other. They are usually embedded in international markets which affect the policies of their governments and the wealth and welfare of their citizens. That requires that they enter into relations with each other. Complete isolation is usually not an option. When states are isolated and are cut off from the state system, either by their own government or by foreign powers, the people usually suffer as a result. That has been the situation recently with regard to Burma, Libya, North Korea, Iraq, and Iran. The state system is a system of social relations, that is, a system of relations between groups of human beings. Like most other social systems, international relations can have certain advantages and disadvantages for the participants. IR is the study of the nature and consequences of these relations.

The state system is a distinctive way of organizing political life on earth which has deep historical roots. There have been state systems or quasi-state systems at different times and places in different parts of the world: for example, in ancient India, in ancient Greece, and in Renaissance Italy (Watson 1992). However, the subject of IR conventionally dates back to the early modern era (sixteenth and seventeenth centuries) in Europe, when sovereign states based on adjacent territories were initially established. Ever since the eighteenth century the relations between such independent states have been labeled 'international relations'. In the nineteenth and twentieth centuries the state system was expanded to encompass the entire territory of the earth. The world of states is basically a territorial world: it is a way of politically organizing the world's populated territory, a distinctive kind of territorial political organization which is based on numerous different governments that are legally independent of each other. The only large territory that is not a state is Antarctica, and it is administered by a consortium of states. Today IR is the study of the global state system from

---

Box 1.1 **Key concepts**

State sovereignty
a state's characteristic of being politically independent of all other states

State system
relations between politically organized human groupings which occupy distinctive territories, are not under any higher authority or power, and enjoy and exercise a measure of independence from each other

Five basic values of a state system
security, freedom, order, justice, and welfare

Major traditional IR approaches
realism, liberalism, International Society, and IPE

The security dilemma
states are both a source of security and a threat to security for human beings

Medieval authority
an arrangement of dispersed political authority

Modern state authority
an arrangement of centralized political authority

Hegemony
power and control exercised by a leading state over the other states

Balance of power
a doctrine and an arrangement whereby the power of one state (or group of states) is checked by the countervailing power of other states

---

various scholarly perspectives, the most important of which shall be discussed in this book.

To understand the significance of IR it is necessary to grasp what living in states basically involves. What does it imply? How important is it? How should we think about it? This book is centrally concerned with these questions and especially with the last one. The chapters which follow deal with various answers to that fundamental question. This chapter examines the core historical subject-matter of IR: the evolution of the state system and the changing contemporary world of states.

To begin to respond to these questions it may be helpful to examine our everyday life as citizens of particular states to see what we generally expect from it. There are at least five basic social values that states are usually expected to uphold: security, freedom, order, justice and welfare. These are social values that are so fundamental to human well-being that they must be protected or ensured in some way. That could be by social organizations other than the state: e.g. by family, clan, ethnic or religious organizations. In the modern era, however, the state has usually been involved as the leading institution in that regard: it is expected to insure these basic values. For example, people generally assume that the state should and will underwrite the value of security, which involves the protection of citizens from internal and external threat. That is a fundamental concern or interest of states. However, the very existence of independent states affects the value of security: we live in a world of many states, almost all of which are armed at least to some degree. Thus states can both defend and threaten peoples' security, and that paradox of the state system is usually referred to as the 'security dilemma'. In other words, just like any other human organization, states present problems as well as provide solutions.

Most states are likely to be friendly, non-threatening, and peace-loving. But a few states may be hostile and aggressive and there is no world government to constrain them. That poses a basic and age-old problem of state systems: national security. To deal with that problem most states possess armed forces. Military power is usually considered a necessity so that states can coexist and deal with each other without being intimidated or subjugated. Unarmed states are extremely rare in the history of the state system. That is a basic fact of the state system that we should never lose sight of. Many states also enter into alliances with other states to increase their national security. To ensure that no great power succeeds in achieving a hegemonic position of overall domination, based on intimidation, coercion, or the outright use of force, it is also necessary to construct and maintain a balance of military power. Security is obviously one of the most fundamental values of international relations. That approach to the study of world politics is typical of realist theories of IR (Morgenthau 1960). It operates on the assumption that relations of states can be best characterized as a world in which armed states are competing rivals and periodically go to war with each other.

The second basic value that states are usually expected to uphold is freedom, both personal freedom and national freedom or independence. A fundamental reason for having states and putting up with the burdens that governments place on citizens, such as tax burdens or obligations of military service, is the condition of national freedom or independence which states exist to foster. We cannot be free unless our country is free too: that was made very clear to millions of Czech, Polish, Danish, Norwegian, Belgian, and Dutch citizens as well as citizens of other countries that were invaded and occupied by Nazi Germany during the Second World War. Even if our country is free we may still not be free personally, but at least then the problem of our freedom is in our own hands. War threatens and sometimes destroys freedom. Peace fosters freedom. Peace also makes progressive international change possible, that is, the creation of a better world. Peace and progressive change are obviously among the most fundamental values of international relations. That approach to the study of world politics is typical of liberal theories of IR (Claude 1971). It operates on the assumption that international relations can be best characterized as a world in which states cooperate with each other to maintain peace and freedom and to pursue progressive change.

The third and fourth basic values that states are usually expected to uphold are order and justice. States have a common interest in establishing and maintaining international order so that they can coexist and interact on a basis of stability, certainty, and predictability. To that end, states are expected to uphold international law: to keep their treaty commitments and to observe the rules, conventions, and customs of the international legal order. They are also expected to follow accepted practices of diplomacy and to support international organizations. International law, diplomatic relations, and international organizations can only exist and operate successfully if these expectations are generally met by most states most of the time. States are also expected to uphold human rights. Today there is an elaborate international legal framework of human rights—civil, political, social, and economic—which has been developed since the end of the Second World War. Order and justice obviously are among the most fundamental values of international relations. That approach to the study of world politics is typical of International Society theories of IR (Bull 1995). It operates on the assumption that international relations can be best characterized as a world in which states are socially responsible actors and have a common interest in preserving international order and promoting international justice.

The final basic value that states are usually expected to uphold is the population's socioeconomic wealth and welfare. People expect their government to adopt appropriate policies to encourage high employment, low inflation, steady investment, the uninterrupted flow of trade and commerce, and so forth. Because national economies are rarely isolated from each other, most people also expect that the state will respond to the international economic environment in such a way as to enhance or at least defend and maintain the national standard of living.

States nowadays try to frame and implement economic policies that can maintain the stability of the international economy upon which they are all increasingly dependent. That usually involves economic policies that can deal adequately with international markets, with the economic policies of other states, with foreign investment, with foreign exchange rates, with international trade, with international transportation and communications, and with other international economic relations that affect national wealth and welfare. Economic interdependence, meaning a high degree of mutual economic dependence among countries, is a striking feature of the contemporary state system. Some people consider that to be a good thing because it may increase overall freedom and wealth by expanding the global marketplace and thereby increasing participation, specialization, efficiency, and productivity. Other people consider it to be a bad thing because it may promote overall inequality by allowing rich and powerful countries, or countries with financial or technological advantages, to dominate poor and weak countries that lack those advantages. But either way, wealth and welfare obviously are among the most fundamental values of international relations. That approach to the study of world politics is typical of IPE (international political economy) theories of IR (Gilpin 1987). It operates on the assumption that international relations can be best characterized as fundamentally a socioeconomic world and not merely a political and military world.

Box 1.2 IR values and theories

FOCUS	THEORIES
• **Security** power politics, conflict, and war	• **Realism**
• **Freedom** cooperation, peace, and progress	• **Liberalism**
• **Order and justice** shared interests, rules, and institutions	• **International Society**
• **Welfare** wealth, poverty, equality	• **IPE theories**

Most people usually take these basic values (security; freedom; order and justice; welfare) for granted. They only become aware of them when something goes wrong—for example, during a war or a depression, when things begin to get beyond the control of individual states. On those learning occasions people wake up to the larger circumstances of their lives which in normal times are a silent or invisible background. At those moments they are likely to become sharply aware of what they take for granted, and of how important these values really are in their everyday lives. We become aware of national security when a foreign power rattles its saber or engages in hostile actions against our country or one of our allies. We become aware of national independence and our freedom as citizens when peace is no longer guaranteed. We become aware of international order and justice when some states, especially major powers, abuse, exploit, denounce, or disregard international law or trample on human rights. We become aware of national welfare and our own personal socioeconomic well-being when foreign countries or international investors use their economic clout to jeopardize our standard of living.

There were significant moments of heightened awareness of these major values during the twentieth century. The First World War made it dreadfully clear to most people just how devastatingly destructive of lives and living conditions modern mechanized warfare between major powers can be, and just how important it is to reduce the risk of great power war. That recognition led to the first major developments of IR thought which tried to find effective legal institutions— e.g. the Covenant of the League of Nations—to prevent great-power war. The Great Depression brought home to many people around the world how their economic livelihood could be adversely affected, in some cases destroyed, by market conditions not only at home but also in other countries. The Second World War not only underlined the reality of the dangers of great-power war but also revealed how important it is to prevent any great power from getting out of control and how unwise it is to pursue a policy of appeasement— which was adopted by Britain and France in regard to Nazi Germany just prior to the war with disastrous consequences for everybody, including the German people.

There also were moments of heightened awareness of the fundamental importance of these values after the Second World War. The Cuban missile crisis of 1962 brought home to many people the dangers of nuclear war. The anti-colonial movements in Asia and Africa of the 1950s and 1960s and the secessionist movements in the former Soviet Union and former Yugoslavia at the end of the Cold War made it clear how important self-determination and political independence continue to be. The global inflation of the 1970s and early 1980s caused by a sudden dramatic increase in oil prices by the OPEC cartel of oil-exporting countries was a reminder of how the interconnectedness of the global economy can be a threat to national and personal welfare anywhere in the world. For example, the oil shock of the 1970s made it abundantly clear to countless American, European, and Japanese motorists—among others—that economic policies of Middle-East and other major oil producing countries could suddenly raise the price of gas or petrol at the pump and lower their standard of living. The Gulf War (1990–1) and the conflicts in the Balkans, particularly Bosnia (1992–5) and Kosovo (1999) were a reminder of the importance of international order and respect for human rights. The attacks on New York and Washington (2001) awakened many people in the United States and elsewhere to the dangers of international terrorism.

For a long time there has been a basic assumption that life inside properly organized and well managed states is better than life outside states or without states at all. For example, the Jews spent more than half a century trying to get a state of their own in which they could be secure: Israel. As long as states and the state system manage to maintain the foregoing core values, that assumption holds. That has generally been the case for developed countries, especially the states of Western Europe, North America, Japan, Australia, New Zealand, and some others. That gives rise to more conventional IR theories which regard the state system as a valuable core institution of modern life. The traditional IR theories discussed in this book tend to adopt that positive view. They recognize the significance of these basic values even if they disagree about which ones are most important—e.g. realists emphasize the importance of security and order, liberals emphasize freedom and justice, and IPE scholars emphasize economic equality and welfare.

But if states are not successful in that regard the state system can easily be understood in the opposite light: not as upholding basic social conditions and values, but rather as undermining them. That is the case with regard to many states in the Third World, especially sub-Saharan Africa. It is also the case with regard to some states which emerged as a result of the breakup of the Soviet Union and Yugoslavia at the end of the Cold War. Many of these states more or less fail to provide or protect even to a minimal standard at least some of the five basic values discussed above. More than a few states fail to ensure any of them. The plight of countless men, women, and children in those countries puts into question the credibility and perhaps even the legitimacy of the state system. It promotes a corresponding assumption that the international system fosters or at least tolerates human suffering, and that the system should be changed so that people everywhere can flourish, and not just those in the developed countries of the world. That gives rise to more critical IR theories which regard the state and the state system as a less beneficial and more problematical institution. The alternative IR theories discussed later in this book tend to adopt that critical view.

Box 1.3 **Views of the state**

TRADITIONAL VIEW

- States are valuable institutions: they provide security, freedom, order, justice, welfare

- People benefit from the state system

ALTERNATIVE VIEW

- States and the state system create more problems than they solve

- The majority of the world's people suffer more than they benefit from the state system

---

To sum up thus far: states and the system of states are territory-based social organizations which exist primarily to establish, maintain, and defend basic social conditions and values, including particularly security, freedom, order, justice, and welfare. These are the main reasons for having states. Many states and certainly all developed countries uphold these conditions and values at least to minimal standards and often at a higher level. Indeed, they have been so successful in doing that for the past several centuries that the standards have steadily increased and are now higher than ever. These countries set the international standard for the entire world. But many states and most underdeveloped countries fail to meet even minimal standards, and as a consequence their presence in the contemporary state system raises serious questions not only about those states but also about the state system of which they are an important part. That has provoked a debate in IR between traditional theorists who by and large accept the existing state system and radical theorists who by and large reject it.

Brief Historical Sketch of the State System

States and the state system are such basic features of modern political life that it is easy to assume that they are permanent features: that they have always been and will always be present. That assumption is false. It is important to emphasize that the state system is a historical institution. It is not ordained by God or determined by Nature. It has been fashioned by certain people at a certain time: it is a social organization. Like all social organizations, the state system has advantages and disadvantages which change over time. There is nothing about the state system that is necessary to human existence, even though there may be many things about it that are advantageous to high standards of living.

People have not always lived in sovereign states. For most of human history people have organized their political lives in different ways, the most common being that of political empire such as the Roman empire. In the future the world may not be organized into a state system either. People may eventually give up on sovereign statehood and abandon the institution. People throughout history have abandoned many other ways of organizing their political lives, including city-states, feudalism, and colonialism, to mention a few. It is not unreasonable to suppose that a form of global political organization that is better or more advanced than states and the state system will eventually be adopted. Some IR scholars discussed in later chapters believe that such an international transformation, connected with growing interdependence among states (i.e. globalization), is already well under way. But the state system has been a central institution of world politics for a very long time, and still remains so. Even though world politics is in flux, in the past states and the state system have always managed to adapt to significant historical change. But nobody can be sure that that will continue to be the case in the future. This issue of present and future international change is discussed later in the chapter.

There were no clearly recognizable sovereign states before the sixteenth century, when they first began to be instituted in Western Europe. But for the past three or four centuries, states and the system of states have structured the political lives of an ever-increasing number of people around the world. They have become universally popular. Today the system is global in extent. The era of the sovereign state coincides with the modern age of expanding power, prosperity, knowledge, science, technology, literacy, urbanization, citizenship, freedom, equality, rights, etc. This could be a coincidence, but that is not very likely when we remember how important states and the state system have been in shaping the five fundamental human values discussed above. Of course, it is difficult to say whether states were the effect or the cause of modern life, and whether they will have any place in a postmodern age. Those questions must be set aside for later.

However, we do know that the state system and modernity are closely related historically. In fact, they are completely coexistent: the system of adjoining territorial states arose in Europe at the start of the modern era. And the state system has been a central if not a defining feature of modernity ever since. Although the sovereign state emerged in Europe, it extended to North America in the late eighteenth century and to South America in the early nineteenth century. As modernity spread around the world the state system spread with it. Only slowly did it expand to cover the entire globe. Sub-Saharan Africa, for example, remained isolated from the expanding Western state system until the late nineteenth century, and it only became an independent regional state system after the middle of the twentieth century. Whether the end of modernity will also bring the end of the state system is an important question that must be left for later in this book.

Of course, there is evidence of political systems that resembled sovereign states long before the modern age. They obviously had relations of some sort with each other. The historical origin of international relations in that more general sense lies deep in history and can only be a matter of speculation. But, speaking conceptually, it was a time when people began to settle down on the land and form themselves into separate territory-based political communities. The first examples of that date back more than 5,000 years.

Each political group faced the inescapable problem of coexisting with neighboring groups whom they could not ignore or avoid because they were right there next door. Each political grouping also had to deal with groups that were further away but were still capable of affecting them. Their geographical closeness must have come to be regarded as a zone of political proximity, if not a frontier or border of some kind. Where group contact occurred, sometimes it must have involved rivalry, disputes, threats, intimidation, intervention, invasion, conquest, and other hostile and warlike interactions. But sometimes and perhaps most of the time, it must also have involved mutual respect, cooperation, commerce, conciliation, dialogue, and similar friendly and peaceful relations. A very significant form of dialogue between autonomous political communities—diplomacy—has ancient roots. There are recorded formal agreements among ancient political communities which date as far back as 1390 BC, and records of quasi-diplomatic activity as early as 653 BC (Barber 1979: 8–9).

Here in prototype is the classical problem of IR: war and peace, conflict and cooperation. Here, too, are the different aspects of international relations emphasized by realism and liberalism.

These relations between independent political groups make up the core problem of international relations. They are built on a fundamental distinction between our collective selves and other collective selves in a territorial world of many such separate collective selves in contact with each other. Here we arrive at a preliminary definition of a 'state system': it stands for relations between politically organized human groupings which occupy distinctive territories, are not under any higher authority or power, and enjoy and exercise a measure of independence from each other. International relations are relations between such independent groups.

The first relatively clear historical manifestation of a state system is that of ancient Greece (500 BC–100 BC), then known as Hellas. It comprised a large number of mostly small city-states (Wight 1977; Watson 1992). Ancient Greece was not a nation-state the way it is today. Rather, it was a system of city-states. Athens was the largest and most famous, but there were also many other city-states, such as Sparta and Corinth. Together they formed the first state system in Western history. There were extensive and elaborate relations between the city-states of Hellas. But the ancient Greek city-states were not modern sovereign states with extensive territories. They were far smaller in population and territory than most modern states. Greek intercity relations also lacked the institution of diplomacy, and there was nothing comparable to international law and international organization. The state system of Hellas was based on a shared language and a common religion more than anything else.

The ancient Greek state system was eventually destroyed by more powerful neighboring empires, and in due course the Greeks became subjects of the Roman Empire (200 BC–500 AD). The Romans developed a huge empire in the course of conquering, occupying, and ruling most of Europe and a large part of the Middle East and North Africa. The Romans had to deal with the numerous political communities that occupied these areas, but they did that by subordinating them rather than recognizing them. Instead of international relations or quasi-international relations, under the Roman empire the only option for political communities was either submission to Rome or revolt. Eventually those communities on the periphery of the empire began to revolt; the Roman army could not contain the revolts and began to retreat, and on several occasions the city of Rome itself was invaded and shattered by the 'barbarian' tribes. In that way the Roman empire was finally brought to an end after many centuries of political success and survival.

Empire was the prevalent pattern of political organization that gradually emerged in Christian Europe over several centuries after the fall of the Roman empire. Rome's two main successors in Europe also were empires: in Western Europe the medieval (Catholic) empire based at Rome (Christendom); in Eastern Europe and the near east the Byzantine (Orthodox) empire centered on Constantinople or what is today Istanbul (Byzantium). Byzantium claimed to be the continuation of the Christianized Roman empire. The European medieval

---

Box 1.4 The Roman Empire

Rome began as a city state in central Italy . . . Over several centuries the city expanded its authority and adapted its methods of government to bring first Italy, then the western Mediterranean and finally almost the whole of the Hellenistic world into an empire larger than any which had existed in that area before . . . This unique and astonishing achievement, and the cultural transformation which it brought about, laid the foundations of European civilization . . . Rome helped to shape European and contemporary practice and opinion about the state, about international law and especially about empire and the nature of imperial authority.

Watson (1992: 94)

Christian world (500–1500) was thus divided geographically most of the time into two politico-religious empires. There were other political systems and empires further afield. North Africa and the Middle East were a world of Islamic civilization which originated in the Arabian peninsula in the early years of the seventh century. There were empires in what is today Iran and India. The oldest empire was the Chinese which survived, under different dynasties, for about 4,000 years until the early twentieth century. Perhaps it still exists in the form of the Chinese Communist state, which resembles an empire in its hierarchical political and ideological structure. The Middle Ages were thus an era of empire and the relations and conflicts of different empires. But contact between empires was intermittent at best: communications were slow and transportation was difficult. Most empires at that time consequently were a world unto themselves.

Can we speak of 'international relations' in Western Europe during the medieval era? Only with difficulty because, as already indicated, medieval

---

Box 1.5 City-states and empires

500 BC–100 BC	Greek city-states
200 BC–500 AD	Roman Empire
500–1500 Medieval Christian World	Catholic Christendom: The Pope in Rome
	Orthodox Christendom: Byzantine Empire, Constantinople
Other historical empires	Islam Iran, India, China

Christendom was more like an empire than a state system. States existed, but they were not independent or sovereign in the modern meaning of these words. There were no clearly defined territories with borders. The medieval world was not a geographical patchwork of sharply differentiated colors which represented different independent countries. Instead, it was a complicated and confusing intermingling of lines and colors of varying shades and hues. Power and authority were organized on both a religious and a political basis: the Pope and the Emperor were the heads of two parallel and connected hierarchies, one religious and the other political. Kings and other rulers were subjects of those higher authorities and their laws. They were not fully independent. And much of the time local rulers were more or less free from the rule of kings: they were semi-autonomous but they were not fully independent either. The fact is that territorial political independence as we know it today was not present in medieval Europe.

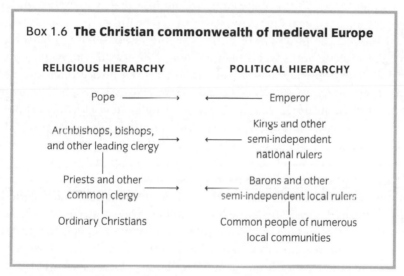

Box 1.6 **The Christian commonwealth of medieval Europe**

The medieval era was also one of considerable disarray, disorder, conflict, and violence which stemmed from this lack of clear lines of territorial political organization and control. Sometimes wars were fought between religious civilizations—for example, the Christian Crusades against the Islamic world (1096–1291). Sometimes wars were fought between kings—for example, the Hundred Years War between England and France (1337–1453). But often war was feudal and local and was fought between rival groups of knights whose leaders had a quarrel. The authority and power to engage in war was not monopolized by the state: kings did not control war as they were later able to do. Instead, war-making rights and capacities belonged to members of a distinctive caste—the armed knights and their leaders and followers—who fought sometimes for the Pope, sometimes for the Emperor, sometimes for their king, sometimes for their master, and sometimes and indeed quite regularly for themselves. There was no clear distinction between civil war and international war. Medieval wars were more likely to be fought over issues of rights and wrongs: wars to defend the faith, wars to resolve conflicts over dynastic inheritance, wars to punish outlaws, wars to collect debts, etc. (Howard 1976: ch. 1). Wars were less likely to be fought over the exclusive control of territory or over state or national interests. In medieval Europe there was no exclusively controlled territory, and no clear conception of the nation or the national interest.

The values connected with sovereign statehood were arranged differently in medieval times. The key to that difference is the fact that no one political organization, such as the sovereign state, catered for all these values. Instead, they were looked after by different organizations which operated at different levels of social life. Security was provided by local rulers and their knights who operated from fortified castles and towns. Freedom was not freedom for the individual or the nation; rather, it was freedom for feudal rulers and their followers and clients. Order was the responsibility of the emperor, but his capacity to enforce order was very limited and medieval Europe was punctuated by turbulence and discord at all levels of society. The provision of justice was the responsibility of both political and religious rulers, but it was a highly unequal justice. Those higher up in the political and religious hierarchies had easier access to justice than those at the bottom. There were different courts for different classes of people. There was no police, and often justice was meted out by people themselves in the form of revenge or reprisal. The Pope was responsible not only for ruling the Church through his hierarchy of bishops and other clergy but also for overseeing political disputes between kings and other semi-independent national rulers. Members of the clergy were often senior advisers to kings and other secular rulers. Kings were sometimes 'Defenders of the Faith'—such as Henry VIII of England. Knights often thought of themselves as Christian soldiers. Welfare was connected to security and was based on feudal ties between local rulers and common people in which those rulers provided protection in exchange for a share of the labor, crops and other resources and products of a local peasant economy. Peasants were not free to live wherever they wished. Instead, they were tied to feudal landlords who could be members of the nobility or the clergy or both.

What did the political change from medieval to modern basically involve? The short answer is: it eventually consolidated the provision of these values within the single framework of one unified and independent social organization: the sovereign state. In the early modern era European rulers liberated themselves from the overarching religious-political authority of Christendom. They also freed themselves from their dependence on the military power of barons and other local feudal leaders. The kings subordinated the barons and defied the Emperor and the Pope. They became defenders of state sovereignty against internal disorder and external threat. Peasants began their long journey to escape from their dependence on local feudal rulers to become the direct subjects of the King: they eventually became 'the people'.

In short, power and authority were concentrated at one point: the King and his government. The King now ruled a territory with borders which were defended against outside interference. The King became the supreme authority over all the people in the country, and no longer had to operate via intermediate authorities and rulers. That fundamental political transformation marks the advent of the modern era.

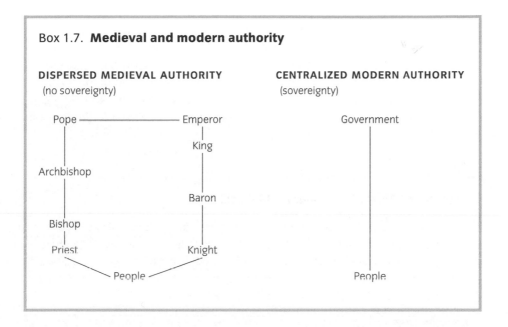

Box 1.7. **Medieval and modern authority**

DISPERSED MEDIEVAL AUTHORITY
(no sovereignty)

CENTRALIZED MODERN AUTHORITY
(sovereignty)

Pope ——————— Emperor

King

Archbishop

Baron

Bishop

Priest   Knight

People

Government

People

One of the major effects of the rise of the modern state was its monopoly of the means of warfare. The King first created order at home and became the sole centre of power within the country. Knights and barons who had formerly controlled their own armies now took orders from the King. Many kings then looked outward with an ambition to expand their territories. As a result international rivalries developed which often resulted in wars and the enlargement of some countries at the expense of others. At various times Spain, France, Austria, England, Denmark, Sweden, Holland, Poland, Russia, Prussia and other states of the new European state system were at war. Some wars were spawned by the Protestant Reformation which profoundly divided the European Christian population in the sixteenth and seventeenth centuries. But other wars, and increasingly most wars, were provoked by the mere existence of independent states whose rulers resorted to war as a means of defending their interests, pursuing their ambitions and, if possible, expanding their territorial holdings. War became a key international institution for resolving conflicts between sovereign states.

The political change from medieval to modern thus basically involved the construction of the independent territorial state. The state captured its territory and

turned it into state property, and it captured the population of that territory and turned them into subjects and later citizens. In many countries, indeed most, the Christian churches fell under state control. There was no room within modern states for semi-independent territory or people or institutions. In the modern international system territory is consolidated, unified, and centralized under a sovereign government. The population of the territory owe their allegiance to that government and they have a duty to obey its laws. That includes bishops as well as barons, merchants as well as aristocrats. All institutions are now subordinate to state authority and public law. The familiar territorial patchwork map of the world is in place in which each patch is under the exclusive jurisdiction of a particular state. All of the territory of Europe and eventually the entire planet is partitioned in that way by independent governments. The historical end point of the medieval era and the starting-point of the modern international system, speaking very generally, is usually identified with the Thirty Years War (1618–48) and the Peace of Westphalia which brought it to an end.

Box 1.8 **The Thirty Years War (1618–1648)**

Starting initially in Bohemia as an uprising of the Protestant aristocracy against Spanish authority, the war escalated rapidly, eventually incorporating all sorts of issues . . . Questions of religious toleration were at the root of the conflict . . . But by the 1630s, the war involved a jumble of conflicting stakes, with all sorts of cross-cutting dynastic, religious, and state interests involved . . . Europe was fighting its first continental war.

Holsti (1991: 26–8)

From the middle of the seventeenth century states were seen as the only legitimate political systems of Europe based on their own separate territories, their own independent governments, and their own political subjects. That emergent state system had several prominent characteristics which can be summarized. First, it consisted of adjoining states whose legitimacy and independence was mutually recognized. Second, that recognition of states did not extend outside of the European state system. Non-European political systems were not members of the state system. They were usually regarded as politically inferior and most of them were eventually subordinated to European imperial rule. Third, the relations of European states were subject to international law and diplomatic practices. In other words, they were expected to observe the rules of the international game. Fourth, there was a balance of power between member states which was intended to prevent any one state from getting out of control and making a successful bid for hegemony which would in effect re-establish an empire over the continent.

> ### Box 1.9 The Peace of Westphalia (1648)
>
> The Westphalian settlement legitimized a commonwealth of sovereign states. It marked the triumph of the *stato* [the state], in control of its internal affairs and independent externally. This was the aspiration of princes [rulers] in general—and especially of the German princes, both Protestant and Catholic, in relation to the [Holy Roman or Habsburg] empire. The Westphalian treaties stated many of the rules and political principles of the new society of states . . . The settlement was held to provide a fundamental and comprehensive charter of all Europe.
>
> Watson (1992: 186)

There were several major attempts by different powers to impose their political hegemony on the continent. The Habsburg empire (Austria) made the attempt during the Thirty Years War (1618–1648), and was blocked by a coalition led by France and Sweden. France made the attempt under King Louis XIV (1661–1714) and was blocked by an English–Dutch alliance. Napoleon (1795–1815) made the attempt and was blocked by Britain, Russia, Prussia, and Austria. A post-Napoleonic balance of power among the great powers (the Concert of Europe) held for most of the period between 1815 and 1914. Germany made the attempt under Hitler (1939–45) and was blocked by the United States, the Soviet Union, and Britain. For the past 350 years the European state system has managed to resist the main political tendency of world history, which is the attempt by strong powers to bend weaker powers to their political will and thereby establish an empire. Whether the sole remaining superpower after the Cold War, the United States, was becoming a global hegemon was an issue at the time of writing.

. . . .

The Global State System and the World Economy

Yet, while Europeans resisted empire in Europe, at the very same time they also constructed vast overseas empires and a world economy by which they controlled most non-European political communities in the rest of the world. The Western states that could not dominate each other succeeded in dominating much of the rest of the world both politically and economically. That outward control of the non-European world by Europeans began at the start of the early modern era in the sixteenth century, at the same time that the European state system was coming into existence. It lasted down to the middle of the twentieth century, when the last non-Western peoples finally broke free of Western colonialism and acquired political independence. The fact that Western states were never able to dominate each other but were capable of dominating almost everybody else has been crucially important in shaping the modern international system. The global ascendancy and supremacy of the West is crucial for understanding IR even today.

The history of modern Europe is a history of political and economic conflict and war between its sovereign states. States made war, and war made and unmade states (Tilly 1992). European state rivalries were conducted not only in Europe but wherever European ambitions and power could be projected—and that was, eventually, throughout the world. European states entered into competition with each other to penetrate and control militarily useful and economically desirable areas in other parts of the world. European states felt they had every right to do that. The idea that non-Western peoples had rights of independence and self-determination only came much later. Huge non-European territories and populations consequently fell under the control of European states, by military conquest, commercial domination, or political annexation.

Western imperial expansion made possible for the first time the formation and operation of a global economy (Parry 1966) and a global polity (Bull and Watson 1984). The expansion of trade between the Western world and the non-Western world began at about the same time that the modern state was emerging in Europe—around the year 1500. That expansion was based on the long-distance and heavily armed sailing-ship which Europeans used both for transporting goods and for projecting military and political power. By such means European states expanded their power far beyond Europe. The American continents were gradually brought into the world trading system via the mining of silver and other precious metals, the trade in furs, and the production of agricultural commodities—much of it produced on large plantations by slave labor. About the same time the East Indies and then continental parts of South Asia and South-East Asia came under European colonization and control. While the Spanish, the Portuguese, the Dutch, the English, and the French expanded their empires over-seas, the Russians expanded theirs overland. By the late eighteenth century the Russian empire based on the fur trade extended across Siberia, into Alaska, and down the west coast of North America as far as northern California. The Western powers also forced the opening of trade with China and Japan—although neither country was colonized politically. Large territories of the non-European world were settled by Europeans and later became independent member states of the state system under the control of their settler populations: the United States, the states of Latin America, Canada, Australia, New Zealand and—for a long time—South Africa. The Middle East and tropical Africa were the last continents that Europeans colonized.

During the era of economic and political imperialism by European states a few fundamental points should be kept in mind which shed light on the state system at that time. First, European states made expedient alliances with non-

---

Box 1.10 **President McKinley on American imperialism in the Philippines (1899)**

When I realized that the Philippines [a Spanish colony] had dropped into our laps [as a result of America's military defeat of Spain] . . . I did not know what to do . . . one night late it came to me this way . . . (1) That we could not give them back to Spain—that would be cowardly and dishonorable; (2) that we could not turn them over to France or Germany—our commercial rivals in the Orient—that would be bad business and discreditable; (3) that we could not leave them to themselves—they were unfit for self-government—and they would soon have anarchy and misrule over there worse than Spain's was; and (4) that there was nothing left for us to do but take them . . . [and] put the Philippines on the map of the United States . . .

Bridges *et al.* (1969: 184)

European political systems—such as the alliances arranged by the British and by the French with different Indian 'tribes' (i.e. nations) of North America. Second, almost wherever they could, European states conquered and colonized those non-Western political systems and made them a subordinate part of their empires. Third, those far-flung empires became a basic source of the wealth and power of the European states for several centuries. Thus the development of Europe was achieved in significant part on the basis of the control of extensive territories outside Europe and by the exploitation of their natural and human resources. Fourth, some of those overseas colonies fell under the control of European settler populations, and many of those new 'settler states' were eventually allowed to become members of the state system. The successful American revolution against the British empire first opened that door in the late eighteenth century. That launched the transition from a European state system to a Western state system. Lastly, throughout the era of Western imperialism, from the sixteenth century until the early twentieth century, there was no interest or desire to incorporate non-Western political systems into the state system on a basis of equal sovereignty. That only happened on a large scale after the Second World War.

The first stage of the globalization of the state system was via the incorporation of non-Western states that could not be colonized by the West. Not every non-Western country fell under the political control of a Western imperial state; but countries that escaped colonization were still obliged to accept the rules of the Western state system. The Ottoman empire (Turkey), is one example: it was forced to accept those rules by the Treaty of Paris in 1854. Japan is another example: it acquiesced to them later in the nineteenth century. Japan rapidly acquired the organizational substance and constitutional shape of a modern state, and by the early twentieth century that country had become a great power—as demonstrated by its military defeat of an existing great power, Russia, on the battlefield: the Russo-Japanese war of 1904–5. China was obliged to accept the rules of the

Western state system during the nineteenth and early twentieth century. China was not acknowledged and fully recognized as a great power until 1945. The second stage of the globalization of the state system was brought about via anti-colonialism by the colonial subjects of Western empires. In that struggle indigenous political leaders made political claims for decolonization and independence based on European and American ideas of self-determination. That 'revolt against the West', as Hedley Bull put it, was the main vehicle by which the state system expanded dramatically after the Second World War (Bull and Watson 1984). In a short period of some twenty years, beginning with the independence of India and Pakistan in 1947, most colonies in Asia and Africa became independent states and members of the United Nations.

> ### Box 1.11 President Ho Chi-minh's 1945 declaration of independence of the Republic of Vietnam
>
> 'All men are created equal. They are endowed by their Creator with certain inalienable rights, among these are life, liberty and the pursuit of happiness.' . . . All the peoples on the earth are equal from birth, all the peoples have a right to live, be happy and free . . . We members of the provisional Government, representing the whole population of Vietnam, have declared and renew here our declaration that we break off all relations with the French people and abolish all the special rights the French have unlawfully acquired in our Fatherland . . . We are convinced that the Allied nations which have acknowledged at Teheran and San Francisco the principles of self-determination and equality of status will not refuse to acknowledge the independence of Vietnam . . . For these reasons we . . . declare to the world that Vietnam has the right to be free and independent . . .
>
> R. Bridges et al. (1969: 311–12)

European decolonization in the Third World more than tripled the membership of the UN from about 50 states in 1945 to over 160 states by 1970. About 70 per cent of the world's population were citizens or subjects of independent states in 1945 and were thus represented in the state system. By 1995 that figure was virtually 100 per cent. The spread of European political and economic control beyond Europe thus eventually proved to be an expansion of the state system which became completely global in the second half of the twentieth century. The final stage of the globalization of the state system was the dissolution of the Soviet Union together with the simultaneous breakup of Yugoslavia and Czechoslovakia at the end of the Cold War. That expanded UN membership to almost 200 states at the end of the twentieth century.

Today the state system is a global institution that affects the lives of virtually everybody on earth whether they realize it or not. That means that IR is now more than ever a universal academic subject. That also means that world politics at the start of the twenty-first century must accommodate a range and variety of states which are far more diverse—in terms of their cultures, religions, languages, ideologies, forms of government, military capacity, technological sophistication, levels of economic development, etc.—than ever before. That is a fundamental change in the state system and a fundamental challenge for IR scholars to theorize.

Box 1.12 **Global expansion of the state system**

1600s	Europe (European system)
1700s	+ North America (Western system)
1800s	+ South America, Japan (globalizing system)
1900s	+ Asia, Africa, Caribbean, Pacific (global system)

IR and the Changing Contemporary World of States

Many important questions in the study of IR are connected with the theory and practice of sovereign statehood which, as indicated, is the central historical institution of world politics. But there are other important issues as well. That has led to ongoing debates about the proper scope of IR. At one extreme the scholarly focus is exclusively on states and interstate relations; but at another extreme IR includes almost everything that has to do with human relations across the world. It is important to study these different perspectives if we hope to have a balanced and rounded knowledge of IR.

Our reason for linking the various IR theories to states and the state system is to acknowledge the historical centrality of that subject. Even theorists who seek to get beyond the state usually take it as a starting-point: the state system is the main point of reference both for traditional and for new approaches. Later chapters will explore how each tradition of IR scholarship has attempted to come to grips with the sovereign state. There are debates about how we should conceptualize the state and different IR theories take somewhat different approaches. In later chapters we shall present contemporary debates on the future of the state. Whether its central importance in world politics may now be changing is a very important question in contemporary IR scholarship. But the fact is that states and the state system remain at the center of academic analysis and discussion in IR.

We must of course be alert to the fact that the sovereign state is a contested theoretical concept. When we ask the questions 'what is the state?' and 'what is

the state system?' there will be different answers depending on the theoretical approach adopted: the realist answer will be different from the liberal answer, and those answers will be different from the International Society answer and from the answer given by IPE theories. None of these answers are strictly speaking either correct or incorrect because the truth is: the state is a multifaceted and somewhat confusing entity. There is disagreement about the scope and purpose of the state. The state system consequently is not an easy subject to understand, and it can be understood in different ways and with different points of emphasis.

But there are ways of simplifying. It is helpful to think of the state as having two different dimensions, each divided into two broad categories. The first dimension is the state as a government versus the state as a country. Viewed from within, the state is the national government: it is the highest governing authority in a country: it possesses internal sovereignty. That is the *internal* aspect of the state. Main questions in regard to the internal aspect concern *state-society* relations: how the government rules the domestic society, the means of its power and the sources of its legitimacy, how it deals with the demands and concerns of individuals and groups which compose that domestic society, how it manages the national economy, what its domestic policies are, and so forth.

Viewed internationally, however, the state is not merely a government: it is a populated territory with a national government and a society. In other words, it is a country. From that angle, both the government and the domestic society make up the state. If a country is a sovereign state it will be generally recognized as politically independent. That is the *external* aspect of the state in which the main questions concern *interstate* relations: how the governments and societies of states relate to each other and deal with each other, what the basis of those interstate relations are, what the foreign policies of particular states are, what the international organizations of the states are, how people from different states interact with each other and engage in transactions with each other, and so forth.

That brings us to the second dimension of the state, which divides the external aspect of sovereign statehood into two broad categories. The first category is the state viewed as a *formal* or legal institution in its relation with other states. That is the state as an entity which is recognized as sovereign or independent, enjoys membership in international organizations, and possesses various international rights and responsibilities. We shall refer to that first category as *juridical statehood*. Recognition is an essential element of juridical statehood. Recognition qualifies states for membership of International Society, including membership of the United Nations. The absence of recognition denies it. Not every country is recognized as independent: an example is Quebec, which is a province of Canada. To become independent it must be recognized as such by existing sovereign states, by far the most important of which for Quebec are first Canada and second the United States.

Box 1.13 **External dimension of statehood**

The state as a country
- Territory, government, society

Legal, juridical statehood
- Recognition by other states

Actual, empirical statehood
- Political institutions, economic basis, national unity

The countries that are recognized as sovereign states are always fewer than the countries that are not recognized but conceivably could be recognized. That is because independence is generally regarded as politically valuable. But the countries that are recognized as sovereign states usually have no desire to see new countries recognized because it would involve partition: existing states would lose territory, population, resources, power, status, etc. If partition became an accepted practice it would undermine international stability. Partition would set a dangerous precedent that could destabilize the state system if a growing number of currently subordinated but potentially independent countries lined up to demand recognition as sovereign states. So, there may always be somebody knocking on the door of state sovereignty, but there is a great reluctance to open the door and let them in. That would be disruptive of the present state system—especially now that there are no more colonies and the entire inhabited territory of the world is enclosed within one global state system. So juridical statehood is carefully rationed by existing sovereign states.

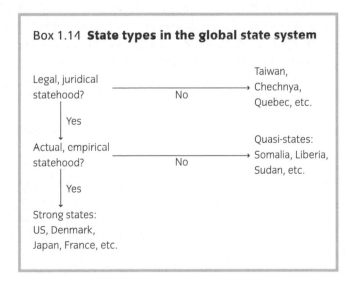

Box 1.14 **State types in the global state system**

Legal, juridical statehood? —— No ——→ Taiwan, Chechnya, Quebec, etc.

↓ Yes

Actual, empirical statehood? —— No ——→ Quasi-states: Somalia, Liberia, Sudan, etc.

↓ Yes

Strong states: US, Denmark, Japan, France, etc.

The second category is the state viewed as a *substantial* political-economic organization. That category has to do with the extent to which states have developed efficient political institutions, a solid economic basis, and a substantial degree of national unity, that is, of popular unity and support for the state. We shall refer to that second category as *empirical statehood*. Some states are very strong in the sense that they have a high level of empirical statehood. Most states in the West are like that. Many of those states are small, for example Sweden, Holland, and Luxembourg. A strong state in the sense of a high level of empirical statehood should be held separate from the notion of a strong power in the military sense. Some strong states are not militarily powerful; Denmark is an example. Some powers in the military sense, such as Russia, are not strong states. Canada is the unusual case of a highly developed country with an effective democratic government but with a major weakness in its statehood: the threat of Quebec to secede. On the other hand, the United States is both a strong state and a strong power: indeed, it is the strongest power on earth.

Box 1.15 Strong/weak states—strong/weak powers

	STRONG POWER	WEAK POWER
STRONG STATE	USA, France, UK, Japan	Denmark, Switzerland, New Zealand, Singapore
WEAK STATE	Russia, Iraq, Pakistan	Somalia, Liberia, Chad, etc.

This distinction between empirical statehood and juridical statehood is of fundamental importance because it helps to capture the very significant differences that exist between the almost 200 currently independent and formally equal states of the world. States differ enormously in the legitimacy of their political institutions, the effectiveness of their governmental organizations, their economic wealth and productivity, their political influence and status, and their national unity. Not all states posses effective national governments. Some states, including both large and small, are solid and capable organizations: they are strong states. Most states in the West are more or less like that. Some tiny island microstates in the Pacific ocean are so small that they can hardly afford to have a government at all. Other states may be fairly large in terms of territory or population or both—e.g. Nigeria or the Congo (formerly Zaïre)—but they are so poor, so inefficient, and so corrupt that they are barely able to carry on as an effective government. A large number of states, especially in the Third World, have a low degree of empirical statehood. Their institutions are weak, their economic basis is frail and underdeveloped, there is little or no national unity. We can refer to these states as 'quasi-states': they possess juridical statehood but they are severely deficient in empirical statehood (Jackson 1990). If we summarize the various distinctions made here, we get the picture of the global state system shown in Box 1.16.

One of the most important conditions that throws light on the existence of so many quasi-states in the Third World is that of economic underdevelopment. Their poverty and consequent shortages of investment, infrastructure (roads, schools, hospitals, etc.), modern technology, trained and educated people, and

---

Box 1.16 **The global state system**

- 5 Great Powers: US, Russia, China, Britain, France

- Approx. 30 highly substantial states: Europe, N. America, Japan

- Approx. 75 moderately substantial states: Asia and Latin America

- Approx. 90 insubstantial quasi-states: Africa, Asia, Caribbean, Pacific

- Numerous unrecognized territorial political systems submerged in existing states

---

other socioeconomic assets or resources are among the most important factors that help us to understand why these states are so weak. The government and its institutions in these countries demonstrate little in the way of a solid foundation. The weakness of these states is a mirror of their poverty and technological backwardness, and as long as those conditions persist their incapacity as states is likely to persist as well. That profoundly affects the nature of the state system and also, therefore, the character of our IR theories.

Different conclusions can be drawn from the fact that empirical statehood varies so widely in the contemporary state system, from economically and techno-logically advanced and mostly Western states at one extreme to economically and technologically backward and mostly non-Western states at the other. Realist IR scholars focus mainly on the states at the center of the system: the major powers and especially the great powers. They see Third World states as marginal players in a system of power politics that has always rested on 'the inequality of nations' (Tucker 1977). Such marginal or peripheral states do not affect the system in any very significant way. Other IR scholars, usually liberals and International Society theorists, see the adverse conditions of quasi-states as a fundamental problem for the state system which raises issues not only of international order but also of international freedom and justice.

Some IPE scholars, usually Marxists, make underdevelopment of peripheral countries and the unequal relations between the center and the periphery of the global economy the crucial explanatory element of their theory of the modern international system (Wallerstein 1974). They investigate international linkages between the poverty of the Third World, or the South, and the enrichment of America, Europe, and other parts of the North. They see the international economy as one overall 'world system', with the developed capitalist states at the center advancing at the expense of the weak, underdeveloped states at the periphery. According to these scholars, legal equality and political independence—what we have designated as 'juridical statehood'—is scarcely more than a polite façade that merely obscures the extreme vulnerability of poor Third World states and their domination and exploitation by the rich capitalist states of the West.

The underdeveloped countries certainly disclose in a striking way the profound empirical inequalities of contemporary world politics. But it is their possession of juridical statehood which reflects their membership of the state system that places that issue in sharp perspective, for it highlights the fact that the populations of some states—the developed countries—enjoy far better living conditions in virtually every respect than the populations of other states—the underdeveloped countries. The fact that underdeveloped countries belong to the same global state system as developed countries raises different questions than if they belonged to entirely separate systems, which was the case before the global state system was created. We can see the issues of security, freedom and progress, order and justice, and wealth and poverty far more clearly when it involves members of the same international system. For *inside* a system the same general standards and expectations apply. So if some states cannot meet common standards or expectations because of their underdevelopment, that becomes an international problem and not only a domestic problem or somebody else's problem. That is a major change from the past when most non-Western political systems either were *outside* the state system and operated according to different standards or they were colonies of Western imperial powers who were responsible for them as a matter of domestic policy rather than foreign policy.

Box 1.17 **Insiders and outsiders in the state system**

PREVIOUS STATE SYSTEM	PRESENT STATE SYSTEM
• Small core of insiders, all strong states	• Virtually all states are recognized insiders, possessing formal or juridical statehood
• Many outsiders: colonies, dependencies, etc.	• Big differences between insiders: some strong states, some weak quasi-states

---

These developments are a reminder that the world of states is a dynamic, changing world and not a static, unchanging one. In international relations, as in other spheres of human relations, nothing stands still for very long. International relations change along with everything else: politics, economics, science, technology, education, culture, and the rest. An obvious case in point is technological innovation, which has profoundly shaped international relations from the beginning and continues to shape it in significant ways that are never entirely predictable. Over the centuries new or improved military technology has had a profound impact on the balance of power, arms races, imperialism and colonialism, military alliances, the nature of war, and much else. Economic growth has permitted greater wealth to be devoted to military budgets, and has provided a foundation for the development of larger, better-equipped, and more effective military forces. Scientific discoveries have made possible new technologies, such as transportation or information technologies, which have had the effect of knitting the world more closely together and making national borders more permeable. Literacy, mass education, and expanded higher education have enabled governments to increase the capacity of their state and expand their activities into more and more specialized spheres of society and economy.

It cuts both ways, of course, because highly educated people do not like being told what to think or what to do. Changing cultural values and ideas have affected not only the foreign policy of particular states but also the shape and direction of international relations. For example, the ideologies of anti-racism and anti-imperialism that were first articulated by intellectuals in Western countries eventually undermined Western overseas empires in Asia and Africa, and helped bring about the decolonization process by making the moral justification of colonialism increasingly difficult and eventually impossible.

The examples of the impact of social change on international relations are almost endless in their number and variety. However, this should suffice to make the point that social change affects states and the state system. The relationship is undoubtedly reversible: the state system also has an impact on politics, economics, science, technology, education, culture, and the rest. For example, it has been compellingly argued that it was the development of a state system in Europe that was decisive in propelling that continent ahead of all other continents during the modern era. The competition of the independent European states within their state system—their military competition, their economic competition, their scientific and technological competition—catapulted those states ahead of non-European political systems which were not spurred by the same degree of competition. One scholar has made the point as follows: 'The states of Europe . . . were surrounded by actual or potential competitors. If the government of one were lax, it impaired its own prestige and military security. . . . The state system was an insurance against economic and technological stagnation' (Jones 1981: 104–26). We should not conclude, therefore, that the state system merely reacts to change; it is also a cause of change.

The fact of social change raises a more fundamental question. At some point should we expect states to change so much that they are no longer states in the sense discussed here? For example, if the process of economic globalization continues and makes the world one single market-place and one single production site, will the state system then be obsolete? We have in mind the following activities which might bypass states: ever-increasing international trade and investment, expanding multinational business activity, enlarged NGO (non-governmental organization) activities, increasing regional and global communications, the growth of the Internet, expanding and ever-extending transportation networks, exploding travel and tourism, massive human migration, cumulative environmental pollution, expanded regional integration, the growth of trading communities, the global expansion of science and technology, continuous downsizing of government, increased privatization, and other activities which have the effect of increasing interdependence across borders.

Or will sovereign states and the state system find ways of adapting to those social changes, just as they have adapted time and again to other major changes during the past 350 years? Some of those changes were just as fundamental: the scientific revolution of the seventeenth century, the enlightenment of the eighteenth century, the encounter of Western and non-Western civilizations over the course of several centuries, the growth of Western imperialism and colonialism, the Industrial Revolution of the eighteenth and nineteenth centuries, the rise and spread of nationalism in the nineteenth and twentieth centuries, the revolution of anti-colonialism and decolonization in the twentieth century, the spread of mass public education, the growth of the welfare state, and much else. These are some of the most fundamental questions of contemporary IR scholarship, and we should keep them in mind when we speculate about the future of the state system.

. . . .

Conclusion

The state system is a historical institution, fashioned by people. The population of the world has not always lived in sovereign states. For most of recorded human history people have lived under different kinds of political organization. In medieval times, political authority was chaotic and dispersed. Most people were dependent on a large number of different authorities—some of them political, some religious—with diverse responsibilities and power, from the local ruler and landlord to the King in a distant capital city, from parish priest to the Pope in far away Rome. In the modern state, authority is centralized in one legally supreme government, and people live under the standard laws of that government. The development of the modern state went a long way towards organizing political authority and power along rational and national lines.

The state system was a European state system in the first instance. During the era of Western imperialism the rest of the world was dominated by Europeans, both politically and economically. Only with Asian and African decolonization, after the Second World War, did the state system become a global institution. The globalization of the state system vastly increased the variety of its member states and consequently its diversity. The most important difference is between strong states with a high level of empirical statehood and weak quasi-states, which have formal sovereignty but very little substantial statehood. In other words, decolonization contributed to a huge and deep internal division in the state system between the rich North and the poor South: i.e. between developed countries at the center, which dominate the system politically and economically, and under-developed countries at the peripheries, which have limited political and economic influence.

People often expect states to uphold certain key values: security, freedom, order, justice, and welfare. IR theory concerns the ways in which states do or do not ensure those values. Historically the system of states consists of many heavily armed states, including a small number of great powers which often have been military rivals and sometimes have gone to war with each other. That reality of the state as a war machine underlines the value of security. That is the starting-point for the realist tradition in IR. Until states cease to be armed rivals, realist theory will have a firm historical basis. Following the end of the Cold War there are some signs that that may be changing: the great powers have cut back very significantly their military budgets and reduced the size of their armed forces. They have modernized their armies and navies and air forces, but they have not even considered abandoning their armed forces. That suggests that realism will be a relevant IR theory for some time to come.

But it is also a fact that most of the time states cooperate with each other more or less routinely, and without much political drama, for mutual advantage. They carry on diplomatic relations, they trade, they support international markets, they exchange scientific and technological knowledge, they open their doors to investors, businessmen, tourists, and travelers from other countries. They collaborate in order to deal with various common problems, from the environment to the traffic in illegal drugs. They commit themselves to bilateral and multilateral treaties for that purpose. In short, states interact in accordance with norms of reciprocity. The liberal tradition in IR is based on the idea that the modern state in that quiet and routine way makes a strategic contribution to international freedom and progress.

How do states uphold order and justice in the state system? Mainly through the rules and norms of international law, and through international organizations and diplomatic activity. There has been a huge expansion of those elements of international society since 1945. The International Society tradition in IR emphasizes the importance of such international relations. Finally the system of states is also a socioeconomic system; wealth and welfare is a core concern of most states. That fact is the starting-point for the IPE theories in IR. IPE theorists also discuss the consequences of Western expansion and the eventual incorporation of the Third World into the state system. Is that process bringing modernization and progress to the Third World, or is it bringing inequality, underdevelopment, and misery? This question also leads to the larger issue of whether the state system is worth upholding and defending or whether it ought to be replaced by another system. IR theories are not in agreement on this issue; but the discipline of IR is based on the conviction that sovereign states and their development are of crucial importance for understanding how basic values of human life are being, or not being, provided to people around the world.

The following chapters will introduce the theoretical traditions of IR in further detail. We begin this task by introducing IR as an academic discipline. Whereas this chapter has concerned the actual development of states and the state system, the next chapter will focus on how our thinking about states and their relations has developed over time.

KEY POINTS

- The main reason why we should study IR is the fact that the entire population of the world is living in independent states. Together those states form a global state system.

- The core values that states are expected to uphold are security, freedom, order, justice, and welfare. IR theory is about the effects that states and the state system have for these core values.

- The system of sovereign states emerged in Europe at the start of the modern era, in the sixteenth century. Medieval political authority was dispersed; modern political authority is centralized, residing in the government and the head of state.

- The state system was European first; now it is global. The global state system contains states of very different type: great-powers and small states; strong, substantial states and weak quasi-states.

- There is a link between the expansion of the state system and the establishment of a world market and a global economy. Some Third World countries have benefited from integration into the global economy; others remain poor and underdeveloped.

- Economic globalization and other developments challenge the sovereign state. We cannot know for certain whether the state system is now becoming obsolete, or whether states will find ways of adapting to new challenges.

QUESTIONS

- What is a state? Why do we have them? What is a state system?

- When did independent states and the modern system of states emerge? What is the difference between a medieval and a modern system of political authority?

- We expect states to sustain a number of core values: security, freedom, order, justice, and welfare. Do states meet our expectations?

- What are the effects on Third World countries of integration into the global economy?

- Should we strive to preserve the system of sovereign states? Why or why not?

- Explain the main differences between strong, substantial states, weak quasi-states, great powers, and small powers. Why is there such diversity in the state system?

 For additional material and resources see the companion web site at:
www.oup.co.uk/best.textbooks/politics/jacksonsorensen2e/

GUIDE TO FURTHER READING

Bull, H., and Watson, A. (eds.) (1984). *The Expansion of International Society*. Oxford: Clarendon Press.

Oslander, A. (1994). *The States System of Europe, 1640–1990*. Oxford: Clarendon Press.

Tilly, C. (1992). *Coercion, Capital and European States*. Oxford: Blackwell.

Wallerstein, I. (1974). *The Modern World System*, i. New York: Academic Press.

Watson, A. (1992). *The Evolution of International Society*. London: Routledge.

WEB LINKS

http://www.yale.edu/lawweb/avalon/westphal.htm
Full text of the 1648 Treaty of Westphalia, which established modern European international society. Hosted by the Avalon Project at Yale Law School.

http://plato.stanford.edu/entries/war/
Discussion of the concept of war as well as links to related web resources. Hosted by Stanford Encyclopaedia of Philosophy.

http://carlisle-www.army.mil/usawc/Parameters/96spring/creveld.htm
Martin van Creveld discusses 'The Fate of the State'. Hosted by the US Army War College.

http://www.jeanmonnetprogram.org/papers/00/00f0801.html
Jan Zielonka discusses whether a neo-medieval empire is likely to develop in Europe. Hosted by the Jean Monnet Center at the New York University School of Law.

2 | IR as an Academic Subject

SUMMARY

This chapter shows how thinking about international relations has evolved since IR became an academic subject around the First World War. Theoretical approaches are a product of their time: they address those problems of international relations that are seen as the most important ones in their day. The established traditions deal nonetheless with international problems that are of lasting significance: war and peace, conflict and cooperation, wealth and poverty, development and underdevelopment. In this chapter we shall focus on four established IR traditions. They are realism, liberalism, International Society, and International Political Economy (IPE). We shall also introduce some recent, alternative approaches which challenge the established traditions.

. . . .

Introduction

The traditional core of IR has to do with issues concerning the development and change of sovereign statehood in the context of the larger system or society of states. That focus on states and the relations of states helps explain why war and peace is a central problem of traditional IR theory. However, contemporary IR is concerned not only with political relations between states but also with a host of other subjects: economic interdependence, human rights, transnational corporations, international organizations, the environment, gender inequalities, development, terrorism, and so forth. For this reason, some scholars prefer the label 'International Studies' or 'World Politics.' We shall stay with the label 'International Relations' but we shall interpret it to cover the broad range of issues.

There are four major theoretical traditions in IR: realism, liberalism, International Society, and IPE. In addition, there is a more diverse group of alternative approaches which have gained prominence in recent years. The main task of this book is to present and discuss all these theories. In this chapter we shall examine IR as an evolving academic subject. IR thinking has developed through distinct phases, characterized by specific debates between groups of scholars. At most times during the twentieth century there has been a dominant way of thinking about IR and a major challenge to that way of thinking. Those debates and dialogues are the main subject of this chapter.

There are a great many different theories in IR. They can be classified in a number of ways; what we call a 'main theoretical tradition' is not an objective entity. If you put four IR theorists in a room you will easily get ten different ways of organizing theory, and there will also be disagreement about which theories that are relevant in the first place! At the same time, we have to group theories into main categories. Without drawing together main paths in the development of IR thinking, we are stuck with a large number of individual contributions, pointing in different and sometimes rather confusing directions. But the reader should always be wary of selections and classifications, including the ones offered in this book. They are analytical tools created to achieve overview and clarity; they are not objective truths that can be taken for granted.

Of course, IR thinking is influenced by other academic subjects, such as philosophy, history, law, sociology, or economics. IR thinking also responds to historical and contemporary developments in the real world. The two world wars, the Cold War between East and West, the emergence of close economic cooperation between Western states, and the persistent development gap between North and South are examples of real-world events and problems that stimulated IR scholarship in the twentieth century. And we can be certain that future events and episodes will provoke new IR thinking in the years to come: that is already

---

Box 2.1 **The development of IR thinking**

HISTORICAL CONTEXT

Development and change of sovereign statehood

↓

THEORETICAL DISCUSSION BETWEEN IR SCHOLARS

Major debates

↑

OTHER DISCIPLINES

(philosophy, history, economics, law, etc.)
New insights and new methods influence IR

---

evident with regard to the end of the Cold War, which is stimulating a variety of innovative IR thought at the present time. The terrorist attack of September 11, 2001, is the latest major challenge to IR thinking.

There have been three major debates since IR became an academic subject at the end of the First World War and we are now in the early stages of a fourth. The first major debate is between utopian liberalism and realism; the second between traditional approaches and behavioralism; the third between neo-realism/neoliberalism and neo-Marxism. The emerging fourth debate is between established traditions and post-positivist alternatives. We shall review these major debates in this chapter because they provide us with a map of the way the academic subject of IR has developed over the past century. We need to become familiar with that map in order to comprehend IR as a dynamic academic subject which continues to evolve, and to see the directions of that continuing evolution of IR thought.

. . . .

Utopian Liberalism: The Early Study of IR

The decisive push to set up a separate academic subject of IR was occasioned by the First World War (1914–18), which produced millions of casualties; it was driven by a widely felt determination never to allow human suffering on such a scale to happen again. That desire not to repeat the same catastrophic mistake required coming to grips with the problem of total warfare between the mechanized armies of modern industrial states which were capable of inflicting mass destruction. The war was a devastating experience for millions of people, and particularly for young soldiers who were conscripted into the armies and were slaughtered by the million, especially in the trench warfare on the Western Front. Some battles resulted in tens of thousands and sometimes 100,000 casualties or even more. The famous battle of the Somme (France) in July–August 1916 inflicted casualties on that scale. It was referred to as a 'bloody holocaust' (Gilbert 1995: 258). The justification for all that death and destruction became less and less clear as the war years went by, as the number of casualties kept on increasing to historically unprecedented levels, and as the war failed to disclose any rational purpose. On first learning of the war's devastation one man who had been isolated was quoted as follows: 'Millions are being killed. Europe is mad. The world is mad' (Gilbert 1995: 257). That has come to be our historical image of the First World War.

Why was it that the war began in the first place? And why did Britain, France, Russia, Germany, Austria, Turkey, and other powers persist in waging war in the face of such slaughter and with diminishing chances of gaining anything of real value from the conflict? These questions and others like them are not easy to answer. But the first dominant academic theory of IR was shaped by the search for answers to them. The answers that the new discipline of IR came up with were profoundly influenced by liberal ideas. For liberal thinkers, the First World War was in no small measure attributable to the egoistic and short-sighted calculations and miscalculations of autocratic leaders in the heavily militarized countries involved, especially Germany and Austria.

Box 2.2 **Leadership misperceptions and war**

It is my conviction that during the descent into the abyss, the perceptions of statesmen and generals were absolutely crucial. All the participants suffered from greater or lesser distortions in their images of themselves. They tended to see themselves as honorable, virtuous, and pure, and the adversary as diabolical. All the nations on the brink of the disaster expected the worst from their potential adversaries. They saw their own options as limited by necessity or 'fate', whereas those of the adversary were characterized by many choices. Everywhere, there was a total absence of empathy; no one could see the situation from another point of view. The character of each of the leaders was badly flawed by arrogance, stupidity, carelessness, or weakness.

Stoessinger (1993: 21–3)

Unrestrained by democratic institutions and under pressure from their generals, these leaders were inclined to take the fatal decisions that led their countries into war. And the democratic leaders of France and Britain, in turn, allowed themselves to be drawn into the conflict by an interlocking system of military alliances.

The alliances were intended to keep the peace, but they propelled *all* the European powers into war once *any* major power or alliance embarked on war. When Austria and Germany confronted Serbia with armed force, Russia was duty-bound to come to the aid of Serbia, and Britain and France were treaty-bound to support Russia. For the liberal thinkers of that time the 'obsolete' theory of the balance of power and the alliance system had to be fundamentally reformed so that such a calamity would never happen again.

Why was early academic IR influenced by liberalism? That is a big question, but there are a few important points that we should keep in mind in seeking an answer. The United States was eventually drawn into the war in 1917. Its military intervention decisively determined the outcome of the war: it guaranteed victory for the democratic allies (US, Britain, France) and defeat for the autocratic central powers (Germany, Austria, Turkey). At that time the United States had a President, Woodrow Wilson, who had been a university professor of political science and who saw it as his main mission to bring liberal democratic values to Europe and to the rest of the world. Only in that way, he believed, could another great war be prevented. In short, the liberal way of thinking had a solid political backing from the most powerful state in the international system at the time. Academic IR developed first and most strongly in the two leading liberal-democratic states: the United States and Great Britain. Liberal thinkers had some clear ideas and strong beliefs about how to avoid major disasters in the future; e.g. by reforming the international system, and also by reforming the domestic structures of autocratic countries.

Box 2.3 **Making the world safe for democracy**

We are glad now that we see the facts with no veil of false pretense about them, to fight thus for the ultimate peace of the world and for the liberation of its peoples; the German peoples included: for the right of nations great and small and the privilege of men everywhere to choose their way of life and of obedience. The world must be made safe for democracy. We have no selfish ends to serve. We desire no conquest, no dominion. We seek no indemnities for ourselves, no material compensation for the sacrifices we shall freely make. We are but one of the champions of the right of mankind. We shall be satisfied when those rights have been made as secure as the faith and the freedom of nations can make them.

Woodrow Wilson, from 'Address to Congress Asking for Declaration of War', 1917
Quoted in Vasquez (1996: 35–40)

President Wilson had a vision of making the world 'safe for democracy' that had wide appeal for ordinary people. It was formulated in a fourteen-point program delivered in an address to Congress in January 1918. He was awarded the Nobel

Peace Prize in 1919. His ideas influenced the Paris Peace Conference which followed the end of hostilities and tried to institute a new international order based on liberal ideas. Wilson's peace program calls for an end to secret diplomacy: agreements must be open to public scrutiny. There must be freedom of navigation on the seas and barriers to free trade should be removed. Armaments should be reduced to 'the lowest point consistent with domestic safety'. Colonial and territorial claims shall be settled with regard to the principle of self-determination of peoples. Finally, 'a general association of nations must be formed under specific covenants for the purpose of affording mutual guarantees of political independence and territorial integrity of great and small nations alike' (Vasquez 1996: 40). This latter point is Wilson's call to establish a League of Nations, which was instituted by the Paris Peace Conference in 1919.

Two major points in Wilson's ideas for a more peaceful world deserve special emphasis (Brown 1997: 24). The first concerns his promotion of democracy and self-determination. Behind this point is the liberal conviction that democratic governments do not and will not go to war against each other. It was Wilson's hope that the growth of liberal democracy in Europe would put an end to autocratic and warlike leaders and put peaceful governments in their place. Liberal democracy should therefore be strongly encouraged. The second major point in Wilson's program concerned the creation of an international organization that would put relations between states on a firmer institutional foundation than the realist notions of the Concert of Europe and the balance of power had provided in the past. Instead, international relations would be regulated by a set of common rules of international law. In essence that was Wilson's concept of the League of Nations. The idea that international institutions can promote peaceful co-operation among states is a basic element of liberal thinking; so is the notion about a relationship between liberal democracy and peace. We shall return to both ideas in Chapter 4.

Wilsonian idealism can be summarized as follows. It is the conviction that, through a rational and intelligently designed international organization, it should be possible to put an end to war and to achieve more or less permanent peace. The claim is not that it will be possible to do away with states and statespeople, foreign ministries, armed forces, and other agents and instruments of international conflict. Rather, the claim is that it is possible to tame states and statespeople by subjecting them to the appropriate international organizations, institutions, and laws. The argument liberal idealists make is that traditional power politics— so-called 'Realpolitik'—is a 'jungle', so to speak, where dangerous beasts roam and the strong and cunning rule, whereas under the League of Nations the beasts are put into cages reinforced by the restraints of international organization, i.e. into a kind of 'zoo'. Wilson's liberal faith that an international organization could be created that could guarantee permanent peace is clearly reminiscent of the thought of the most famous classical liberal IR theorist: Immanuel Kant in his pamphlet *Perpetual Peace*.

Norman Angell is another prominent liberal idealist of the same era. In 1909 Angell published a book entitled *The Great Illusion*. The illusion is that many states-people still believe that war serves profitable purposes; that success in war is beneficial for the winner. Angell argues that exactly the opposite is the case: in modern times territorial conquest is extremely expensive and politically divisive because it severely disrupts international commerce. The general argument set forth by Angell is a forerunner of later liberal thinking about modernization and economic interdependence. Modernization demands that states have a growing need of things 'from "outside"—credit, or inventions, or markets or materials not contained in sufficient quantity in the country itself' (Navari 1989: 345). Rising interdependence, in turn, effects a change in relations between states. War and the use of force become of decreasing importance, and international law develops in response to the need for a framework to regulate high levels of interdependence. In sum, modernization and interdependence involve a process of change and progress which renders war and the use of force increasingly obsolete.

The thinking of Wilson and Angell is based on a liberal view of human beings and human society: human beings are rational, and when they apply reason to international relations they can set up organizations for the benefit of all. Public opinion is a constructive force; removing secret diplomacy in dealings between states and, instead, opening diplomacy to public scrutiny assures that agreements will be sensible and fair. These ideas had some success in the 1920s; the League of Nations was indeed established and the great powers took some further steps to assure each other of their peaceful intentions. The high point of these efforts came with the Kellogg–Briand pact of 1928, which practically all countries signed. The pact was an international agreement to abolish war; only in extreme cases of self-defense could war be justified. In short, liberal ideas dominated in the first phase of academic IR. In the international relations of the 1920s these ideas could claim some success.

Why is it, then, that we tend to refer to such ideas by the somewhat pejorative term of 'utopian liberalism', indicating that these liberal arguments were little more than the projection of wishful thinking? One plausible answer is to be found in the political and economic developments of the 1920s and 1930s. Liberal democracy suffered hard blows with the growth of fascist and Nazi dictatorship in Italy, Germany, and Spain. Authoritarianism also increased in many of the new states of Central and Eastern Europe—for example Poland, Hungary, Romania, and Yugoslavia—that were brought into existence as a result of the First World War and the Paris Peace Conference and were supposed to become democracies. Thus, contrary to Wilson's hopes for the spread of democratic civilization, it failed to happen. In many cases what actually happened was the spread of the very sort of state that he believed provoked war: autocratic, authoritarian, and militaristic states.

The League of Nations never became the strong international organization that liberals hoped would restrain powerful and aggressively disposed states. Germany

---

Box 2.4 **The League of Nations**

The League of Nations (1920–46) contained three main organs: the Council (fifteen members including France, the United Kingdom and the Soviet Union as permanent members) which met three times a year, the Assembly (all members) which met annually and a Secretariat. All decisions had to be by unanimous vote. The underlying philosophy of the League was the principle of collective security which meant that the international community had a duty to intervene in international conflicts: it also meant that parties to a dispute should submit their grievances to the League. The centre-piece of the [League] Covenant was Article 16, which empowered the League to institute economic or military sanctions against a recalcitrant state. In essence, though, it was left to each member to decide whether or not a breach of the Covenant had occurred and so whether or not to apply sanctions.

Evans and Newham (1992: 176)

---

and Russia failed to sign the Versailles Peace Treaty initially, and their relationship to the League was always strained. Germany joined the League in 1926 but left in the early 1930s. Japan also left at about that time, while embarking on war in Manchuria. Russia finally joined in 1934, and was expelled in 1940 because of the war with Finland. But by that time the League was effectively dead. Although Britain and France were members from the start, they never regarded the League as an important institution and refused to shape their foreign policies with League criteria in mind. Most devastating, however, was the refusal of the United States Senate to ratify the covenant of the League. Isolationism had a long tradition in US foreign policy, and many American politicians were isolationists even if President Wilson was not; they did not want to involve their country in the entangling and murky affairs of Europe. So, much to Wilson's chagrin, the strongest state in the international system—his own—did not join the League. With a number of important states outside the League, including the most important, and with the two major powers inside the organization lacking any real commitment to it, the League never achieved the central position marked out for it in Wilson's blueprint.

Norman Angell's high hopes for a smooth process of modernization and inter-dependence also foundered on the harsh realities of the 1930s. The Wall Street crash of October 1929 marked the beginning of a severe economic crisis in Western countries that would last until the Second World War and would involve severe measures of economic protectionism. World trade shrank dramatically, and industrial production in developed countries declined rapidly to become only one third of what it was a few years before. In ironic contrast to Angell's vision, it was every country for itself, each country trying as best it could to look after its own interests, if necessary to the detriment of others—the 'jungle' rather than the 'zoo'. The historical stage was being set for a less hopeful and more pessimistic understanding of international relations.

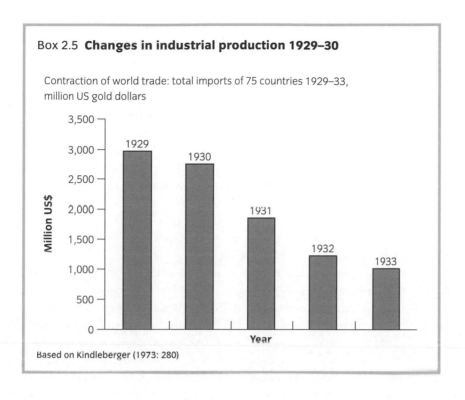

Box 2.5 **Changes in industrial production 1929–30**

Contraction of world trade: total imports of 75 countries 1929–33, million US gold dollars

Based on Kindleberger (1973: 280)

Realism and the Twenty Years' Crisis

Liberal idealism was not a good intellectual guide to international relations in the 1930s. Interdependence did not produce peaceful cooperation; the League of Nations was helpless in the face of the expansionist power politics conducted by the authoritarian regimes in Germany, Italy, and Japan. Academic IR began to speak the classical realist language of Thucydides, Machiavelli, and Hobbes in which the grammar and the vocabulary of power was central.

The most comprehensive and penetrating critique of liberal idealism was that of E. H. Carr, a British IR scholar. In *The Twenty Years' Crisis* (1964 [1939]) Carr argued that liberal IR thinkers profoundly misread the facts of history and misunderstood the nature of international relations. They erroneously believed that such relations could be based on a harmony of interest between countries and people. According to Carr, the correct starting-point is the opposite one: we should assume that there are profound conflicts of interest both between countries and between people. Some people and some countries are better off than others. They will attempt to preserve and defend their privileged position. The underdogs, the 'have-nots', will struggle to change that situation. International relations is in a basic sense about the struggle between such conflicting interests and desires. That is why IR is far more about conflict than about cooperation. Carr astutely labeled the liberal position 'utopian' as a contrast to his own position, which he labeled 'realist', thus implying that his approach was the more sober and correct analysis of international relations.

The other significant realist statement from this period was produced by a German scholar who fled to the United States in the 1930s to escape from the Nazi regime in Germany: Hans J. Morgenthau. More than any other European émigré scholar Morgenthau brought realism to the US, and with great success. His *Politics Among Nations: The Struggle for Power and Peace*, first published in 1948, was for several decades the most influential American book on IR (Morgenthau 1960). There were other authors writing along the same realist lines: among the most important were Reinhold Niebuhr, George Kennan, and Arnold Wolfers. But Morgenthau gave the clearest summary of realism's core claims and had the widest appeal to IR scholars and their students.

For Morgenthau, human nature was at the base of international relations. And humans were self-interested and power-seeking and that could easily result in aggression. In the late 1930s it was not difficult to find evidence to support such a view. Hitler's Germany, Mussolini's Italy, and Imperial Japan pursued blatantly aggressive foreign policies aimed at conflict, not cooperation. Armed struggle for the creation of *Lebensraum*, of a larger and stronger Germany, was at the core of Hitler's political program. Furthermore, and ironically from a liberal perspective, both Hitler and Mussolini enjoyed widespread popular support despite the fact that they were autocratic and even tyrannical leaders. Even the most horrendous component of Hitler's political project—elimination of the Jews—enjoyed such popular support (Goldhagen 1996).

Why should international relations be egoistic and aggressive? Observing the growth of fascism in the 1930s, Einstein wrote to Freud that there must be 'a human lust for hatred and destruction' (Ebenstein 1951: 802–4). Freud confirmed that such an aggressive impulse did indeed exist, and he remained deeply sceptical about the possibilities for taming it.

Another possible explanation draws on Christian religion. According to the Bible, humans have been endowed with original sin and a temptation for evil ever since Adam and Eve were thrown out of Paradise. The first murder in history is Cain's killing of his brother Abel out of pure envy. Human nature is plain bad; that is the starting-point for realist analysis.

The second major element in the realist view concerns the nature of international relations. 'International politics, like all politics, is a struggle for power. Whatever the ultimate aims of international politics, power is always the immediate aim' (Morgenthau 1960: 29). There is no world government. On the contrary, there is a system of sovereign and armed states facing each other. World politics is an international anarchy. The 1930s and 1940s appeared to confirm this proposition. International relations was a struggle for power and for survival. The quest for power certainly characterized the foreign policies of Germany,

---

Box 2.6 **Freud's reply to Einstein**

Freud's reply [to Einstein] drew on his theoretical work. We see this necessity for repression, Freud explained, in the imposition of discipline by parents over children by institutions over individuals, and by the state over society. From this he deduced, and Einstein agreed, that a world government was needed to impose the necessary discipline on the otherwise danger-ously anarchic international system. But whereas Einstein became a supporter of the United World Federalists and other groups working toward the establishment of world government, Freud doubted that humans have the requisite capacity to overcome their irrational attach-ments to national and religious groups. The father of psychoanalysis, therefore, remained deeply pessimistic about the prospects for fundamentally reducing the role of war in world politics.

Brown (1994: 10–11)

Italy, and Japan. The same struggle, in response, applied to the Allied side during the Second World War. Britain, France, and the United States were the 'haves' in Carr's terms, the satisfied powers who wanted to hold on to what they already had, and Germany, Italy, and Japan were the 'have-nots.' So it was only natural, according to realist thinking, that the 'have nots' would try and redress the international balance through the use of force.

Following realist analysis, the sole appropriate response to such attempts is the creation of countervailing power and the intelligent utilization of that power to provide for national defense and to deter potential aggressors. In other words, it was essential to maintain an effective balance of power as the only way to preserve peace and prevent war. This is a view of international politics that denies that it is possible to reorganize the 'jungle' into a 'zoo'. The strongest animals will never allow themselves to be captured and put in cages. Germany following the First World War was seen as proof of that truth. The League of Nations failed to put Germany in a cage. It took a world war, millions of casualties, heroic sacrifice, and vast material resources finally to defeat the challenge from Nazi Germany, Fascist Italy, and Imperial Japan. All of that might have been avoided if a realistic foreign policy based on the principle of countervailing power had been followed by Britain, France, and the United States right from the start of Germany's, Italy's, and Japan's saber-rattling. Negotiations and diplomacy by themselves can never bring security and survival in world politics.

The third major component in the realist view is a cyclical view of history. Contrary to the optimistic liberal view that qualitative change for the better is possible, realism stresses continuity and repetition. Each new generation tends to make the same sort of mistake as previous generations. Any change in this situation is highly unlikely. As long as sovereign states are the dominant form of political organization, power politics will continue and states will have to look after their security and prepare for war. In other words, the Second World War was no extraordinary event; neither was the First World War. Sovereign states can live in peace with each other for long periods when there is a stable balance of power. But every now and then that precarious balance will break down and war is likely to follow. There can of course be many different causes of such breakdown. Some realist scholars think that the Paris Peace Conference of 1919 contained the seeds of the Second World War because of the harsh conditions that the peace treaty imposed on Germany. But domestic developments in Germany, the emergence of Hitler, and many other factors are also relevant in accounting for that war.

In sum, the classical realism of Carr and Morgenthau combine a pessimistic view of human nature with a notion of power politics between states which exist in an international anarchy. They see no prospects of change in that situation: for classical realists, independent states in an anarchic international system are a permanent feature of international relations. The classical realist analysis appeared to capture the essentials of European politics in the 1930s and world politics in the 1940s far better than liberal optimism. When international relations took the shape of an East–West confrontation, or Cold War, after 1945 realism again appeared to be the best approach for making sense of what was going on.

The debate between the utopian liberalism of the 1920s and the realism of the 1930s–1950s make up the two contending positions in the first major debate in IR (see Box 2.7).

Box 2.7 **First major debate in IR**

UTOPIAN LIBERALISM 1920s		REALIST RESPONSE 1930s–1950s
Focus	⟵——————⟶	*Focus*
• International law		• Power politics
• International organization		• Security
• Interdependence		• Aggression
• Cooperation		• Conflict
• Peace		• War

The first major debate was clearly won by Carr, Morgenthau, and the other realist thinkers. Realism became the dominant way of thinking about international relations not only among scholars but also among politicians and diplomats. Morgenthau's summary of realism in his 1948 book became the standard introduction to IR in the 1950s and 1960s. Yet it is important to emphasize that liberalism did not disappear. Many liberals conceded that realism was the better guide to international relations in the 1930s and 1940s, but they saw this as an extreme and abnormal historical period. Liberals of course rejected the deeply pessimistic realist idea that humans were 'plain bad' (Wight 1991: 25) and they had some strong counter-arguments to that effect, as we shall see in Chapter 4. Finally, the postwar period was not only about a struggle for power and survival between the United States and the Soviet Union and their political-military alliances. It was also about cooperation and international institutions, such as the United Nations and its many special organizations. Although realism had won the first debate, there were still competing theories in the discipline that refused to accept permanent defeat.

The Voice of Behavioralism in IR

The second major debate in IR concerns methodology. In order to understand how that debate emerged, it is necessary to be aware of the fact that the first generations of IR scholars were trained as historians or academic lawyers, or were former diplomats or journalists. They often brought a humanistic and historical approach to the study of IR. This approach is rooted in philosophy, history, and law, and is characterized 'above all by explicit reliance upon the exercise of judgment' (Bull 1969). Locating judgment at the heart of international theory serves to emphasize the normative character of the subject which at its core involves some profoundly difficult moral questions that neither politicians nor diplomats nor anyone else who is involved can escape, such as the deployment of nuclear weapons and their justified uses, military intervention in independent states, and so forth. That is because the deployment and use of power in human relations, military power especially, always has to be justified and can thus never be divorced completely from normative considerations. This way of studying IR is usually referred to as the traditional, or classical, approach.

After the Second World War, the academic discipline of IR expanded rapidly. That was particularly the case in the United States, where government agencies and private foundations were willing to support 'scientific' IR research which they could justify as being in the national interest. That support produced a new generation of IR scholars who adopted a rigorous methodological approach. They were usually trained in political science, economics, or other social sciences, sometimes in mathematics and the natural sciences, rather than diplomatic history, international law, or political philosophy. These new IR scholars thus had a very different academic background and equally different ideas concerning how IR should be studied. These new ideas came to be summarized under

> Box 2.8 **Behavioralist science in brief**
>
> Once the investigator has mastered the existing knowledge, and has organized it for his purposes he pleads a 'meaningful ignorance'. 'Here is what I know; what do I not know that is worth knowing'. Once an area has been selected for investigation the questions should be posed as clearly as possible, and it is here that quantification can prove useful provided that mathematical tools are combined with carefully constructed taxonomic schemes. Surveying the field of international relations, or any sector of it, we see many disparate elements . . . wondering whether there may be any significant relationships between A and B, or between B and C. By a process which we are compelled to call 'intuition' . . . we perceive a possible correlation, hitherto unsuspected or not firmly known, between two or more elements. At this point, we have the ingredients of a hypothesis which can be expressed in measurable referents, and which, if validated, would be both explanatory and predictive.
>
> Dougherty and Pfaltzgraff (1921: 36–7)

the term 'behavioralism', which signified not so much a new theory as a novel methodology which endeavored to be 'scientific' in the natural-science meaning of that term.

Just as scholars of science are able to formulate objective and verifiable 'laws' to explain the physical world, the ambition of behavioralists in IR is to do the same for the world of international relations. The main task is to collect empirical data about international relations, preferably large amounts of data, which can then be used for measurement, classification, generalization, and, ultimately, the validation of hypotheses, i.e. scientifically explained patterns of behavior. Behavioralism is thus not a new IR theory; it is a new method of studying IR. Behavioralism is more interested in observable facts and measurable data, in precise calculation, and the collection of data in order to find recurring behavioral patterns, the 'laws' of international relations. According to behavioralists, facts are separate from values. Unlike facts, values cannot be explained scientifically. The behavioralists were therefore inclined to study facts while ignoring values. The scientific procedure that behavioralists support is laid out as in Box 2.9.

The two methodological approaches to IR briefly described above, the traditional and the behavioral, are clearly very different. The traditional approach is a holistic one that accepts the complexity of the human world, sees international relations as part of the human world, and seeks to understand it in a humanistic way by getting *inside* it. That involves imaginatively entering into the role of states-people, attempting to understand the moral dilemmas in their foreign policies, and appreciating the basic values involved, such as security, order, freedom, and justice. To approach IR in that traditional way involves the scholar in understanding the history and practice of diplomacy, the history and role of

---

Box 2.9 **The scientific procedure of behavioralists**

The hypothesis must be validated through testing. This demands the construction of a verifying experiment or the gathering of empirical data in other ways . . . The results of the data-gathering effort are carefully observed, recorded and analyzed, after which the hypothesis is discarded, modified, reformulated or confirmed. Findings are published and others are invited to duplicate this knowledge-discovering adventure, and to confirm or deny. This, very roughly, is what we usually mean by 'the scientific method'.

Dougherty and Pfaltzgraff (1971: 37)

---

international law, the political theory of the sovereign state, and so forth. IR is on that view a broadly humanistic subject; it is not and could never be a strictly scientific or narrowly technical subject.

The other approach, behavioralism, has no place for morality or ethics in the study of IR because that involves values, and values cannot be studied objectively, i.e. scientifically. Behavioralism thus raises a fundamental question which continues to be discussed today: can we formulate scientific laws about international relations (and about the social world, the world of human relations, in general)? Critics emphasize what they see as a major mistake in that method: the mistake of treating human relations as an external phenomenon in the same general category as nature so that the theorist stands *outside* the subject—like an anatomist dissecting a cadaver. The anti-behavioralists hold that the theorist of human affairs is a human being who can never divorce himself or herself completely from human relations: he or she is always *inside* the subject (Hollis and Smith 1990; Jackson 2000). The scholar can strive for detachment and moral neutrality but can never succeed completely. Some scholars attempt to reconcile these approaches: they seek to be historically conscious about IR as a sphere of human relations while also trying to come up with general models that seek to explain and not merely understand world politics. Morgenthau might be an example of that. In studying the moral dilemmas of foreign policy he is in the traditionalist camp; yet he also sets forth general 'laws of politics' which are supposed to apply at all times in all places, and that would appear to put him in the behavioralist camp.

The behavioralists did not win the second major debate, but neither did the traditionalists. After a few years of vigorous controversy the second great debate petered out. A compromise resulted which has been portrayed as 'different ends of a continuum of scholarship rather than completely different games . . . Each type of effort can inform and enrich the other and can as well act as a check on the excesses endemic in each approach' (Finnegan 1972: 64). Yet behavioralism did have a lasting effect in IR. That was largely because of the domination of the discipline after the Second World War by US scholars the vast majority of whom supported the quantitative, scientific ambitions of behavioralism. They also led the way in setting a research agenda focused on the role of the two super-powers, especially the United States, in the international system. That paved the way to new formulations of both realism and liberalism that were heavily influenced by behavioralist methodologies. These new formulations—neorealism and neoliberalism—led to a replay of the first major debate under new historical and methodological conditions.

Box 2.10 Second major debate in IR

TRADITIONAL APPROACHES	BEHAVIORALIST RESPONSE
Focus	*Focus*
UNDERSTANDING ⟷	EXPLAINING
• Norms and values	• Hypothesis
• Judgment	• Collection of data
• Historical knowledge	• Scientific knowledge
Theorist inside subject	Theorist outside subject

Neoliberalism: Institutions and Interdependence

Having won the first major debate, realism remained the dominant theoretical approach in IR. The second debate about methodology did not immediately change that situation. After 1945 the center of gravity in international relations was the Cold War struggle between the United States and the Soviet Union. The East–West rivalry lent itself easily to a realist interpretation of the world.

Yet during the 1950s, 1960s, and 1970s a good deal of international relations concerned trade and investment, travel and communication, and similar issues which were especially prevalent in the relations between the liberal democracies of the West. Those relations provided the basis for a new attempt by liberals to formulate an alternative to realist thinking that would avoid the utopian excesses of earlier liberalism. We shall use the label 'neoliberalism' for that renewed liberal approach. Neoliberals share old liberal ideas about the possibility of progress and change, but they repudiate idealism. They also strive to formulate theories and apply new methods which are scientific. In short, the debate between liberalism and realism continued, but it was now colored by the post-1945 international setting and the behavioralist methodological persuasion.

In the 1950s a process of regional integration was getting under way in Western Europe which caught the attention and imagination of neoliberals. By 'integration' we refer to a particularly intensive form of international cooperation. Early theorists of integration studied how certain functional activities across borders (trade, investment, etc.) offered mutually advantageous longterm cooperation. Other neoliberal theorists studied how integration fed on itself: cooperation in one transactional area paved the way for cooperation in other areas (Haas 1958; Keohane and Nye 1975). During the 1950s and 1960s Western Europe and Japan developed mass-consumption welfare states, as the United States had done already before the war. That development entailed a higher level of trade, communication, cultural exchange, and other relations and transactions across borders.

Box 2.11 OECD countries, total import/export, million current US$

	1965	1970	1975	1980	2000
IMPORTS, C.I.F.	10,804	18,803	48,945	114,086	4,379,185
EXPORTS, F.O.B.	10,455	18,333	47,315	103,487	4,041,170

Based on OECD and UNCTAD trade statistics

This provides the basis for *sociological liberalism*, a strand of neoliberal thinking which emphasizes the impact of these expanding cross-border activities. In the 1950s Karl Deutsch and his associates argued that such interconnecting activities helped create common values and identities among people from different states and paved the way for peaceful, cooperative relations by making war increasingly costly and thus more unlikely. They also tried to measure the integration phenomenon scientifically (Deutsch *et al.* 1957).

In the 1970s Robert Keohane and Joseph Nye developed such ideas further. They argued that relationships between Western states (including Japan) are characterized by complex interdependence: there are many forms of connections between societies in addition to the political relations of governments, including transnational links between business corporations. There is also an 'absence of hierarchy among issues': i.e. military security does not dominate the agenda any more. Military force is no longer used as an instrument of foreign policy (Keohane and Nye 1977: 25). Complex interdependence portrays a situation that is radically different from the realist picture of international relations. In Western democracies there are other actors besides states, and violent conflict clearly is not on their international agenda. We can call this form of neoliberalism *interdependence liberalism*. Robert Keohane and Joseph Nye (1977) are among the main contributors to this line of thinking.

When there is a high degree of interdependence, states will often set up international institutions to deal with common problems. Institutions promote cooperation across international boundaries by providing information and by reducing costs. Institutions can be formal international organizations, such as the WTO or EU or OECD, or they can be less formal sets of agreements (often called regimes) which deal with common activities or issues, such as agreements about shipping, aviation, communication, or the environment. We can call this form of neoliberalism *institutional liberalism*. Robert Keohane (1989a) and Oran Young (1986) are among the main contributors to this line of thinking.

The fourth and final strand of neoliberalism—*republican liberalism*—picks up on a theme developed in earlier liberal thinking. It is the idea that liberal democracies enhance peace because they do not go to war against each other. It has been strongly influenced by the rapid spread of democratization in the world after the end of the Cold War, especially in the former Soviet satellite countries in Eastern Europe. An influential version of the theory of democratic peace was set forth by Michael Doyle (1983). Doyle finds that the democratic peace is based on three pillars: the first is peaceful conflict resolution between democratic states; the second is common values among democratic states—a common moral foundation; the final pillar is economic cooperation among democracies. Republican liberals are generally optimistic that there will be a steadily expanding 'Zone of Peace' among liberal democracies even though there may also be occasional setbacks.

Box 2.12 **Neoliberalism: progress and cooperation**

Sociological liberalism	Cross-border flows, common values
Interdependence liberalism	Transactions stimulate cooperation
Institutional liberalism	International institutions, regimes
Republican liberalism	Liberal democracies living in peace with each other

---

These different strands of neoliberalism are mutually supportive in providing an overall consistent argument for more peaceful and cooperative international relations. They consequently stand as a challenge to the realist analysis of IR. In the 1970s there was a general feeling among IR scholars that neoliberalism was on the way to becoming the dominant theoretical approach in the discipline. But a reformulation of realism by Kenneth Waltz (1979) once again tipped the balance towards realism. Neoliberal thinking could make convincing reference to relations between industrialized liberal democracies to argue its case about a more cooperative and interdependent world. But the East–West confrontation remained a stubborn feature of international relations in the 1970s and 1980s. The new reflections on realism took their cue from that historical fact.

Neorealism: Bipolarity and Confrontation

Kenneth Waltz broke new ground in his book *Theory of International Politics* (1979), which sets forth a substantially different realist theory inspired by the scientific ambitions of behavioralism. His theory is most often referred to as 'neorealism', and we shall employ that label. Waltz attempts to formulate 'law-like statements' about international relations that achieve scientific validity. He thus departs sharply from classical realism in showing virtually no interest in the ethics of statecraft or the moral dilemmas of foreign policy—concerns that are strongly evident in the realist writings of Morgenthau.

Waltz's focus is on the 'structure' of the international system and the consequences of that structure for international relations. The concept of structure is defined as follows. First, Waltz notes that the international system is an anarchy; there is no worldwide government. Second, the international system is composed of like units: every state, small or large, has to perform a similar set of government functions such as national defense, tax collection, and economic regulation. However, there is one respect in which states are different and often very different: in their power, what Waltz calls their relative capabilities. Waltz thus draws a very parsimonious and abstract picture of the international system with very few elements. International relations is thus an anarchy composed of states that vary in only one important respect: their relative power. Anarchy is likely to endure, according to Waltz, because states want to preserve their autonomy.

The international system that came into existence after the Second World War was dominated by two superpowers, the United States and the Soviet Union: i.e. it was a bipolar system. The demise of the Soviet Union has resulted in a different system with several great powers but with the United States as the predominant power in the system: i.e. it is moving towards a multipolar system. Waltz does not claim that these few pieces of information about the structure of the international system can explain everything about international politics. But he believes that they can explain 'a few big and important things' (Waltz 1986: 322–47). What are they? First, great powers will always tend to balance each other. With the Soviet Union gone, the United States dominates the system. But 'balance-of-power theory leads one to predict that other countries . . . will try to bring American power into balance' (Waltz 1993: 52). Second, smaller and weaker states will have a tendency to align themselves with great powers in order to preserve their maximum autonomy. In making this argument Waltz departs sharply from the classical realist argument based on human nature viewed as 'plain bad' and thus leading to conflict and confrontation. For Waltz states are power-seeking and security-conscious not because of human nature but rather because the structure of the international system compels them to be that way.

This last point is also important because it is the basis for neorealism's counterattack against the neoliberals. Neorealists do not deny all possibilities for cooperation among states. But they do maintain that cooperating states will always strive to maximize their relative power and preserve their autonomy. In other words, just because there is cooperation, as for example in relations between industrialized liberal democracies (e.g. between the United States and Japan), it does not mean that the neoliberal view has been vindicated. We shall return to the details of this debate in Chapter 4. Here we merely draw attention to the fact that neorealism succeeded in putting neoliberalism on the defensive in the 1980s. Theoretical arguments were significant in this development. But historical events also played an important role. In the 1980s the confrontation between the United States and the Soviet Union reached a new level. US President Ronald Reagan referred to the Soviet Union as an 'evil empire', and in that hostile international climate the arms race between the superpowers was sharply intensified. At about that time the United States was also feeling the increasing competitive pressure from Japan and to some extent from Europe too. Armed conflict between the liberal democracies was certainly not on the agenda; but there were 'trade wars' and other disputes between the Western democracies which appeared to confirm the neorealist hypothesis about competition between self-interested countries who were fundamentally concerned about their power position relative to each other.

During the 1980s some neorealists and neoliberals came close to sharing a common analytical starting-point that is basically neorealist in character: i.e. states are the main actors in what is still an international anarchy and they constantly look after their own best interests (Baldwin 1993). Neoliberals still argued that institutions, interdependence, and democracy led to more thoroughgoing cooperation than is predicted by neorealists. But many current versions of neorealism and neoliberalism were no longer diametrically opposed. In methodological terms there was even more common ground between neorealists and neoliberals. Both strongly supported the scientific project launched by the behavioralists, even though republican liberals were a partial exception in that regard.

As indicated earlier, the debate between neorealism and neoliberalism can be seen as a continuation of the first major debate in IR. But unlike the earlier debate this one resulted in most neoliberals accepting most of the neorealist assumptions as starting-points for analysis. Robert Keohane (1986) attempted to formulate a synthesis of neorealism and neoliberalism coming from the neoliberal side. Barry Buzan *et al.* (1993) made a similar attempt coming from the neorealist side. However, there is still no complete synthesis between the two traditions. Some neorealists (e.g. Mearsheimer 1991; 1995*b*) and neoliberals (e.g. Rosenau 1990) are far from reconciled to each other and keep arguing exclusively in favor of their side of the debate. The debate is therefore a continuing one.

....

International Society: The English School

The behavioralist challenge was most strongly felt among IR scholars in the United States. The neorealist and neoliberal acceptance of that challenge also came predominantly from the American academic community. As indicated earlier, during the 1950s and 1960s American scholarship completely dominated the developing but still youthful IR discipline. Stanley Hoffman made the point that the discipline of IR was 'born and raised in America', and he analyzed the profound consequences of that fact for thinking and theorizing in IR (Hoffmann 1977: 41–59). Among the most important of such consequences is the fact that IR continues to be dominated by American scholars even though their pre-eminence may be declining. In the 1970s and 1980s the IR agenda was preoccupied with the neoliberalism/neorealism debate. In the 1990s after the end of the Cold War American predominance in the discipline became less pronounced. IR scholars in Europe and elsewhere became more self-confident and less ready to accept an agenda largely written by US scholars.

In the United Kingdom a school of IR had existed throughout the period of the Cold War which was different in two major ways. It rejected the behavioralist challenge and emphasized the traditional approach based on human understanding, judgment, norms, and history. It also rejected any firm distinction between a strict realist and a strict liberal view of international relations. The IR school to which we refer is sometimes called 'the English School'. But that name is far too narrow: it overlooks the fact that several of its leading figures were not English and many were not even from the United Kingdom; rather, they were from Australia, Canada, and South Africa. For that reason we shall use its other name: International Society. Two leading International Society theorists of the twentieth century are Martin Wight and Hedley Bull.

International Society theorists recognize the importance of power in international affairs. They also focus on the state and the state system. But they reject the narrow realist view that world politics is a Hobbesian state of nature in which there are no international norms at all. They view the state as the combination of a *Machtstaat* (power state) and a *Rechtsstaat* (constitutional state): power and law are both important features of international relations. It is true that there is an international anarchy in the sense that there is no world government. But international anarchy is a social and not an antisocial condition: i.e. world politics is an 'anarchical society' (Bull 1995). International Society theorists also recognize the importance of the individual, and some of them argue that individuals are prior to states. Unlike many contemporary liberals, however, International Society theorists tend to regard IGOs and NGOs (intergovernmental and nongovernmental organizations) as marginal rather than central features of world

> ### Box 2.13 **International Society**
>
> A *society of states* (or international society) exists when a group of states, conscious of certain common interests and common values form a society in the sense that they conceive themselves to be bound by a common set of rules in their relations with one another, and share in the working of common institutions. My contention is that the element of a society has always been present, and remains present, in the modern international system.
>
> Bull (1995: 13, 39)

politics. They emphasize the relations of states and they play down the importance of transnational relations.

International Society theorists find that realists are correct in pointing to the importance of power and national interest. But if we push the realist view to its logical conclusion, states would always be preoccupied with playing the tough game of power politics; in a pure anarchy, there can be no mutual trust. That view is clearly misleading; there is warfare, but states are not continually preoccupied with each other's power, nor do they conceive of that power exclusively as a threat. On the other hand, if we take the liberal idealist view to the extreme, it means that all relations between states are governed by common rules in a perfect world of mutual respect and the rule of law. That view too is clearly misleading. Of course there are common rules and norms that most states can be expected to observe most of the time; in that sense relations between states constitute an international society. But these rules and norms cannot by themselves guarantee international harmony and cooperation; power and the balance of power still remain very important in the anarchical society.

The United Nations system demonstrates how both elements—power and law—are simultaneously present in international society. The Security Council is set up according to the reality of unequal power among states. The great powers (the United States, China, Russia, Britain, France) are the only permanent members with the authority to veto decisions. That simply recognizes the reality of unequal power in world politics. The great powers have a de facto veto anyway: it would be very difficult to force them to do anything that they were not prepared to do. That is the 'realist power and inequality element' in international society. The General Assembly—by contrast with the Security Council—is set up according to the principle of international equality: every member state is legally equal to every other state; each state has one vote, and the majority rather than the most powerful prevail. That is the rationalist 'common rules and norms' element in international society. Finally, the UN also provides evidence about the importance of individuals in international affairs. The UN has promoted the international law of human rights, beginning with the Universal Declaration of Human Rights (1948). Today there is an elaborate structure of humanitarian law which defines the basic civil, political, social, economic, and cultural rights that are intended to promote an acceptable standard of human existence in the contemporary world. That is the Cosmopolitan or Solidarist element of international society.

For International Society theorists the study of international relations is not about singling out one of these elements and disregarding the others. They do not seek to make and test hypotheses with the aim of constructing scientific laws of IR. They are not trying to explain international relations scientifically; rather, they are trying to understand it and interpret it. International Society theorists thus take a broader historical, legal, and philosophical approach to international relations. IR is about discerning and exploring the complex presence of all these elements and the normative problems they present to state leaders. Power and national interests matter; so do common norms and institutions. States are important, but so are human beings. Statesmen and stateswomen have a national responsibility to their own nation and its citizens; they have an international responsibility to observe and follow international law and respect the rights of other states; and they have a humanitarian responsibility to defend human rights around the world. But as the 1990s crises in Bosnia, Somalia, and the Persian Gulf clearly demonstrated, carrying out these responsibilities in a justifiable way is no easy task (Jackson 2000).

In sum, International Society is an approach which tells us something about a world of sovereign states where power and law are both present. The ethics of prudence and the national interest claim the responsibilities of statespeople alongside their duty to observe international rules and procedures. World politics is a world of states but it is also a world of human beings, and it will often be difficult to reconcile the demands and claims of both. The main elements of the International Society approach are summarized in Box 2.14.

The challenge posed by the International Society approach does not count as a new major debate. It should rather be seen as an extension of the first debate and

---

Box 2.14 International Society (the English School)

METHODOLOGICAL FOCUS	MAIN ELEMENTS IN THE INTERNATIONAL SYSTEM
• Understanding	1. Power, national interest (realist element)
• Judgment	2. Rules, procedures, international law (liberal element)
• Values and norms	3. Universal human rights, one world for all (cosmopolitan element)
• Historical knowledge	
Theorist inside subject	

a repudiation of the seeming behavioralist triumph in the second debate. International Society builds on classical realist and liberal ideas, combining and expanding them in ways which provides an alternative to both. International Society adds another perspective to the first great debate between realism and liberalism by rejecting the sharp division between them. Although International Society scholars did not enter that debate directly, their approach clearly suggests that the difference between realism and liberalism is drawn too sharply: the historical world does not choose between power and law in quite the categorical way that the debate implies. As regards the second great debate between the traditionalists and the behavioralists, International Society theorists did enter that debate by firmly rejecting the latter approach and upholding the former approach (Bull 1969). International Society scholars do not see any possibility of the construction of 'laws' of IR on the model of the natural sciences. For them, that project is flawed: it is based on an intellectual misreading of the character of international relations. For International Society scholars IR is entirely a field of human relations: it is thus a normative subject and it cannot be fully understood in non-normative terms. IR is about understanding, not explaining; it involves the exercise of judgment: putting oneself in the place of statespeople to try better to understand the dilemmas they confront in their conduct of foreign policy. The notion of an international society also provides a perspective for studying issues of human rights and humanitarian intervention which figured prominently on the IR agenda at that time.

To sum up: International Society scholars emphasize the simultaneous presence in international society of both realist and liberal elements. There is conflict and there is cooperation; there are states and there are individuals. These different elements cannot be simplified and abstracted into a single theory that emphasizes only one explanatory variable—e.g. power. That would be a much too simple view of world politics and would distort reality. International Society theorists argue for a humanist approach that recognizes the simultaneous presence of all these elements, and the need for holistic and historical study of the problems and dilemmas that arise in that complex situation.

International Political Economy (IPE)

The academic IR debates presented so far are mainly concerned with international politics. Economic affairs play a secondary role. There is little concern with the weak states in the Third World. As we noted in Chapter 1, the decades after the Second World War were a period of decolonization. A large number of 'new' countries appeared on the map as the old colonial powers gave up their control and the former colonies were given political independence. Many of the 'new' states are weak in economic terms: they are at the bottom of the global economic hierarchy and constitute a 'Third World'. In the 1970s Third World countries started to press for changes in the international system to improve their economic position in relation to the developed countries. Around this time, neo-Marxism emerged as an attempt to theorize about economic underdevelopment in the Third World.

This became the basis for a third major debate in IR about international wealth and international poverty—i.e. about international political economy or IPE for short. IPE is basically about who gets what in the international economic and political system. The third debate takes the shape of a neo-Marxist critique of the capitalist world economy together with liberal IPE and realist IPE responses concerning the relationship between economics and politics in international relations.

Neo-Marxism is an attempt to analyze the situation of the Third World by applying the tools of analysis first developed by Karl Marx. Marx, a famous nineteenth-century political economist, focused on capitalism in Europe; he argued that the bourgeoisie or capitalist class used its economic power to exploit and oppress the proletariat, or working class. Neo-Marxists extend that analysis to the Third World by arguing that the global capitalist economy controlled by the wealthy capitalist states is used to impoverish the world's poor countries. 'Dependence' is a core concept for neo-Marxists. They claim that countries in the Third World are not poor because they are inherently backward or undeveloped. Rather, it is because they have been actively underdeveloped by the rich countries of the First World. Third World countries are subject to unequal exchange: in order to participate in the global capitalist economy they must sell their raw materials at cheap prices, and they have to buy finished goods at high prices. In marked contrast, rich countries can buy low and sell high. It is important to emphasize that for neo-Marxists that situation is imposed upon poor countries by the wealthy capitalist states.

Andre Gunder Frank claims that unequal exchange and appropriation of economic surplus by the few at the expense of the many are inherent in capitalism (Frank 1967). As long as the capitalist system exists there will be underdevelopment in the Third World. A similar view is taken by Immanuel Wallerstein (1974; 1983), who has analyzed the overall development of the capitalist world system since its beginning in the sixteenth century. Wallerstein allows for the possibility that some Third World countries can 'move upwards' in the global capitalist hierarchy. But only a few can do that; there is no room at the top for everybody. Capitalism is a hierarchy based on the exploitation of the poor by the rich, and it will remain that way unless and until it is replaced.

The liberal view of IPE is very different and almost exactly the opposite. Liberal IPE scholars argue that human prosperity can be achieved by the free global expansion of capitalism beyond the boundaries of the sovereign state, and by the decline of the significance of these boundaries. Liberals draw from the economic

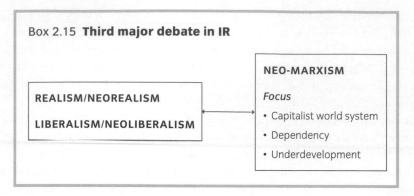

Box 2.15 **Third major debate in IR**

REALISM/NEOREALISM

LIBERALISM/NEOLIBERALISM

NEO-MARXISM

Focus

• Capitalist world system

• Dependency

• Underdevelopment

analysis of Adam Smith and other classical liberal economists, who argue that free markets together with private property and individual freedom create the basis for self-sustaining economic progress for everybody involved. People would not conduct exchange on the free market unless it was to their benefit: 'Since the household always has the alternative of producing directly for itself, it need not enter into any exchange unless it benefits from it. Hence, no exchange will take place unless both parties do benefit from it' (Friedman 1962: 13–14). Thus, whereas Marxist IPE views international capitalism as an instrument for the exploitation of the Third World by the developed countries, liberal IPE views it as an instrument of progressive change for all countries regardless of their level of development.

Realist IPE is different again. It can be traced back to the thought of Friedrich List, a nineteenth-century German economist. It is based on the idea that economic activity should be put in the service of building a strong state and supporting the national interest. Wealth should thus be controlled and managed by the state; that statist IPE doctrine is often referred to as 'Mercantilism' or 'economic nationalism'. For Mercantilists, the creation of wealth is the necessary basis for increased power of the state. Wealth is therefore an instrument in the creation of national security and national welfare. Moreover, the smooth functioning of a free market depends on political power. Without a dominant or hegemonic power, there can be no liberal world economy (Gilpin 1987: 72). The United States has had the role of hegemon since the end of the First World War. But beginning in the early 1970s the US was increasingly challenged economically by Japan and by Western Europe. And according to realist IPE that decline of US leadership has weakened the liberal world economy, because there is no other state that can perform the role of global hegemon.

These different views of IPE show up in analyses of three important and related IPE issues of recent years. The first issue concerns economic globalization: that is, the spread and intensification of all kinds of economic relations between countries. Does economic globalization undermine 'national' economies by erasing national borders and by subjecting national economies to the exigencies of the global economy? The second issue is about who wins and who loses in the process of economic globalization. The third issue concerns how we should view the relative importance of economics and politics. Are global economic relations ultimately controlled by states who set out the framework of rules that economic actors have to observe? Or are politicians increasingly subject to anonymous market forces over which they have lost effective control? Underlying many of these questions is the issue of state sovereignty: are the forces of global economics making the sovereign state obsolete? The three approaches to IPE come up with very different answers to these questions, as we shall see in Chapter 6.

In short, the third major debate further complicates the discipline of IR because it shifts the subject away from political and military issues and towards economic and social issues, and because it introduces the distinct socioeconomic problems of Third World countries. It is not a debate like the previous two IR debates discussed above. Rather, it is a marked expansion of the academic IR research agenda to include socioeconomic questions of welfare as well as political-military questions of security. Yet both the realist and the liberal tradition have specific views on IPE, and those views have been attacked by neo-Marxism. And all three perspectives are in rather sharp disagreement with each other: they take fundamentally different views of the international political economy in terms of both concepts and values. In that sense we do indeed have a third debate. The debate was focused on North–South relations at first, but it has long since expanded to include IPE issues in all areas of international relations. There was no clear winner in the third debate, as we shall see in Chapter 6.

. . . .

Dissident Voices: Alternative Approaches to IR

The debates introduced so far have concerned the established theoretical traditions in the discipline: realism, liberalism, International Society, and the theories of international political economy (IPE). Currently a fourth debate is under way in IR. It involves various critiques of the established traditions by alternative approaches, sometimes identified as post-positivism (Smith *et al.* 1996).

There have always been 'dissident voices' in the discipline of IR: philosophers and scholars who have rejected established views and tried to replace them with alternatives. But in recent years these voices have increased in number.

Two factors help explain that development. The end of the Cold War changed the international agenda in some fundamental ways. In place of a clear-cut East/West conflict dominated by two contending superpowers a number of diverse issues emerged in world politics, including for example: state partition and disintegration, civil war, terrorism, democratization, national minorities,

> ## Box 2.16 **Post-positivist approaches**
>
> In the last few years a number of powerful attacks on realism have been mounted by scholars from a diffuse grouping of positions . . . there are four main groupings involved in this challenge. The first comes from critical theory. A second strand of thought has developed . . . under the general heading of historical sociology . . . The third grouping comprises feminist writers. Finally, there are those writers concerned to develop postmodern readings of international relations.
>
> Smith (1995: 24–5)

humanitarian intervention, ethnic cleansing, mass migration and refugee problems, environmental security, and so forth. An increasing number of IR scholars expressed dissatisfaction with the dominant Cold War approach to IR: the neorealism of Kenneth Waltz. Many IR scholars now take issue with Waltz's claim that the complex world of international relations can be squeezed into a few law-like statements about the structure of the international system and the balance of power. They consequently reinforce the anti-behavioralist critique first put forward by International Society theorists such as Hedley Bull (1969). Many IR scholars also criticize Waltzian neorealism for its conservative political outlook: there is not much in neorealism which can point to change and the creation of a better world.

In sum, there are new debates in IR that address methodological issues (i.e. *how* to approach the study of IR) and substantial issues (i.e. *which* issues should be considered the most important ones for IR to study). We have chosen to present these debates in three chapters: one debate deals with what could be called 'post-positivist methodologies' (Chapters 8 and 9); the other debate addresses 'new' (or rediscovered) issues which we shall review under the label of 'new issues' (Chapter 10).

In Chapters 8 and 9 we shall look into different methodological currents in post-positivist IR. These different methodologies are rival answers to the question: if behavioralist methodology, as employed by neorealism and neoliberalism, is abandoned, what should it be replaced with? The various currents are thus in agreement about criticizing the behavioralist attempts to formulate scientific laws of international relations; but they disagree about what is the best replacement for the methods that are now being rejected. In Chapter 10 we shall look into four important issues that have captured the attention of IR scholars since the end of the Cold War: the environment; gender; sovereignty and changes in statehood. They are rival answers to the question: what is the most important issue or concern in world politics now that the Cold War has come to an end, and IR's realist preoccupation with superpower rivalry and nuclear security along with it?

The new issues and methodologies mentioned here have something in common: they claim that established traditions in IR fail to come to grips with the post-Cold War changes of world politics. These recent approaches should thus be seen as 'new voices' that are trying to point the way to an academic IR discipline that is more in tune with international relations at the start of a new millennium. In short, many scholars argue that a fourth IR debate has been thrown open in the 1990s between the established traditions on the one hand and these new voices on the other.

Box 2.17 A fourth major debate

ESTABLISHED TRADITIONS	NEW VOICES
• Realism/neorealism	• Post-positivist methodologies
• Liberalism/neoliberalism	• Post-positivist issues
• International Society	
• International political economy (IPE)	

Which Theory?

This chapter has introduced the main theoretical traditions in IR. It is necessary to be familiar with theory, because facts do not speak for themselves. We always look at the world, consciously or not, through a specific set of lenses; we may think of those lenses as theory. Is development taking place in the Third World or is it underdevelopment? Is the world a more secure or a more dangerous place after the end of the Cold War? Are contemporary states more prone to cooperate or to compete with each other? The facts alone cannot answer these questions; we need help from theories. They tell us which facts are important and which are unimportant, that is, they structure our view of the world. They are based on certain values, and often they also contain visions of how we want the world to be. Early liberal thinking about IR, for example, was driven by the determination never to repeat the disaster of the First World War. Liberals hoped the creation of new international organizations would foster a more peaceful and cooperative world.

Because theory is necessary in thinking systematically about the world it is better to get the most important theories out in the open and subject them to scrutiny. We should examine their concepts, their claims about how the world hangs together and what the important facts are; we should probe their values and visions. That is what we set out to do in the following chapters. The presentation of different theories always begs a big question: which theory is best? It may seem an innocent question, but it raises a number of difficult and complex issues. One answer is that the question about the best theory is not really meaningful, because different theories, such as realism and liberalism, are like different games, played by different people (Rosenau 1967; see also Smith 1997). If there was only one game, say tennis, we could easily find one winner by setting up a tournament. But when there is more than one game, say both tennis and badminton, the badminton player will not stop playing just because a tennis player comes along and claims that tennis is a much better game. Maybe the theories that most appeal to us are like the games that we most enjoy watching or playing.

Another answer to the question about the best theory is that even if theories are different in many ways, it does make sense to rank them, just as it makes sense to point out the athlete of the year even if the candidates for that honor compete in very different athletic disciplines. What would be the criteria for identifying the best theory? We may think of several relevant criteria, among them:

- Coherence: the theory should be consistent, i.e. free of internal contradictions.

- Clarity of exposition: the theory should be formulated in a clear and lucid manner.

- Unbiased: the theory should not be based on purely subjective valuations. No theory is value-free, but the theory should strive to be candid about its normative premises and values.

- Scope: the theory should be relevant for a large number of important issues. A theory with limited scope, for example, is a theory about US decisionmaking in the Gulf War. A theory with wide scope is a theory about foreign policy decision-making in general.

- Depth: the theory should be able to explain and understand as much as possible of the phenomenon which it purports to tackle. For example, a theory of European integration has limited depth if it explains only some part of that process and much more depth if it explains most of it.

Other possible criteria could be set forth (see Chapter 7); but it must be emphasized that there is no objective way of choosing between the evaluative criteria. And it is clear that some criteria can load the dice in favor of some types of theory and against others. There is no simple way around the problem. A further complication is that people's values and political priorities play a role in choosing one theory ahead of another.

As textbook-writers, we see it as our duty to present what we consider the most important theories in a way that draws out the strength of each theory but is also critical of its weaknesses and limitations. This book is not aimed at guiding the reader towards one single theory which we see as the best; it is aimed at identifying the pros and cons of several important theories in order to enable the reader to make his or her own well-considered choices from the available possibilities.

Conclusion

The foregoing traditional and alternative theories constitute the main analytical tools and concerns of contemporary IR. We have seen how the subject developed through a series of debates between different theoretical approaches. We noted that these debates were not conducted in splendid isolation from everything else: they were shaped and influenced by historical events, by the major political and economic problems of the day. They were also influenced by methodological developments in other areas of scholarship. These elements are summarized in Box 2.1.

No single theoretical approach has clearly won the day in IR. The main theoretical traditions and alternative approaches that we have outlined are all actively employed in the discipline today. That situation reflects the necessity of different approaches to capture different aspects of a very complicated historical and contemporary reality. World politics is not dominated by one single issue or conflict; on the contrary, it is shaped and influenced by many different issues and conflicts. The pluralist situation of IR scholarship also reflects the personal preferences of different scholars: they often prefer particular theories for reasons that may have as much to do with their personal values and world-views as with what takes place in international relations and what is required to understand those events and episodes.

KEY POINTS

- IR thinking has evolved in stages that are marked by specific debates between groups of scholars. The first major debate is between *utopian liberalism* and *realism*; the second debate is on method, between *traditional approaches* and *behavioralism*. The third debate is between *neorealism/neoliberalism* and *neo-Marxism*; and an emerging fourth debate is between *established traditions* and *post-positivist* alternatives.

- The first major debate was won by the realists. During the Cold War realism became the dominant way of thinking about international relations not only among scholars but also among politicians, diplomats, and so-called 'ordinary people'. Morgenthau's (1960) summary of realism became the standard introduction to IR in the 1950s and 1960s.

- The second major debate is about method. The contenders are traditionalists and behavioralists. The former tries to understand a complicated social world of human affairs and the values fundamental to it, such as order, freedom, and justice. The latter approach, behavioralism, finds no place for morality or ethics in international theory. Behavioralism wants to classify, measure, and explain through the formulation of general laws like those formulated in the 'hard' sciences of chemistry, physics, etc. The behavioralists seemed to triumph for a time but in the end neither side won the debate. Today both types of method are used in the discipline. There was a revival of traditional normative approaches to IR after the end of the Cold War.

- In the 1960s and 1970s, neoliberalism challenged realism by arguing that interdependence, integration, and democracy is changing IR. Neorealism responded that anarchy and the balance of power are still at the heart of IR.

- International Society theorists maintain that IR contains both 'realist' elements of conflict and 'liberal' elements of cooperation, and that these elements cannot be collapsed into a single theoretical synthesis. They also emphasize human rights and other cosmopolitan features of world politics, and they defend the traditional approach to IR.

- The third debate is characterized by a neo-Marxist attack on the established positions of realism/neorealism and liberalism/neoliberalism. This debate concerns international political economy (IPE). It creates a more complex situation in the discipline because it expands the terrain towards economic issues and because it introduces the distinct problems of Third World countries. There is no clear winner of the third debate. Within IPE, the discussion between the main contenders continues.

- Currently a fourth debate is under way in IR; it involves an attack on the established traditions by alternative approaches, sometimes identified as 'post-positivist alternatives'. The debate raises both methodological issues (i.e. *how* to approach the study of an issue) and substantial issues (i.e. *which* issues should be considered the most important ones). These approaches also reject the scientific claims of neorealism and neoliberalism.

....

QUESTIONS

- Identify the major debates within IR. Why do the debates often linger on without any clear winner emerging?

- Which are the established theoretical traditions in IR? How can they be seen as 'established'?

- Why was early IR strongly influenced by liberalism?

- Seen over the long term, realism is the dominant theoretical tradition in IR. Why?

- Why do scholars have pet theories? What are your own theoretical preferences?

For additional material and resources see the companion web site at:
www.oup.co.uk/best.textbooks/politics/jacksonsorensen2e/

GUIDE TO FURTHER READING

Angell, N. (1909). *The Great Illusion*. London: Weidenfeld & Nicolson.

Carr, E. H. (1964). *The Twenty Years Crisis*. New York: Harper & Row.

Cox, M. (ed.) (2002). 'The World Crisis and the Origins of International Relations', *International Relations*, 16/1, April (Issue on the origins of the IR discipline).

Kahler, M. (1997). 'Inventing International Relations: International Relations Theory after 1945', in M. Doyle and G. J. Ikenberry (eds.), *New Thinking in International Relations Theory*, Boulder: Westview, 20–54.

Knutsen, T. L. (1997). *A History of International Relations Theory*. Manchester: Manchester University Press.

Schmidt, B. C. (1998). *The Political Discourse of Anarchy. A Disciplinary History of International Relations*. Albany: SUNY Press.

Smith, S. (1995). 'The Self-Images of a Discipline: A Genealogy of International Relations Theory', in K. Booth and S. Smith (eds.), *International Relations Theory Today*. Oxford: Polity Press, 1–38.

Smith, S., Booth, K., and Zalewski, M. (eds.) (1996). *International Theory: Positivism and Beyond*. Cambridge: Cambridge University Press.

Vasquez, J. A. (1996). *Classics of International Relations*. Upper Saddle River, NJ: Prentice-Hall.

WEB LINKS

http://www.geocities.com/Athens/2391/
Articles, speeches, and biographies of Woodrow Wilson, as well as links to Wilson's Fourteen Points and other materials. Hosted by Yahoo! GeoCities.

http://www.mtholyoke.edu/acad/intrel/carr.htm
An extract (chapters 4 and 5) of *The Twenty Year's Crisis* which contains E. H. Carr's famous critique of Utopian Liberalism as well as a presentation of Realist thought. Hosted by Mount Holyoke College.

http://www.globalpolicy.org/globaliz/econ/histneol.htm
Susan George provides 'A Short History of Neoliberalism'. Hosted by Global Policy Forum.

http://www.ukc.ac.uk/politics/englishschool/
A comprehensive list of links to papers as well as information about conferences and working groups related to the English School. Hosted by Barry Buzan, University of Kent.

3 Realism

SUMMARY

This chapter sketches the realist tradition in IR. The chapter takes note of an important dichotomy in realist thought between classical and contemporary approaches to realism. Classical and neoclassical realists emphasize the normative aspects of realism as well as the empirical aspects. Most contemporary realists pursue a social scientific analysis of the structures and processes of world politics, but they tend to ignore norms and values. The chapter discusses both classical and contemporary strands of realist thought. It examines a debate among realists concerning the wisdom of NATO expansion into Eastern Europe. It also reviews two critiques of realist doctrine: an international society critique and an emancipatory critique. The concluding section assesses the prospects for the realist tradition as a research program in IR.

Introduction: Elements of Realism

Basic realist ideas and assumptions are: (1) a pessimistic view of human nature; (2) a conviction that international relations are necessarily conflictual and that international conflicts are ultimately resolved by war; (3) a high regard for the values of national security and state survival; (4) a basic skepticism that there can be progress in international politics that is comparable to that in domestic political life. These ideas and assumptions steer the thought of most leading realist IR theorists, both past and present.

In realist thought humans are characterized as being preoccupied with their own well-being in their competitive relations with each other. They desire to be in the driver's seat. They do not wish to be taken advantage of. They consequently strive to have the 'edge' in relations with other people—including international relations with other countries. In that regard at least, human beings are considered to be basically the same everywhere. Thus the desire to enjoy an advantage over others and to avoid domination by others is universal. This pessimistic view of human nature is strongly evident in the IR theory of Hans Morgenthau (1965; 1985), who was probably the leading realist thinker of the twentieth century. He sees men and women as having a 'will to power'. That is particularly evident in politics and especially international politics: 'Politics is a struggle for power over men, and whatever its ultimate aim may be, power is its immediate goal and the modes of acquiring, maintaining, and demonstrating it determine the technique of political action' (Morgenthau 1965: 195).

Thucydides, Machiavelli, Hobbes, and indeed all classical realists share that view to a greater or lesser extent. They believe that the goal of power, the means of power, and the uses of power are a central preoccupation of political activity. International politics is thus portrayed as—above all else—'power politics': an arena of rivalry, conflict, and war between states in which the same basic problems of defending the national interest and ensuring the continued survival of the state repeat themselves over and over again.

Realists thus operate with a core assumption that world politics unfolds in an international anarchy: i.e. a system with no overarching authority, no world government. The state is the pre-eminent actor in world politics. International relations are primarily relations of states. All other actors in world politics—individuals, international organizations, NGOs, etc.—are either less important or unimportant. The main point of foreign policy is to project and defend the interests of the state in world politics. But states are not equal: on the contrary, there is an international hierarchy of power among states. The most important states in world politics are the great powers. International relations are understood by realists as primarily a struggle among the great powers for domination and security.

> ### Box 3.1 **President Nixon on the balance of power (1970)**
>
> We must remember the only time in the history of the world that we have had any extended periods of peace is when there has been balance of power. It is when one nation becomes infinitely more powerful in relation to its potential competitor that the danger of war arises. So I believe in a world in which the United States is powerful. I think it will be a safer world and a better world if we have a strong, healthy United States, Europe, Soviet Union, China, Japan, each balancing the other, not playing one against the other, an even balance.
>
> Quoted in Kissinger (1994: 705)

The normative core of realism is national security and state survival: these are the values that drive realist doctrine and realist foreign policy. The state is considered to be essential for the good life of its citizens: without a state to guarantee the means and conditions of security and to promote welfare, human life is bound to be, in the famous phrase of Thomas Hobbes (1946: 82), 'solitary, poor, nasty, brutish and short'. The state is thus seen as a protector of its territory, of the population, and of their distinctive and valued way of life. The national interest is the final arbiter in judging foreign policy. Human society and morality is confined to the state and does not extend into international relations, which is a political arena of considerable turmoil, discord, and conflict between states in which the great powers dominate everybody else.

The fact that all states must pursue their own national interest means that other countries and governments can never be relied upon completely. All international agreements are provisional and conditional on the willingness of states to observe them. All states must be prepared to sacrifice their international obligations on the altar of their own self-interest if the two come into conflict. That makes treaties and all other agreements, conventions, customs, rules, laws, etc. between states merely expedient arrangements which can and will be set aside if they conflict with the vital interests of states. There are no international obligations in the moral sense of the word—i.e. bonds of mutual duty—between independent states. As indicated above, the only fundamental responsibility of statespeople is to advance and to defend the national interest. That is nowhere stated more brutally than by Machiavelli in his famous book *The Prince* (see Box 3.2).

That means that there can be no progressive change in world politics comparable to the developments that characterize domestic political life. That also means that realist IR theory is considered to be valid not only at particular times but at all times, because the foregoing basic facts of world politics never change. That, at any rate, is what most realists argue and evidently believe.

There is an important distinction in realist IR theory between classical realism and contemporary realism. Classical realism is one of the 'traditional' approaches

Box 3.2 **Machiavelli on the Prince's obligations**

A prince . . . cannot observe all those things for which men are considered good, for in order to maintain the state he is often obliged to act against his promise, against charity, against humanity, and against religion. And therefore, it is necessary that he have a mind ready to turn itself according to the way the winds of fortune and the changeability of [political] affairs require . . . as long as it is possible, he should not stray from the good, but he should know how to enter into evil when necessity commands.

Machiavelli (1984: 59–60)

to IR that was prominent prior to the behavioralist revolution of the 1950s and 1960s as outlined in Chapter 2. It is basically normative in approach, and focuses on the core political values of national security and state survival. Classical realists have lived in many different historical periods; from ancient Greece right down to the present time. Contemporary realism, on the other hand and as the name implies, is a recent IR doctrine: it is basically scientific in approach and focuses on the international system or structure. It is largely (although not exclusively) American in origin. Indeed, it has been and perhaps still is the most prominent IR theory in the United States, which is home to by far the largest number of IR scholars in the world. That fact alone makes contemporary realism a particularly important IR theory.

Classical Realism

What is classical realism? Who are the leading classical realists? What are their key ideas and arguments? In this section we shall examine, briefly, the international thought of three outstanding classical realists of the past: (1) the ancient Greek historian Thucydides; (2) the Renaissance Italian political theorist Niccolò Machiavelli; and (3) the seventeenth-century English political and legal philosopher Thomas Hobbes. In the next section we shall single out for special treatment the neoclassical realist thought of the twentieth-century German-American IR theorist Hans J. Morgenthau.

Thucydides

What we call inter*national* relations Thucydides saw as the inevitable competitions and conflicts between ancient Greek city-states (which together composed the cultural-linguistic civilization known as Hellas) and between Hellas and neighboring non-Greek empires, such as Macedonia or Persia. Neither the states of Hellas nor their non-Greek neighbors were in any sense equal. On the contrary, they were substantially unequal: there were a few 'great powers'—such as Athens, Sparta, the Persian empire—and many smaller and lesser powers—such as the tiny island statelets of the Aegean sea. That inequality was considered to be inevitable and natural. A distinctive feature of Thucydides' brand of realism is thus its naturalist character. Aristotle said that 'man is a political animal'. Thucydides said in effect that political animals are highly unequal in their powers and capabilities to dominate others and to defend themselves. All states, large and small, must adapt to that given reality of unequal power and conduct themselves accordingly. If states do that, they will survive and perhaps even prosper. If states fail to do that, they will place themselves in jeopardy and may even be destroyed. Ancient history is full of many examples of states and empires, small and large, that were destroyed.

Box 3.3 **International relations in Ancient Greece**

The Greeks established the Hellenic League . . . and placed it under the leadership of Sparta and Athens. Despite the semblance of Greek unity during the Persian Wars (492–477 BC) there were serious conflicts between members of the League, mostly occasioned by the smaller city-states' fear of Athenian imperialism and expansion. Thus, after the Greek victories over the Persians, Athens' competitors, led by Sparta, formed a rival organization, the Peloponnesian League, an intricate alliance and collective security system designed to deter further Athenian expansion . . . A bitter competition over trade and naval supremacy between Corinth and Athens led ultimately to the Peloponnesian Wars involving the two military alliances.

Holsti (1988: 38–9)

So Thucydides emphasizes the limited choices and the restricted sphere of maneuver available to statespeople in the conduct of foreign policy. He also emphasizes that decisions have consequences: before any final decision is made a decisionmaker should have carefully thought through the likely consequences, bad as well as good. In pointing that out, Thucydides is also emphasizing the ethics of caution and prudence in the conduct of foreign policy in an international world of great inequality, of restricted foreign-policy choices, and of ever-present danger as well as opportunity. Foresight, prudence, caution, judgment are the characteristic political ethics of classical realism which Thucydides and most other classical realists are at pains to distinguish from private morality and the principle of justice. If a country and its government wish to survive and prosper, they had better pay attention to these fundamental political maxims of international relations.

In his famous study of the Peloponnesian war (431–404 BC) Thucydides (1972: 407) put his realist philosophy into the mouths of the leaders of Athens—a great power—in their dialogue with the leaders of Melos—a minor power—during a moment of conflict between the two city-states in 416 BC. The Melians made an appeal to the principle of justice, which to them meant that their honor and dignity as an independent state should be respected by the powerful Athenians. But according to Thucydides, justice is of a special kind in international relations. It is not about equal treatment for all; it is about knowing your proper place, about adapting to the natural reality of unequal power. Thucydides therefore let the Athenians reply to the Melian appeal as set out in Box 3.4.

Box 3.4 **Thucydides on the strong and the weak**

The standard of justice depends on the equality of power to compel and that in fact the strong do what they have the power to do and the weak accept what they have to accept . . . this is the safe rule—to stand up to one's equals, to behave with deference to one's superiors, and to treat one's inferiors with moderation. Think it over again, then, when we have withdrawn from the meeting, and let this be a point that constantly recurs to your minds—that you are discussing the fate of your country, that you have only one country, and that its future for good or ill depends on this one single decision which you are going to make.

Thucydides (1972: 406)

That is probably the most famous example of the classical realist understanding of international relations as basically an anarchy of separate states that have no real choice except to operate according to the principles and practices of power politics in which security and survival are the primary values and war is the final arbiter.

Machiavelli

Power (the Lion) and deception (the Fox) are the two essential means for the conduct of foreign policy, according to the political teachings of Machiavelli (1984: 66). The supreme political value is national freedom, i.e. independence. The main responsibility of rulers is always to seek the advantages and to defend the interests of their state and thus ensure its survival. That requires strength: if a state is not strong it will be a standing invitation for others to prey upon it; the ruler must be a lion. That also requires cunning and—if necessary—ruthlessness in the pursuit of self-interest: the ruler must also be a fox. If rulers are not astute, crafty, and adroit they might miss an opportunity that could bring great advantages or benefits to them and their state. Even more important, they might fail to notice a menace or threat which if not guarded against might harm or even destroy them, their regime, and possibly even the state as well. That statesmen and stateswomen must be both lions and foxes is at the heart of Machiavelli's (1984: 66) realist theory. Classical realist IR theory is primarily a theory of survival (Wight 1966).

The overriding Machiavellian assumption is that the world is a dangerous place. But it is also, by the same token, an opportune place too. If anybody hopes to survive in such a world, he or she must always be aware of dangers, must anticipate them, and must take the necessary precautions against them. And if they hope to prosper, to enrich themselves, and to bask in the reflected glory of their accumulated power and wealth, it is necessary for them to recognize and to exploit the opportunities that present themselves and to do that more quickly, more skillfully and—if necessary—more ruthlessly than any of their rivals or enemies. The conduct of foreign policy is thus an instrumental or 'Machiavellian' activity based on the intelligent calculation of one's power and interests as against the power and interests of rivals and competitors.

That shrewd outlook is reflected in some typical Machiavellian maxims of realist statecraft, including the following: Be aware of what is happening. Do not wait for things to happen. Anticipate the motives and actions of others. Do not wait for others to act. Act before they do. The prudent state leader acts to ward off any threat posed by his or her neighbors. He or she should be prepared to engage in pre-emptive war and similar initiatives. The realist state leader is alert to opportunities in any political situation, and is prepared and equipped to exploit them.

Above all, according to Machiavelli, the responsible state leader must not operate in accordance with the principles of Christian ethics: love thy neighbor, be peaceful, and avoid war except in self-defense or in pursuit of a just cause; be charitable, share your wealth with others, always act in good faith, etc. Machiavelli sees these moral maxims as the height of political irresponsibility: if political leaders act in accordance with Christian virtues, they are bound to come to grief and they will lose everything. Not only that: they will sacrifice the property and perhaps the freedom and even the lives of their citizens, who depend upon their statecraft. The implication is clear: if a ruler does not know or respect the maxims of power politics, his or her statecraft will fail, and with it the security and welfare of the citizens who depend absolutely upon it. In other words, political responsibility flows in a very different vein than ordinary, private morality. The fundamental, overriding values are the security and the survival of the state: that is what must guide foreign policy.

Machiavelli's realist writings are sometimes portrayed (Forde 1992: 64) as 'manuals on how to thrive in a completely chaotic and immoral world'. But that view is misleading. It overlooks the responsibilities of rulers not merely to themselves or to their personal regimes but also to their country and its citizens: what Machiavelli, thinking of Florence, refers to as 'the republic'. This is the civic-virtue aspect of Machiavellian realism: rulers have to be both lions and foxes because their people depend upon them for their survival and prosperity. That dependence of the people upon their ruler, and specifically upon the wisdom of his or her foreign policy, is owing to the fact that their fate is entangled in the same state: that is the normative heart not only of Machiavellian realism but of classical realism generally.

Hobbes and the Security Dilemma

Thomas Hobbes thinks we can gain a fundamental insight into political life if we imagine men and women living in a 'natural' condition prior to the invention and institution of the sovereign state. He refers to that pre-civil condition as the 'state of nature'. For Hobbes (1946: 82) the 'state of nature' is an extremely adverse human circumstance in which there is a permanent 'state of war' 'of every man against every man': in their natural condition every man, woman, and child is endangered by everybody else, life is constantly at risk, and nobody can be confident about his or her security and survival for any reasonable length of time. People are living in constant fear of each other. Hobbes characterizes that precivil condition as shown in Box 3.5. It is obviously not only desirable but also extremely urgent to escape from those intolerable circumstances at the earliest moment if that is possible.

Box 3.5 **Hobbes on the state of nature**

In such condition, there is no place for industry; because the fruit thereof is uncertain: and consequently no culture of the earth, no navigation, nor use of the commodities that may be imported by sea; no commodious building . . . no arts; no letters; no society, and which is worst of all, continual fear, and danger of violent death; and the life of man, solitary, poor, nasty, brutish, and short.

Hobbes (1946: 82)

Hobbes believes that there is an escape route from the state of nature into a civilized human condition, and that is via the creation and maintenance of a sovereign state. The means of escape is by men and women turning their fear of each other into a joint collaboration with each other to form a security pact that can guarantee each other's safety. Men and women paradoxically cooperate politically because of their fear of being hurt or killed by their neighbors: they are 'civilized by fear of death' (Oakeshott 1975: 36). Their mutual fear and insecurity drives them away from their natural condition: the war of all against all. In other words, they are basically driven to institute a sovereign state not by their reason (intelligence) but, rather, by their passion (emotion). With the value of peace and order firmly in mind, they willingly and jointly collaborate to create a state with a sovereign government that possesses absolute authority and credible power to protect them from both internal disorders and foreign enemies and threats. In the civil condition—i.e. of peace and order—under the protection of the state men and women have an opportunity to flourish in relative safety: they no longer live under the constant threat of injury and death. Being secure and at peace, they are now free to prosper. As Hobbes puts it, they can pursue and enjoy 'felicity', i.e. happiness, well-being.

However, that statist solution to the problem of the natural condition of humankind automatically poses a serious political problem. The very act of instituting a sovereign state to escape from the fearful state of nature simultaneously creates another state of nature between states. That poses what is usually referred to as 'the security dilemma' in world politics: the achievement of personal security and domestic security through the creation of a state is necessarily accompanied by the condition of national and international insecurity that is rooted in the anarchy of the state system.

There is no escape from the international security dilemma in the way that there is an escape from the personal security dilemma, because there is no possibility of forming a global state or world government. Unlike individual men and women in the primary state of nature, sovereign states are not willing to give up their independence for the sake of any global security guarantee. That is because the international state of nature between states is not as threatening and dangerous as the original state of nature: it is easier for states to provide security than it is for individual men and women to do it on their own; states can mobilize the collective power of large numbers of people; states can arm themselves and defend themselves against foreign-security threats in a credible and continuous way. Individual men and women are vulnerable because they sometimes have to let their guard down: e.g. they have to sleep. But states never sleep: while some citizens sleep, other citizens are awake and on guard. If states do their job of protecting their own people, then the international state of nature can even be seen as a good thing because it gives particular groups of people freedom from other groups of people. In other words, international anarchy based on sovereign states is a system of freedom for groups. But the main point about the international state of nature is that it is a condition of actual or potential war; there can be no permanent or guaranteed peace between sovereign states. War is necessary, as a last resort, for resolving disputes between states that cannot agree and will not acquiesce.

According to Hobbes, states can also contract treaties with each other to provide a legal basis for their relations: international law can moderate the international state of nature by providing a framework of agreements and rules that are of advantage to all states. The classical realism of Hobbes thus emphasizes both military power and international law. But international law is created by states, and it will only be observed if it is in the security and survival interests of states to do that; otherwise it will be ignored. For Hobbes, as for Machiavelli and Thucydides, security and survival are values of fundamental importance. But the core value of Hobbesian realism is domestic peace—peace within the framework

Box 3.6 **Basic values of three classical realists**

THUCYDIDES	MACHIAVELLI	HOBBES
• Political fate	• Political agility	• Political will
• Necessity and security	• Opportunity and security	• Security dilemma
• Political survival	• Political survival	• Political survival
• Safety	• Civic virtue	• Peace and felicity

of the sovereign state—and the opportunity that only civil peace can provide for men and women to enjoy felicity. The state is organized and equipped for war in order to provide domestic peace for its subjects and citizens.

We can summarize the discussion thus far by briefly stating what these classical realists basically have in common. First, they agree that the human condition is a condition of insecurity and conflict which must be addressed and dealt with. Second, they agree that there is a body of political knowledge, or wisdom, to deal with the problem of security, and each of them tries to identify the keys to it. Finally, they agree that there is no final escape from this human condition, which is a permanent feature of human life. In other words, although there is a body of political wisdom—which can be identified and stated in the form of political maxims—there are no permanent or final solutions to the problems of politics—including international politics. This sober and somewhat pessimistic view is at the heart of the IR theory of the leading neoclassical realist of the twentieth century, Hans J. Morgenthau.

. . . .

Morgenthau's Neoclassical Realism

According to Morgenthau (1965), men and women are by nature political animals: they are born to pursue power and to enjoy the fruits of power. Morgenthau speaks of the *animus dominandi*, the human 'lust' for power (Morgenthau 1965: 192). The craving for power dictates a search not only for relative advantage but also for a secure political space within which to maintain oneself and to enjoy oneself free from the political dictates of others. That is the security aspect of the *animus dominandi*. The ultimate political space within which security can be arranged and enjoyed is, of course, the independent state. Security beyond the state is impossible.

The human *animus dominandi* inevitably brings men and women into conflict with each other. That creates the condition of power politics which is at the heart not only of Morgenthau's realism but of all classical and neoclassical realist conceptions of international relations. 'Politics is a struggle for power over men, and whatever its ultimate aim may be, power is its immediate goal and the modes of acquiring, maintaining, and demonstrating it determine the technique of political action' (Morgenthau 1965: 195). Here Morgenthau is clearly echoing Machiavelli and Hobbes. If people desire to enjoy a political space free from the intervention or control of foreigners, they will have to mobilize their power and deploy their power for that purpose. That is, they will have to organize themselves into a capable and effective state by means of which they can defend their interests. The system of states leads to international anarchy and conflict.

The struggle between states in turn leads to the problem of justifying power in human relations. Here we arrive at the central normative doctrine of classical and neoclassical realism. Morgenthau follows in the tradition of Thucydides and Machiavelli: there is one morality for the private sphere and another and very different morality for the public sphere. Political ethics allows some actions that would not be tolerated by private morality. Morgenthau is critical of those theorists and practitioners, such as American President Woodrow Wilson, who believed that it was necessary for political ethics to be brought into line with private ethics. For example, in a famous address to the US Congress in 1917 President Wilson said he could discern 'the beginning of an age in which it will be insisted that the same standards of conduct and of responsibility for wrong shall be observed among nations and their governments that are observed among the individual citizens of civilized states' (Morgenthau 1965: 180).

Morgenthau considers that outlook to be not only ill-advised but also irresponsible: it is not only mistaken intellectually but also fundamentally wrong morally. It is a gross intellectual mistake because it fails to appreciate the important difference between the public sphere of politics, on the one hand, and the private sphere or domestic life, on the other hand. According to classical realists, the difference is fundamental. As indicated, Machiavelli made that point by noting that if a ruler operated in accordance with Christian private ethics he or she would come to grief very quickly because political rivals could not be counted on to operate in the same Christian way. It would thus be an ill-advised and irresponsible foreign policy; and all the people who depended on the policy would suffer from the disaster it created.

Such a policy would be reckless in the extreme, and would thus constitute a moral failure because political leaders bear a very heavy responsibility for the security and welfare of their country and its people. They are not supposed to expose their people to unnecessary perils or hardships. Sometimes—for example, during crises or emergencies—it may be necessary to carry out foreign policies and engage in international activities that would clearly be wrong according to private morality: spying, lying, cheating, stealing, conspiring, etc. are only a few of the many activities that would be considered at best dubious and at worst evil by the standards of private morality. Sometimes it may be necessary to trample on human rights for the sake of the national interest: during war, for example. Sometimes it may be necessary to sacrifice a lesser good for a greater good and to choose between evils: for realists that tragic situation is virtually a defining feature of international politics especially during times of war. Here Morgenthau is reiterating an insight into the ethically compromised nature of statecraft that was noted by the ancient Greek philosopher Plato (1974: 82, 121), who spoke of the 'noble lie': 'Our rulers will probably have to make considerable use of lies and deceit for the good of their subjects.'

Box 3.7 **Morgenthau on political morality**

Realism maintains that universal moral principles cannot be applied to the actions of states in their abstract universal formulation, but that they must be filtered through the concrete circumstances of time and place. The individual may say for himself: '*fiat justitia, pereat mundus* (let justice be done even if the world perish)', but the state has no right to say so in the name of those who are in its care.

Morgenthau (1985: 12)

For Morgenthau the heart of statecraft is thus the clear-headed knowledge that political ethics and private ethics are not the same, that the former cannot be and should not be reduced to the latter, and that the key to effective and responsible statecraft is to recognize this fact of power politics and to learn to make the best of it. That involves statecraft of the kind that Machiavelli advocated, as well as action in defense of the state and the national interest such as Hobbes recommended.

Box 3.8 **President Nixon on the American national interest (1970)**

Our objective . . . is to support our interests over the long run with a sound foreign policy. The more that policy is based on a realistic assessment of our and others' interests, the more effective our role In the world can be. We are not involved in the world because we have commitments; we have commitments because we are involved. Our interests must shape our commitments, rather than the other way around.

Quoted from Kissinger (1994: 711–12)

It also involves the distinctive political ethics associated with responsible statecraft. Responsible statesmen and stateswomen are not merely free, as sovereign rulers, to act in an expedient way. They must act in full knowledge that the mobilization and exercise of political power in foreign affairs inevitably involves moral dilemmas, morally tainted acts, and sometimes evil actions. The awareness that political ends (i.e. defending the national interest during times of war) must sometimes justify morally questionable or morally tainted means (i.e. the targeting and bombing of cities) leads to situational ethics and the dictates of 'political wisdom': prudence, moderation, judgment, resolve, courage, etc. Those are the cardinal virtues of political ethics. They do not preclude evil actions. Instead, they underline the tragic dimension of international ethics: they recognize the inevitability of moral dilemmas in international politics: that evil actions must sometimes be taken to prevent a greater evil.

Box 3.9 Morgenthau's concept of neoclassical realist statecraft

HUMAN NATURE (basic condition)	POLITICAL SITUATION (means and context)	POLITICAL CONDUCT (goals and values)
• *Animus dominandi*	• Power politics	• Political ethics (prudence, etc.)
• Self-interest	• Political power	• Human necessities (security, etc.)
	• Political circumstances	• National interest
	• Political skills	• Balance of power

Morgenthau (1985: 4–17) encapsulates his IR theory in 'six principles of political realism'. As a conclusion to this section of the chapter we shall briefly reiterate them.

• Politics is rooted in a permanent and unchanging human nature which is basically self-centered, self-regarding, and self-interested.

• Politics is 'an autonomous sphere of action' and cannot therefore be reduced to economics (as Marxist scholars are prone to do) or reduced to morals (as Kantian or liberal theorists are prone to do). State leaders should act in accordance with the dictates of political wisdom.

• Self-interest is a basic fact of the human condition: all people have an interest at a minimum in their own security and survival. Politics is the arena for the expression of those interests which are bound to come into conflict sooner or later. International politics is an arena of conflicting state interests. But interests are not fixed: the world is in flux and interests change over time and over space. Realism is a doctrine that responds to the fact of a changing political reality.

• The ethics of international relations is a political or situational ethics which is very different from private morality. A political leader does not have the same freedom to do the right thing that a private citizen has. That is because a political leader has far heavier responsibilities than a private citizen: he is *responsible to* the people (typically of his country) who depend on him; he is *responsible for* their security and welfare. The responsible state leader should strive not to do the best but, rather, to do the best that circumstances on that particular day permit. That circumscribed situation of political choice is the normative heart of realist ethics.

• Realists are therefore opposed to the idea that particular nations—even great democratic nations such as the United States—can impose their ideologies on other nations and can employ their power in crusades to do that. Realists oppose that because they see it as a dangerous activity that threatens international peace and security. Ultimately, it could backfire and threaten the crusading country.

• Statecraft is a sober and uninspiring activity that involves a profound awareness of human limitations and human imperfections. That pessimistic knowledge of human beings as they are and not as we might wish them to be is a difficult truth that lies at the heart of international politics.

Schelling and Strategic Realism

Classical and neoclassical realists—including Thucydides, Machiavelli, Hobbes, and Morgenthau—provide a normative analysis as well as an empirical analysis of IR. Power is understood to be not only a fact of political life but also a matter of political responsibility. Indeed, power and responsibility are inseparable concepts. For example, the balance of power is not merely an empirical statement about the way that world politics are alleged to operate. The balance of power is also a basic value: it is a legitimate goal and a guide to responsible statecraft on the part of the leaders of the great powers. In other words, for classical realists the balance of power is a desirable institution and a good thing to strive for because it prevents hegemonic world domination by any one great power. It upholds the basic values of international peace and security.

Since the 1950s and 1960s new realist approaches have emerged which are a product of the behavioralist revolution and the quest for a positivist social science of IR. Many contemporary realists seek to provide an empirical analysis of world politics. But they hold back from providing a normative analysis of world politics because that is deemed to be subjective and thus unscientific. That attitude to the study of values in world politics marks a fundamental divide between classical and neoclassical realists on the one hand and contemporary strategic realists and neorealists on the other. In this section we shall examine strategic realism which is exemplified by the thought of Thomas Schelling (1980; 1996). Schelling does not pay much attention to the normative aspects of realism, although he does notice their presence in the background. In the next section we shall turn to neorealism which is associated most closely with Kenneth Waltz (1979). Waltz tends to ignore the normative aspects of realism.

Strategic realism focuses centrally on foreign policy decisionmaking. When state leaders confront basic diplomatic and military issues they are obliged to think strategically—i.e. instrumentally—if they hope to be successful. Schelling (1980; 1996) seeks to provide analytical tools for strategic thought. He views diplomacy and foreign policy, especially that of the great powers and particularly the United States, as a rational-instrumental activity that can be more deeply understood by the application of a form of logical analysis called 'game theory'. He summarizes his thought as shown in Box 3.10.

Box 3.10 **Schelling on diplomacy**

Diplomacy is bargaining: it seeks outcomes that, though not ideal for either party, are better for both than some of the alternatives . . . The bargaining can be polite or rude, entail threats as well as offers, assume a status quo or ignore all rights and privileges, and assume mistrust rather than trust. But . . . there must be some common interest, if only in the avoidance of mutual damage, and an awareness of the need to make the other party prefer an outcome acceptable to oneself. With enough military force a country may not need to bargain.

Schelling (1980: 168)

A central concept that Schelling employs is that of a 'threat': his analysis concerns how statespeople can deal rationally with the threat and dangers of nuclear war. For example, writing about nuclear deterrence Schelling (1980: 6–7) makes the important observation that

the efficacy of . . . [a nuclear] threat may depend on what alternatives are available to the potential enemy, who, if he is not to react like a trapped lion, must be left some tolerable recourse. We have come to realize that a threat of all-out retaliation . . . eliminates lesser courses of action and forces him to choose between extremes . . . [and] may induce him to strike first.

This is a good example of strategic realism which basically concerns how to employ power intelligently in order to get our military adversary to do what we desire and, more importantly, to avoid doing what we fear. The statement from President Kennedy in 1963 (Box 3.11) gives an example of the need for bargaining between strongly armed nuclear powers.

For Schelling the activity of foreign policy is technically instrumental and thus free from moral choice. It is not primarily concerned about what is good or what is right. It is primarily concerned with the question: what is required for our policy to be successful? These questions are clearly similar to those posed above by Machiavelli. Schelling (1980) identifies and dissects with sharp insight various mechanisms, stratagems, and moves which, if followed by the principal actors, could generate collaboration and avoid disaster in a conflict-ridden world of nuclear-armed states. But Schelling does not base his instrumental analysis on an

---

Box 3.11 **President Kennedy on US/Soviet relations (1963)**

Among the many traits the people of [the United States and the Soviet Union] have in common, none is stronger than our mutual abhorrence of war. Almost unique among the major world powers, we have never been at war with each other . . .

Today, should total war ever break out again—no matter how—our two countries would become the primary targets. It is an ironical but accurate fact that the two strongest powers are the two in most danger of devastation . . . We are both caught up in a vicious and dangerous cycle in which suspicion on one side breeds suspicion on the other and new weapons beget counter weapons.

In short, both the United States and its allies, and the Soviet Union and its allies, have a mutually deep interest in a just and genuine peace and in halting the arms race . . .

So let us not be blind to our differences, but let us also direct attention to our common interests and to the means by which those differences can be resolved. And if we cannot end now our differences, at least we can help make the world safe for diversity.

Quoted in Kegley and Wittkopf (1991: 56)

---

underlying political or civic ethics the way that Machiavelli does. The normative values at stake in foreign policy are largely taken for granted. That marks an important divide between classical and neoclassical realism, on the one hand, and contemporary strategic realism and neorealism, on the other.

One of the crucial instruments of foreign policy for a great power, like the United States, is that of armed force. And one of the characteristic concerns of strategic realism is the use of armed force in foreign policy. Schelling devotes considerable thought to this issue. He observes (1996: 169–70) that there is an important distinction between brute force and coercion: 'between taking what you want and making someone give it to you.' He goes on to notice that 'brute force succeeds when it is used, whereas the power to hurt is most successful when held in reserve. It is the threat of damage . . . that can make someone yield or comply.' He adds that to make the use of our coercive apparatus effective 'we need to know what an adversary treasures and what scares him', and we also need to communicate clearly to him 'what will cause the violence to be inflicted [on him] and what will cause it to be withheld'.

Schelling goes on to make a fundamentally realist point: for coercion to be effective as a foreign policy 'requires that our interests and our opponent's [interests] are not absolutely opposed . . . coercion requires finding a bargain.' Coercion is a method of bringing an adversary into a bargaining relationship and getting the adversary to do what we want him or her to do without having to compel it—i.e. the use of brute force, which is usually far more difficult, far less efficient, and far more dangerous. Schelling (1996: 181) summarizes his analysis of the modern diplomacy of violence in Box 3.12.

> ### Box 3.12 **Schelling on diplomacy and violence**
>
> The power to hurt is nothing new in warfare, but . . . modern technology . . . enhances the importance of war and threats of war as techniques of influence, not of destruction; of coercion and deterrence, not of conquest and defense; of bargaining and intimation . . . War no longer looks like just a contest of strength. War and the brink of war are more a contest of nerve and risk-taking, of pain and endurance . . . The threat of war has always been some- where underneath international diplomacy . . . Military strategy can no longer be thought of . . . as the science of military victory. It is now equally, if not more, the art of coercion, of intimidation and deterrence . . . Military strategy . . . has become the diplomacy of violence.
>
> Schelling (1996: 168–82)

There obviously are striking similarities between the realism of Machiavelli and that of Schelling. However, unlike Machiavelli the strategic realism of Schelling (1980) usually does not probe the ethics of foreign policy; it merely presupposes basic foreign goals without comment. The normative aspects of foreign policy and the justifications of intelligent strategy in a dangerous world of nuclear-armed superpowers are intimated by his argument but largely hidden beneath the surface of his text. Schelling speaks quite readily of the 'dirty' and 'extortionate' heart of strategic realism. But he does not inquire why that kind of diplomacy could be called 'dirty' or 'extortionate', and he does not say whether that can be justified. Schelling's realism is fundamentally different from Machiavelli's realism in that important respect.

Strategic realism thus presupposes values and carries normative implications. Unlike classical realism, however, it does not examine them or explore them. For example, Schelling (1980: 4) is well aware that rational behavior is motivated not only by a conscious calculation of advantages but also by 'an explicit and internally consistent value system.' But the role of value systems is not explicitly investigated by Schelling beyond making it clear that behavior is related to values, such as vital national interests. The character and *modus operandi* of the specific values involved in nuclear strategy—threats, mutual distrust, promises, reprisals, and so forth—are not investigated. Values are taken as given and treated instrumentally. In other words, the fundamental point of behaving the way that Schelling suggests foreign policymakers *ought* to behave is not explored, clarified, or even addressed. He provides a strategic analysis but not a normative theory of IR. That is a characteristic of much contemporary realism in IR.

Here we come to a fundamental difference between classical or neoclassical realism and contemporary realism. Here is where Schelling differs fundamentally from Machiavelli. For Machiavelli, the point was the survival and flourishing of the nation. It was the responsibility of state leaders to achieve that desirable political condition which required civic (i.e. political) virtue on their part. Classical

Box 3.13 **Realist statecraft: instrumental realism and strategic realism**

	MACHIAVELLI'S RENAISSANCE STATECRAFT	SCHELLING'S NUCLEAR STATECRAFT
Mode	Instrumental realism	Strategic realism
Means	Strength and cunning	Intelligence, nerve, and risk-taking
	Opportunism and luck	Logic and art of coercion
Goals	Security and survival	Security and survival
Values	Civic virtue	[value-neutral; non-prescriptive]

realists are conscious of the basic values at stake in world politics and they are explicitly concerned about them: they provide a political and ethical theory of IR. Contemporary realists are mostly silent about them and seem to take them more or less for granted without commenting on them or building them into their realist IR theories. They limit their analyses to political structures and processes and they largely ignore political ends. That is evident from a brief analysis of contemporary neorealism.

Waltz and Neorealism

The leading contemporary neorealist thinker is undoubtedly Kenneth Waltz (1979). He takes some elements of classical and neoclassical realism as a starting-point—e.g. independent states existing and operating in a system of international anarchy. But he departs from that tradition by ignoring its normative concerns and by trying to provide a scientific IR theory. Unlike Morgenthau (1985), he gives no account of human nature and he ignores the ethics of statecraft. Waltz's *Theory of International Politics* (1979) seeks to provide a scientific explanation of the international political system. His explanatory approach is heavily influenced by positivist models of economics. A scientific theory of IR leads us to expect states to behave in certain predictable ways. In Waltz's view the best IR theory is a neo-realist systems theory that focuses centrally on the structure of the system, on its interacting units, and on the continuities and changes of the system. In classical realism, state leaders and their subjective valuations of international relations are at the center of attention. In neorealism, by contrast, the structure of the system, in particular the relative distribution of power, is the central analytical focus. Actors are less important because structures compel them to act in certain ways. Structures more or less determine actions.

According to Waltz's neorealist theory, a basic feature of international relations is the decentralized structure of anarchy between states. States are alike in all basic functional respects—i.e. in spite of their different cultures or ideologies or constitutions or personnel they all perform the same basic tasks. All states have to collect taxes, conduct foreign policy, etc. States differ significantly only in regard to their greatly varying capabilities. In Waltz's own words, the state units of an international system are 'distinguished primarily by their greater or less capabilities for performing similar tasks . . . the structure of a system changes with changes in the distribution of capabilities across the system's units' (Waltz 1979: 97). In other words, international change occurs when great powers rise and fall and the balance of power shifts accordingly. A typical means of such change is great-power war.

As indicated, the states that are crucially important for determining changes in the structure of the international system are the great powers. A balance of power between states can be achieved, but war is always a possibility in an anarchical system. Waltz distinguishes between bipolar systems—such as existed during the Cold War between the United States and the Soviet Union—and multipolar systems—such as existed both before and after the Cold War. Waltz believes that bipolar systems are more stable and thus provide a better guarantee of peace and security than multipolar systems. 'With only two great powers, both can be expected to act to maintain the system' (Waltz 1979: 204). That is because in maintaining the system they are maintaining themselves. According to that view, the Cold War was a period of international stability and peace.

That hypothesis may be historically problematical insofar as the United States and the Soviet Union took joint (i.e. cooperative) actions in the early 1990s to terminate their international military rivalry and thus to bring the bipolar system and the Cold War to an end. In the course of that historical change the Soviet Union failed to survive and a number of smaller successor states emerged in its place, the most important of which is Russia. In the light of the ending of the Cold War, presumably, Waltzian neorealism will have to be revised to incorporate the historical possibility that two great powers may in certain circumstances terminate a bipolar system rather than perpetuate it without engaging in a war in which one of them is defeated. It is a matter of debate among IR scholars whether the United States defeated the Soviet Union in the Cold War or the Soviet government, particularly President Gorbachev, terminated it by withdrawing from the contest. Neorealists are inclined to take the first view.

As indicated, Waltz takes classical and neoclassical realism as a starting-point and develops some of its core ideas and assumptions. For example, he employs the concept of international anarchy and focuses exclusively on states. He also focuses on the central feature of anarchical state systems: power politics. He assumes that the fundamental concern of states is security and survival. He also assumes that the major problem of great-power conflict is war, and that the major task of international relations among the great powers is that of peace and security.

> ### Box 3.14 **Waltz's neorealist theory: structure and outcomes**
>
> | INTERNATIONAL STRUCTURE (state units and relations) | INTERNATIONAL OUTCOMES (effects of state competition) |
> |---|---|
> | International anarchy | Balance of power |
> | States as 'like units' | International recurrence and repetition |
> | Unequal state capability | International conflict, war |
> | Great Power relations | International change |

But Waltz departs from classical and neoclassical realism in some fundamental ways which make his approach different from that, say, of Morgenthau. There is no discussion of human nature, such as Morgenthau provides and even Schelling clearly assumes. The focus is on the structure of the system and not on the human beings who create the system or operate the system. State leaders are prisoners of the structure of the state system and its determinist logic which dictates what they must do in their conduct of foreign policy. There is no room in Waltz's theory for foreign policymaking that is independent of the structure of the system. Thus, in the above example neorealists would view Gorbachev's policy of disengaging from the Cold War as dictated by the Soviet Union's 'defeat' at the hands of the United States. On that view, Gorbachev could not have initiated the policy for domestic reasons or for ideological reasons. Waltz's image of the role of state leaders in conducting foreign policy comes close to being a mechanical image in which their choices are shaped by the international structural constraints that they face, as emphasized in Box 3.15.

Unlike Schelling's strategic realism, Waltz's neorealist approach does not provide explicit policy guidance to state leaders as they confront the practical problems of world politics. That is presumably because they have little or no

> ### Box 3.15 **Waltz on the importance of structure**
>
> The ruler's, and later the state's, interest provides the spring of action; the necessities of policy arise from the un-regulated competition of states; calculation based on these necessities can discover the policies that will best serve the state's interests; success is the ultimate test of policy, and success is defined as preserving and strengthening the state . . . structural constraints explain why the methods are repeatedly used despite differences in the persons and states who use them.
>
> Waltz (1979: 117)

choice, owing to the confining international structure in which they must operate. Waltz (1979: 194–210) does address the question of 'the management of international affairs'. However, that discussion is far more about the structural constraints of foreign policy than it is about what Schelling clearly understands as the logic and art of foreign policy. Schelling operates with a notion of situated choice: the rational choice for the situation or circumstances in which leaders find themselves. The choice may be sharply confined by the circumstances but it is a choice nevertheless and it may be made intelligently or stupidly, skillfully or maladroitly, etc. The main point of Schelling's analysis is to reveal the logic and art of making rational foreign policy choices. Waltz's neorealism makes far less provision for statecraft and diplomacy than Schelling's strategic realism. Waltz's argument is at base a determinist theory in which structure dictates policy. This takes the classical realist idea of the importance of international structure in foreign policy to a point beyond classical or neoclassical realism, which always makes provision for the politics and ethics of statecraft (Morgenthau 1985).

However, just beneath the surface of Waltz's neorealist text, and occasionally on the surface, there is a recognition of the ethical dimension of international politics which is virtually identical to classical realist IR. The core concepts that Waltz employs have a normative aspect. For example, he operates with a concept of state sovereignty: 'To say that a state is sovereign means that it decides for itself how it will cope with its internal and external problems' (Waltz 1979: 96). Thus state sovereignty means being in a position to decide, a condition which is usually signified by the term 'independence': sovereign states are postulated as independent of other sovereign states. But what is independence? Waltz (1979: 88) says that each state is formally 'the equal of all the others. None is entitled to command; none is required to obey.' But to say that independence is an 'entitlement' is to take notice of a *norm* which is acknowledged: in this case the norm of 'equal' state sovereignty. Because to say that states are the formal or legal equals of each other is to make not only an empirical statement but also a normative statement. For Waltz, all states are equal only in a formal-legal sense; they are unequal, often profoundly so, in a substantive or material sense. But that means that a norm of state equality exists which all states without exception are expected to observe in their relations with each other regardless of their substantive inequalities of power. Waltz also assumes that states are worth fighting for. That, too, indicates that neorealism is imbued with normative values: those of state security and survival.

Waltz (1979: 113) operates, as well, with a concept of the national interest: 'each state plots the course it thinks will best serve its interests.' For classical realists the national interest is the basic guide of responsible foreign policy: it is a moral idea that must be defended and promoted by state leaders. For Waltz, however, the national interest seems to operate like an automatic signal commanding state leaders when and where to move. The difference here is: Morgenthau believes that state leaders are duty bound to conduct their foreign policies by reference to the guidelines laid down by the national interest, and they may be condemned for failing to do that. Waltz's neorealist theory hypothesizes that they will always do that more or less automatically. Morgenthau thus sees states as organizations guided by leaders whose foreign policies are successful or unsuccessful, depending on the astuteness and wisdom of their decisions. Waltz sees states as structures that respond to the impersonal constraints and dictates of the international system.

Similarly, Waltz (1979: 195) argues that the great powers manage the international system. Classical and neoclassical realists argue that they ought to manage that system and that they can be criticized when they fail to manage it properly—i.e. when they fail to maintain international order. The notion that the Great Powers must be Great Responsibles is not only a traditional realist idea but it is also a core idea of the International Society tradition (see Chapter 5). Great powers are understood by Waltz to have 'a big stake in their system' and for them management of the system is not only something that is possible but also something that is 'worthwhile'. It is perfectly clear that Waltz values international order. It is clear, too, that he is convinced that international order is more likely to be achieved in bipolar systems than in multipolar systems. That discloses his normative values. The difference between neorealism and classical and neoclassical realism in this regard is that Waltz takes it as a given that that will happen, whereas Morgenthau and classical realists take it as an important norm for judging the foreign policy of the great powers.

A distinctive characteristic of neorealism emerges at this point. Waltz wants to present a scientific *explanation* of international politics; but he cannot avoid employing what are inherently normative concepts, and he cannot avoid making what are implicitly normative assumptions and indeed resting his entire case on normative foundations of a traditional realist kind. Thus, although he makes no explicit reference to values or ethics and avoids normative theory, the basic assumptions and concepts he uses and the basic international issues he is concerned with are normative ones. In that respect his neorealism is not as far removed from classical or neoclassical realism as his claims about scientific theory imply. This demonstrates how attempts at scientific explanation can frequently rest on unidentified norms and values (see Chapter 9).

....

Neorealist Stability Theory

Both strategic realism (Schelling 1980; 1996) and neorealism (Waltz 1979) were intimately connected with the Cold War. They were distinctive IR theory responses to that special, if not unique, historical situation. Being strongly influenced by the behavioralist revolution in IR (see Chapters 2 and 8) they both sought to apply scientific methods to the theoretical and practical problems posed by the conflict between the United States and the Soviet Union. Schelling tried to show how a notion of strategy based on game theory could shed light on the nuclear rivalry between the two superpowers. Waltz tried to show how a structural analysis could shed light on 'the long peace' (Gaddis 1987) that was produced by the rivalry between the United States and the Soviet Union during the Cold War. The end of the Cold War thus raises an important question about the future of realist theories that were developed during what could be regarded as an exceptional period of modern international history. In this section we shall address that question in connection with neorealism.

In a widely discussed essay John Mearsheimer (1993) takes up the neorealist argument of Waltz (1979) and applies it to both the past and the future. He says that neorealism has continued relevance for explaining international relations: neorealism is a general theory that applies to other historical situations besides that of the Cold War. He also argues that neorealism can be employed to predict the course of international history beyond the Cold War.

Mearsheimer builds on Waltz's (1979: 161–93) argument (outlined in the previous section) concerning the stability of bipolar systems as compared to multipolar systems. These two configurations are considered to be the main structural arrangements of power that are possible among independent states. As indicated, Waltz claims that bipolar systems are superior to multipolar systems because they provide greater international stability and thus greater peace and security. There are three basic reasons why bipolar systems are more stable and peaceful. First, the number of great power conflicts is fewer, and that reduces the possibilities of great-power war. Second, it is easier to operate an effective system of deterrence because fewer great powers are involved. Finally, because only two powers dominate the system the chances of miscalculation and misadventure are lower. There are fewer fingers on the trigger. In short, the two rival superpowers can keep their eye steadily fixed on each other without the distraction and confusion that would occur if there were a larger number of great powers, as was the case prior to 1945 and arguably has been the case since 1990 (Mearsheimer 1993: 149–50).

The question Mearsheimer (1993: 141) poses is: What would happen if the bipolar system is replaced by a multipolar system? How would that basic system change affect the chances for peace and the dangers of war in post-Cold War Europe? The answer Mearsheimer (p. 142) gives is as follows:

the prospects for major crises and war in Europe are likely to increase markedly if . . . this scenario unfolds. The next decades in a Europe without the superpowers would probably not be as violent as the first 45 years of this century, but would probably be substantially more prone to violence than the past 45 years.

What is the basis for that pessimistic conclusion? Mearsheimer (pp. 142–3) argues that the distribution and nature of military power are the main sources of

---

Box 3.16 **John Gaddis' portrait of the long bipolar peace during the Cold War**

1. The postwar bipolar system realistically reflected the facts of where military power resided at the end of World War II . . .

2. The post-1945 bipolar structure was a simple one that did not require sophisticated leadership to maintain it . . .

3. Because of its relatively simple structure, alliances in this bipolar system have tended to be more stable than they had been in the 19th century and in the 1919–1939 period. It is striking that the North Atlantic Treaty Organization has equalled in longevity the most durable of the pre-World War I alliances, that between Germany and Austria-Hungary; it has lasted almost twice as long as the Franco-Russian alliance, and certainly much longer than any of the tenuous alignments of the interwar period . . .

In short, without anyone's having designed it . . . the nations of the post-war era lucked into a system of international relations that because it has been based upon realities of power, has served the cause of order—if not justice—better than one might have expected.

Gaddis (1987: 221–2)

---

war and peace and says, specifically, that 'the long peace' between 1945 and 1990 was a result of three fundamentally important conditions: the bipolar system of military power in Europe; the approximate military equality between the United States and the Soviet Union; and the reality that both of the rival superpowers were equipped with an imposing arsenal of nuclear weapons. The withdrawal of the superpowers from the European heartland would give rise to a multipolar system consisting of five major powers (Germany, France, Britain, Russia, and perhaps Italy) as well as a number of minor powers. That system would be 'prone to instability'. 'The departure of the superpowers would also remove the large nuclear arsenals they now maintain in Central Europe. This would remove the pacifying effect that these weapons have had on European politics' (Mearsheimer 1993: 143).

Thus, according to Mearsheimer (p. 187), the Cold War between the United States and the Soviet Union 'was principally responsible for transforming a historically violent region into a very peaceful place'. Mearsheimer even argues that the demise of the bipolar Cold War order and the emergence of a multipolar Europe will produce a highly undesirable return to the bad old ways of European anarchy and instability and even a renewed danger of international conflict, crises, and possibly war. He makes the following highly controversial point:

The West has an interest in maintaining peace in Europe. It therefore has an interest in maintaining the Cold War order, and hence has an interest in the continuation of the Cold War confrontation; developments that threaten to end it are dangerous.

Box 3.17   **Mearsheimer's neorealist stability theory**

CONDITIONS OF STABLE BIPOLARITY	CONDITIONS OF UNSTABLE MULTIPOLARITY
• Europe during the Cold War	• Europe before 1945 and after 1990
• Two superpowers	• Several great powers
• Rough superpower equality	• Unequal and shifting balances of power
• Nuclear deterrence	• Conventional military rivalry
• Conquest is difficult	• Conquest is less difficult and more tempting
• Superpower discipline	• Great power indiscipline and risk-taking

---

By way of conclusion, we should notice some contemporary historical places where Mearsheimer's thesis seems to be confirmed by them, and other places where it seems to be refuted by events. His hypothesis seems to be confirmed by the outbreak of conflict and war in the former Yugoslavia (Croatia, Bosnia-Herzegovina, and Kosovo in Serbia) and in the former Soviet Union (Azerbaijan, Armenia, Georgia, Moldova, and Russia itself—in Chechnya).

It is worth pointing out, however, that these places are outside the Central European heartland where the neorealist thesis about the instability of the post-Cold War era is meant to apply most. In that part of Europe since the late 1950s something entirely different has been happening that Mearsheimer's neorealist hypothesis seems to ignore: the integration of the European nation-states into the European Union, the core of which consists of Germany and France, who have created a very close partnership over the past several decades. The end of the Cold War has not put an end to that relationship; if anything, it has made it even more important. In other words, the European Union and particularly the Franco-German core of that emerging political community discloses a new international relationship between the major and minor powers of Europe that neorealism's thesis about bipolarism versus multipolarism seems unable to comprehend. This historical transformation may be better understood by liberal approaches to IR (see Chapter 4).

....

Realism after the Cold War:
The Issue of NATO Expansion

Mearsheimer's arguments raise the important question of how realists should understand the post-Cold War era. There is a major debate that offers important insights into how realism looks upon international relations and particularly the relations of the great powers after the Cold War: the debate over the eastward expansion of NATO to include Poland, the Czech Republic, Slovakia, and Hungary. That is a complicated and in some respects a highly technical subject—especially concerning the equipment and deployment of military forces. But the heart of the debate involves questions of military strategy and ultimately questions of international politics at the highest level. Reduced to essentials, there are two opposing arguments regarding NATO expansion. Both arguments disclose realist ideas and concerns. Each argument can be summarized as follows.

Those who argue in favor of NATO expansion into Eastern Europe (Ball 1998: 52–67) claim that 'the prime objective' is greater regional security. They base their argument on the claim that it could deter Russia from entertaining or engaging in territorial revisionism to recover lost territories or to intimidate its neighbors. It could also promote stability and security in the region by providing reassurance not only to its new East European member states but also to other countries in the region who are not NATO members, for example the Ukraine. If NATO expanded eastward, Russia would be obliged to take into account the strategic fact that any threat or use of force against its neighbors would provoke a response from the alliance. With NATO in the area Russia would have to stop and consider the consequences of any such threats or actions. It could not intimidate smaller and weaker neighbors such as the Baltic republics (Lithuania, Latvia, Estonia).

Box 3.18 In favor of NATO expansion

NATO expansion can provide greater security to all European states, provided that the proper balance among deterrence, reassurance, and diplomatic linkage is maintained. The single best argument for NATO expansion is that the next war is likely to arise out of the uncoordinated pursuit of security by the Central European states, not unprovoked hostile actions by Russia. The fears that Central European countries have about their future security are not unreasonable. Opponents of NATO expansion downplay or ignore the consequences of those fears. The key to the success of NATO expansion is conducting diplomacy that tempers all Central European states' foreign policy while reassuring them of their security.

Ball (1998: 67)

Proponents of NATO expansion claim that it will confer benefits on Russia too. For example, it would restrain Russia's East European neighbors from taking advantage of the present weakness of Russia and thereby provoking regional instability. In other words, it would place a positive West European control on East European states with a history of suspicion, fear, and even enmity *vis-à-vis* Russia. It would also forestall East European states from searching for security outside the alliance. Such states would not have to fear for their security if they became members of NATO. They would not be tempted by nationalism or chauvinism which could provoke regional instability, nor would they be tempted to develop and equip their armed forces with nuclear weapons. They would not be tempted to form alliances among themselves that would complicate the task of building a regional security community, and they would not tempt Germany to play a more independent security role in the region. The risk of any East European state going it alone and becoming a problem for everybody else would be averted if NATO were in charge in the region. The risk of a regional arms race would be lowered if not eliminated, because NATO could ensure that weaponry was consistent with the overall defensive goals of the alliance.

The eastward expansion of NATO, proponents argue, would largely pre-empt any plans and actions by Russia to regard their security in Cold War terms: i.e. the mistake—as a US senior State Department official put it—of 'defining their security at the expense of everyone else's' (Strobe Talbott, quoted by Ball 1998: 60). Instead, with NATO present there would be greater opportunities for cooperative as opposed to competitive security arrangements between Russia and the states to the West. Russian security unilateralism would decrease; consultation would increase. The possibilities of agreements between Russia and NATO to reduce the level of military forces in Eastern Europe would be very much greater in a climate of consultation and agreement than in one of rivalry and suspicion. In short, security in Eastern Europe and international order and stability beyond that region is likely to be worse—i.e. more uncertain, more provocative, more unpredictable, more combative, and ultimately more dangerous—if NATO does not expand.

Those who argue against NATO expansion raise several concerns which they believe are very serious. In June 1997 in an open letter to US President Clinton a group of fifty leading former US Senators, cabinet members in previous administrations, ambassadors, arms control experts, and foreign-policy specialists registered their opposition to expansion in the following stark terms: 'the current US-led effort to expand NATO . . . is a policy error of historical importance' (McGwire 1998: 23–42). They based their negative assessment on four fundamental arguments.

First, it would place in doubt 'the entire post-Cold War settlement' (McGwire 1998: 23). That is because it would threaten Russia. It would drastically undermine those Russian politicians and officials who were in favor of closer and more cooperative relations with the United States and who wanted to bring about democratic reforms in Russia that would align that nation's political system more closely with those of the West. Russia expressed grave concerns about the prospect of NATO eastward expansion. If its concerns were ignored, that would be a sign in Russian eyes that the West did not take Russia seriously and was contemptuous of its fundamental security interests. Further, expansion would undermine NATO's claim to be a purely defensive and peace-loving alliance. It would provoke the antagonism of many Russian politicians and embolden those who were opposed to negotiations with the United States to reduce nuclear and other strategic weapons. It would strengthen those Russian parties and politicians, including Communists, who were opposed to democratic reform. In short, NATO expansion into the former Soviet sphere of Eastern Europe might unite all those nationalist and xenophobic political forces in Russia who opposed closer collaboration between their country and the West, particularly the United States. There was a real and deeply worrying possibility that it would reopen the Cold War division between East and West.

Second, it would draw a new and deep line of division between those former Soviet satellite countries which had moved inside NATO (Poland, the Czech Republic, Slovakia, Hungary) and those which remained outside. It would reduce the security of those nations that were not included: they would be left to fend for themselves and perhaps to seek other security alliances. That would provoke greater instability rather than less.

Third, within NATO itself, expansion would reduce the alliance's credibility at the politically most fundamental point: its promise to defend without exception any member in the event of an attack. As the alliance expanded eastward, according to this argument, its capacity to defend its member states' security and independence would diminish, and maybe its political will to do that would diminish too—if that undertaking risked all-out war with Russia. A significant factor in this argument is that some of those would-be NATO member states are much nearer to Russia, some of them harbor strong historical resentments and animosities towards Russia, some of them have domestic Russian minority problems, and some of them have unstable and undeveloped systems of government. In other words, these states are in awkward locations, have unfortunate historical memories, and lack the political foundations to be solid and reliable members of the alliance. 'NATO could be entrapped by Central European [member] states' (Ball 1998: 49).

Box 3.19 **Against NATO expansion**

Russian ultranationalist Vladimir Zhirinovsky said Saturday that Eastern Europe would become a battlefield in another world war if any of its countries try to join NATO: 'Our neighbors must know that if they let NATO soldiers approach Russia's borders. Russia would destroy both NATO and the territories that are putting the world on the brink of war,' Zhirinovsky said.

Many Russian leaders, including President Boris Yeltsin, have spoken out strongly against NATO's proposed eastward expansion, although none has gone so far as firebrand Zhirinovsky.

Associated Press, 11 February 1996

Finally, NATO expansion into areas of Europe that are inherently more unstable and more difficult to defend might put in jeopardy the United States' commitment to the alliance. That is because of the always latent and sometimes active strain of isolationism in American political culture. This could be a fatal weakening of the alliance, because the United States has always been and would have to continue to be the political and military key to NATO's success as a defensive military organization. NATO expansion might very well encourage American isolationism, which would be a fatal blow to international peace and security.

What are the implications of this important historical debate for realism after the Cold War? It clearly reveals a fundamental point that is often obscured by IR scholars: that realists can have honest and open differences of opinion among themselves on important issues of foreign policy. Both arguments are basically realist in their values: they are both concerned with national security, regional stability, international peace, etc. They both employ instrumental language such as 'danger', 'risk', 'uncertainty', 'threat', 'capability', 'credibility', 'deterrence', 'fear', 'reassurance', 'confidence'. They both clearly understand international relations in strategic realist terms, in which the primary aim is to use foreign policy and military power to defend national interests and promote international order.

In that connection, realists who favor expansion and realists who oppose it both understand statecraft as an activity that involves the responsible use of power. They both operate within the same general realist ethics of statecraft. Their differences only emerge at this point. They are concerned with the same values and they both employ the same language, but they differ in their *judgments* of the proposed policy and their assessments of the circumstances in which it must be carried out. One side views expansion as promoting basic realist values and the other side views it as undermining the same values. Where those in favor see an opportunity in NATO expansion that must be seized, those against see a risk that must be avoided. So each side assesses opportunity and risk differently but both sides are fully alerted to risk and both are concerned about the fundamental values of security and stability.

In that regard, the debate on NATO expansion into Eastern Europe discloses the classical and neoclassical realist emphasis on responsible statecraft and political virtues such as prudence and judgment. Responsible statecraft and political virtue are moral concerns. To understand such concerns involves normative inquiry. That cannot be grasped by neorealism, which aims at scientific explanation that repudiates normative analysis, i.e. the study of values and norms. That brings to the surface one important advantage that classical and neoclassical realism has over neorealism in IR: its ability to engage in inquiry into foreign policy issues that involve basic questions of values: for example, given the fundamental importance of the value of security and stability in world politics, *should* NATO expand eastward or should it stay where it is? Because that is a normative question that involves political judgment, there can be honest differences on the part of both practitioners and observers and there can be no scientific or objective answer. The failure to address such value questions is a clear limitation of neorealism as an IR approach.

Two Critiques of Realism

The dominance of realism in IR during the second half of the twentieth century, especially in the United States, has spawned a substantial literature that criticizes many of its core assumptions and arguments. As indicated in Chapter 2, realism itself rose to a position of academic pre-eminence in the 1940s and 1950s by effectively criticizing the liberal idealism of the interwar period. Contemporary neo-realism has been involved in a renewed debate with contemporary liberalism. We shall investigate that debate in Chapter 4. Here we shall confine our discussion to two important critiques of realism: an International Society critique and an emancipatory critique.

The International Society tradition (see Chapter 5) is critical of realism on two counts. First, it regards realism as a one-dimensional IR theory that is too narrowly focused. Second, it claims that realism fails to capture the extent to which international politics is a dialogue of different IR voices and perspectives. The International Society tradition is not critical of every aspect of realist thought in IR. On the contrary, International Society scholars acknowledge that classical and neoclassical realism provide an important angle of vision on world politics. They agree that there is a strain in human nature that is self-interested and combative. They share a focus of analysis in which states loom large. They operate with a conception of international relations as anarchical. They agree that power is important and that international relations consist significantly of power politics. They also agree that international theory is in some fundamental respects a theory of security and survival. They recognize that the national interest is an important value in world politics. In short, International Society scholars incorporate several elements of realism into their own approach.

However, they do not believe that realism captures all of IR or even its most important aspects. They argue that realism overlooks, ignores, or plays down many important facets of international life. It overlooks the cooperative strain in human nature. It ignores the extent to which international relations form an anarchical *society* and not merely an anarchical system. States are not only in conflict, they also share common interests and observe common rules which confer mutual rights and duties. It ignores other important actors besides states, such as human beings and NGOs. Realism plays down the extent to which the relations of states are governed by international law. It also plays down the extent to which international politics are progressive, i.e. cooperation instead of conflict can prevail. International Society theorists recognize the importance of the national interest as a value, but they refuse to accept that it is the only value that is important in world politics.

Martin Wight (1991), a leading representative of the International Society approach, places a great deal of emphasis on the character of international politics as a historical dialogue between three important philosophies/ideologies: realism (Machiavelli), rationalism (Grotius), and revolutionism (Kant). In order to acquire a holistic understanding of IR it is necessary, according to Martin Wight, to comprehend the dialectical relations of these three basic normative perspectives (see Chapter 5).

At least one leading neoclassical realist appears to agree with Martin Wight. In a monumental study of diplomacy, the American scholar and statesman Henry Kissinger (1994: 29–55) explores the long-standing and continuing dialogue in diplomatic theory and practice between the foreign-policy outlook of pessimistic realism and that of optimistic liberalism. For example, Kissinger discerns that dialogue in the contrasting foreign policies of US Republican President Theodore Roosevelt and Democratic President Woodrow Wilson in the early twentieth century. Roosevelt was 'a sophisticated analyst of the balance of power' while Wilson was 'the originator of the vision of a universal world organization, the League of Nations'. Both perspectives have shaped American foreign policy historically. That dialogue between realism and liberalism is not confined to past and present American foreign policy; it is also evident in British foreign policy historically. Kissinger contrasts the politically cautious and pragmatic nineteenth-century British foreign policy of Conservative Prime Minister Benjamin Disraeli and the morally aroused and interventionist foreign policy of his Liberal counter-part, William Gladstone. Kissinger implies that both these perspectives have a legitimate place in American foreign policy and in British foreign policy, and that neither of them should be ignored. Here, then, is an implied criticism of realism: that it is inclined to ignore or at least to downplay the liberal and democratic voice in world affairs.

We thus have reason to ask whether Kissinger should be classified as a realist at all? Is he a secret member of the International Society school? We believe the correct answer to the first question is 'yes' and to the latter question 'no'. Kissinger should be regarded as a neoclassical realist. Although he portrays the Wilsonian voice in American foreign policy and the Gladstonian voice in British foreign policy as legitimate and important, it is abundantly clear from his lengthy analysis that his preferred basis for any successful foreign policy for America and Britain is the realist outlook disclosed by Roosevelt and Disraeli, with whom Kissinger strongly identifies.

Neoclassical realists could thus reply to the critique as follows. International Society scholars can be criticized for failing to recognize that while the liberal voice is important in world politics the realist voice is always first in importance. That is because it is the best perspective on the core problem of IR: war. According to realists, difficult times, such as war, demand hard choices that realists are better able to clarify than any other IR scholars or practitioners. Liberals—according to classical/neoclassical realists—tend to operate on the assumption that foreign-policy choices are easier and less dangerous than they really may be: they are the foremost theorists of peaceful, prosperous, and easy times. For realists the problem with that is: what shall we do when times are difficult? If we follow the liberals we may fail to respond adequately to the challenge with appropriate hard choices and we may thus place ourselves—and those who depend on our policies and actions—at risk. In other words, realism will always be resorted to during times of crisis when hard choices have to be made, and some criteria for making those choices are required.

An alternative and very different critique of realism is that of emancipatory IR theory. Because realism has been such a dominant IR theory, emancipatory theorists direct their energies at providing what they consider to be a root-and-branch critique of realist assumptions and arguments. That is intended to pave the way for a complete reconceptualization of IR. Their critique of realism is central to their project of global human emancipation. Emancipatory theorists argue that IR should seek to grasp correctly how men and women are prisoners of existing international structures. IR theorists should indicate how they can be liberated from the state and from other structures of contemporary world politics which have the effect of oppressing them and thus preventing them from flourishing as they otherwise would. A central aim of emancipatory theory, then, is the trans-formation of the realist state-centric and power-focused structure of international politics. The goal is human liberation and fulfillment. The role of the emancipatory IR theorist is to determine the correct theory for guiding the practice of human liberation.

An emancipatory critique of realism has been developed by Ken Booth (1991). Booth (pp. 313–26) builds his critique on a familiar realist view of the 'West-phalian system': i.e. it is 'a game' that is 'played by diplomats and soldiers on behalf of statesmen'. The 'security game' that states learned to play was 'power politics, with threats producing counterthreats, alliances, counteralliances and so on'. In IR that produced an 'intellectual hegemony of realism': a conservative or 'status quo' theory based on the security and survival of existing states, and focused on strategic thinking in which the concept of military (sometimes nuclear) threats was the core of realist thought. In other words, Booth is specifically criticizing strategic realism associated with thinkers such as Thomas Schelling (1980) discussed above.

Booth claims that the realist game of power politics and military (including nuclear) strategy is now obsolete because security is now a local problem within disorganized and sometimes failed states. It is no longer primarily a problem of national security and national defense. Security is now more than ever both cosmopolitan and local at the same time: a problem of individual humans (e.g. citizens in failed states) and of the global community of humankind (facing, for example, ecological threats or nuclear extinction). Security is different in scope; it is also different in character:

Emancipation is the freeing of people (as individuals and groups) from those physical and human constraints which stop them carrying out what they would freely choose to do. War and the threat of war is one of those constraints, together with poverty, poor education, political oppression and so on. Security and emancipation are two sides of the same coin. Emancipation, not power or order, produces true security. (Booth 1991:319).

Implicit in this argument is the Kantian 'categorical imperative': the moral idea 'that we should treat people as ends and not means. States, however, should be treated as means and not ends' (Booth 1991: 319). In other words, people always come first; states are merely tools that can be discarded if they are no longer useful.

In a similar vein Andrew Linklater (1989) disputes the realist view of IR and offers an alternative emancipatory perspective to take its place (Box 3.20). Both Booth and Linklater claim that world politics can be constructed along these universal solidarist lines, with IR theorists leading the way. Not only that: they also claim that this social movement away from the anarchical society based on states and power politics and toward a cosmopolitan idea of global human security is well under way. The consequence of that for IR is clear: realism is becoming obsolete as a theoretical apparatus for studying IR, and irrelevant as a practical attitude to world politics.

The realist response to such emancipatory critiques could be expected to include some of the following observations. Linklater's and Booth's declaration of the death of the independent state and thus of the anarchical state system, like the

---

Box 3.20 **Linklater's emancipatory vision of global politics**

A new framework for world politics, based on

1. the construction of a 'global legal and political system' which goes beyond the state and 'affords protection to all human subjects';

2. the decline of self-interest and competitiveness [which allegedly sustains the state and fosters international conflict and ultimately war];

3. the rise and spread of human generosity that transcends state boundaries and extends to people everywhere;

4. the consequent development of a community of humankind to which all people owe their primary loyalty.

Linklater (1989: 199)

famous mistaken announcement of the death of Mark Twain, is premature. People across the world in their almost countless millions continue to cling to the state as their preferred form of political organization. We need only recall the powerful attraction of self-determination and political independence based on the state for the peoples of Asia, Africa, and the Middle East during the demise of European colonialism and for the peoples of Eastern Europe during the demise of the Soviet empire. When states fragment—as in the case of Yugoslavia at the end of the Cold War—the fragments turn out to be new (or old) states—e.g. Slovenia, Croatia, Bosnia. In historical terms all these major movements toward the sovereign state occurred recently—i.e. in the latter half of the twentieth century. Security continues to be based primarily on the state and the state system. It is not based on a global political-legal organization: such an entity does not exist (at least not yet). Where security is based on other social organizations, such as the family or the clan, as sometimes happens in Africa and some other parts of the world, that is because the local state has failed as a security organization. The people are trying to make the best of a bad situation. Their own state has failed them, but that does not mean they have given up on the state. What they want is what the people of many other countries already have: a developed and democratic state of their own. What they do not want is a 'global legal and political system' such as Linklater describes: that would be scarcely distinguishable from Western colonialism which they have just escaped from.

It is also necessary to mark the continuing significance of the major states. Realists underline the centrality of great powers in world politics. Great-power relations shape the international relations and influence the foreign policies of most other states. That is why realists concentrate their attention on the great powers. There is little reason to doubt that the United States, China, Japan, Russia, Germany, France, Britain, India, and a few other core states will continue to assert their leading roles in world politics. There also is little reason to doubt that the people of the world depend on those states, before all others, for maintaining international peace and security. There is nobody else to provide that fundamental service.

. . . .

Research Prospects and Program

Realism is a theory, first about the security problems of sovereign states in an international anarchy, and second about the problem of international order. The normative core of realism is state survival and national security. If world politics continues to be organized on the basis of independent states with a small group of powerful states largely responsible for shaping the most important international events, then it seems clear that realism will continue to be an important IR theory.

The only historical development that could render it obsolete is a world historical transformation that involved abandoning the sovereign state and the anarchical state system. That does not appear very likely in the foreseeable future.

This chapter has discussed the various main strands of realism; a major distinction was made between classical (and neoclassical) realism on the one hand and contemporary strategic realism and neorealism on the other. Which strand of realism contains the most promising research program? John Mearsheimer (1993) says that neorealism is a general theory that applies to other historical situations besides that of the Cold War. He argues that neorealism can be employed to predict the course of international history after the Cold War. We have noted that neorealism formulates a number of important questions about the distribution of power in the international system and the power-balancing of the leading powers. Yet we have also emphasized some limitations of neorealist theory, especially as regards the analysis of cooperation and integration in Western Europe after the end of the Cold War. Some neorealists think that these patterns of cooperation can be addressed without major difficulty through the further development of neorealist analysis (see e.g. Grieco 1997). On a more skeptical view, neorealism (and also strategic realism) appear closely tied to the special historical circumstances of the East/West conflict: (1) a bipolar system based on two rival superpowers (the United States and the Soviet Union) each implacably opposed to the other and prepared to risk nuclear war for the sake of their ideology; and (2) the development of nuclear weapons and the means to deliver them to any point on earth.

Since the end of the Cold War the Soviet Union has disappeared and the bipolar system has given way to one in which there are several major powers, but the United States arguably is now the only genuine superpower. Nuclear weapons remain in existence, of course. There is now a greater danger than before of the spread of nuclear weapons. In 1998 both India and Pakistan tested nuclear-weapon devices and in so doing turned the sub-continent of South Asia into an openly nuclear-weapons region. In 2002 they came to the brink of war which raised widespread anxiety about nuclear conflict and provoked the United States and some members of the European Union into concerted diplomatic efforts to defuse the situation. But none of the major powers that possess nuclear weapons—including Russia and China—give any indication of wishing to restore the Cold War system of nuclear coercion.

We believe that leaves neoclassical realism with the most promising future research program. We have tried to show how the debate on NATO expansion in Eastern Europe emphasized the need for discussing important questions of values when conducting inquiry into foreign policy issues. Neorealists are right in pointing to the risk of a new Cold War, but it is classical realism which is focused on analyzing how the difficult choices made by state leaders may or may not bring about a new Cold War. In the debate on NATO expansion it is clearly evident that both realists in favor of expansion and realists against expansion were very concerned about this, and that they both wanted to avoid a second Cold War—even though they came to opposite conclusions about whether or not expansion would diminish or increase the risks of that happening. Their debate was a good example of the honest differences between neoclassical realists.

On this view, a future research program for realism would build on the work of Hans Morgenthau rather than that of Schelling or Waltz, and would address important issues of the post-Cold War state system that the narrower focus of strategic realism and neorealism cannot so readily come to grips with. Among those issues are: (1) The emergence of the United States as an unrivaled great power following the demise of the Soviet Union, and the reduced significance of Russia in world politics. The role of the United States as a paramount power is somewhat comparable to Great Britain in the nineteenth century. At that time Britain refrained from engaging in wars of conquest in Europe and remained content with employing its political skill and military assets to maintain the balance of power. The United States at the dawn of the twenty-first century is even more benign than Britain was at that time: the US appears prepared to devote itself not only to defending its own national interest but also, albeit to a lesser extent, to being a responsible defender of international peace and security. (2) The return to a contemporary version of the Concert system of great powers in which the permanent members of the UN Security Council assume the main responsibility for safeguarding international peace and security under the leadership of the United States. (3) The threat posed by peripheral 'rogue states' such as Iraq which are prepared to threaten regional peace and security but are not in a position to threaten the global balance of power. (4) The problems posed by 'failed states' and the issue of great power responsibility for the protection of human rights in a world of states. (5) The security crisis presented by audacious acts of international terrorism, particularly the September 11, 2001 attacks on New York and Washington DC, which threaten the personal security of citizens more than either the national security of states or international peace and security.

A plausible research strategy for post-Cold War realism, therefore, would involve the attempt to understand the role of an unrivaled but also a benign paramount power in an international system which must face several fundamental problems: the protection of global peace and security, the coming to grips with 'rogue states' and 'failed states' on the periphery of the state system, and the protection of citizens, particularly those of Western countries, from international terrorism.

. . . .

KEY POINTS

- Realists usually have a pessimistic view of human nature. Realists are skeptical that there can be progress in international politics that is comparable to that in domestic political life. They operate with a core assumption that world politics consists of an international anarchy of sovereign states. Realists see international relations as basically conflictual, and they see international conflicts as ultimately resolved by war.

- Realists believe that the goal of power, the means of power, and the uses of power are a central preoccupation of political activity. International politics is thus portrayed as 'power politics'. The conduct of foreign policy is an instrumental activity based on the intelligent calculation of one's power and one's interests as against the power and interests of rivals and competitors.

- Realists have a high regard for the values of national security, state survival, and international order and stability. They usually believe that there are no international obligations in the moral sense of the word—i.e. bonds of mutual duty—between independent states. For classical and neoclassical realists there is one morality for the private sphere and another and very different morality for the public sphere. Political ethics allows some actions that would not be tolerated by private morality.

- Realists place a great deal of importance on the balance of power, which is both an empirical concept concerning the way that world politics are seen to operate and a normative concept: it is a legitimate goal and a guide to responsible statecraft on the part of the leaders of the great powers. It upholds the basic values of peace and security.

- Many contemporary realists seek to provide an empirical analysis of world politics. But they hold back from providing a normative analysis of world politics because that is deemed to be subjective and thus unscientific. That attitude marks a fundamental divide between classical and neoclassical realists on the one hand and contemporary strategic realists and neorealists on the other.

- Schelling seeks to provide analytical tools for strategic thought. He views diplomacy and foreign policy, especially that of the great powers and particularly the United States, as a rational-instrumental activity that can be more deeply understood by the application of a form of mathematical analysis called 'game theory'. Coercion is a method of bringing an adversary into a bargaining relationship and getting the adversary to do what we want him or her to do without having to compel it—i.e. employ brute force which, in addition to being dangerous, is usually far more difficult and far less efficient.

- Neorealism is an attempt to explain international relations in scientific terms by reference to the unequal capabilities of states and the anarchical structure of the state system, and by focusing on the great powers whose relations determine the most important 'outcomes' of international politics. A scientific theory of IR leads us to expect states to behave in certain predictable ways. Waltz and Mearsheimer believe that bipolar systems are more stable and thus provide a better guarantee of peace and security than multipolar systems. According to that view, the Cold War was a period of international stability and peace.

- The International Society tradition is critical of realism on two counts. First, it regards realism as a one-dimensional IR theory that is too narrowly focused. Second, it claims that realism fails to capture the extent to which international politics is a dialogue of different IR voices and perspectives. Emancipatory theory claims that power politics is obsolete because security is now a local problem within disorganized and sometimes failed states, and at the same time is a cosmopolitan problem of people everywhere regardless of their citizenship. It is no longer exclusively or even primarily a problem of national security and national defense.

QUESTIONS

- Realists are pessimistic about human progress and cooperation beyond the boundaries of the nation-state. What are the reasons given for that pessimism? Are they good reasons?

- Why do realists place so much emphasis on security? Does that make sense? How important is security in world politics?

- Identify the major differences between the neoclassical realism of Hans Morgenthau and the neorealism of Kenneth Waltz. Which approach is best suited for analyzing international relations after the Cold War?

- Outline the main arguments for and against NATO expansion. State your own position including supporting arguments.

- What is the emancipatory critique of realism? Does it make sense?

 For additional material and resources see the companion web site at:
www.oup.co.uk/best.textbooks/politics/jacksonsorensen2e/

GUIDE TO FURTHER READING

Kennan, G. (1954). *Realities of American Foreign Policy*. Princeton: Princeton University Press.

Machiavelli, N. (1984). *The Prince*, trans. P. Bondanella and M. Musa. New York: Oxford University Press.

Morgenthau, H. (1985). *Politics Among Nations: The Struggle for Power and Peace*, 6th edn. New York: Knopf.

Schelling, T. (1980). *The Strategy of Conflict*. Boston: Harvard University Press.

Waltz, K. (1979). *Theory of International Politics*. New York: McGraw-Hill.

WEB LINKS

http://classicals.mit.edu/Thucydides/pelopwar.html
Full text of Thucydides' *The History of the Peloponnesian War*. Hosted by the Internet Classics Archive.

http://www.bigchalk.com/cgi-bin/WebObjects/WOPortal.woa/wa/HWCDA/file?fileid=149329&flt=CAB
An extract from Hans J. Morgenthau's 'Politics among Nations'. Hosted by bigchalk.

http://cs-education.stanford.edu/class/sophomore-college/projects-98/game-theory/
Stanford University provides an excellent account of the basics of game theory.

http://wwics.si.edu/ees/special/2001/peace.htm
The report of the Woodrow Wilson Center on the NATO enlargement process.

4 Liberalism

SUMMARY

This chapter sets forth the liberal tradition in IR. Basic liberal assumptions are: (1) a positive view of human nature; (2) a conviction that international relations can be cooperative rather than conflictual; (3) a belief in progress. In their conceptions of international cooperation liberal theorists emphasize different features of world politics. Sociological liberals highlight transnational non-governmental ties between societies, such as communication between individuals and between groups. Interdependence liberals pay particular attention to economic ties of mutual exchange and mutual dependence between peoples and governments. Institutional liberals underscore the importance of organized cooperation between states; finally, republican liberals argue that liberal democratic constitutions and forms of government are of vital importance for inducing peaceful and cooperative relations between states. The chapter discusses these four strands of liberal thought and a debate with neorealism to which it has given rise. The concluding section evaluates the prospects for the liberal tradition as a research program in IR.

Introduction: Basic Liberal Assumptions

Why read a chapter on the liberal tradition in IR? The short answer is that you need to know the liberal tradition to form your own opinion about the most keenly debated issue in IR: the pessimistic view of realism versus the optimistic view of liberalism. The previous chapter introduced the realist tradition, with its focus on power and conflict. This chapter is about the sharply contrasting liberal view. How can liberals be optimistic? Why do they see a more peaceful world down the road? What are their arguments and beliefs?

The liberal tradition in IR is closely connected with the emergence of the modern liberal state. Liberal philosophers, beginning with John Locke in the seventeenth century, saw great potential for human progress in modern civil society and capitalist economy, both of which could flourish in states which guaranteed individual liberty. Modernity projects a new and better life, free of authoritarian government and with a much higher level of material welfare.

Box 4.1 **Modernization**

Between 1780 and 1850, in less than three generations, a far-reaching revolution, without precedent in the history of Mankind, changed the face of England. From then on, the world was no longer the same. The Industrial Revolution transformed Man from a farmer-shepherd into a manipulator of machines worked by inanimate energy . . . [It] opened up a completely different world of new and untapped sources of energy such as coal, oil, electricity and the atom. From a narrow technological point of view, the Industrial Revolution can be defined as the process by which a society gained control of vast sources of inanimate energy; but such a definition does not do justice to this phenomenon . . . as regards its economic, cultural, social and political implications.

Cipolla (1977: 7–8)

The process of modernization unleashed by the scientific revolution led to improved technologies and thus more efficient ways of producing goods and mastering nature. That was reinforced by the liberal intellectual revolution which had great faith in human reason and rationality. Here is the basis for the liberal belief in progress: the modern liberal state invokes a political and economic system that will bring, in Jeremy Bentham's famous phrase, 'the greatest happiness of the greatest number'.

Liberals generally take a positive view of human nature. They have great faith in human reason and they are convinced that rational principles can be applied to international affairs. Liberals recognize that individuals are self-interested and competitive up to a point. But they also believe that individuals share many interests and can thus engage in collaborative and cooperative social action, domestically as well as internationally, which results in greater benefits for everybody at home and abroad. In other words, conflict and war are not inevitable; when people employ their reason they can achieve mutually beneficial cooperation not only within states but also across international boundaries. Liberal theorists thus believe that human reason can triumph over human fear and the lust for power. But they disagree about the magnitude of the obstacles on the way to human progress (Smith 1992: 204). For some liberals it is a long-term process with many setbacks; for others, success is just around the corner. However, all liberals agree that in the long run cooperation based on mutual interests will prevail. That is because modernization constantly increases the scope and the need for cooperation (Zacher and Matthew 1995: 119).

The belief in progress is a core liberal assumption. But it is also a point of debate among liberals (see Pollard 1971: 9–13). How much progress? Scientific and technological for sure, but also social and political? What are the limits of progress? Are there any limits? Progress for whom? A small number of liberal countries or the entire world? The scope and degree of liberal optimism as regards progress has fluctuated over time. Many early liberals were inclined to be thoroughly optimistic; we have also noted the surge of utopian liberalism around the First World War. After the Second World War, however, liberal optimism became more muted. Robert Keohane, for example, cautiously notes that liberals at a minimum believe 'in at least the possibility of cumulative progress' (Keohane 1989a: 174). Yet there was another surge of liberal optimism after the end of the Cold War, propelled by the notion of 'the end of history' based on the defeat of communism and the expected universal victory of liberal democracy (Fukuyama 1989; 1992). However, the terrorist attack of September 11, 2001, is a setback for liberal optimism.

Progress for liberals is always progress for individuals. The core concern of liberalism is the happiness and contentment of individual human beings. John Locke argued that states existed to underwrite the liberty of their citizens and thus enable them to live their lives and pursue their happiness without undue interference from other people. In contrast to realists, who see the state first and foremost as a concentration and instrument of power, a *Machtstaat*, liberals see the state as a constitutional entity, a *Rechtsstaat*, which establishes and enforces the rule of law that respects the rights of citizens to life, liberty, and property. Such constitutional states would also respect each other and would deal with each other in accordance with norms of mutual toleration. That argument was enlarged by Jeremy Bentham—an eighteenth-century English philosopher—who coined the term 'international law'. He believed that it was in the rational interests of constitutional states to adhere to international law in their foreign policies (Rosenblum 1978: 101). The argument was further expanded by Immanuel Kant, an eighteenth-century German philosopher. He thought that a world of such

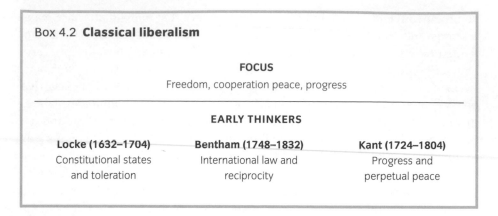

Box 4.2 Classical liberalism

FOCUS

Freedom, cooperation peace, progress

EARLY THINKERS

Locke (1632–1704)	Bentham (1748–1832)	Kant (1724–1804)
Constitutional states and toleration	International law and reciprocity	Progress and perpetual peace

constitutional and mutually respectful states—he called them 'republics'—could eventually establish 'perpetual peace' in the world (Gallie 1978: 8–36). Box 4.2 summarizes the focus of leading classical liberal thinkers.

In summary, liberal thinking is closely connected with the emergence of the modern constitutional state. Liberals argue that modernization is a process involving progress in most areas of life. The process of modernization enlarges the scope for cooperation across international boundaries. Progress means a better life for at least the majority of individuals. Humans possess reason, and when they apply it to international affairs greater cooperation will be the end result.

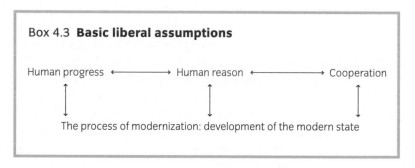

Box 4.3 Basic liberal assumptions

Human progress ←——————→ Human reason ←——————→ Cooperation

The process of modernization: development of the modern state

In Chapter 2, we presented the utopian or idealist liberalism of the 1920s. This chapter focuses on liberal theory after the Second World War. It is useful to divide postwar liberalism into four main strands of thinking: sociological liberalism; interdependence liberalism; institutional liberalism; and republican liberalism (Nye 1988: 246; Keohane 1989*a*: 11; Zacher and Matthew 1995: 121). The following sections of this chapter will focus on each one in turn. It will not be possible to address all the relevant scholarly works or to demonstrate in detail how contemporary liberal thought builds on classical liberal thinking. Our focus will be on important contributions that represent each of these strands. We have chosen this division into four major strands because we find that they bring out the most important aspects of current liberal ideas about international relations.

Sociological Liberalism

For realists, IR is the study of relations between the governments of sovereign states. Sociological liberals reject this view as too narrowly focused and one-sided. IR is not only about state–state relations; it is also about transnational relations, i.e. relations between people, groups, and organizations belonging to different countries. We should note that this emphasis on society as well as the state, on many different types of actor and not just national governments, has led some to identify liberal thought by the term 'pluralism'.

Transnational relations are considered by sociological liberals to be an increasingly important aspect of international relations. James Rosenau defines transnationalism as follows: 'the processes whereby international relations conducted by governments have been supplemented by relations among private individuals, groups, and societies that can and do have important consequences for the course of events' (Rosenau 1980: 1). In focusing on transnational relations, sociological liberals return to an old theme in liberal thinking: the notion that relations between people are more cooperative and more supportive of peace than are relations between national governments. Richard Cobden, a leading nineteenth-century liberal thinker, put the idea as follows: 'As little intercourse betwixt the Governments, as much connection as possible between the nations of the world' (Cobden 1903: 216; Taylor 1957: 49). By 'nations' Cobden was referring to societies and their membership.

Karl Deutsch was a leading figure in the study of transnational relations during the 1950s. He and his associates attempted to measure the extent of communication and transactions between societies. Deutsch argues that a high degree of transnational ties between societies leads to peaceful relations that amount to more than the mere absence of war (Deutsch *et al.* 1957). It leads to a security community: 'a group of people which has become "integrated"'. Integration means that a 'sense of community' has been achieved; people have come to agree that their conflicts and problems can be resolved 'without resort to large-scale physical force' (1957: 5). Such a security community has emerged, argues Deutsch, among the Western countries in the North Atlantic area. He lists a number of conditions that are conductive to the emergence of security communities: increased social communication; greater mobility of persons; stronger economic ties; and a wider range of mutual human transactions.

Many sociological liberals hold the idea that transnational relations between people from different countries help create new forms of human society which exist alongside or even in competition with the nation state. In a book called *World Society* John Burton (1972) proposes a 'cobweb model' of transnational relationships. The purpose is to demonstrate how any nation state consists of many different groups of people which have different types of external tie and different types of interest: religious groups, business groups, labor groups, etc. In marked contrast, the realist model of the world often depicts the system of states as a set of billiard balls: i.e. as a number of independent, self-contained units. According to sociological liberals like Burton, if we map the patterns of communication and transactions between various groups we will get a more accurate picture of the world because it would represent actual patterns of human behavior rather than artificial boundaries of states.

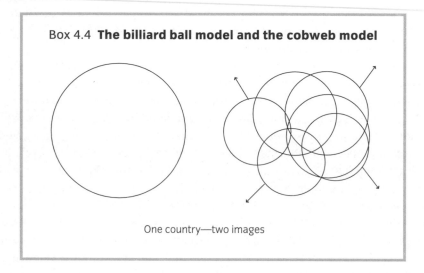

Box 4.4 **The billiard ball model and the cobweb model**

One country—two images

Burton implies that the cobweb model points to a world driven more by mutually beneficial cooperation than by antagonistic conflict. In this way the cobweb model builds on an earlier liberal idea about the beneficial effects of cross-cutting or overlapping group memberships. Because individuals are members of many different groups, conflict will be muted if not eliminated; overlapping memberships minimize the risk of serious conflict between any two groups (Nicholls 1974: 22; Little 1996: 72).

James Rosenau has further developed the sociological liberal approach to transnational relations (Rosenau 1990; 1992). He focuses on transnational relations at the macro-level of human populations in addition to those conducted at the micro-level by individuals. Rosenau argues that individual transactions have important implications and consequences for global affairs. First, individuals have greatly extended their activities owing to better education and access to electronic means of communication as well as foreign travel. Second, states' capacity for control and regulation is decreasing in an ever more complex world. The consequence is a world of better-informed and more mobile individuals who are far less tied than before to 'their' states. Rosenau thus sees a profound transformation of the international system that is underway: the state-centric, anarchic system has not disappeared but a new 'multi-centric world has emerged that is composed of diverse "sovereignty-free" collectivities which exist apart from and in competition with the state-centric world of "sovereignty-bound" actors' (Rosenau 1992: 282). Rosenau thus supports the liberal idea that an increasingly pluralist world, characterized by transnational networks of individuals and groups, will be more peaceful. In some respects it will be a more unstable world, because the old order built on state power has broken down; but only rarely will conflicts lead to the use of force, because the numerous new cosmopolitan individuals that are members of many overlapping groups will not easily become enemies divided into antagonistic camps.

We can summarize sociological liberalism as follows. IR is not only a study of relations between national governments; IR scholars also study relations between private individuals, groups, and societies. Overlapping interdependent relations between people are bound to be more cooperative than relations between states because states are exclusive and, according to sociological liberalism, their interests do not overlap and cross-cut. A world with a large number of transnational networks will thus be more peaceful.

Box 4.5 **The importance of individuals in global politics**

Citizens have become important variables . . . in global politics   [for] at least five reasons:

1. The erosion and dispersion of state and governmental power.

2. The advent of global television, the widening use of computers in the workplace, the growth of foreign travel and the mushrooming migrations of peoples, the spread of educational institutions . . . has enhanced the analytic skills of individuals.

3. The crowding onto the global agenda of new, interdependence issues (such as environmental pollution, currency crises, the drug trade, AIDS, and terrorism) has made more salient the processes whereby global dynamics affect the welfare and pocketbooks of individuals.

4. The revolution of information technologies has made it possible for citizens and politicians literally to 'see' the aggregation of micro actions into macro outcomes. People can now observe support gather momentum as street rallies, the pronouncements of officials, the responses of adversaries, the comments of protesters . . . and a variety of other events get portrayed and interpreted on television screens throughout the world.

5. This new-found capacity of citizens to 'see' their role in the dynamics of aggregation has profoundly altered . . . possibly even reduced, the extent to which organization and leadership are factors in the mobilization of publics . . . Leaders are increasingly becoming followers because individuals are becoming increasingly aware that their actions can have consequences.

Rosenau (1992: 274–6)

Interdependence Liberalism

Interdependence means mutual dependence: peoples and governments are affected by what happens elsewhere, by the actions of their counterparts in other countries. Thus, a higher level of transnational relations between countries means a higher level of interdependence. That also reflects the process of modernization, which usually increases the level of interdependence between states. The twentieth century, especially the period since 1950, has seen the rise of a large number of highly industrialized countries. Richard Rosecrance (1986; 1995; 1999) has analyzed the effects of these developments on the policies of states. Throughout history states have sought power by means of military force and territorial expansion. But for highly industrialized countries economic development and foreign trade are more adequate and less costly means of achieving prominence and prosperity. That is because the costs of using force have increased and the benefits have declined. Why is force less beneficial for states and trade increasingly so? The principal reason, according to Rosecrance, is the changing character and basis of economic production, which is linked to modernization. In an earlier age the possession of territory and ample natural resources were the key to greatness. In today's world that is no longer the case; now a highly qualified labor force, access to information, and financial capital are the keys to success.

The most economically successful countries of the postwar period are the 'trading states' such as Japan and Germany. They have refrained from the traditional military-political option of high military expenditure and economic self-sufficiency; instead, they have chosen the trading option of an intensified international division of labor and increased interdependence. Many small countries are also 'trading states'. For a long time the very large countries, most notably the former Soviet Union and the United States, pursued the traditional military-political option, thereby burdening themselves with high levels of military expenditure. That has changed in recent decades. According to Rosecrance, the end of the Cold War has made that traditional option less urgent and thus less attractive. Consequently, the trading-state option is increasingly preferred even by very large states.

Basically these liberals argue that a high division of labor in the international economy increases interdependence between states, and that discourages and reduces violent conflict between states. There still remains a risk that modern states will slide back to the military option and once again enter into arms races and violent confrontations. But that is not a likely prospect. It is in the less developed countries that war now occurs, according to Rosecrance, because at lower levels of economic development land continues to be the dominant factor of production, and modernization and interdependence are far weaker.

During the Second World War, David Mitrany (1966) set forth a functionalist theory of integration, arguing that greater interdependence in the form of transnational ties between countries could lead to peace. Mitrany believed, somewhat naïvely, that cooperation should be arranged by technical experts, not by politicians. The experts would devise solutions to common problems in various functional areas: transport, communication, finance, etc. Technical and economic collaboration would expand when the participants discovered the mutual benefits that could be obtained from it. When citizens saw the welfare improvements that resulted from efficient collaboration in international organizations, they would transfer their loyalty from the state to international organizations. In that way, economic interdependence would lead to political integration and to peace.

Ernst Haas developed a so-called neofunctionalist theory of international integration that was inspired by the intensifying cooperation between the countries of Western Europe that began in the 1950s. Haas builds on Mitrany. But he rejects the notion that 'technical' matters can be separated from politics. Integration has to do with getting self-interested political élites to intensify their cooperation. Integration is a process whereby 'political actors are persuaded to shift their loyalties . . . toward a new center whose institutions possess or demand jurisdiction over the preexisting national states' (Haas 1958: 16). This 'functional' process of integration depends on the notion of 'spillover', when increased cooperation in one area leads to increased cooperation in other areas. Spillover would ensure that political élites marched inexorably towards the promotion of integration. Haas saw that happening in the initial years of West European cooperation in the 1950s and early 1960s.

From the mid-1960s, however, West European cooperation entered a long phase of stagnation and even backsliding. That was due primarily to President de Gaulle of France, who opposed the limitations on French sovereignty that resulted from interdependence. Functional and neofunctional theory did not allow for the possibility of setbacks in cooperation; integration theorists had to rethink their theories accordingly. Haas concluded that regional integration ought to be studied in a larger context: 'theory of regional integration ought to be subordinated to a general theory of interdependence' (Haas 1976: 179).

It was indeed such a general theory of interdependence that was attempted in the next phase in liberal thinking. But we should also note that theories of integration have seen a revival in the 1980s and 1990s due to a new momentum in West European cooperation (Moravcsik 1991; Tranholm-Mikkelsen 1991; Keohane and Hoffmann 1991). A core issue in these recent studies concerns whether integration is best explained by a liberal, neofunctionalist approach, or by a realist approach emphasizing national interest? We return to that debate between liberals and realists below.

An ambitious attempt to set forth a general theory of what they called 'complex interdependence' was made in the late 1970s in a book by Robert Keohane and Joseph Nye, *Power and Interdependence* (1977; 2001). They argue that postwar 'complex interdependence' is qualitatively different from earlier and simpler kinds

Box 4.6 **Major EU institutions**

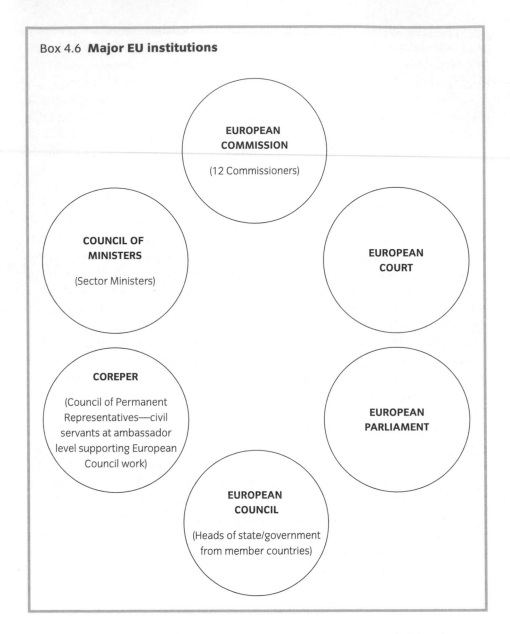

of interdependence. Previously, international relations were directed by state leaders dealing with other state leaders. The use of military force was always an option in the case of conflict between those national leaders. The 'high politics' of security and survival had priority over the 'low politics' of economics and social affairs (Keohane and Nye 1977: 23). Under conditions of complex interdependence, however, that is no longer the case, and for two reasons. First, relations between states nowadays are not only or even primarily relations between state leaders; there are relations on many different levels via many

different actors and branches of government. Second, there is a host of transnational relations between individuals and groups outside of the state. Furthermore, military force is a less useful instrument of policy under conditions of
complex interdependence.

Consequently, international relations are becoming more like domestic politics:
'Different issues generate different coalitions, both within governments and
across them, and involve different degrees of conflict. Politics does not stop at the
water's edge' (Keohane and Nye 1977: 25). In most of these conflicts military
force is irrelevant. Therefore, power resources other than military ones are of
increasing importance, for example, negotiating skills. Finally, under complex
interdependence states become more preoccupied with the 'low politics' of
welfare and less concerned with the 'high politics' of national security (Nye 1993:
169; Keohane and Nye 1977: 24–6).

We typify the receding old realist world and the advancing new world of
complex interdependence in Box 4.7.

Box 4.7 **Types of international relation**

REALISM	COMPLEX INTERDEPENDENCE
• States dominant actors and coherent units	• Transnational actors increasingly important. States not coherent units
• Force usable and effective	• Military force less useful. Economic and institutional instruments more useful
• Military security dominates the agenda	• Military security less important. Welfare issues increasingly important

Based on Keohane and Nye (1977)

Complex interdependence clearly implies a far more friendly and cooperative
relationship between states. According to Keohane and Nye (1977: 29–38) several
consequences follow. First, states will pursue different goals simultaneously and
transnational actors, such as NGOs and transnational corporations, will pursue
their own separate goals free from state control. Second, power resources will
most often be specific to issue areas. For example, in spite of their comparatively
small size, Denmark and Norway will command influence in international
shipping because of their large merchant and tanker fleets, but that influence does
not easily translate to other issue areas. Third, the importance of international
organizations will increase. They are arenas for political actions by weak states,
they animate coalition formation, and they oversee the setting of international
agendas.

Where do we locate complex interdependence in time and space? On the time
dimension, it appears to be connected with social modernization or what Keohane

and Nye (1977: 227) call 'the long-term development of the welfare state' which picked up speed after 1950. In space, complex interdependence is most evident in Western Europe, North America, Japan, Australia, and New Zealand: in short, the industrialized, pluralist countries (1977: 27). The relevance of complex interdependence grows as modernization unfolds, and it is thus especially applicable to the relations between advanced Western countries.

Keohane and Nye are nevertheless at pains to emphasize that realism is not irrelevant or obsolete.

It is not impossible to imagine dramatic conflict or revolutionary change in which the use of threat of military force over an economic issue or among advanced industrial countries might become plausible. Then realist assumptions would again be a reliable guide to events. (Keohane and Nye 1977: 28)

In other words, even among industrialized countries of the West an issue could still become 'a matter of life and death' (p. 29), because even that world is still in some basic respects a world of states. In that eventuality, realism would be the more relevant approach to events.

Realists claim that any issue can become a matter of life and death in an anarchic world. Interdependence liberals will reply that that is too simplistic and that a large number of issues on the international agenda are important bread-and-butter items in line with the complex interdependence assumptions. Therefore, interdependence liberals suggest a compromise:

The appropriate response to the changes occurring in world politics today is not to discredit the traditional wisdom of realism and its concern for the military balance of power, but to realize its limitations and to supplement it with insights from the liberal approach. (Nye 1990: 177)

Interdependence liberals are thus more balanced in their approach than some other liberals for whom everything has changed for the better and the old world of violent conflict, unbridled state power, and the dictatorship of the national interest is gone forever. However, in adopting this middle-of-the-road position interdependence liberals face the problem of deciding exactly how much has changed, how much remains the same, and what the precise implications are for IR. We return to this debate later in the chapter.

Meanwhile, interdependence liberalism can be summarized as follows. Modernization increases the level and scope of interdependence between states. Under complex interdependence, transnational actors are increasingly important, military force is a less useful instrument, and welfare—not security—is becoming the primary goal and concern of states. That means a world of more cooperative international relations.

Institutional Liberalism

This strand of liberalism picks up on earlier liberal thought about the beneficial effects of international institutions. In Chapter 2, we noted Woodrow Wilson's vision about transforming international relations from a 'jungle' of chaotic power politics to a 'zoo' of regulated and peaceful intercourse. This transformation was to be achieved through the building of international organizations, most importantly the League of Nations. Present-day institutional liberals are less optimistic than their more idealist predecessors. They do agree that international institutions can make cooperation easier and far more likely, but they do not claim that such institutions can by themselves guarantee a qualitative transformation of inter-national relations, from a 'jungle' to a 'zoo'. Powerful states will not easily be completely constrained. However, institutional liberals do not agree with the real-ist view that international institutions are mere 'scraps of paper', that they are at the complete mercy of powerful states. International institutions are more than mere handmaidens of strong states. They are of independent importance, and they can promote cooperation between states (Keohane 1989a; Young 1989; Rittberger 1993; Levy *et al.* 1995).

What is an international institution? According to institutional liberals, it is an international organization, such as NATO or the European Union; or it is a set of rules which govern state action in particular areas, such as aviation or shipping. These sets of rules are also called 'regimes'. Often the two go together: the trade regime, for example, is shaped primarily by the World Trade Organization (WTO). There may also be regimes without formal organizations: for example, the Law of the Sea conferences held under the auspices of the United Nations do not have a formal international organization. Finally, we should note that there is an additional type of international institution which is of a more fundamental kind, such as state sovereignty or the balance of power. These fundamental institutions are not what institutional liberals focus on; but they are main objects of study for International Society theorists, as we shall see in Chapter 5.

Institutional liberals claim that international institutions help promote co-operation between states. In order to evaluate that claim, institutional liberals adopt a behavioralistic, scientific approach. An empirical measure of the extent of institutionalization among states is devised. The extent to which these inter-national institutions have helped advance cooperation is then assessed. The extent of institutionalization can be measured on two dimensions, scope and depth. 'Scope' concerns the number of issue areas in which there are institutions. Are they only in a few crucial economic areas, such as trade and investment, or are they in many other economic areas as well, and also in military and sociopolitical areas? For assessing the 'depth' of institutionalization, three measures have been suggested:

- **Commonality:** the degree to which expectations about appropriate behavior and understanding about how to interpret action are shared by participants in the system

- **Specificity:** the degree to which these expectations are clearly specified in the form of rules

- **Autonomy:** the extent to which the institution can alter its own rules rather than depending on outside agents (i.e. states) to do so (From Keohane 1989*a*: 4)

Box 4.8 **A typology of international and transnational organizations**

		GOAL OF ORGANIZATION	
		SPECIFIC	GENERAL
REGIONAL	Intergovernmental	NATO NAFTA	OAU (Organization of African Unity)
REGIONAL	Supranational	ECSC (European Coal and Steel Community) EURATOM	(Parts of) European Union
REGIONAL	Transnational	European Anti-poverty Network	European Movement
UNIVERSAL	Intergovernmental	WHO (World Health Organization) IAEA (International Atomic Energy Agency)	UN
UNIVERSAL	Supranational	—	—
UNIVERSAL	Transnational	Amnesty International	World Federalist Association

TERMS OF MEMBERSHIP

Adapted from Heurlin (1996)

Current research on international institutions has two main aims. First, there is an effort to collect more data on the existence of regimes in various issue areas of international relations. Second, a number of theoretical questions require further study, as indicated in a recent survey (Levy *et al.* 1995: 268):

- Under what conditions and through what mechanisms do international regimes come into existence?

- Do regimes persist even when the circumstances in which they came into existence change?

- What consequences of regimes for state behavior and problem-solving can we observe?

- What long-term effects do regimes have on national political systems and the structure of world politics?

It is clear that a thorough analysis of the scope and depth of institutionalization among a group of states is a substantial research task. A complete absence of institutionalization is highly unlikely; there will always be some rules of coordination. The difficulty is to determine the exact level of institutionalization. A number of studies have addressed the question about the extent to which institutions have helped advance cooperation (Krasner 1983; Keohane 1984; 1989*a*; Rittberger 1993; Underdal 1992; Young 1989; Oye 1986; Haftendorn *et al.* 1999; Lake 2001; Botcheva and Martin 2001). One way of doing that is to look at a group of states where we immediately believe that the scope and depth of institutionalization are high and then evaluate the ways in which institutions matter.

One such group of states is Western Europe, especially the European Union countries. EU countries cooperate so intensively that they share some functions of government, for example in agricultural and industrial policies; they have established the regulatory framework for a single market in the economic sector, and they are in the process of intensifying their cooperation in other areas. EU Europe, in other words, is a good test case for examining the importance of institutions. Institutional liberals do claim that institutions have made a significant difference in Western Europe after the end of the Cold War (Keohane *et al.* 1993). Institutions acted as 'buffers' which helped absorb the 'shocks' sent through Western Europe by the end of the Cold War and the reunification of Germany.

One way to assess the institutional liberal view is to set it against that of neorealist analysis. Neorealists argue that the end of the Cold War is most likely to bring the return of instability to Western Europe which could lead to a major war. It threatens to be a repetition of the first half of the twentieth century. Peace in Europe during the Cold War rested on two pillars that made up the balance of power between the United States and the Soviet Union. They were, first, bipolarity with its stable distribution of military power and, second, the large arsenals of nuclear weapons almost entirely monopolized by those superpowers. With the revival of multipolarity, however, instability and insecurity is sharply increased. At the root of all this is the anarchic structure of the international system. According to neorealist John Mearsheimer, '[a]narchy has two principal consequences. First, there is little room for trust among states. . . . Second, each state must guarantee its own survival since no other actor will provide its security' (Mearsheimer 1991: 148).

The argument made by institutional liberals (Keohane 1989*a*: 2; Nye 1993: 38; Keohane *et al.* 1993) is that a high level of institutionalization significantly reduces the destabilizing effects of multipolar anarchy identified by Mearsheimer.

Institutions make up for lack of trust between states. They do that by providing a flow of information among their member states, which consequently are much less in the dark about what other states are doing and why. Institutions thus help reduce member states' fear of each other. In addition, they provide a forum for negotiation between states. For example, the European Union has a number of fora with extensive experience in negotiation and compromise, including the Council of Ministers, the European Commission, and the European Parliament. Institutions provide continuity and a sense of stability. They foster cooperation between states for their mutual advantage. For example, European states can use the EU machinery to try to ensure that the other parties will respect commitments already made. Institutions help 'create a climate in which expectations of stable peace develop' (Nye 1993: 39). The constructive role of institutions as argued by institutional liberals is summarized in Box 4.9.

Box 4.9 Institutional liberalism: the role of institutions

Provide a flow of information and opportunities to negotiate;

Enhance the ability of governments to monitor others' compliance and to implement their own commitments—hence their ability to make credible commitments in the first place;

Strengthen prevailing expectations about the solidity of international agreements.

Based on Keohane (1989a: 2)

Institutional liberalism can be summarized as follows. International institutions help promote cooperation between states and thereby help alleviate the lack of trust between states and states' fear of each other which are considered to be the traditional problems associated with international anarchy. The positive role of international institutions for advancing cooperation between states continues to be questioned by realists. We return to that debate below.

....

Republican Liberalism

Republican liberalism is built on the claim that liberal democracies are more peaceful and law-abiding than are other political systems. The argument is not that democracies never go to war; democracies have gone to war as often as have non-democracies. But the argument is that democracies do not fight each other. This observation was first articulated by Immanuel Kant (1992) in the late eighteenth century in reference to republican states rather than democracies. It was resurrected by Dean Babst in 1964 and it has been advanced in numerous studies since then. One liberal scholar even claims that the assertion that democracies do not fight each other is 'one of the strongest nontrivial or non-tautological statements that can be made about international relations' (Russett 1989: 245). This finding, then, is the basis of the present optimism among many liberal scholars and policymakers concerning the prospects of long-term world peace. Their reasoning goes as follows. Because the number of democracies in the world has increased rapidly in recent years we can look forward to a more peaceful world with international relations characterized by cooperation instead of conflict (parts of this section draw on Sørensen 1993*a*).

Why are democracies at peace with one another? The answer to that question has been most systematically addressed by Michael Doyle (1983; 1986). Doyle based his argument on the classical liberal treatment of the subject by Immanuel Kant. There are three elements behind the claim that democracy leads to peace with other democracies (see Box 4.11). The first is the existence of domestic political cultures based on peaceful conflict resolution. Democracy encourages peaceful international relations because democratic governments are controlled by their citizens, who will not advocate or support wars with other democracies.

The second element is that democracies hold common moral values which lead to the formation of what Kant called a 'pacific union'. The union is not a formal peace treaty; rather, it is a zone of peace based on the common moral foundations of all democracies. Peaceful ways of solving domestic conflict are seen as morally superior to violent behavior, and this attitude is transferred to international relations between democracies. Freedom of expression and free communication promote mutual understanding internationally, and help to assure that political representatives act in accordance with citizens' views.

Finally, peace between democracies is strengthened through economic cooperation and interdependence. In the pacific union it is possible to encourage what Kant called 'the spirit of commerce': mutual and reciprocal gain for those involved in international economic cooperation and exchange.

Of the different strands of liberalism considered in this chapter, republican liberalism is the one with the strongest normative element. For most republican liberals there is not only confidence but also hope that world politics is already developing and will develop far beyond rivalry, conflict, and war among independent states. Republican liberals are optimistic that peace and cooperation will eventually prevail in international relations, based on progress towards a more democratic world. Not only that (and here the normative element shows itself clearly): they see it as their responsibility to promote democracy worldwide, for in doing so they are promoting peace, which is one of the most fundamental of all political values.

The end of the Cold War helped launch a new wave of democratization; that led to growing liberal optimism as regards the future of democracy. Yet most liberals are well aware of the fragility of democratic progress. When republican liberals examine the conditions for a democratic peace in the light of recent democratic transformations in Eastern Europe, Latin America, and Africa, the evidence is not

Box 4.10 **Democracy's progress**

The Freedom House Index Classification of Independent Countries (with greater than one million inhabitants), 2001–2002

(1 = highest rating)

Average rating: 1

Andorra	Finland	New Zealand
Australia	Grenada	Norway
Austria	Iceland	Portugal
Bahamas	Ireland	San Marino
Barbados	Kirbati	Sweden
Belize	Liechtenstein	Switzerland
Canada	Luxembourg	Tuvalu
Cyprus (G)	Malta	United States
Denmark	Marshall Islands	Uruguay
Dominica	Netherlands	

Average rating: 1.5

Argentina	Latvia	Sao Tome and Principe
Belgium	Lithuania	Slovakia
Cape Verde	Mauritius	Slovenia
Costa Rica	Micronesia	South Africa
Czech Republic	Monaco	Spain
Estonia	Palau	Suriname
France	Panama	Taiwan
Germany	Poland	United Kingdom
Hungary	St. Kitts and Nevis	
Italy	St. Lucia	
Japan	St. Vincent and Grenadines	

Average rating: 2

Benin	Greece	Nauru
Bolivia	Guyana	Peru
Botswana	Israel	Romania
Chile	Jamaica	Samoa
Dominican Republic	Korea, South	Vanuatu

Average rating: 2.5

Bulgaria	India	Namibia
Croatia	Mali	Papua New Guinea
El Salvador	Mexico	Philippines
Ghana	Mongolia	Thailand

Based on data from www.freedomhouse.org (2001): 14. The index employs one dimension for political rights and one dimension for civil liberties. For each dimension a seven-point scale is used, so that the highest ranking countries (that is, those with the highest degree of democracy) are one–ones (1–1's) and the lowest ranking are seven–seven's (7–7's). Countries with an average rating between 1 and 2.5 are considered free.

Box 4.11 **Republican liberalism: three conditions of peace among liberal democracies**

1. Democratic norms of peaceful resolution of conflict
2. Peaceful relations among democratic states, based on a common moral foundation
3. Economic cooperation among democracies: ties of interdependence

---

supportive of any profound optimism. With regard to the first condition (see Box 4.11), it is evident that a democratic culture with norms of peaceful conflict resolution has not yet taken root in the new democracies. Democratic norms must be ingrained before the domestic basis of the democratic peace will be secure, and such development of the political culture usually takes a long time. There will be setbacks; some countries will revert to non-democratic forms of rule.

As regards the second condition, peaceful relations have indeed developed among the consolidated democracies of the West. There is reason to hope that the new democracies of Eastern Europe will come to be included in this zone—provided that there are no severe setbacks in their further democratization. The democracies of the South are more problematic in that regard. The foundations between North and South are not strong. During the Cold War the United States was hostile and even aggressive towards some southern democracies, e.g. the Dominican Republic in the early 1960s or Chile in the early 1970s. That reflected American determination to defend its perceived economic and security interests in its competition with the Soviet Union (for further analysis, see Sørensen 1993a: 101–12). It remains to be seen whether the end of the Cold War will also put an end to such divisions and mistrust between old and new democracies.

Turning to the final condition, economic cooperation and interdependence is highly developed among the consolidated democracies of the West. At least some of the new democracies of Eastern Europe are on course to be integrated into these economic networks through membership of the European Union, e.g. Poland, Hungary, and the Czech Republic. Yet the complex negotiations about EU enlargement demonstrate the considerable difficulties involved in close economic cooperation between countries at highly different levels of development. For the democracies of the South, continued one-sided economic dependence on the North rather than interdependence is the order of the day, even after the end of the Cold War. That relation of basic inequality augurs less well for the development of peaceful relations even if both parties have democratic governments.

In short, the emergence of a global pacific union embracing all the new and old democracies is not guaranteed. Indeed, most of the new democracies fail to meet at least two of the three conditions for a democratic peace identified above. And instead of exhibiting further progress, they may backslide towards authoritarian rule. Most republican liberals are therefore less optimistic than was Francis

Fukuyama when he predicted 'the end of history as such: that is, the end point of mankind's ideological evolution and the universalization of Western liberal democracy as the final form of human government' (1989: 4). Most liberals argue that there is a democratic 'zone of peace' among the consolidated liberal democracies, including Western Europe, North America, and Japan. But the expansion of that zone is far from assured (Russett 1993: 138).

Most republican liberals thus emphasize that democratic peace is a dynamic process rather than a fixed condition. A pacific union does not spring into existence between countries as soon as they meet a minimum definition of democracy. Peace is built on all three foundation stones (Box 4.11) only over a long period of time. There can be setbacks. There can even be reversions to non-democratic rule. There is a weakness even in this qualified republican liberal argument, however. Republican liberals need to specify the exact ways in which democracy leads to peace, and they need to sort out in more precise terms when there is a democratic peace between a group of democracies and why. In that context a more thorough evaluation of the current processes of democratization is necessary. There is already a number of contributions that address these issues (Thompson 1996; Sørensen 1992; Adler and Barnett 1996; Schweller 1992; Lake 1992; Russett 1993).

Republican liberalism can be summarized as follows. Democracies do not go to war against each other owing to their domestic culture of peaceful conflict resolution, their common moral values, and their mutually beneficial ties of economic cooperation and interdependence. These are the foundation-stones upon which their peaceful relations are based. For these reasons an entire world of consolidated liberal democracies could be expected to be a peaceful world.

We have already introduced a number of specific points where realists are sceptical of liberalism. Realists are sceptical about this version of liberalism too. Behind their disbelief is a larger debate which sets liberalism against realism in IR. The core question in that debate is: can a liberal world escape the perils of anarchy? Will a more liberal world, with more democracies, with a higher level of interdependence, and with more international institutions mean that anarchy is eclipsed? Will it mean that war is permanently ended? The next two sections take up the most important debates between liberals and neorealists.

. . . .

Neorealist Critiques of Liberalism

Liberalism's main contender is neorealism. We saw in Chapter 2 that the first major debate in IR was between idealist liberalism and pessimist realism. The debate between liberalism and realism continues to this day. We shall see that this debate has created divisions in the liberal camp. There is now a group of 'weak liberals' who have moved closer to the realist camp; and there is a group of 'strong liberals' who continue to support a more distinctively liberal view of world politics.

A main point of contention in previous debates between liberals and realists, around the Second World War, concerned 'human nature'. We have seen that liberals generally take a positive view of human nature whereas realists tend to hold a negative view: they see human beings as capable of evil. That issue was at the core of Hans Morgenthau's realist critique of liberals. The substance of that critique can be expressed as follows: 'You have misunderstood politics because you have misestimated human nature' (Waltz 1959: 40).

These diverging views of human nature continue to separate realists from liberals. But 'human nature' is no longer a major point of debate for two reasons. First, it was increasingly realized among neorealists as well as liberals that 'human nature' is highly complex. It is behind 'good' things as well as 'bad' things: peace and war, philanthropy and robbery, Sunday schools and brothels. Our attention must therefore shift to the social and political context to help us explain when humans (having the potential for being good as well as bad) will behave in either one way or another way (Waltz 1959: 16–41). Second, there was the influence from the behavioral movement in political science. That influence led scholars away from the study of human actions and their 'internal' moral qualities and capabilities towards the analysis of observable facts and measurable data in the 'external' world, i.e. overt evidence of patterns of human behavior. How should scholars conceive of the external world? How should we view history?

We noted earlier that classical realists have a non-progressive view of history. States remain states in spite of historical change. They continue to reside in an unchanging anarchical system. Anarchy leads to self-help: states have to look after themselves; nobody will do it for them. To be secure they arm themselves against potential enemies; one state's security is another state's insecurity. The result can be an arms race and, eventually, war. That was the case 2,000 years ago. According to neorealists it is still the case today, because the basic structure of the state system remains the same. History is 'the same damn things over and over again' (Layne 1994: 10).

For liberals, however, history is at least potentially progressive. We identified the main conditions of liberal progress earlier and summarized them in the four major strands of liberal thought. Neorealists are not impressed. They note that such 'liberal' conditions have existed for a long time without being able to prevent violent conflict between states. For example, economic interdependence is nothing new. As a percentage of world GNP, world exports in 1970 were below the 1880–1910 level. Put differently, the rapid increase in world trade between 1950 and 1975 which liberals view as the great era of interdependence was nothing more than a recovery from abnormally low levels of interdependence caused by two world wars and the Great Depression in the first half of the twentieth century.

Box 4.12 **Trade as percentages of world GNP, various years**

YEAR	WORLD EXPORTS/ WORLD GNP
1830	4.6
1840	5.7
1850	6.8
1860	9.3
1870	9.8
1880	11.4
1890	11.1
1900	10.4
1910	10.4
1913	11.4
1950	8.1
1960	9.2
1970	10.0
1980	16.9

Based on tables in Thompson and Krasner (1989: 199, 201)

Financial flows reveal a similar story. Measured as a percentage of GNP, total foreign investment from Western developed countries were much higher over the entire period from 1814 to 1938 than during the 1960s and 1970s. International banking has been important for more than two centuries (Thompson and Krasner 1989). In sum, economic interdependence is nothing new, and in the past it has done little to prevent wars between states, such as the Second World War.

Neorealists are also critical of the role that liberals attach to international institutions. While states cooperate through institutions, they still do it solely on the basis of their own decision and self-interest. The strong prevail in international relations. Institutions are no more than theater stages where the power play unfolds. But the play has been written by the playwright: the states. Institutions are not important in their own right (Mearsheimer 1995b: 340). Finally, as we indicated, neorealists are critical of republican liberalism. They emphasize that there is always the possibility that a liberal or democratic state will revert to authoritarianism or another form of non-democracy. Furthermore, today's friend might very well turn out to be tomorrow's enemy, whether they are a democracy or not.

There is thus a common thread running through the realist critique of the various strands of liberalism: the persistence and permanence of anarchy and the insecurity that that involves. According to neorealists, anarchy cannot be eclipsed. Anarchy means that even liberal states must contemplate the possibility that their liberal friends will some day perhaps turn against them. 'Lamentably, it is not possible for even liberal democracies to transcend anarchy' (Mearsheimer 1991: 123). No amount of sociological, interdependence, institutional, or republican liberalism can do the trick. And as long as anarchy prevails, there is no escape from self-help and the security dilemma. Liberal optimism is not warranted.

The Retreat to Weak Liberalism

Liberals have reacted to these neorealist objections in basically two different ways. One group is somewhat defensive, accepting several realist claims including the essential point about the persistence of anarchy. We shall call this group 'weak liberals'. Another group, whom we shall call the 'strong liberals', will not budge; they claim that the world is changing in some fundamental ways which are in line with liberal expectations. Note that the labels 'weak' and 'strong' say nothing about the solidity of the arguments made. They are purely descriptive labels, indicating different degrees of disagreement with realism.

The work of Robert Keohane, one of the leading scholars in the debate between liberals and neorealists, illustrates how a liberal adjusted to realist critiques. As indicated, his early work with Joseph Nye (Keohane and Nye 1971) is characteristic of sociological liberalism. In that work they draw an important distinction between a 'state-centric' paradigm and a 'world politics paradigm'; the former focus is on 'interstate interactions' whereas the latter focus is on 'transnational interactions' in which non governmental actors play a significant role (1971: xii, 380). The implication is that world politics is changing dramatically from a state system to a transnational political system. That argument is an example of strong liberalism.

This sociological liberal view was popular in the early 1960s; realists were on the defensive. But sociological liberalism appeared to be a prisoner of history and the circumstances of the time. It turned out that the flutter of transnational relations upon which sociological liberals built their argument could only develop smoothly within a framework created by dominant American power (Little 1996: 78). That was true for a period following the Second World War. Then came a period when American power appeared to wane; the country was tied up in a difficult and unpopular war in Vietnam. On the economic front there was also trouble; President Nixon terminated the dollar's convertibility into gold in 1971. The United States' political and economic distress sent shock waves through the entire international system. That put realism back on the offensive: if sociological liberalism only worked within a realist framework of power, progress had hardly gone very far.

Keohane turned his attention away from transnational relations and back toward states. The result was the theory of complex interdependence described earlier. That analysis was a movement in the direction of realism: the primary importance of states was acknowledged. But it was unclear to what extent realism should be supplemented with liberal insights. Keohane increasingly focused his analysis on international institutions. That brought him one step closer to neorealism. The analytical starting-point is now clearly realist. States are the major actors, the international system is anarchical, and the power of states is highly significant. The strong can prevail over the weak. Still, as we saw above, a liberal core remained, namely the idea that international institutions can facilitate cooperation.

Even though this brand of liberalism is fairly close to a neorealist position, most such realists remained dissatisfied with the revised and very much weakened liberal thesis. They claim that Keohane as well as several other liberal institutional-ists overlook one crucial item, that of relative gains. 'Gains' are benefits that accrue to participants that cooperate. Institutional liberals claim that institutions facilitate cooperation and thus make it less likely that states will cheat on each other. That is because international institutions are transparent. They provide information to all member states and they thus foster an environment in which it is easier for states to make reliable commitments. Neorealists reply that cheating is not the main problem in negotiation between states. The main problem is relative gains. States must worry that other states gain more from cooperation than they do. Neorealists claim that institutional liberals take no account of that problem; they 'ignore the matter of relative gains . . . in doing so, they fail to identify a major source of state inhibitions about international cooperation' (Grieco 1993: 118).

This neorealist critique led Keohane to emphasize a qualification which further moderated his liberal position. That qualification concerned the conditions for cooperation among states. The single most important condition is the existence of common interests between states (Keohane 1989a: 3; 1993: 277). If states have interests in common they will not worry about relative gains. In that situation institutions can help advance cooperation. In the absence of common interests states will be competitive, apprehensive, and even fearful. In those circumstances institutions will not be of much help.

This way of responding to the neorealist critique does make the liberal position less vulnerable to realist attacks, and it does help us to understand why there can be cooperation under anarchy. But it leads liberalism closer and closer to neo-realism: less and less remains of a distinctive and genuine liberal theory. In other words, liberal institutionalism is open to the criticism that it is merely neorealism 'by another name' (Mearsheimer 1995a: 85). If we define weak liberals as those who accept basic neorealist assumptions as a starting-point for analysis, other members of that group include Axelrod (1984), Lipson (1984), and Stein (1990). However, the end of the Cold War gave a strong boost to a more pronounced liberal posture.

Box 4.13 **Absolute and relative gains**

Absolute gains   As long as we do well it doesn't matter if others do even better.
Example: The United States economy grows by 25% over the next decade; China grows by 75%.

Relative gains   We will do our best, but the number one priority is that the others don't get ahead of us.
Example: The United States economy grows by 10% over the next decade; China grows by 10.3%.

The American that chooses the latter scenario over the first is concerned with relative gains.

The Counterattack of Strong Liberalism

The neorealist attack on liberal theory looks strong. Their spare and parsimonious theory builds on two basic assumptions: history is 'the same damn things over and over again'; there is anarchy leading to insecurity and the risk of war. A terse and bold starting-point makes for strong statements. But parsimony can also be a weakness, because so many things are not taken into consideration. Can we really seriously believe that nothing has changed in international relations over the past several hundred years? Neorealism, as one experienced observer noticed, 'manages to leave most of the substance of the field [of IR] outside the straitjacket' (Hoffmann 1990). In order to argue for such a bald thesis, you have to close your eyes to a lot of things.

That is where strong liberals begin their counterattack on neorealism. They maintain that qualitative change has taken place. Today's economic inter-dependence ties countries much closer together; economies are globalized; pro-duction and consumption take place in a worldwide market-place. It would be extremely costly in welfare terms for countries to opt out of that system (Holm and Sørensen 1995; Cerny 1993). Today there is also a group of consolidated liberal democracies for whom reversion to authoritarianism is next to unthinkable, because all major groups in society support democracy. These countries conduct their mutual international relations in new and more cooperative ways. For them there is no going back; historical change is irreversible. 'Strong liberals' include Rosenau (1990), Doyle (1983), Deutsch (1957), Burton (1972), Rosecrance (1986), Zürn (1995), and Russett (1993).

Neorealists do not insist that there has been no change at all; but they do maintain that such change has not led to the disappearance of anarchy. The self-help system of states remains in place. In that fundamental respect the realist analysis continues to apply. From this fact, neorealists draw the conclusion that

> ### Box 4.14 **Globalization in practice**
>
> First, information is now universally available, in real time, simultaneously, in every financial center of the world. Second, technology has tied all the principal countries and world financial and banking centers together into one integrated network. Few countries or parts of the world can any longer remain insulated from financial shocks and changes, wherever they may occur. Third, technology has made possible the establishment of a new, comprehensive system and highly efficient world market to match lenders and borrowers, to pool resources and share risks on an international scale without regard to boundaries.
>
> Blumenthal (1988)

there is a huge difference between domestic and international politics. In domestic affairs there is 'authority, administration and law', while international politics 'is the realm of power, struggle, and of accommodation' (Waltz 1979: 113). Strong liberals, however, dispute that crucial premise: the assertion that anarchy—as understood by realists—remains in place. Strong liberals do not argue that anarchy has been replaced by hierarchy: that a world government has been created or is in the making. Rather, they argue that anarchy is a far more complex international relationship than is recognized by neorealists, and they question the conclusions that neorealists draw from the existence of anarchy.

What does it mean that there is anarchy in the international system? It means that there is no single, overarching government. It does not mean that there is no government at all. It follows that the distinction between domestic and international politics is not as clear as neorealists claim. The fact is that some states lack an effective and legitimate system of government: e.g. Chad, Somalia, Liberia, Afghanistan, Bosnia. The fact also is that some groups of states are acquiring a governmental system, e.g. the EU. Politics is not 'stopping at the water's edge'. Anarchy does not necessarily mean complete absence of legitimate and effective authority in international politics.

Strong liberals take their cue from that reality. International politics need not be a 'raw anarchy' with fear and insecurity all around. There can be significant elements of legitimate and effective international authority. And strong liberals see examples in the international relations of firmly consolidated, liberal democracies, because here we have combined the key elements of sociological liberalism, interdependence liberalism, institutional liberalism, and republican liberalism. One way of characterizing these relations is by Karl Deutsch's term, 'security communities'. The consolidated liberal democracies of Western Europe, North America, and Japan constitute a security community (Singer and Wildawsky 1993). It is extremely unlikely—indeed, it is unthinkable—that there will be violent conflict between any of these countries in the future.

Strong liberals thus underline the need for a more nuanced view of peace and war. Peace is not merely the absence of war, as most realists believe. There are different kinds or degrees of peace. The 'warm peace' between the countries of the security community of liberal democracies is far more secure than the 'cold peace' between, say, the United States and the Soviet Union during the height of the Cold War (Boulding 1979; Adler and Barnett 1996). A more nuanced view of war is also required. War has changed dramatically in the course of history. War has grown more and more destructive, spurred by technological and industrial development, culminating in the two world wars of the twentieth century. In addition, there is now the risk of unlimited destruction through nuclear war. Strong liberals argue that these developments increase the incentives for states to cooperate (Mueller 1990; 1995); neorealists do not deny that nuclear weapons help decrease the risk of war (Waltz 1993). But strong liberals go one step further. They argue that large-scale war has moved 'toward terminal disrepute because of its perceived repulsiveness and futility' (Mueller 1990: 5).

Box 4.15 **The obsolescence of major war**

Dueling and slavery no longer exist as effective institutions and have faded from human experience except as something one reads about in books . . . There are signs that, at least in the developed world . . . [war] has begun to succumb to obsolescence. Like dueling and slavery, war does not appear to be one of life's necessities—it is not an unpleasant fact of existence that is somehow required by human nature or by the grand scheme of things. One can live without it, quite well in fact. War may be a social affliction, but in important respects it is also a social affliction that can be shrugged off.

John Mueller (1990: 13)

Strong liberals, then, argue that in important parts of the world anarchy does not produce the insecurity that realists claim. Peace is fairly secure in many important places. There are two main types of peace in the world today. The first type is among the heavily armed powers, especially the nuclear powers, where total war threatens self-destruction. It rests primarily (but not solely) on the balance created by military power. It is the least secure peace. The second main type of peace is among the consolidated democracies of the OECD. This is a far more secure, 'liberal' peace, predicated upon liberal democratic values, a high level of economic interdependence, and a dense network of institutions facilitating cooperation (Cooper 1996; Russett 1993; Maoz and Russett 1993; Sørensen 1992; 1997).

For these reasons strong liberals remain optimistic about the future. They argue that genuine progress is possible, and that it is taking place in important parts of the world. There is no world government, of course, but in several areas the world has moved far beyond the neorealist condition of raw anarchy, with all its

Box 4.16 **Prospects for war and peace**

REALISTS	STRONG LIBERALS
↓	↓
Raw anarchy	Anarchy need not be raw
↓	↓
Self-help	
↓	Legitimate authority exists
Security dilemma	in international relations
↓	↓
Balance of power	Two types of peace:
↓	1. among heavily armed powers
Risk of war	2. among consolidated democracies

negative consequences for international relations. Liberals thus appear better equipped than most realists when it comes to the study of change as progress. Whereas many realists always see more of the same in international relations, namely anarchy and power politics, most liberals have a notion of modernization and progress built into their theoretical foundation which makes them more receptive to the study of social, economic, institutional, and political change. The end of the Cold War has boosted the liberal position; the world seems to be moving in a more liberal direction. At the same time, liberals are less well prepared for lack of progress or retrogress. For example, we saw how liberal theories of integration did not allow for setbacks in the process of cooperation in Europe. In the Third World a number of very poor countries have experienced lack of development and even state collapse in some instances. Liberal theory has difficulty handling such cases because it is fundamentally based on a conception of irreversible moderniza- tion (Zacher and Matthew 1995: 138). It is the beneficial consequences of that process which is the core theme of liberal thinking. Consequently, when that process does not take place for some reason or when it backfires, liberal analysis falters.

Liberals also are not as precise in their claims as realists are. How much has actually changed? How secure is a democratic peace? What is the exact link between the various liberal elements in international relations—such as democracy or transnational relations—and more peaceful and cooperative relations between governments? Liberals have problems with these questions. That is because liberals try to theorize historical change, which is by its very nature complex, fluid, open-ended, and thus uncertain in the course it will take.

Recent liberal thinking has gone to work on these problems. Andrew Moravcsik has set forth a reformulation of liberal theory that attempts to be 'non-ideological and non-utopian' (Moravcsik 1997: 513). The fundamental actors in international politics are rational individuals and private groups. The policies of states represent what individuals and groups in society (and inside the state apparatus) want. In other words, government policy reflects the preferences of different combinations of groups and individuals in domestic society. In the international system, each state seeks to realize its preferences—to get what it wants—under the constraints imposed by the preferences of other states.

This reformulation of liberal theory avoids prior assumptions about the prevalence of cooperation over conflict or the inavoidability of progress. At the same time, it contains both a 'domestic' component (state preferences) and an international, 'systemic' component (state preferences constrained by other states). The core element in the theory is the set of preferences pursued by states. The preferences may be influenced liberal factors. To the extent that they are, peace and cooperation may follow. To the extent that they are not, conflict may prevail. According to Moravcsik, there are three major variants of liberal theory: ideational, commercial, and republican. Republican liberalism, for example, 'stresses the impact on state behavior of varying forms of domestic representation and the resulting incentives for social groups to engage in rent seeking' (Moravcsik 1997).

Moravcsik's efforts demonstrates the attempt to provide a 'a general restatement of positive liberal IR theory' (p. 515) which is based on strong liberal assumptions. The assertion is that such a liberal theory is better than both realism and neoliberal institutionalism at explaining foreign policy, historical change in the international system, and the peaceful relations between consolidated liberal democracies.

Another recent attempt by strong liberals to update liberal thinking is the theory of 'structural liberalism' by Daniel Deudney and G. John Ikenberry (1999). They seek to characterize the major features of the Western order, that is, the relations between Western liberal democracies. Five elements of that order are singled out:

- security co-binding

- penetrated reciprocal hegemony

- semi-sovereign and partial great powers

- economic openness

- civic identity

Security co-binding refers to the liberal practice of states locking one another into mutually constraining institutions, such as NATO. That organization has joint force planning, coordinated military command structures, and a network for making political and military decisions. Penetrated reciprocal hegemony is the special way in which the United States leads the Western order. The U.S. is an open and diverse political system that is also receptive to pressures from her partners. Transnational and transgovernmental political networks play an increasing role in this.

Semi-sovereign and partial great powers refers to the special status of Germany and Japan. They have imposed constraints on themselves as great powers; an important part of that is they have foregone the acquisition of nuclear weapons. The features of these 'trading states' are an anomaly seen from neorealism, but from a liberal view they are an integrated part of the Western political order. Economic openness is another major aspect of the Western liberal order. In a world of advanced industrial capitalism, the benefits from absolute gain derived from economic openness are so great that liberal states try to cooperate so as to avoid the incentive to pursue relative gains. Finally, civic identity expresses a common Western support for the values of political and civil liberties, market economics, and ethnic toleration.

Deudney and Ikenberry argue that these features of the Western liberal order are so strong and entrenched that they will survive the collapse of the common external threat, the Soviet Union. In short, the liberal order rests on a liberal foundation, not on a particular balance of power or a certain external threat.

....

Liberalism: The Current Research Agenda

With the end of the Cold War some traditional issues on the liberal research agenda have been endowed with a new urgency. More than previously, it is now important to know precisely how democracy leads to peace, and to understand the exact extent to which new democracies need to be consolidated in order to secure a democratic peace. The concept of the 'security community' proposed by Karl Deutsch requires further development. This notion is helpful in emphasizing that peace is more than merely the absence of war. However, it is less precise than it ought to be as an effective research tool (for current research building on Deutsch, see e.g. Adler and Barnett 1996; Kacowicz 1995; Schneider 1995; Deudney 1996; Parish and Peany 2002).

A similar urgency of need for more solid knowledge pertains to international institutions. Newer institutions, such as the OSCE (Organization for Security and Cooperation in Europe) and the WTO (World Trade Organization), have appeared on the world stage. Older institutions, such as NATO, are changing significantly. (Core questions regarding the emergence, change, and effects of institutions were set forth in the section on institutional liberalism.)

Sociological and interdependence liberals have emphasized the importance of the development of transnational relations. It appears that this process is continuing with increasing intensity, at least among some countries (Keohane and Milner 1996; Risse-Kappen 1995). In Western Europe it has helped foster a policy of integration with qualitatively new elements: states are pooling their sovereignty in order to improve their collective capacity for regulation (Keohane

1995; Zürn 1995). (For the prospects and problems involved, see Keohane and Hoffmann 1991; Lodge 1993; Sbragia 1992; Baun 1996.)

The atrocities of September 11, 2001 present a challenge to liberal IR theory. Mass murder terrorism, such as the attack on New York and Washington DC, obviously is a very ominous threat to the physical security of citizens of Western liberal democracies, especially the United States. It clearly is the case that easy movement of people across international boundaries around the world has a dark side. Some individuals may exploit that freedom to plot and carry out acts of mass murder against citizens of the country in which they are residing. That new security threat demands greater police and intelligence surveillance within countries. That could extend to infringing on some of the civil liberties associated with liberal democracy—as in the case of the US Patriot Act passed in the aftermath of the attack. It also demands greater security at international borders and other entry points of countries. That could extend to closer inspection of the international transport of goods. It could interfere with the open borders advocated by liberals. At the same time, however, the event could also strengthen international cooperation between countries that perceive a terrorist threat to the security of their citizens. That has happened in connection with the terrorist attack on New York and Washington DC. The main point is: such events may oblige theorists to rethink their theories, and that includes liberals and liberalism

In sum, all students of IR need to take note of the processes of change which are taking place, and to evaluate the possible consequences for international relations. That is an important lesson that liberal IR theory teaches us.

. . . .

KEY POINTS

- The theoretical point of departure for liberalism is the individual. Individuals plus various collectivities of individuals are the focus of analysis: first and foremost states, but also corporations, organizations, and associations of all kinds. Liberals maintain that not only conflict but also cooperation can shape international affairs.

- Liberals are basically optimistic: when humans employ their reason they can arrive at mutually beneficial cooperation. They can put an end to war. Liberal optimism is closely connected with the rise of the modern state. Modernization means progress in most areas of human life, including international relations.

- Liberal arguments for more cooperative international relations are divided into four different strands: sociological liberalism, interdependence liberalism, institutional liberalism, and republican liberalism.

- Sociological liberalism: IR not only studies relations between governments; it also studies relations between private individuals, groups, and societies. Relations between people are more cooperative than relations between governments. A world with a large number of transnational networks will be more peaceful.

- Interdependence liberalism: Modernization increases the level of interdependence between states. Transnational actors are increasingly important, military force is a less useful instrument, and welfare, not security, is the dominant goal of states. That 'complex interdependence' signifies a world of more cooperative international relations.

- Institutional liberalism: International institutions promote cooperation between states. Institutions alleviate problems concerning lack of trust between states and they reduce states' fear of each other.

- Republican liberalism: Democracies do not go to war against each other. That is due to their domestic culture of peaceful conflict resolution, to their common moral values, and to their mutually beneficial ties of economic cooperation and interdependence.

- Neorealists are critical of the liberal view. They argue that anarchy cannot be eclipsed and therefore that liberal optimism is not warranted. As long as anarchy prevails, there is no escape from self-help and the security dilemma.

- Liberals react differently to these neorealist objections. One group of 'weak liberals' accepts several neorealist claims. Another group, 'strong liberals', maintain that the world is changing in fundamental ways that are in line with liberal expectations. Anarchy does not have the exclusively negative consequences that neorealists claim: there can be positive anarchy that involves secure peace among consolidated liberal democracies.

. . . .

QUESTIONS

- Liberals are optimistic about human progress, cooperation, and peace. What are the reasons given for that optimism? Are they good reasons?

- Has international history been as progressive as liberals claim? Use examples.

- Identify the arguments given by the four strands of liberalism discussed in this chapter. Is any strand of liberalism more fundamentally important, or are all strands equally important?

- What arguments can you make, for and against, the assertion that democracy has made striking progress in the world during the past decade?

- Realists argue that anarchy cannot be transcended. Strong liberals say it can. Who is right and for which reasons?

- Is September 11, 2001, a setback for liberal ideas?

- Think of one or two research projects based on liberal theory.

For additional material and resources see the companion web site at:
www.oup.co.uk/best.textbooks/politics/jacksonsorensen2e/

GUIDE TO FURTHER READING

Deudney, D. and **Ikenberry, G. J.** (1999). 'The Nature and Sources of Liberal International Order', *Review of International Studies*, 25/2:179–96.

Deutsch, K. W. *et al.* (1957). *Political Community and the North Atlantic Area*. Princeton: Princeton University Press.

Doyle, M. W. (1986). 'Liberalism and World Politics', *American Political Science Review*, 80/4: 1151–69.

Keohane, R. O. (1989a). *International Institutions and State Power: Essays in International Relations Theory*. Boulder: Westview Press.

—— and **Nye, J. S.** (1977). *Power and Interdependence: World Politics in Transition*. Boston: Little, Brown, 3rd edn. (2001). New York: Longman.

Moravcsik, A. (1997). 'Taking Preferences Seriously: A Liberal Theory of International Politics', *International Organization*, 51/4.513–53.

Mueller, J. (1990). *Retreat from Doomsday: The Obsolescence of Major War*. New York: Basic.

Nye, J. S., Jr. (1988). 'Neorealism and Neoliberalism', *World Politics*, 40/2: 235–51.

Rosecrance, R. (1995). 'The Obsolescence of Territory', *New Perspectives Quarterly*, 12/1: 44–50.

—— (1999). *The Rise of the Virtual State*. New York: Basic.

Rosenau, J. N. (1997). *Along the Domestic–Foreign Frontier: Exploring Governance in a Turbulent World*. Cambridge: Cambridge University Press.

Zacher, M. and **Matthew, R. A.** (1995). 'Liberal International Theory: Common Threads, Divergent Strands', in C.W. Kegley, Jr., *Controversies in International Relations: Realism and the Neoliberal Challenge*, New York: St. Martin's Press, 107–50.

WEB LINKS

http://www.constitution.org/kant/perpeace.htm
Full text of Immanuel Kant's 'Perpetual Peace'. Hosted by Constitution Society.

http://www.revise.it/reviseit/EssayLab/Undergraduate/Politics/e313.htm
Short criticism of the theory of complex interdependence. Hosted by Revise.it.

http://europa.eu.int/
The official website of the European Union.

http://www.hawaii.edu/powerkills/welcome.html
Several links to papers and other documents on the theory of democratic peace. Hosted by the University of Hawaii.

5

International Society

SUMMARY

The International Society tradition is a historical and institutional approach to world politics that focuses on human beings and their political values. Central to this approach is the study of ideas and ideologies that shape world politics. The basic assumptions are: (1) a claim that international relations are a branch of human relations at the heart of which are basic values such as independence, security, order, and justice; (2) a human-focused approach: the IR scholar is called upon to interpret the thoughts and actions of the people involved in international relations; (3) acceptance of the premise of international anarchy. But International Society scholars argue that world politics is an anarchical society with distinctive rules, norms, and institutions that statespeople employ in conducting foreign policy. The chapter discusses contributions of the International Society tradition as well as critiques of the tradition. The concluding section evaluates the current research agenda of the tradition and its prospects.

Basic International Society Approach

According to a leading exponent of this approach (Wight 1991: 1) international politics 'is a realm of human experience' with its own distinctive characteristics, problems, and language. To study IR means 'entering this tradition' and 'joining in the conversation' with the aim of understanding it. The main point of this approach is that international relations ought to be understood as a 'society' of sovereign states.

Understanding the society of states is not a question of applying social-science models. Rather, it is a question of becoming familiar with the history of international relations as it is experienced by the people involved, the most important of whom are statespeople: presidents, prime ministers, foreign ministers, defense ministers, diplomats, military commanders, and other people who act on behalf of states in foreign affairs. IR scholars should try to understand what inclines the practitioners of international relations to act the way they do by seeking to gain insight into the ideas and thought behind their foreign policies. In short, IR scholarship involves getting as close as possible to the social world of international relations by trying to grasp the experience of practitioners past as well as present.

Hedley Bull (1969: 20) summarized this 'traditional' International Society approach as follows: it derives from 'philosophy, history and law' and it 'is characterized above all by explicit reliance upon the exercise of judgement'. By 'the exercise of judgement' Bull meant that IR scholars should fully understand that foreign policy sometimes presents difficult moral choices to the statespeople involved—i.e. choices about conflicting political values and goals. IR scholars should be able to evaluate those choices in terms of the situations in which they are made and the values at stake. A difficult foreign-policy choice in this regard would be the decision to go to war or the decision to engage in humanitarian intervention. Two recent examples of such decisions are discussed later in this chapter: the 1990 UN Security Council decision to use armed force to expel the Iraqi army from occupied Kuwait and the 1995 UN and NATO decisions to intervene in former Yugoslavia.

One of the important IR debates identified in Chapter 2 was that between traditionalists and behavioralists (Bull 1969). International Society scholars are squarely on the traditionalist side of that debate. They do not see IR theory as a value-neutral science in which models and hypotheses are applied and tested. They reject 'positivist' social science methodologies. They disagree fundamentally with Kenneth Waltz's claim that there is a 'structure' of international politics which operates with 'law-like regularity', and which thus makes possible a 'scientific' theory of international politics from which 'predictions' can be derived (Waltz 1979). States are not things: they do not exist or interact on their own. States do not have an existence separate from the human beings—the citizens and governments—who compose them and who act on their behalf. International Society theorists view international relations as a special branch of human relations that occur in historical time and involve rules, norms, and values. IR is a study of that historical human world.

Box 5.1 **Traditionalism and behavioralism**

TRADITIONAL CLASSICAL APPROACH	BEHAVIORALIST APPROACH
Human-focused	Structure-focused
Interpretive	Explanatory
Normative	Positive
Historical-concrete	Analytical-abstract

The International Society tradition is one of the classical IR approaches. But it seeks to avoid the stark choice between (1) state egotism and conflict and (2) human goodwill and cooperation presented by the debate between realism and liberalism. On the one hand, International Society scholars reject classical realists' singularly pessimistic view of states as self-sufficient and self-regarding political organizations which relate to each other and deal with each other only on an instrumental basis of narrow self interest: international relations conceived as a state 'system' that is prone to recurrent discord, conflict, and—sooner or later—war. On the other hand, they reject classical liberalism's singularly optimistic view of international relations as a developing world community that is conducive to unlimited human progress and perpetual peace.

The International Society tradition is a middle way in classical IR scholarship: it carves out a place between classical realism and classical liberalism and builds that place into a separate and distinctive IR approach. It regards international relations as a 'society' of states in which the principal actors are statespeople who are specialized in the practice of statecraft. It views statecraft as a very important human activity that encompasses foreign policy, military policy, trade policy, political recognition, diplomatic communication, intelligence-gathering and spying, forming and joining military alliances, threatening or engaging in the use of armed force, negotiating and signing peace treaties, entering into commercial agreements, joining and participating in international organizations, and engaging in countless international contacts, interactions, transactions, and exchanges. That means that the foreign-policy inclinations of states and statespeople must be a central focus of analysis: their interests, concerns, intentions, ambitions, calculations and miscalculations, desires, beliefs, hopes, fears, doubts, uncertainties, and so forth.

The discussion so far can be summarized: international relations consist of the foreign-oriented policies, decisions, and activities of statespeople who act on behalf of territory-based political systems that are independent of each other and are subject to no higher authorities than themselves, i.e. sovereign states. 'International organizations', 'non-governmental organizations', 'multinational corporations', and so forth are important human organizations that are also involved in international relations. But they are subordinate to sovereign states. They cannot act completely independently of those states. That is why International Society theorists consider sovereign states to be the foundation of world politics. That is the basic image of the 'society of states' that International Society scholars operate with.

For International Society theorists IR typically is a study of war and peace; of declaring war, making peace, and rejecting or accepting peace offers; of giving assurances, forming alliances, and entering into secret pacts; of saber-rattling and appeasing; of negotiating and breaking off negotiations; of establishing and severing diplomatic communications; of attacking and defending; of intervening, liberating, isolating, terrorizing, 'ethnic cleansing', hostage taking, and spying; of broadcasting propaganda and jamming foreign broadcasts; of trading and investing, claiming and offering humanitarian assistance, receiving and repatriating refugees; and of many other distinctive international activities in which human engage. All these international activities have important normative aspects which are of central concern to International Society scholars.

At the heart of the International Society approach are states conceived as human organizations. As indicated, the key concept is that of a 'society of states' (Wight 1977). International politics is understood to be that special branch of politics that is lacking in hierarchical authority—i.e. there is no world 'government' that is above sovereign states. To that extent they agree with classical realists. However, there are still common interests, rules, institutions, and organizations which are created and shared by states and which help to shape the relations of states. That international social condition is summed up by Hedley Bull's (1995) phrase 'the anarchical society': there is a worldwide social order of independent states. Bull made an important distinction between an 'international system' and an 'international society' (see Box 5.2).

The 'system of states' is a realist concept; the 'society of states' is a liberal concept. The more international relations constitute a society and the less international relations merely compose a system is an indication of the extent to which world politics forms a distinctive human civilization with its own norms and values. For example, during the Cold War international society between the United States and the Soviet Union was reduced to being not much more than a system in which the foreign policy of each side was based on its calculation about the intentions and capabilities of the other side. After the Cold War, however, Russia became associated with the Western-centered world of international

---

Box 5.2 **International system, international society**

A system of states (or international system) is formed when two or more states have sufficient contact between them, and have sufficient impact on one another's decisions . . . to make the behaviour of each a necessary element in the calculations of the other. A society of states (or international society) exists when a group of states, conscious of certain common interests and common values, form a society in the sense that they conceive themselves to be bound by a common set of rules in their relations with one another and share in the working of common institutions.

Bull (1995: 9–13)

---

organizations such as the G-8, OECD, IMF, EBRD, OSCE, and NATO. In order to do that Russia had to take on board the common interests and observe the common values and obligations of those international organizations—in short, Russia had to become a reliable citizen of Western-centred international society.

Another important set of distinctions are the concepts of realism, rationalism, and revolutionism (Wight 1991). These are three different ways of looking at the relations of states. The first concept views states as power agencies that pursue their own interests. It thus conceives of international relations solely as instrumental relations. That is the realist view of Machiavelli. The second concept views states as legal organizations that operate in accordance with international law and diplomatic practice. It thus conceives of international relations as rule-governed activities based on the mutually recognized authority of sovereign states. That is the rationalist view of Grotius. The third concept downplays the importance of states and places the emphasis on human beings. Humans are seen to compose a primordial 'world community' or 'community of humankind' that is more fundamental than the society of states. That is the revolutionist view of Kant.

According to Martin Wight (1991), however, IR cannot be adequately understood through any one of these conceptualizations alone. IR can only be adequately understood through all of them together. If properly carried out, the International Society approach should be an exploration of the conversation or dialogue between these three different theoretical perspectives. Realists, rationalists, and revolutionists each represent a distinctive normative position, or 'voice', in a continuing dialogue about the conduct of foreign policy and other international human activities. That will be set out in the next section.

All three voices broadcast the fact that international relations is basically a human activity concerned with fundamental values. Two of the most fundamental values are given special attention by Hedley Bull (1995): international order and international justice. By 'international order' Bull means 'a pattern or disposition of international activity that sustains' the basic goals of the society of states. By 'international justice' he means the moral rules which 'confer rights and duties upon states and nations' such as the right of self-determination, the right of non-intervention, and the right of all sovereign states to be treated on a basis of equality (Bull 1995: 78). These two basic values of the international society tradition will be discussed in a later section.

Box 5.3 **Basic International Society approach**

Methodology	Humanism
	Interpretation
	Historical, jurisprudential, philosophical
Core concepts	Human relations
	States
	Anarchical Society
	State system
	Society of states
Basic values	Order
	Justice
	State sovereignty
	Human rights

Two international values that are closely related to order and justice are given special emphasis by John Vincent (1986): state sovereignty and human rights. On the one hand, states are supposed to respect each other's independence; that is the value of state sovereignty and non-intervention. On the other hand, international relations involve not only states but also human beings, who possess human rights regardless of the state of which they happen to be a citizen. There can be and sometimes there is a conflict between the right of non-intervention and human rights. When that happens, which of these values should have priority? If human rights are being massively violated from within a state, does the government retain its right of non-intervention? In such circumstances, is there a right of humanitarian intervention to rescue people? How should the two rights be balanced? That is one of the basic value conflicts of international relations at the present time.

The International Society approach presents two main answers to these questions. The first answer is *pluralist*, stressing the importance of state sovereignty. According to this view, rights and duties in the international society are conferred upon sovereign states; individuals have only the rights given to them by their own states. Therefore, the principles of respect for sovereignty and non-intervention always come first. States have no right to intervene in other states for humanitarian reasons. The second answer given by the International Society approach to the above questions is *solidarist*, stressing the importance

---

Box 5.4 **United Nations Charter, Article 2**

1. The Organization is based on the principle of the sovereign equality of all its Members . . . 4. All Members shall refrain in their international relations from the threat or use of force against the territorial integrity of political independence of any state . . . 7. Nothing contained in the present Charter shall authorize the United Nations to intervene in matters which are essentially within the domestic jurisdiction of any state . . .

---

of individuals as the ultimate members of international society. On this view, there is both a right and a duty for states to conduct intervention in order to mitigate extreme cases of human suffering.

We return to this discussion later. Here we may stress that, according to the International Society approach, problems of intervention and human rights can be studied normatively, i.e. philosophically, historically, and legally. But they cannot be studied scientifically because they are essentially human issues and are thus value-laden. There can be no value-neutral scientific answer to them. There can be no abstract or general answer either. Every answer will be affected by the situation and will thus be essentially historical in character.

Box 5.5 **UN Secretary-General Javier Perez de Cuellar on human rights (1991)**

It is now increasingly felt that the principle of non-interference with the essential domestic jurisdiction of States cannot be regarded as a protective barrier behind which human rights can be massively or systematically violated with impunity.

UN Press Release SG/SM/4560, 24 Apr. 1991

The International Society approach views world politics as a totally human world. That means that it is attuned to the normative aspects and value dilemmas of international relations. That also means that the approach is basically situational or historical. World politics is open to all the potential that human beings have for improving their lives, including the progress and peace that classical liberals emphasize. But world politics is also exposed to all the shortcomings and limitations that human beings exhibit, with all the possibilities of risk, uncertainty, danger, conflict, etc. that that implies; including the insecurity and disorder emphasized by classical realists. The International Society approach refuses to choose between liberal optimism and realist pessimism; that may be its main strength.

The Three Traditions: Theory

Martin Wight (1991) taught that the leading ideas of the most outstanding classical theorists of IR—theorists such as Machiavelli, Grotius, and Kant—fall into three basic categories: realist, rationalist, and revolutionist. Realists are those who emphasize and concentrate on the aspect of 'international anarchy'; rationalists are those who emphasize and concentrate on the aspect of 'international dialogue and intercourse'; and revolutionists are those who emphasize and concentrate on the aspect of 'moral unity' of international society (Wight 1991: 7–8). Wight considered these to be the foundational ideas of international relations. As indicated, the three Rs are not isolated from each other but are in dialogue, and all three voices must be heard by IR scholarship. Wight sees IR as a never-ending dialogue between realist, revolutionist, and rationalist ideas. All three Rs are necessary for gaining a rounded and balanced understanding of IR. However, there is a tendency for International Society theorists to listen most carefully to the moderate voice of Grotian rationalism.

Box 5.6 Wight's three IR traditions

REALISM	RATIONALISM	REVOLUTIONISM
Anarchy	Society	Humanity
Power politics	Evolutionary change	Revolutionary change
Conflict and warfare	Peaceful coexistence	Anti-state Utopianism
Pessimism	Hope without illusions	

The key to the International Society approach is the role of these leading ideas in world politics. While history is emphasized, it is the history of ideas that is at the heart of the tradition. None of these ideas is 'true' and none is 'false'. They simply represent different basic normative outlooks on world politics that compete with each other. Each is incomplete in that it only captures one aspect or dimension of international relations. Each by itself is an inadequate theory of IR. But together they play an indispensable role in IR theory. Realism is the 'controlling' or disciplining factor, revolutionism is the 'vitalizing' or energizing factor, and rationalism is the 'civilizing' or moderating factor in world politics.

Realism is the doctrine that rivalry and conflict between states is 'inherent' in their relations. Realists emphasize 'the element of anarchy, of power politics, and of warfare' (Wight 1991: 15–24). Realism concentrates on the actual—what is—rather than the ideal—what ought to be. It thus involves the avoidance of wishful thinking and 'the frank acceptance of the disagreeable side of life'. Realists therefore tend to be pessimistic about human nature: humankind is divided into 'crooks and fools', and realists survive and succeed by outsmarting the crooks and taking advantage of those who are stupid or naïve. That implies that world politics cannot progress but always remains basically the same from one time or place to another. Realism taken to the extreme is a denial that an international society exists; what exists is a Hobbesian state of nature. The only political society and, indeed, moral community is the state. There are no international obligations beyond or between states.

Rationalists are those theorists who believe that humans are reasonable, can recognize the right thing to do, and can learn from their mistakes and from others (Wight 1991: 14–24). Rationalists believe that people can reasonably manage to live together even when they share no common government, as in the anarchical condition of international relations. Rationalism taken to the extreme—if it is possible to push to the limit that which is the soul of moderation—is a perfect world of mutual respect, concord, and the rule of law between states. In this way rationalism defines a 'middle road' of international politics, separating the pessimistic realists on one side from the optimistic revolutionists on the other side.

Revolutionists are those theorists who identify themselves with humanity and believe in 'the moral unity' of human society beyond the state (Wight 1991: 8–12). They are 'cosmopolitan' rather than state-centric thinkers, solidarists rather than pluralists, and their international theory has a progressive and even a missionary character in that it aims at changing the world for the better. Revolutionary social change is the goal. That involves bringing into existence an ideal world of some kind, whether that ideal world is based on a revolutionary religion, such as Christianity, or a revolutionary ideology, such as republican liberalism or Marxism-Leninism. For revolutionists history is not merely a sequence of events and happenings. Rather, history has a purpose; human beings have a destiny. Revolutionists are optimistic about human nature: they believe in human perfectibility. The ultimate purpose of international history is to enable humans to achieve fulfillment and freedom. For Kant, revolution involved instituting a system of constitutional states—'Republics'—that could jointly build perpetual peace. For Marx, revolution involved destroying the capitalist state, overthrowing the class system upon which it was based, and instituting a classless society. When that was achieved, humanity would be not only liberated but also reunited, and there would be no place either for states or for international relations. Revolutionism taken to the extreme is a claim that the only real society on earth is a world society consisting of every human being, that is, humankind.

The Three Traditions: Practice

When Wight (1991) elaborated on realism or rationalism or revolutionism, he illustrated and illuminated his argument with historical and contemporary examples that probed the thought of statespeople or leading commentators. During the depths of the Cold War in 1956, for example, the leader of the Soviet Union, Nikita Khrushchev, was quoted as saying: 'a little country doesn't count any more in the modern world. In fact, the only two countries that matter are Russia and the United States. And Russia is superior. The other countries have no real say' (Wight 1991: 33). This comment is an expression of the idea of realism in world politics.

　Wight (1991: 47) distinguishes moderate realism from both realism proper and extreme realism (see Box 5.7). Extreme realists deny the existence of an international society: they see international relations as a morally neutral and thus instrumental condition between sovereign states; society is possible within states but not between states. No sovereign state has the authority to command any other sovereign state. No sovereign state has the obligation to obey any other sovereign state. Moderate realists are closer to rationalists in recognizing international law. But they see international law as based on the interests and responsibilities of the great powers.

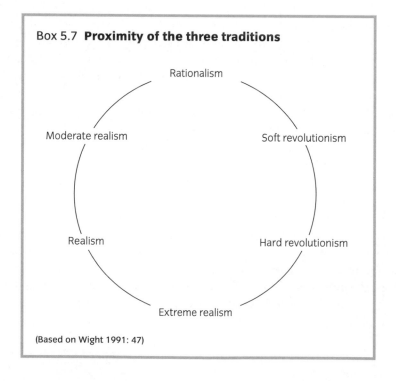

Box 5.7　**Proximity of the three traditions**

Rationalism

Moderate realism　　Soft revolutionism

Realism　　Hard revolutionism

Extreme realism

(Based on Wight 1991: 47)

Wight draws no important distinctions within rationalism. He does, however, draw a distinction between rationalism and moderate realism. Wight quotes George Kennan, an influential American commentator on US foreign policy during the Cold War: 'I do not wish ever to see the conduct of this nation in . . . its foreign relations animated by anything else than decency, generosity, moderation and consideration for others' (Wight 1991: 120–1). Kennan recognized the guiding importance of the national interest in the conduct of foreign policy. But he also recognized the legitimacy of the national interest of other countries and not merely of his own country, including rivals and even enemies. Kennan is usually seen as a moderate realist, but these remarks come very close to expressing ideas characteristic of rationalism. Wight (p. 267) claims: 'Kennan is really a rationalist because he maintains that the national interest should be guided by justice.'

Box 5.8 The authority of the Security Council under the UN Charter (1945)

The Security Council shall determine the existence of any threat to the peace, breach of the peace, or act of aggression and shall make recommendations, or decide what measures shall be taken [Article 39] . . . it may take action by air, sea or land forces as may be necessary to maintain or restore international peace and security. [Article 42]

Realist and rationalist ideas are also embedded in international organization. Wight regards the UN Charter as an instance of moderate realism by giving commanding authority on questions of peace and security to five great powers. He points to the UN Security Council: the Council is given the exclusive constitutional responsibility for maintaining international peace and security, and in that way it acts as 'the Hobbesian sovereign of the United Nations'. States can join the United Nations or remain outside, but either way they have no right to refuse the commands of the Security Council, which is controlled by five great powers that possess a permanent veto: the United States, Russia, China, Britain, and France. On the other hand, Wight regards the Covenant of the League of Nations as an instance of rationalism by binding 'the organs of the League to observe the rules of law and existing treaties' much more definitely and explicitly than does the UN. In short, according to Wight, the League Covenant was based on the *consent* of member states, whereas the UN Charter is based on the *interests* of the great powers (Wight 1991: 34).

Revolutionism, as its name implies, is a doctrine of overthrowing and eradicating existing regimes, if necessary by violence. There is no particular ideology associated with the doctrine: revolutionists could be left-wing or right-wing. Wight quotes a leading Russian Communist during the Russian civil war in 1920 and an interview with the leader (Franco) of the Spanish Fascists during the

> ### Box 5.9 **The Covenant of the League of Nations (1920)**
>
> The High Contracting Parties, in order to promote international co-operation and to achieve international peace and security, by the acceptance of obligations not to resort to war, by the prescription of open, just and honorable relations between nations, by the firm establishment of the understandings of international law as the actual rule of conduct among Governments and by the maintenance of justice and a scrupulous respect for all treaty obligations in the dealings of organized peoples with one another, agree to this Covenant of the League of Nations.

Spanish civil war in 1936: both disclose the same basic attitude to revolutionary violence (see Box 5.10). Wight (1991: 228) notes that each of these revolutionary leaders 'expresses very simply the revolutionist principle of holy war: divide mankind into good and bad on a criterion provided by your doctrine, and then kill all the bad'. That is the 'hard' version of militant and violent revolutionism. Hard revolutionists seek the violent destruction of the system or society of sovereign states and its replacement by a world government or global order of some kind which is based on an exclusive ideology. Among hard revolutionists he names Lenin. They are close to the tough-minded position of extreme realists—except that hard revolutionists want to destroy the state system, whereas extreme realists want to preserve it.

> ### Box 5.10 **Revolutionist ideology: left and right**
>
> Comrades! Brothers! The time has come when you can start on the organization of a true and holy people's war against the robbers and oppressors . . . The Communist International turns today to the peoples of the East and says to them: 'Brothers we summon you to a holy war, in the first place against English imperialism.'
>
> **Soviet Communist Grigory Zinoviev, 1920**
>
> How long . . . is the massacre to go on? There can be no compromise, no truce. I shall go on preparing my advance to Madrid. I shall advance. I shall take the capital. I shall save Spain from Marxism, at whatever cost. That means you will have to shoot half Spain. I repeat, at whatever cost.
>
> **Spanish Fascist Francisco Franco, 1936 Quoted in Wight (1991: 223, 226)**

There is also a 'soft' version of revolutionism that proclaims 'a world society of individuals which overrides nations or states . . . rejects the idea of a society of states and says that the only true international society is one of individuals'

(Wight 1991: 45). Christian pacifists and secular humanitarians are examples of soft revolutionists. Soft revolutionists also want to abolish states and the state system but they are committed to achieve that peacefully by a revolution of ideas rather than by violence. Among the soft revolutionists he names the German philosopher Immanuel Kant, American President Woodrow Wilson, and India's first Prime Minister, Jawaharlal Nehru. One could add the names of the Indian pacifist Mohandas K. Gandhi and his disciple, the American civil rights leader Martin Luther King. Soft revolutionists are close to the tender-minded position of the rationalist.

This cosmopolitan world society idea is not as far-fetched as it may seem. For example, there is a historical tendency in American foreign policy to be suspicious of secret diplomacy and to be in favor of open relations between the citizens of different countries. President Woodrow Wilson made a famous speech in 1918 containing Fourteen Points for ending the First World War and establishing a world safe for democracy. That outlook, discussed in Chapters 2 and 4, is usually referred to as the 'idealist' or 'liberal' tendency in American foreign policy and is undoubtedly rooted in the democratic traditions of the United States.

Box 5.11 President Wilson's 1917 war message

There is one choice we cannot make . . . we will not choose the path of submission and suffer the most sacred rights of our nation and our people to be ignored or violated . . . We have no quarrel with the German people. We have no feeling towards them but one of sympathy and friendship. It was not upon their impulse that their government acted in entering this war. It was not with their previous knowledge or approval. It was a war determined upon as wars used to be . . . in the old, unhappy days when peoples were nowhere consulted by their rulers and wars were provoked and waged in the interest of dynasties or of little groups of ambitious men who were accustomed to use their fellow men as pawns and tools . . .

Address to Congress Asking for Declaration of War, 2 Apr. 1917. Quoted in Vasquez (1996: 35–40)

Henry Kissinger explored in great historical detail the diplomatic dialectic of American foreign policy between an outward impulse towards idealism and the creation of a new world order based on human freedom, and a countervailing inward pull of national self-indulgence and isolationism. According to Kissinger, American statesmen and citizens have to balance 'hope and possibility': 'the fulfillment of America's ideals will have to be sought in the patient accumulation of partial successes' (Kissinger 1994: 836). The world cannot be made permanently safe for democracy: that is a naïve hope that cannot be fulfilled. But in recognizing that impossibility it is not necessary or desirable to retreat into Fortress America, because that would leave the management of international order to others by default, and that would not be in the national interest of the

United States. According to Kissinger, American foreign policy has to be guided by a realistic assessment of the limited choices available, even for a superpower like the United States, in a far-flung and diverse world of numerous independent states expressing different foreign policies, political ideologies, systems of government, cultures, civilizations, etc. Here Kissinger discloses his own moderately realist and almost rationalist foreign-policy philosophy: his doctrine of 'hope and possibility' is virtually identical to the rationalist position of 'hope without illusions'.

There are four key emphases in International Society theory. The first is the emphasis on leading operative ideas that are seen to shape the thought, policies, and activities of the people involved in international relations: statespeople especially. The second is the emphasis on the dialogue between the leading ideas, values, and beliefs which come into play in the conduct of foreign policy. A proper academic understanding cannot be obtained by adopting only a realist or only a revolutionist or only a rationalist approach. To adopt only one of these approaches is to give a one-dimensional and thus partial and incomplete analysis which distorts our understanding of international relations. The third is the emphasis on the historical dimension of international relations. To ignore history is to fail to appreciate the great length of time these traditions have been in existence and the significance of that. The fourth is the emphasis on the most fundamental and the least ephemeral aspect of international relations: the normative aspect as seen in a historical light. To ignore the normative dimension is to fail to understand the essentially human character of international relations and the extremely difficult moral problems involved.

. . . .

Order and Justice

As indicated, the International Society approach emphasizes philosophy and history as well as law. Martin Wight was essentially a diplomatic historian who reflected on the dynamic interplay of foundational ideas in international relations. Hedley Bull, on the other hand, was primarily a philosopher of world politics who tried to work out a systematic theory of international society (Jackson 1995: 110–28). Both Wight and Bull saw IR theory as a branch of political theory. They believed that it was only possible to theorize IR within the context of concrete historical events and episodes. They were deeply skeptical of abstract social science theorizing based on game theory or other scientific models that are divorced from history and human experience.

The main point of the anarchical society, according to Bull (1995: 16–19), is promotion and preservation of international *order*, which is defined as 'a pattern or disposition of international activity that sustains those goals of the society of states that are elementary, primary or universal'. He identifies four such goals: preservation of international society, upholding the independence of member states, maintaining peace, and helping to secure the normative foundations of all social life, which includes 'the limitation of violence' (expressed in the laws of war), 'the keeping of promises' (expressed in the principle of reciprocity), and 'the stability of possession' (expressed in the principle of mutual recognition of state sovereignty). According to Bull, these are the most fundamental goals of the anarchical society. All these goals are moral in character: they are not merely instrumental or wholly self-interested; they are for others as well as ourselves. Bull, like most other International Society theorists, presents a normative analysis of world politics.

Bull distinguishes three kinds of order in world politics (Bull 1995: 3–21). The first kind is 'order in social life', which is an essential element of human relations regardless of the form taken; the second is 'international order', which is order between states in a system or society of states; and the last is 'world order', which is order among humankind as a whole. He goes on to say that 'world order is more fundamental and primordial than international order because the ultimate units of the great society of all mankind are not states . . . but individual human beings'. States and the society of states are merely temporary—i.e. historical—arrangements of human relations, but 'individual human beings . . . are permanent and indestructible in a sense in which groupings of them . . . are not'. That is a cosmopolitan or solidarist inclination of Bull's IR theory. But most of Bull's analysis is concerned with states and the society of states: it is pluralist rather than solidarist.

The responsibility for sustaining international order—order between states—belongs to the great powers, and is achieved by 'managing their relations with one another'. Bull adds the important qualifier that this is not an empirical statement about what great powers actually do. Rather, it is a normative statement of their special role and responsibility in world politics which derives from the reality of the profound inequality of power between states. He notes that 'great powers, like small powers, frequently behave in such a way as to promote disorder rather than order' (Bull 1995: 199–201). That of course happened on two major occasions in the twentieth century which shook the foundations of world politics: the First World War (1914–18) and the Second World War (1939–45). The latter in particular was a profound failure of responsibility on the part of the great powers whose fundamental duty is to maintain the balance of power and prevent any great power from getting out of hand and creating a disaster—as Germany and Japan did in the 1930s and 1940s. Bull argued that during the 1960s and early 1970s the United States and the Soviet Union made some attempt to act 'as responsible managers of the affairs of international society as a whole'. The Cold War at times produced international order. But he also said that at certain other times during the Cold War, specifically in the late 1970s and early 1980s, the two superpowers behaved more like 'the great irresponsibles' (Bull 1984: 437). That clearly is a more ambivalent view of the Cold War than that held by contemporary neorealists (see Chapter 3).

Bull's argument on the balance of power comes very close to that of a moderate realist in Wight's terms. He employed history to draw some important distinctions, for example between a 'simple balance of power' and a 'complex balance of power'. The former corresponds roughly to the realist concept of bipolarity; the latter corresponds roughly to the realist concept of multipolarity. In the same vein, he went on to use historical illustrations to distinguish between a general balance of power and a local balance of power, and between an objective balance of power and a subjective balance of power. The general balance of power between the United States and the Soviet Union during the Cold War could be distinguished from the local balance of power between Israel and the Arab states in the Middle East, or between India and Pakistan in South Asia.

Box 5.12 Walter Lippmann (a famous American journalist) on Cold War containment of the Soviet Union (1947)

For more than a hundred years all Russian governments have sought to expand over Eastern Europe. But only since the Red Army reached the Elbe River [in Germany, 1945] have the rulers of Russia been able to realize the ambitions of the Russian Empire and the ideological purposes of communism . . . American power must be available, not to 'contain' the Russians at scattered points, but to hold the whole Russian military machine in check, and to exert a mounting pressure in support of a diplomatic policy which has as its concrete objective a settlement that means withdrawal [from Germany and other occupied countries of Eastern Europe].

Quoted in Kissinger (1994: 465)

The objective balance of power is a factual reality, but the subjective balance is a matter of belief and even faith: the doctrine of promoting and maintaining a balance of power to achieve and maintain the value of international order. That is the fundamental moral point of the balance of power which scientific theories often fail to grasp. Writing in the 1970s Bull (1995: 109) noted that at that time there was no general agreement between the great powers that the maintenance of the balance of power was a common objective, much less a valuable goal for them to pursue. That is misleading, because the Soviet Union and the United States did in fact work out rules between themselves for regulating nuclear weapons and other military aspects of their relationship: they collaborated in the pursuit of nuclear peace, and in doing so they disclosed a recognition of shared interests and at least a minimal sociability in their Cold War relationship (Hoffmann: 1991).

Hedley Bull also uses historical and contemporary illustrations to make his argument about the nature of war in an anarchical society. In writing on war his argument is characteristic of a rationalist in Wight's terms. That is clear from his definition of war as an institution. Bull employs historical and contemporary examples to illustrate this rationalist notion of war. He notes (1995: 179) that war between states is often contrasted unfavorably with peace between states, but that can be misleading. He points out that 'the historical alternative to war between states was more ubiquitous violence', such as the social anarchy that existed during the medieval era before modern states monopolized the activity and means of warfare (see Chapter 1). Historically the state system has sought to suppress such violence by restricting warfare to armed combat between states. So the monopoly of war by states has promoted the value of order.

Since 1945 international society has succeeded in limiting interstate war but not intrastate war. Wars between great powers have been almost nonexistent—except for 'wars fought "by proxy" between the superpowers', such as the Korean War or the Vietnam War (Bull 1995: 187). The wars that have occurred since 1945 have predominantly been revolutionary wars, wars of national liberation, civil wars, secessionist wars, the 'war' against international terrorism, and so forth. These are the non-state 'wars of a third kind' (Holsti 1996) that characterize the contemporary era. Bull notes that 'international war, as a determinant of the shape of the international system, has declined in relation to civil war', which he attributed largely to the Cold War stand-off between the superpowers, but which could also be attributed to the norms of the UN Charter, which outlaw aggressive war, and to international public opinion which stands behind them.

During the Cold War social-science positivists—such as strategic realists and neorealists—saw the rivalry between the United States and the Soviet Union in instrumental or structural terms (see Chapter 3). They did not see the Cold War in normative terms as involving basic human values. However, as an exponent of the International Society tradition, Hedley Bull saw nuclear deterrence and other aspects of the American/Russian rivalry as a conflict involving fundamental human values. For Bull (1995: 112–21, emphasis added) nuclear deterrence was an *'institution* or quasi-institution' involving human values which could be captured in the following statement: 'To say that Country A deters Country B from something is to imply . . . that Country A conveys to Country B a threat to inflict *punishment* or deprivation of values if it embarks on a certain course of action.' Bull points out that mutual nuclear deterrence, is a special case of general deterrence which has always been a defense policy of states. It is special in the sense that it becomes 'a prime object of policy' because of the reluctance of nuclear armed powers 'to use nuclear weapons in actual war'. Clearly what is at stake in deterrence, and what is at greater stake in the case of nuclear deterrence, is human *values*: security, survival, the continuation of a national way of life, international order, etc. Those normative goals are the fundamental purpose of the game of nuclear deterrence.

According to Bull, international society involves concern not only about order but also about *justice*. He identifies various conceptions of justice, but he draws particular attention to the distinction between commutative justice and distributive justice in international relations. Commutative justice is about procedures and reciprocity. It involves 'a process of claim and counter-claim' among states. States are like firms in the market-place; each firm does its best to succeed within the framework of economic competition. That presupposes a level playing-field: all firms play by the same rules of the market; all states play by the same rules of international society. Justice is fairness of the rules of the game: the same rules are applied in the same way to everybody. The rules of the game are expressed by international law and diplomatic practices. That is commutative justice, the principal form of international justice.

Distributive justice is about goods. It involves the issue of how goods should be distributed between states, as 'exemplified by the idea that justice requires a transfer of economic resources from rich countries to poor'. Distributive justice is the idea that the poor and weak deserve special treatment, such as development aid.

That means that not all states play by the same rules: some get special treatment. That form of justice takes a back seat to commutative justice because sovereign states are usually understood as the most appropriate framework *within* which normative issues of distributive justice ought to be resolved: in other words, distributive justice is usually understood as an issue of domestic politics rather than international politics. However, in the twentieth century issues of distributive justice have increasingly encroached on international relations as the globe has shrunk.

Bull distinguishes three levels of justice in world politics: 'international or interstate justice', which basically involves the notion of equal state sovereignty; 'individual or human justice', which basically involves ideas of human rights; and 'cosmopolitan or world justice', which basically involves 'what is right or good for the world as a whole', as evident, for example, in global environmental standards. Historically the interstate level has usually prevailed in world politics. In the twentieth century the latter two levels of justice have become more prominent, but they have not overtaken the interstate level which is the level at which most issues of justice in world politics are still addressed.

Box 5.15 **Order and Justice**

ORDER	JUSTICE
Order in social life	Human justice
International order	Interstate justice
World order	World justice

Bull ends his discussion of order and justice by considering the relative weight of these two values in world politics. In that comparison, order is seen to be more fundamental: 'it is a condition for the realization of other values' (Bull 1995: 93). Order is prior to justice. However, Bull makes a point of saying that that is a general statement, but in any particular case justice may come first. An example is the international justice of self-determination and state sovereignty for colonized peoples in Asia and Africa that was widely regarded as morally prior to the international order of Western colonialism in those parts of the world. Bull's main point is that world politics involves questions of both order and justice, and that world politics cannot be adequately understood by focusing on either value to the exclusion of the other.

Statecraft and Responsibility

The International Society approach leads to the study of moral choices in foreign policy that responsible statespeople are confronted with (Jackson 2000). We can discern at least three distinctive dimensions or levels of responsibility which correspond to Wight's three traditions noted above: (1) devotion to one's own nation and the well-being of its citizens; (2) respect for the legitimate interests and rights of other states and for international law; and (3) respect for human rights.

National Responsibility

According to this conception, statespeople are responsible for the well-being of their citizens. The only fundamental standard of conduct that they should adhere to in their foreign policies is that of national self-interest. National security is the foundational value that they are duty-bound to protect. This realist standard for evaluating foreign policies gives rise to Machiavellian precepts such as the following: always put your nation and its citizens first; avoid taking unnecessary risks with their security and welfare; collaborate with other countries when it is advantageous or necessary but avoid needless foreign entanglements; do not subject your population to war unless it is absolutely necessary. These normative considerations are characteristic of a system of autonomous states, i.e. realism.

Box 5.16 President de Gaulle on national responsibility (1961)

It is intolerable for a great State [France] to leave its destiny up to the decisions and action of another State [the United States], however friendly it may be . . . the integrated country loses interest in its national defense, since it is not responsible for it.

Quoted in Kissinger (1994: 605)

What is the normative basis for claiming that statespeople are only responsible for defending the national interest of their own country? The answer can be derived from a familiar theory of political obligation which regards the state—whether it is formed by a social contract, by historical evolution, by conquest, or by any other method—as a self-contained political community that is morally prior to any international associations it may subsequently join. That normative view is typical of many American policymakers who regard the United States Constitution as above international law. States have no international obligations that come before their national interests: international law and international organizations are merely instrumental considerations in determining the national interest of states. Human beings have rights only by virtue of being citizens of states: each statesperson is responsible for defending his or her own citizens, but not the citizens of other states.

International Responsibility

According to this conception, statespeople have foreign obligations deriving from their state's membership of international society, which involves rights and duties as defined by international law. This interstate standard for evaluating foreign policies gives rise to Grotian precepts such as the following: be a good citizen of international society; recognize that other states have international rights and legitimate interests which deserve respect; act in good faith; observe international law; comply with the laws of war. These normative considerations are characteristic of a pluralist society of states based on international law, i.e. rationalism.

Box 5.17 President Franklin Roosevelt on international responsibility (1945)

Nothing is more essential to the future peace of the world than continued cooperation of the nations which had to muster the force necessary to defeat the conspiracy of the Axis powers to dominate the world. While the great states have a special responsibility to enforce the peace, their responsibility is based upon the obligations resting upon all states, large and small, not to use force in international relations except in defense of law.

Quoted in Kissinger (1994: 427)

What is the normative basis for believing that statesmen have a separate responsibility to international society and its members? The usual answer comes from a conception of international obligation: states are not isolated or autonomous political entities, responsible only to themselves. On the contrary, states are related to each other, and constitute the external sovereignty of each other by the practices of recognition, diplomacy, commerce, etc. States consequently have foreign obligations to other states and to international society as a whole from which they derive important rights and benefits. Those foreign obligations are independent of and additional to the domestic obligations of statespeople.

Humanitarian Responsibility

According to this conception, statespeople first and foremost are human beings and as such they have a fundamental obligation to respect human rights not only in their own country but in all countries around the world. This cosmopolitan

---

Box 5.18 **Three dimensions of responsibility**

	RESPONSIBLE TO WHOM?	RESPONSIBLE FOR WHAT?
National	Our citizens	National security
International	Other states	International peace
Humanitarian	Humans everywhere	Human rights

---

standard for evaluating foreign policies gives rise to Kantian precepts such as the following: always remember that people in other countries are human beings just like yourself; respect human rights; give sanctuary to those who are fleeing from persecution; assist those who are in need of material aid which you can supply at no sacrifice to yourself; in waging war spare non-combatants. These normative considerations are characteristic of a solidarist world society based on the community of humankind, i.e. revolutionism.

Box 5.19 **Russian Foreign Minister Andrei Kozyrev on humanitarian responsibility**

Wherever threats to democracy and human rights occur, let alone violations thereof, the international community can and must contribute to their removal . . . Such measures are regarded today not as interference in internal affairs but as assistance and cooperation ensuring everywhere a 'most favored regime' for the life of the peoples—one consistent with each state's human rights commitments under the UN Charter, international covenants and other relevant instruments.

Quoted in Weller (1993)

This cosmopolitan criterion of responsible statecraft obviously goes well beyond international responsibility. What is the normative basis for believing that states-people are responsible for human rights around the world? The usual answer derives from a theory of human obligation: before one can be a citizen of a state and a member of its government, one must be a human being. This naturally entails fundamental obligations that every human being must observe. The traditional way of expressing one's obligations as a human being is by claiming that there is a natural law, a universal law of reason and of conscience, and natural rights—what we now call 'human rights'—which statespeople no less than anyone else are duty-bound to respect.

If these criteria and precepts are operative standards of conduct, it becomes clear that we should expect normative dilemmas and conflicts to be a feature of contemporary statecraft. It is equally clear that all three of these dimensions of responsibility must be a focus of analysis. To reduce responsible statecraft to only one or two of these dimensions is to carry out at best a partial analysis and at worse a biased account which would underestimate the normative complexity of international relations and consequently the actual difficulty of making normatively defensible choices in foreign policy. No criterion can predictably trump all other considerations in all circumstances. There is an underlying normative pluralism which statespeople cannot escape from, which IR scholars should not ignore, and which perhaps is what Wight (1991) is referring to when he said he encountered all three perspectives when he canvassed his own mind on such questions. That is evident from two important post-Cold War conflicts: the Gulf War and the crisis in Bosnia (Mayall 1996).

When the armed forces of Saddam Hussein's Iraq invaded Kuwait in August 1990, other countries and international society as a whole were presented with a military action that was in clear violation of the UN Charter and threatened the legitimate national interests of many states. Some response had to be made. But no response would be easy. Even the decision to do nothing would be difficult, owing to the extreme seriousness of Iraq's offense against international law and the threat it posed to the Persian Gulf and its huge oil supplies, upon which many states were heavily dependent. As it happened, a series of major decisions were taken by the UN Security Council and its member states which eventually led to a war against Iraq. It is convenient and instructive to assess those decisions from an International Society perspective (Jackson 1992). The decision to commit member states of the UN to a war with Iraq was taken with reluctance, and only after extensive debate and many previous decisions failed to persuade Saddam Hussein to withdraw his armed forces from occupied Kuwait.

The difficulty of the decision is clearly indicated by a debate in the US Congress in January 1990 regarding whether the United States should participate in the UN action against Iraq by committing its armed forces. Senators and Congressmen had to make that decision jointly with the President. They were attentive to the seriousness of their decision, i.e. the anticipated consequences of passing the resolution versus the expected consequences of defeating the resolution. On the one hand, they were acutely aware that an affirmative decision would inevitably result in the wounding and killing of American and Allied soldiers; it would also bring death, destruction, and suffering to the people of Kuwait and Iraq where the war would be waged. On the other hand, they were equally aware that a negative decision would probably allow Iraq to get away with a serious act of aggression that heaped contempt upon the UN Charter and particularly the principle of non-intervention and on the value of international peace and security, and that threatened to disrupt the flow of Middle East oil supplies. As it turned out, the US Senate passed the resolution by a narrow vote of 52 to 47. That is a telling indication of the normative weight and difficulty of the decision.

In short, all three normative criteria of responsible statecraft were evident in the Gulf War. Realists would notice that the West's vital interest in an uninterrupted

---

Box 5.20 United States declared foreign policy in the Persian Gulf

(1) the immediate, unconditional and complete withdrawal of all Iraqi forces from Kuwait;

(2) the restoration of Kuwait's legitimate government;

(3) the security and stability of the Persian Gulf region;

(4) the protection of American citizens abroad, and the release of all those held hostage by Iraq; and

(5) the fostering of a new world order, free from the threat of terror, stronger in the pursuit of justice, and more secure in the quest for peace.

Weller (1993: 276)

---

supply of Middle East oil—i.e. the norm of national responsibility—was uppermost in the minds of US President George Bush and other Western leaders when they embarked upon a course of war to evict Saddam Hussein's armed forces from Kuwait in January 1991. Rationalists would notice the nearly universal condemnation of Iraq's invasion and occupation of Kuwait. Iraq's conduct in this episode was widely construed as an act of aggression and thus a violation of the UN Charter—i.e. the norm of international responsibility was also evident. Soft revolutionists would notice that many UN Security Council resolutions addressed the problem of human-rights violations by Iraq: against citizens of occupied Kuwait, against Western citizens living in Kuwait and Iraq, and against Iraqi citizens who belong to minority groups, such as the Kurds. It is clear that the norm of humanitarian responsibility was evident in the Gulf War too.

Box 5.21 President Bush's justification of war against Iraq (January 1991)

Just 2 hours ago, allied air forces began an attack on military targets in Iraq and Kuwait . . . This military action, taken in accord with United Nations resolutions and with the consent of the United States Congress, follows months of constant and virtually endless diplomatic activity on the part of the United Nations, the United States, and many, many other countries . . . the 28 countries with forces in the Gulf area have exhausted all reasonable efforts to reach a peaceful resolution—have no choice but to drive Saddam Hussein from Kuwait by force. . . . Our objectives are clear. Saddam Hussein's forces will leave Kuwait. The legitimate government of Kuwait will be restored to its rightful place, and Kuwait will once again be free . . . it is our hope that [in the future] Iraq will live as a peaceful and cooperative member of the family of nations, thus enhancing the security and stability of the Gulf.

Quoted in Weller (1993: 279)

The most perplexing post-Cold War conflict was the war in the former Yugoslav republic of Bosnia-Herzegovina (1992–5). Statespeople were confronted with three basic courses of action: absolute non-intervention, in which responsibility for events would reside in the hands of the parties to the conflict (the Bosnian army and the Serbian and Croatian militias); full-scale military intervention, in which International Society would assume a heavy responsibility for events; or a path somewhere between these extremes. The course that was embarked upon and followed during most of the conflict was a normatively ambiguous middle way of muddling through, by means of a limited UN humanitarian intervention which attempted to protect non-combatants, deliver humanitarian aid, and arrange a negotiated settlement. That path was finally abandoned in 1995, when NATO became involved in a major armed peace enforcement operation in Bosnia.

Box 5.22 UN Security Council Resolution 688 on safe havens in Iraq

The Security Council, mindful of its duties and its responsibilities under the Charter of the United Nations for the maintenance of international peace and security . . .

(1) *Condemns* the repression of the Iraqi civilian population in many parts of Iraq, including most recently in Kurdish populated areas, the consequences of which threaten international peace and security in the region;

(2) *Demands* that Iraq . . . immediately end this repression . . .

(3) *Insists* that Iraq allow immediate access by international humanitarian organizations to all those in need of assistance in all parts of Iraq . . .

UN Security Council, 5 Apr. 1991. Quoted in Weller (1993: 13)

For three years (1992–5) the UN Security Council in cooperation with the European Union were reluctant to commit to that second course of action. The leading argument against intervention was the moderate realist claim that it was a civil war, that it presented no threat to international peace and security, and that it did not affect the vital national interests of the great powers. But there was already a major international intervention in Bosnia-Herzegovina. In 1992 the country became a sovereign state as a direct result of recognition by member states of the European Union and the United States. They bore a crucial international responsibility for Bosnia's independence from Yugoslavia. Furthermore, international society subsequently intervened massively by imposing an arms embargo on former Yugoslavia, which put the Bosnian government at a big military disadvantage. The Serbian and Croatian militias were supplied with arms by their kindred states, Serbia and Croatia. That made it possible for them to carry out an undeclared war of state partition against Bosnia-Herzegovina.

Box 5.23 **UN Security Council Resolution 713 on Yugoslavia**

The Security Council . . .

(5) *Appeals urgently to and encourages* all parties to settle their disputes peacefully and through negotiation . . .

(6) *Decides*, under Chapter VII of the Charter of the United Nations, that all States shall, for the purposes of establishing peace and stability in Yugoslavia, immediately implement a general and complete embargo on all deliveries of weapons and military equipment to Yugoslavia . . .

(7) *Calls on* all States to refrain from any action which might contribute to increasing tension and to impeding or delaying a peaceful and negotiated outcome to the conflict in Yugoslavia, which would permit all Yugoslavs to decide upon and to construct their future in peace . . .

UN Security Council, 21 September 1995. Quoted in Mayall (1996: 174–5)

By 1994–5 the leaders of the great powers began to be confronted by a difficult decision that grew out of the failure of their initial middle course. Should they continue with a restricted UN intervention that was proving to have morally intolerable consequences, such as its failure to persuade the parties to settle their conflict at the peace table and its failure to prevent 'ethnic cleansing' and other human rights violations? Or should they engage in a stepped-up major military intervention, with all the risks and dangers that that would involve? Withdrawal was clearly out of the question, and in the mean time the human tragedy of Bosnia was continuing and even deepening. The United States began to assert its leadership role. NATO air power was employed in 1994, and eventually the military option was used as a threat to bring the parties to a peace conference. In late 1995 a peace treaty was signed and a substantial NATO force was deployed to Bosnia to implement the terms of the Dayton Agreement and to help bring about a permanent settlement of the conflict.

The International Society approach to responsible statecraft says that we must imagine ourselves in the shoes of the statespeople at the time they are confronted by a moral dilemma. If we do that in the case of Bosnia, it is not so difficult to understand why a middle course of muddling through was originally chosen: it is the response that one would expect from any statesman or stateswoman who had a genuine desire to safeguard humanitarian values but no compelling national interest to become directly involved in a conflict and persuasive pruden- tial reasons to stay out. Non-intervention would involve disregarding the com- pelling humanitarian claims of the Bosnian people; but full military intervention would involve taking incalculable risks with the lives of everybody involved, civilians as well as soldiers. As it turned out, the middle course of limited UN

Box 5.24 **The General Framework Agreement for Peace in Bosnia and Herzegovina (Dayton Agreement)**

The parties shall conduct their relations in accordance with the principles set forth in the United Nations Charter, as well as the Helsinki Final Act . . . In particular, the parties shall fully respect the sovereign equality of one another . . . and shall refrain from any action, by threat or use of force or otherwise, against the territorial integrity or political independence of Bosnia and Herzegovina or any other state. [Article I]

The Federal Republic of Yugoslavia and the Republic of Bosnia and Herzegovina recognize each other as sovereign independent States within their international borders. [Article X]

Dayton Peace Accord, 21 Nov. 1995

---

humanitarian intervention probably prolonged the conflict and proved to have tragic consequences. But that was not clear in advance. In world politics only hindsight gives you the full picture.

The length, intensity, and circuitous course of the debate over Bosnia did not indicate an exclusively realist preoccupation with national interests or any lack of humanitarian concern. If national responsibility was all that mattered, the Bosnia-Herzegovina conflict would have been left to the people who live in those countries to sort out themselves. In fact, the humanitarian crisis in Bosnia created a great deal of frustration and anguish for the leaders of major Western powers. What that debate did indicate was an absence of confidence that military intervention in Bosnia-Herzegovina would be successful; many statespeople feared that it would actually make the problem worse. The Bosnia-Herzegovina case illustrates the deeply troubling moral choices that sometimes confront statespeople in a pluralist world in which they have a responsibility to safeguard their own country and its citizens but also a responsibility to defend international law and protect human rights around the world. In other words, the case is a reminder of how statesmen and stateswomen must try to come to grips with and find a way to reconcile their diverging foreign policy responsibilities.

In order to construe these episodes in the correct light, according to the International Society approach, it is necessary to take account of all dimensions of responsible statecraft. National responsibility (realism) is a necessary, but it is not a sufficient guide to the ethics of statecraft in contemporary world politics. To account for the normative complexity and ambiguity of international relations today, IR scholarship must also take into account international responsibility (rationalism) and humanitarian responsibility (revolutionism).

Critics of International Society

Several major criticisms can be made of the International Society approach to IR. First, there is the realist critique that the evidence of international norms as determinants of state policy and behavior is weak or non-existent. Second, there is the liberal critique that the International Society tradition downplays domestic politics—e.g. democracy—and cannot account for progressive change in international politics. Third, there is the IPE critique that it fails to give an account of international economic relationships. Finally, there are several solidarist critiques that emerge from within the International Society tradition itself that focus on its limitations as a theory of political modernity that cannot come to grips with an emerging postmodern world.

Box 5.25 Three traditional critiques of International Society

REALISM	LIBERALISM	IPE
Weak evidence of norms	Ignores domestic society	Ignores economics
Interests dominate	Ignores democracy	Ignores Third World
	Ignores progress	

The realist critique of the International Society approach rests on a deep skepticism that there is an 'international society' as Hedley Bull (1995: 13) characterizes it: a group of states that 'conceive themselves to be bound by a common set of rules in their relations with one another, and share in the working of common institutions'. Realists believe that states are bound only by their own national interests. Where is the evidence, realists ask, that states are also 'bound by certain rules . . . that they should respect one another's claims to independence, that they should honour agreements into which they enter, and that they should be subject to certain limitations in exercising force against one another' (Bull 1995: 13)? Realists are skeptical that states really do behave that way. States may respect such rules, but only because it is in their interest to do so. If it is not deemed to be in their interest they are not likely to respect them. Realists thus see states as being 'bound by a common set of rules in their relations with one another' only as long as there is an advantage in doing that. When there is a conflict between international obligations and national interests the latter will always win, because the fundamental concern of states is always their own advantage and ultimately their security and survival. That is the concern that guides foreign policy.

The International Society approach is not as soft a target as the realist critique claims. As pointed out, realism is built into the approach as one of its three basic elements. Wight (1966) characterizes IR as a 'theory of survival' which is an acknowledgment of the primacy of states, their right to exist, and the legitimacy of their interests. But the International Society approach does not stop there. It emphasizes that states bind themselves to other states via treaties, and that the justification for that can be more than merely self-interest (realism) or even enlightened self-interest (moderate realism). It emphasizes that states have legitimate interests that other states recognize and respect; it also emphasizes that states recognize the general advantages of observing a principle of reciprocity in international affairs (rationalism). Likewise, it notices that states do not observe treaties only when it is in their best interests to do so. Rather, they enter into treaty commitments with caution because they know that they are binding themselves to the terms of such treaties. If states really acted the way realists claim there would be no binding treaties, because no state could be expected to keep their promise when it was no longer in their interest to do so. Yet binding treaties are commonplace in world politics.

A more damaging criticism of the International Society approach is the theoretical incoherence that could result from trying to combine realism, rationalism, and revolutionism within a single framework of interpretation, and from emphasizing not only international order but also international justice.

Liberals have directed most of their critical attention at realism, and the debate between liberals [or idealists] and realists was the most conspicuous IR debate in the twentieth century. However, one implied liberal critique is the lack of interest of International Society theorists in the role of domestic politics in international relations. Like realists, International Society theorists draw a firm line between international relations and the internal politics of states. They are not inclined to investigate the domestic aspects of foreign policy. A second implied liberal critique derives from the claim that liberal democracies are more peace-loving than non-democratic political systems. Here, republican liberals are criticizing not only realists but also—by implication—International Society theorists who tend to ignore the subject. A third implied liberal critique is the inability of the International Society approach to account for progressive change in international relations. Wight (1966: 33) claims that domestic politics is a sphere of progressive change, but that international politics is a sphere of recurrence and repetition and IR is a 'theory of survival'. That view is identical to that of realism.

The implied liberal critique does not really hit the mark. Wight's concept of rationalism and Bull's concept of International Society are very close to ideas of institutional liberalism which focus on institution-building and reject the realist claim that institutions are 'scraps of paper'. There is also room in Wight's notion of revolutionism and Bull's notion of international justice for progressive change. Both notions take the Kantian cosmopolitan tradition into account, and that is the philosophical basis for the republican liberal claim that democracies do not fight each other.

The main criticisms that IPE scholars could direct at the International Society approach is its neglect of economics and the social-class aspect of international relations. International Society scholars have only a limited defense against such a criticism, because the fact is that Martin Wight and Hedley Bull give their overwhelming attention to international politics and largely ignore international economics. There is little discussion of economic issues in their writings, and it is possible to conclude from reading them that economics has little role in IR. However, economics are not entirely ignored. Wight (1991: 1) includes in his definition of rationalism the idea of 'commerce' as one of the basic relations between sovereign states. Bull (1995: 261–9) explores the role of 'economic factors in international relations' and specifically that of 'multinational corporations', 'regional economic associations', and 'transnational society'. Robert Jackson (1990: 109–38) investigates the role of 'international development assistance', 'Third World debt', and the obstacles that existing international society based on state sovereignty present to Third World development.

The 'transnational society' critique basically argues that international society conceived in terms of a 'society of states' is deficient because it fails to take into account 'the transnational activities of individuals, firms, interest associations and social groups' (Peterson 1992: 371). The state 'does not monopolize the public sphere' and, accordingly, the relations of states do not exhaust international relations. These transnational actors and activities should neither be underestimated nor overestimated: they 'coexist' with sovereign states and interstate relations. International relations are both public and private. There is an international 'civil society' that consists of various transnational actors, but the operation of that society 'relies on the state' to provide 'the conditions under which it can flourish' (Peterson 1992: 376). Those conditions include peace, security, reciprocity—in other words, Bull's basic goals of international order.

That pinpoints the debate between the traditional International Society theorists of IR, discussed above, and their transnational critics. The question is: how important are these conditions, and how important is the state in providing them? It is hard to see any practical and viable alternative to the state at present. If the state is the only institution that can provide these conditions, then the transnational critique loses much of its force, and becomes merely an added, secondary feature of International Society which is still, basically, a society of states. If transnational society flourishes in the conditions of the society of states, the transnational critique is less a critique of the traditional International Society approach than a modest reform which expands on that approach.

The 'global society' critique basically argues that International Society is deficient because it operates with 'a fundamentally state-centric approach' that regards states as actors 'akin to individuals', and neglects 'the complex social relations which bind individuals and states' (Shaw 1992: 423–8). International Society theory is really a thinly disguised ideology which basically serves the purpose of justifying the system of sovereign states. It also is blind to 'world society', which it is ill-equipped to come to grips with conceptually. 'World society exists through the social relations involved in global commodity production and exchange, through global culture and mass media, and through the increasing development of world politics' (Shaw 1992: 429). That global society has priority, including moral priority, over the society of states. It involves 'global responsibility' for human needs, human rights and the environment regardless of state jurisdiction and international boundaries. To the extent that national leaders fail to exercise global responsibility they disclose the moral bankruptcy of traditional International Society based on independent states and, at the same time, the conceptual inadequacy and ideological blinkers of International Society theory.

Box 5.26 Three solidarist critiques of International Society

TRANSNATIONAL SOCIETY	GLOBAL SOCIETY	GLOBAL INJUSTICE
State and non-state	Anti-statist	Anti-statist
Transnational activities	Complex global relations	Global protection racket
International civil society	World society	Human wrongs
Public–private coexistence	Global responsibility	World injustice

---

The core of this critique is the Marxist claim that there is a primary world society in existence in relation to which the society of states is secondary and subordinate. World society is the basic structure. The corresponding claim is that International Society theorists ignore that underlying 'reality' and dispense an 'ideology' of state primacy, the national interest, the law of nations, etc. The reader has to decide whether the state and, by extension, the society of states is more or less substantial and important than other international relations in world politics. A response that International Society theorists might make to Shaw's critique is to point to the way that statespeople actually conceive of and exercise responsibility in world politics, which is by giving priority, first to their own citizens (national responsibility), second to other states (international responsibility), and only third to human beings, regardless of their citizenship or to the world as a whole. In other words, the ethic of pluralism is more significant than that of solidarism in shaping and taking responsibility in world politics.

The 'global injustice' critique acknowledges that state interests and concerns still have primacy in world politics, but goes on to make a cosmopolitan critique of the morality, or rather the immorality, of the sovereign state. Ken Booth (1995) argues that International Society conceived in terms of a 'society of states' sacrifices human beings on the altar of the sovereign state. Statism is the problem rather than the solution as far as human well-being is concerned. Far from ensuring the protection of citizens in particular states primarily through the mechanisms of respect for state sovereignty and defense of the national interest, International Society actually 'bears an uncomfortable resemblance to a global protection racket'. Ordinary people in many underdeveloped countries are 'slaves' who are abused and exploited by their rulers, the 'slave-masters'. Instead of protecting human rights, the state system actually produces 'human wrongs' on a global scale.

Booth thus extends Shaw's critique by arguing that statespeople, far from acting responsibly, have created an exclusive club—the society of states—whose rules of equal sovereignty and non-intervention exist to serve their own selfish interests at the expense of a suffering humanity. International Society theorists, by trying to understand and appreciate the difficult choices that statespeople face, actually end up by apologizing for their actions and being 'fetishizers of Foreign Offices' (Booth, quoted by Wheeler 1996: 129). However, this critique ignores or plays down the goal of international order and coexistence without which, arguably, there can be no global justice. It also ignores the fact that Hedley Bull was a critical theorist and anything but an apologist when it came to the behavior of the great powers, and specifically the United States and the Soviet Union, which he said were 'not well suited to fulfil the normative requirements of great powerhood' (1984: 437–47).

. . . .

The Current Research Agenda

Since the end of the Cold War the research agenda of International Society has expanded and changed to a degree. The central normative concern has moved at least some distance away from order and toward justice in world politics. Not only has there been a shift of scholarly concern in the direction of justice in world politics, but there has also been a movement away from a concern about international justice and towards a concern about human justice. There has also been an enlargement of the subject to include issues of world justice—such as environmental protection or the law of the sea—and the question of what shape International Society might take in the future if state sovereignty ceases to be the foundation institution of world politics as it has been for the past three and a half centuries.

This raises the age-old question of state sovereignty. We still live in a world of state sovereignty and non-intervention and there is a strong feeling, in our age of democracy, that countries should govern themselves and should not be governed by foreigners, whether they are colonial powers or international trusteeships. However, the same democratic age has produced numerous declarations of human rights which reduce, at least in theory, the sphere of state sovereignty and non-intervention. John Vincent observes that 'boundaries' between domestic societies and international society became 'fuzzier' in the last half of the twentieth century with the accumulation of many international declarations and conventions on human rights (Vincent 1990: 254–5). In other words, there is an ambiguous and confusing relation in international law today between the responsibilities of citizenship, on the one hand, and universal human rights, on the other. A leading item on the research agenda of International Society has been the analysis of that ambiguity in contemporary world politics.

John Vincent and Peter Wilson (1993: 128–9) have argued in more reformist International Society terms that a new idea of 'international legitimacy' is emerging because the international law of human rights 'opens up the state to scrutiny from outsiders and propels us beyond non-intervention.' There is a 'new order of things' which is the interdependent and transnational world propelled by the technological revolution in communications that is 'nudging international society in the direction of a world society'. They argue that the pluralist society of states based on the principle of non-intervention 'has now been replaced by a much more complex world'. There must be a 'new order of thoughts' that explores the conceivable directions that such a change could and should take in the future. They call for a cosmopolitan or solidarist theory of International Society 'which recognizes that the principle of non-intervention no longer sums up the morality of states'. That theory could be pursued by developing a new idea of international legitimacy in which presumably the sovereign state no longer has pride of place, but is instead merely one component, along with human beings and the world itself, of an expanded and far more complex international society: a world society in Hedley Bull's terms.

Another area where we can see an expanding research agenda is 'the greening' of International Society theory (Hurrell and Kingsbury 1992). It is often believed that the environment presents normative problems to which international society cannot respond in the usual terms of state sovereignty and international law. For example, Robert Goodin (1990: 93) considers 'that the traditional structure of international law—guided as it is by notions of autonomous national actors with strong rights that all other national actors similarly share—is wildly inappropriate to many of the new environmental challenges'. That argument suggests that traditional International Society based on state sovereignty is beyond its useful life, and now serves more as an obstacle than an asset as far as addressing world environmental problems is concerned. International Society theorists argue that the society of states is more flexible and adaptable than that critique implies. The clear implication is that international society can be green (Jackson 1996a). Indeed, only if sovereign states get involved will environmental problems get the recognition and environmental norms the respect that they deserve. On that view, international law has not obstructed or even discouraged environmental concerns; on the contrary, it has been employed and adjusted to accommodate and indeed to promote such concerns (Birnie 1992: 51–84) by fitting them into the practices of state sovereignty.

As the above discussion indicates, there has been an enlargement of the scope of International Society theory well beyond its traditional focus on state sovereignty and the society of states. That raises a final question: what shape should international society be expected to take in the future if these trends continue? Are they an indication that state sovereignty will eventually cease to be the foundation institution of world politics, as it has been for the past three and a half centuries? Or are they an indication that state sovereignty is an adapting, evolving international institution which has presented a somewhat different face to the world in the past, and which can be expected to change its shape and substance again in the future?

Hedley Bull (1995: 254–66) speculated on whether the classical society of states based on state sovereignty 'may be giving place to a secular reincarnation of the system of overlapping or segmented authority that characterized medieval Christendom' (see Chapter 1). He saw preliminary evidence of such a trend in 'five features of contemporary world politics': (1) the regional integration of states, such as the European Union; (2) the disintegration of states, such as the breakup of the Soviet Union and former Yugoslavia; (3) the expansion of private international violence, such as the rise of international terrorism; (4) the growth of transnational organizations, including the rise of multinational corporations; and (5) the increasing 'unification' of the world by means of advancing technology, such as the spread of electronic communications. Richard Falk (1985: 651) answered that question in the affirmative: 'the reorganization of international life has two principal features—increased central guidance and increased roles for non-territorial actors.' Bull disagreed with Falk's revolutionist assessment: 'there is no clear evidence that in the next few decades the states system is likely to give place to any of the alternatives to it that have been nominated.' However, Bull did emphasize 'that there is now a wider world political system of which the states system is only a part'. That larger system is a 'world-wide network of interaction' that embraces not only states but also other political actors, both 'above' the state and 'below' it.

In short, the difference between Falk and Bull on the question of the future of International Society is a matter of scholarly judgment. Falk judges world politics to be in a process of fundamental, revolutionary change. Bull judges world politics to be in a process of evolutionary adaptation. The reader will have to make up his or her own mind as to which of these theorists is closer to getting it right.

. . . .

KEY POINTS

- The International Society approach is a middle way in classical IR scholarship: it carves out a place between classical realism and classical liberalism and builds that place into a separate and distinctive IR approach. It regards international relations as a 'society' of states in which the principal actors are statespeople who are specialized in the art of statecraft.

- A system of states is formed when two or more states have sufficient contact between them to make the behavior of each a necessary element in the calculations of the other. A society of states exists when a group of states form a society in the sense that they conceive themselves to be bound by a common set of rules in their relations with one another.

- IR is a never-ending dialogue between realism, rationalism, and revolutionism. Realism emphasizes anarchy and power politics. Rationalism emphasizes society and international law. Revolutionism emphasizes humanitarianism, human rights, and human justice.

- The main point of international society is the promotion and preservation of international order. The responsibility for sustaining order between states belongs to the great powers.

- International society also involves concerns about justice. Commutative justice is the principal form of international justice. But issues of distributive justice are of increasing importance on the international agenda.

- Statespeople face difficult dilemmas because of the different kinds of responsibility that they have to consider. There are three distinctive dimensions of responsibility: national, international, and humanitarian.

....

QUESTIONS

- What are the core elements of the International Society approach?

- What is the difference between order and justice in world politics? Is Hedley Bull correct in claiming that order comes before justice?

- Compare the realist, rationalist, and revolutionist views of the (1990) Gulf War. Which view is the most persuasive?

- What are the most important responsibilities that state leaders in international society must take into consideration when deciding their course of action in cases such as Bosnia?

- Some International Society theorists argue that human rights are of increased importance in world politics since the end of the Cold War. Are they correct? What is the evidence in favor of such a view?

- International Society theorists are sometimes accused of being realists in disguise. Is that accusation warranted?

For additional material and resources see the companion web site at:
www.oup.co.uk/best.textbooks/politics/jacksonsorensen2e/

GUIDE TO FURTHER READING

Bull, H. (1995). *The Anarchical Society: A Study of Order in World Politics*, 2nd edn. London: Macmillan.

——and **Watson, A.** (eds.) (1984). *The Expansion of International Society*. Oxford: Clarendon Press.

Jackson, R. (2000). *The Global Covenant: Human Conduct in a World of States*. Oxford: Oxford University Press.

Vincent, R. J. (1990). 'Grotius, Human Rights, and Intervention', in H. Bull, B. Kingsbury, and A. Roberts (eds.), *Hugo Grotius and International Relations*. Oxford: Clarendon Press.

Wight, M. (1991). *International Theory: The Three Traditions*. Leicester: Leicester University Press.

WEB LINKS

http://www.iyoco.org/hedleybull.pdf
Erol Hofman's essay 'Hedley Bull and the Sociology in International Relations Theory: International Society Revisited' focuses on the main elements in Hedley Bull's theory of International Society: international order, international institutions, and the concept of international society itself. Hosted by IYOCO.

http://www.cis.org.au/policy/aut2001/polaut01–6.pdf
Thorough introduction to Realism, Rationalism, and Revolutionism is found in Sam Roggeveen's 'Towards a Liberal Theory of International Relations'. Hosted by Centre for Independent Studies.

http://www.un.org/
Information about the UN as well as links to institutions operating within the UN framework.

http://www.deakin.edu.au/IRonline/links/themes/issues/humint.html
IR Online provides a comprehensive collection of links to web sites on humanitarian intervention. Hosted by Deakin University.

6 | International Political Economy (IPE): Classical Theories

SUMMARY

This chapter is about the relationship between politics and economics, between states and markets in world affairs. Ultimately, IPE is about wealth and poverty, about who gets what in the international economic and political system. The most important classical theories in this area are mercantilism, economic liberalism, and neo-Marxism. They are 'theories' in the very broad sense of a set of assumptions and values from which the field of IPE can be approached. We present each of these theories in some detail; the next chapter moves on to the most important debates between them.

··

Introduction: What is IPE?

In some fundamental ways, our lives are about political economy. To survive, we need food, clothes, and many other goods. Most of us obtain these provisions in the marketplace, paying for them with money we have earned. We cannot buy anything without money; to demand goods we need some measure of wealth as opposed to poverty. A modern market is based on political rules (if not, it would be a 'Mafia market' based on threats, bribes, and force). Political rules and regulations constitute a framework within which the market functions. At the same time, economic strength is an important basis for political power. If economics is about the pursuit of wealth and politics about the pursuit of power, the two interact in complicated and puzzling ways (Polanyi 1957; Gilpin 1987; 2001). It is this complex interplay in the international context between politics and economics, between states and markets, which is the core of IPE.

The theoretical traditions introduced in earlier chapters have issues of war and peace, of conflict and cooperation between states, as their main subject of study. IPE shifts our attention to issues of wealth and poverty, and to who gets what in the international system. The present chapter is also different from the previous ones in that it does not focus on a single theoretical tradition. Instead, it introduces the three most important classical theories within the field of IPE; the next chapter adds the major current theories. This approach reflects the development of the discipline of IR in which International Political Economy has emerged as a field of study in its own right. Some scholars even argue that IPE is the more comprehensive discipline and that IR should consequently be seen as a subfield of IPE. Alternatively, both IR and IPE could be subfields within a broader discipline of International Studies (Strange 1995). Many economists believe that methods and theories from the discipline of economics can be applied other areas of human affairs, including politics and IR. Many political scientists will argue against this tendency to reduce politics to a branch of economics. This debate is fundamentally about which theories and which research questions are the most important ones.

As we saw in Chapter 2, a core normative argument for the establishment of the academic discipline of IR at the beginning of the twentieth century was that it should help promote a more peaceful world. That focus on war and peace continued during the 1950s and 1960s in the context of the Cold War. For those academics as well as politicians whose international outlook was shaped by the experiences of two world wars this was a natural choice of focus. French president (and general) Charles de Gaulle, for example, considered economic affairs 'quartermaster's stuff' and 'low politics' which could be looked after by lesser minds while statesmen such as himself took care of the 'high politics' which concerned the larger issues of war and peace.

There is another reason for this attitude. It concerns the nature of economic activity in modern society: the separation between a political sphere of the state and an economic sphere of the market is a feature of modern, capitalist society. As we shall see below, economic liberalism holds that the economic system works most efficiently when left to itself, free from political interference. But this liberal idea should not be taken to mean that economics and politics have nothing to do with each other. The term 'free market' does not imply freedom from politics. Many kinds of political regulation concerning contracts, consumer and producer protection, taxation, working conditions, etc. make up the framework within which the 'free market' functions. Politics and economics are entangled in complex ways, even in the most liberal 'free market' economies.

In the 1950s and 1960s one could easily get the impression that many IR scholars committed the misunderstanding of separating economics and politics. For a long time, economics and politics in international relations were seen as almost totally isolated from each other, as qualitatively different activities being studied with qualitatively different approaches. As one scholar pointed out in 1970, international economics and international politics were 'a case of mutual neglect' (Strange 1970). But this sharp distinction between politics and economics was increasingly questioned from the beginning of the 1970s.

Box 6.1 **The Bretton Woods system**

The rules of Bretton Woods . . . provided for a system of fixed exchange rates. Public officials, fresh from what they perceived as a disastrous experience with floating rates in the 1930s, concluded that a fixed exchange rate was the most stable and the most conducive to trade . . . The rules further encouraged an open system, by committing members to the convertibility of their respective currencies into other currencies and to free trade . . .

On August 15, 1971, President Nixon—without consulting the other members of the international monetary system and, indeed, without consulting his own State Department—announced his new economic policy: henceforth, the dollar would no longer be convertible into gold, and the United States would impose a 10 percent surcharge on dutiable imports. August 15, 1971, marked the end of the Bretton Woods period . . .

Spero (1985: 37, 54)

Why the change of attitude? First, the system that politicians had set up to foster economic growth and international exchange after World War II—the so-called Bretton Woods system—showed signs of crisis. In particular, the United States was in economic difficulties which grew out of its deep involvement in the Vietnam war (1961–1973). To halt the drain on US gold reserves the gold-convertibility of the American dollar had to be abandoned. That measure was taken by American President Richard Nixon. In other words, political measures were taken that changed the rules of the game for the economic marketplace. The oil crisis from 1973 onwards contributed to a sense of lost invulnerability. In times of economic crisis it usually becomes clearer that politics and economics hang together. Second, decolonization had created a new group of politically weak and economically poor states in the international system. Most newly independent countries were far from satisfied with their subordinate position in the international economic system. At the UN during the 1970s they called for a 'New International Economic Order,' i.e. political proposals designed to improve the economic position of Third World countries in the international system. Although far less important than the Bretton Woods foreign exchange crisis, these proposals did reveal how the economic position of countries in the international order is closely connected to political measures. Finally, the end of the Cold War also underlined the connection between politics and economics. After 1989 Eastern Europe and the former Soviet Union began to be reintegrated in the international system created by the West. They wanted both political integration, such as membership of Western organizations, and economic integration, meaning more intensive links of economic interdependence with the advanced economies of Western Europe, North America, and Japan.

In summary, there is a complex relationship between politics and economics, between states and markets, that IR has to be able to grasp. That relationship is the subject of IPE. We need different theoretical ways of approaching the connection between politics and economics. From the possible theories to choose from (Caporaso 1993) we have selected three theories which most scholars see as the main theories of IPE: mercantilism, economic liberalism, and Marxism. These are 'theories' in the very broad sense of a set of assumptions and values from which the field of IPE can be approached. As will be apparent, the outlook of mercantilism has much in common with realism, while economic liberalism is an addition to liberal theory. These two theories thus represent views on IPE that are basically realist and liberal. Marxism has its own original theoretical position and we will spend a little more time on that because the Marxist approach has not been presented earlier.

Mercantilism

We begin with mercantilism because this theory is intimately connected to the establishment of the modern, sovereign state during the sixteenth and seventeenth centuries. Mercantilism was the world view of political elites that were at the forefront of building the modern state. They took the approach that economic activity is and should be subordinated to the primary goal of building a strong state. In other words, economics is a tool of politics, a basis for political power. That is a defining feature of mercantilist thinking. Mercantilists see the international economy as an arena of conflict between opposing national interests, rather than an area of cooperation and mutual gain. In brief, economic competition between states is a 'zero-sum game' where one state's gain is another state's loss. States have to be worried about relative economic gain, because the material wealth accumulated by one state can serve as a basis for military-political power which can be used against other states. We should notice the close affinity between this mercantilist way of thinking and neorealist thought about competition between states in an anarchic realm.

Box 6.2 A mercantilist view

Anglo-American *theory* instructs Westerners that economics is by nature a 'positive sum game' from which all can emerge as winners. Asian *history* instructs many Koreans, Chinese, Japanese, and others that economic competition is a form of war in which some win and others lose. To be strong is much better than to be weak; to give orders is better than to take them. By this logic, the way to be strong, to give orders, to have independence and control, is to keep in mind the difference between 'us' and 'them'. This perspective comes naturally to Koreans (when thinking about Japan), or Canadians (when thinking about the United States), or Britons (when thinking, even today, about Germany), or to Chinese or Japanese (when thinking about what the Europeans did to their nations).

Fallows (1994: 231)

Economic rivalry between states can take two different forms (Gilpin 1987: 32). The first is called defensive or 'benign' mercantilism: states look after their national economic interests because that is an important ingredient in their national security; such policies need not have overly negative effects on other states. The other form, however, is aggressive or 'malevolent' mercantilism. Here states attempt to exploit the international economy through expansionary policies: for example, the imperialism of the European colonial powers in Asia and Africa. Mercantilists thus see economic strength and military-political power as complementary, not competing goals, in a positive feedback loop. The pursuit of economic strength supports the development of the state's military and political power; and military-political power enhances and strengthens the state's economic power.

This contrasts sharply with the liberal view introduced in Chapter 4. Liberals posit a radically different choice: the pursuit of economic prosperity through free trade and open economic exchange versus the pursuit of power by the means of military force and territorial expansion. In other words, states can choose the road of economic development and trade and thus become 'trading states,' as did West Germany and Japan after World War II. Or they can choose the road of military force and territorial expansion and thus base their prominence on military power, as did Russia under Communist rule. Mercantilists reject that liberal view. More national wealth and more military-political power are complementary stratagems that serve the same fundamental end: a stronger, more powerful state. A choice between the two appears only in specific situations; one example is the limits that Western powers put on economic exchange with the Eastern Bloc during the Cold War. Here, the West makes an economic sacrifice for reasons of military security. Mercantilists see that as an extraordinary situation. Normally, wealth and power can be pursued simultaneously, in support of each other.

Mercantilists maintain that the economy should be subordinated to the primary goal of increasing state power: politics must have primacy over economics. But the content of the concrete policies recommended to serve that goal has changed over time. Sixteenth century mercantilists noted how Spain benefited from the supply of gold and silver bullion from the Americas; that led them to call for the acquisition of bullion as the main road to national wealth. However, when the Netherlands emerged as the leading country in Europe without directly acquiring bullion mainly because of its vast overseas trading empire, mercantilists started to emphasize trade and the creation of the largest possible trade surplus as the road to national prosperity. Ever since Britain obtained a leading role in world politics through industrialization, mercantilists have underlined the need for countries to industrialize as the best way to obtain national power. Mercantilism has been particularly popular in countries which lagged behind Britain in industrial development; they felt an urgent need to catch up industrially in order to compete with Britain. That catching-up could not be left to market forces; it called for political measures to protect and develop local industry.

Mercantilism has been advocated by some eminent politicians and economists. Alexander Hamilton, one of the founding fathers of the United States, was a strong proponent of mercantilism in the form of protectionist policies aimed at promoting domestic industry in the United States. Another eloquent spokesman for mercantilism was Friedrich List, a German economist. In the 1840s he developed a theory of 'productive power' which stressed that the ability to produce is more important than the result of producing. In other words, the prosperity of a state depends not primarily on its store of wealth, but on the extent to which it has developed its 'powers of production': 'A nation capable of developing a manufacturing power, if it makes use of the system of protection, thus acts quite in the same spirit as the landed proprietor did who by the sacrifice of some material wealth allowed some of his children to learn a production trade' (List 1966: 145). Recent mercantilist thinking focuses on the successful 'developmental' states in East Asia: Japan, South Korea, and Taiwan. They emphasize that economic success has always been accompanied by a strong, commanding role for the state in promoting economic development. In Japan, for example, the Japanese state has played a very comprehensive role in the economic development of the country. The state has singled out strategic industries, protected them from outside competition and supported their development even by regulating the competition between firms. We shall have more to say about these theorists in the next chapter.

In summary, mercantilism posits the economy as subordinate to the polity and, particularly, the government. Economic activity is seen in the larger context of increasing state power. The organization that is responsible for defending and advancing the national interest, namely the state, rules over private economic interests. Wealth and power are complementary, not competing goals. Economic dependence on other states should be avoided as far as possible. When economic and security interests clash, security interests have priority.

Box 6.3 **Mercantilism summarized**

Relationship between economics and politics:	Politics decisive
Main actors/units of analysis:	States
The nature of economic relations:	Conflictual, a zero-sum game
Economic goals:	State power

Hettne (1996: 66)

. . . .

Economic Liberalism

Economic liberalism emerged as a critique of the comprehensive political control and regulation of economic affairs which dominated European state-building in the sixteenth and seventeenth centuries: i.e., mercantilism. Economic liberals reject theories and policies which subordinate economics to politics. Adam Smith (1723–1790), the father of economic liberalism, believed that markets tend to expand spontaneously for the satisfaction of human needs—provided that governments do not interfere. He builds on the body of liberal ideas that are summarized in Chapter 4. These core ideas include the rational individual actor, a belief in progress, and an assumption of mutual gain from free exchange. But Smith also adds some elements of his own to liberal thinking, including the key notion that the economic marketplace is the main source of progress, cooperation, and prosperity. Political interference and state regulation, by contrast, is uneconomical, retrogressive, and can lead to conflict.

Liberal economics has been called 'a doctrine and a set of principles for organizing and managing economic growth, and individual welfare' (Gilpin 1987: 27). It is based on the notion that if left to itself the market economy will

---

Box 6.4 **A liberal view**

Under a system of perfectly free commerce, each country naturally devotes its capital and labour to such employments as are most beneficial to each. The pursuit of individual advantage is admirably connected with the universal good of the whole. By stimulating industry, by rewarding ingenuity, and by using most efficaciously the peculiar powers bestowed by nature, it distributes labour most effectively and most economically: while, by increasing the general mass of productions, it diffuses general benefit and binds together, by one common tie of interest and intercourse, the universal society of nations throughout the civilized world.

Ricardo [1772–1823] (1973: 81)

---

operate spontaneously according to its own mechanisms or 'laws'. These laws are considered to be inherent in the process of economic production and exchange. One example is the 'law of comparative advantage' developed by David Ricardo (1772–1823). He argued that free trade—i.e. commercial activities that are carried on independently of national borders—will bring benefits to all participants because free trade makes specialization possible and specialization increases efficiency and thus productivity. Paul Samuelson summarized the argument as follows: 'Whether or not one of two regions is absolutely more efficient in the production of every good than is the other, if each specializes in the product in which it has a comparative advantage (greatest relative efficiency), trade will be mutually profitable to both regions' (Samuelson 1967: 651). In a world economy based on free trade all countries will benefit through specialization and global wealth will increase.

Economic liberals thus reject the mercantilist view that the state is the central actor and focus when it comes to economic affairs. The central actor is the individual as a consumer and a producer. The marketplace is the open arena where individuals come together to exchange goods and services. Individuals are rational in pursuing their own economic interests, and when they apply that rationality in the marketplace, all participants gain. Economic exchange via the market is thus a positive-sum game: everybody gains more than they put in because of increased efficiency. Individuals and companies would not be active in the marketplace unless it was to their benefit. Liberal economists find that this view of individuals as rational and self-seeking (wanting to make themselves better off) can be used as a starting point for understanding not only market economics but also politics. That particular perspective goes under the name of rational choice theory (see Chapters 7 and 8). Liberals thus reject the mercantilist zero-sum view where one state's economic gain necessarily is another state's economic loss. The road to human prosperity, then, goes through the unfettered expansion of the free market economy, capitalism, not only in each country but also across international boundaries.

There is a recurring debate among economic liberals, however, about the extent to which political interference by governments may be necessary. Early economic liberals called for 'laissez-faire': i.e. for the freedom of the market from all kinds of political restriction and regulation. Yet even the early economic liberals were aware of the need for a politically constructed legal framework as a basis for the market. Laissez-faire does not mean the absence of any political regulation whatsoever; it means that the state shall only set up those minimal underpinnings that are necessary for the market to function properly. This is the classical version of economic liberalism. At the present time this view is also put forward under labels such as 'conservatism' or 'neoliberalism'; the content is basically the same, however. The 'conservative/neoliberal' economic policies of Margaret Thatcher in Britain and of Ronald Reagan in the Unites States were both based on classical laissez-faire doctrines.

Economic liberals have from early on been aware that in some cases the market may not work according to expectations of efficiency and mutual gain; such cases are usually called instances of 'market failure'. Political regulation may be necessary to correct or avoid market failures. Some economic liberals thus argue for a larger degree of state interference in the market. John Stuart Mill was in many ways a laissez-faire economic liberal, but he was also critical of the extreme inequalities of income, wealth, and power, which he observed in nineteenth century Britain. That made him call for limited state action in some areas, including education and relief for the poor. In the 1930s John Maynard Keynes, the leading economist of the early twentieth century, went one step further. According to Keynes the market economy is a great benefit to man, but it also entails potential evils of 'risk, uncertainty and ignorance'. That situation could be remedied through improved political management of the market. Keynes thus argued in favor of a market which was 'wisely managed' by the state (Keynes 1963: 321).

This positive view of the state amounted to a major shift in liberal economic doctrine. Keynesian ideas paved the way for a significantly reformed liberal theory: one which was still based on a market economy, but with a considerable degree of state interference and direction. That Keynesian view was popular in Europe in the decades following World War II. In the 1980s, however, the pendulum swung back to classical laissez-faire liberalism. One major reason for this renewed liberal faith in the unfettered market is the belief that economic globalization will bring prosperity to all. We shall return to that issue in the next chapter.

In summary, economic liberals argue that the market economy is an autonomous sphere of society which operates according to its own economic laws. Economic exchange is a positive-sum game and the market will tend to maximize benefits for the rational, self-seeking individuals, the households, and the companies that participate in market exchange. The economy is a sphere of co-operation for mutual benefit among states as well as among individuals. The international economy should thus be based on free trade. Classical liberal economists view the role of the state as that of leaving the market alone, including international markets as well as national markets: laissez-faire. But some twentieth century economic liberals favor increased state involvement in the marketplace.

Box 6.5 Liberalism summarized

Relationship between economics and politics: Economics autonomous

Main actors/units of analysis: Individuals and private firms

The nature of economic relations: Cooperative, a positive-sum game

Economic goals: Maximum individual and social well-being

Hettne (1996: 66)

. . . .

Marxism

The political economy of the nineteenth century German philosopher and economist Karl Marx in many ways represents a fundamental critique of economic liberalism. We saw above that economic liberals view the economy as a positive-sum game with benefits for all. Marx rejected that view. Instead, he saw the economy as a site of human exploitation and class inequality. Marx thus takes the zero-sum argument of mercantilism and applies it to relations of classes instead of relations of states. Marxists agree with mercantilists that politics and economics are closely intertwined; both reject the liberal view of an economic sphere operating under its own laws. But where mercantilists see economics as a tool of politics, Marxists put economics first and politics second. For Marxists, the capitalist economy is based on two antagonistic social classes: One class, the bourgeoisie, owns the means of production; the other class, the proletariat, owns only its labor power which it must sell to the bourgeoisie. But labor puts in more work than it gets back in pay; there is a surplus value appropriated by the bourgeoisie. That is capitalist profit and it is derived from labor exploitation.

Even if a capitalist economy controlled by the bourgeoisie is exploitative of labor, Marx did not see the growth of capitalism as a negative or retrogressive event. On the contrary, capitalism means progress for Marx, in two ways: first, capitalism destroys previous relations of production, such as feudalism, which were even more exploitative, with peasants subsisting under slave-like conditions. Capitalism is a step forward in the sense that labor is free to sell its labor power and seek out the best possible pay. Second, and most important for Marx, capitalism paves the way for a socialist revolution where the means of production will be placed under social control for the benefit of the proletariat who are the vast majority. That is the revolutionary goal that Marxist economic thought is aiming at.

The Marxist view is materialist: it is based on the claim that the core activity in any society concerns the way in which human beings produce their means of existence. Economic production is the basis for all other human activities, including politics. The economic basis consists, on the one hand, of the forces of production; i.e. the technical level of economic activity (e.g. industrial machinery versus artisan handicraft). On the other hand, it consists of the relations of production: i.e. the system of or social ownership which determines the actual control over the productive forces (e.g. private ownership versus collective ownership). Taken together, forces of production and relations of production form a specific mode of production, for example capitalism, which is based on industrial machinery and private ownership. The bourgeoisie which dominates the capitalist economy through control of the means of production will also tend to dominate in the political sphere because economics is the basis of politics according to Marxists.

Box 6.6 A Marxist view

Modern industry has converted the little workshop of the patriarchal master into the great factory of the industrial capitalist. Masses of laborers, crowded into the factory, are organized like soldiers. As privates of the industrial army they are placed under the command of a perfect hierarchy of officers and sergeants. Not only are they slaves of the bourgeois class, and of the bourgeois state; they are daily and hourly enslaved by the machine, by the overlooker, and above all, by the individual bourgeois manufacturer himself. The more openly this despotism proclaims gain to be its end and aim, the more petty, the more hateful and the more embittering it is.

Marx and Engels (1955: 17)

This brings us to the Marxist framework for the study of IPE. First, states are not autonomous; they are driven by ruling class interests and capitalist states are primarily driven by the interests of their respective bourgeoisies. That means that struggles between states, including wars, should be seen in the economic context of competition between capitalist classes of different states. For Marxists, class conflict is more fundamental than conflict between states. Second, as an economic system, capitalism is expansive: there is a never-ending search for new markets and more profit. Because classes cut across state borders class conflict is not confined to states; instead, it expands around the world in the wake of capitalism. Such expansion first took the form of imperialism and colonization, but it continues after the colonies have been granted independence. It now takes the form of economic globalization led by giant transnational corporations. The history of IPE can thus be seen by Marxists as the history of capitalist expansion across the globe.

Lenin, the communist leader of the Russian revolution of 1917, analyzed this process. He argued that the process of capitalist expansion must always be unequal or uneven, between countries, industries, and firms. For example, Britain was ahead of Germany for most of the eighteenth and nineteenth centuries. Consequently, Britain had secured for herself a vast colonial empire whereas Germany had very little. At the beginning of the twentieth century, however, Germany was catching up economically and Britain was declining. Therefore, Lenin noted, Germany wanted a redivision of the international spheres of influence, according to the new relative strength of the countries. That demand led to war between Germany and Britain. Such disparities and conflicts will always develop under capitalist conditions, argued Lenin. That is the 'law of uneven development.'

Box 6.7 **Lenin and the Law of Uneven Development**

There can be no other conceivable basis under capitalism for the division of spheres of influence ... than a calculation of the strength of the participants in the division, their general economic, financial, military strength, etc. And the strength of these participants in the division does not change to an equal degree, for under capitalism the development of different undertakings, trusts, branches of industry, or countries cannot be even.

Lenin 1917, quoted from Gilpin (1987: 38)

The notion of uneven development points to the need for an historical analysis of capitalist expansion. A Marxist analysis must therefore also be clear about history. Events must always be analyzed in their specific historical context. For example, there was a high economic interdependence between countries around World War I; there is also a high economic interdependence between many countries today. But we need to look at the precise nature of that interdependence in its historical context in order to be able to understand the processes taking place and their significance for international relations: interdependence around World War I was often arms-length import/export relations between independent companies. Today it is frequently integrated circuits of production between subsidiaries of the same transnational company; a Ford car, for example, contains parts produced in many different countries. Such global networks of production make for a different and closer type of economic integration than traditional imports and exports between separate companies.

Box 6.8 **A neo-Marxist view**

It is widely believed that the United States and other developed capitalist countries contribute more capital to the underdeveloped countries than they receive from them. Nonetheless, all available statistics . . . show precisely the opposite . . . For the seven largest Latin American countries . . . the United States Department of Commerce's conservatively calculated figures for the years 1950 to 1961 indicate $2,962 million of investment flows on private account out of the United States and remittances of profits and interest of $6,875 million; adding American public loans and their Latin American servicing between the same years still leaves a conservatively calculated net capital outflow of $2,081 million *to* the United States.

Frank (1971: 237–8)

The difference between Marxist and realist analysis should be brought to attention. Both views agree on the perennial competition and conflict between states. But realists explain this by pointing to the existence of independent states in a condition anarchy. Therefore, the struggle between states has taken place for several millennia, ever since the emergence of states (i.e. independent political units) on the world stage. Marxists reject that view as abstract and unhistorical. It is abstract because there is no concrete specification of the social forces that actually sustain the conflict between states. These social forces, so the Marxist claim, are exactly the ruling classes of capitalists (and their allies); they ultimately control and determine what 'their' states do. When states are rivals and sometime come into conflict it is because they pursue the economic and political interests for international dominance and control sought after by the ruling classes.

The realist view is also unhistorical according to Marxists. That is because history is seen as always repeating itself; it's 'the same damned things over and over again': states competing in anarchy. But Marxists argue that conflict between states varies substantially across history. Conflict between capitalist states— and ultimately between capitalist ruling classes—is of course connected to the capitalist historical era. Consequently, competition and conflict of earlier historical phases require a different explanation, tying it in with the contest between the social forces of those periods of feudalism and antiquity.

Realists argue that the Marxist view of the state is reductionist, that is, it reduces the state to a simple tool in the hands of the ruling classes, with no will of its own. States are strong actors in their own right. They embody powerful institutions, they control the means of violence (army, police), and they have substantial economic resources. It is simply wrong to view the state as a mere instrument for others. More recent Marxist analysis has conceded this point. The state has some autonomy from the ruling classes, but it is a *relative* autonomy: the basic function of the capitalist state remains the safeguarding of the capitalist system. Yet within this general framework, the state should not be reduced to a simple tool of others (Carnoy 1984: ch. 4).

Current Marxist thinking has developed this view further. Robert Cox is a prominent neo-Marxist analyst of world politics and political economy (Cox 1996). Cox begins with the concept of historical structures, defined as 'a particular configuration of forces' (Cox 1996: 97). These historical structures are made up of three categories of forces that interact: material capabilities, ideas, and institutions. Note how Cox moves away from the traditional Marxist emphasis on materialism through the inclusion of ideas and institutions. In the next step, historical structures are identified at three different levels; they are labelled 'social forces', 'forms of state', and 'world orders', as outlined in Box 6.9.

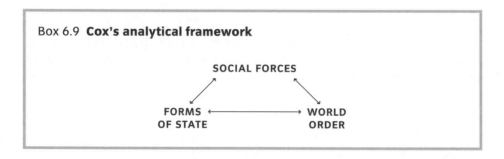

Box 6.9 **Cox's analytical framework**

'Social forces' are a shorthand for the process of capitalist production. An analysis of this aspect will inform us about the present state of development of the capitalist economy on a global scale. 'Forms of state' point to the ways in which states change in the interplay with the social forces of capitalist development. 'World orders' refers to the current organization of international relations including relations between major states and groups of states, the status of international law, and international institutions.

In sum, Cox theorizes a complex interplay between politics and economics, specified as the interaction between social forces, forms of state, and world orders. The task for the analyst is to find out how these relationships play out in the current phase of human history. It is not possible to fully present Cox's analysis of these matters here, but the gist of his argument is as follows (Cox 1992). As regards the social forces of capitalism, they are currently involved in an intense process of economic globalization meaning an internationalizing of production as well as migration movements from South to North. Globalization has been driven by market forces, but Cox foresees that new social movements critical of globalization will grow increasingly strong and this will open a new phase of struggle between social forces concerning the control and regulation of economic globalization.

As regards forms of state, there is variation between states because they link into the global political economy in different ways. Furthermore, states have changed from a role of 'bulwark or buffer protecting the domestic economy from harmful influences' towards a 'transmission belt from world economy to domestic economy' (Cox 1992: 144). That is to say, states compete for advantage, but they do it on the premise that integration in the global economy is unavoidable. Non-territorial power is becoming more important for states; they compete for markets and economic opportunities across the globe. Transnational corporations and civil society organizations operating across borders (i.e. NGOs) are of increasing importance.

Finally, as regards world order, the long-term tendency will be for replacement of the current global US dominance. Several scenarios are possible; one is an international order of 'conflicting power centres' (Cox 1996: 114) structured around leading states or groups of states, such as the EU in Europe and China and Japan in East Asia. Another possibility is a 'post-hegemonic order' (Cox 1993: 142) where states agree on rules and norms of peaceful cooperation for mutual benefit and a common framework for the resolution of possible conflicts. Robert Cox's framework is one example of a recent development of neo-Marxist analysis; we shall return to some of the issues he takes up in the next chapter.

Another recent neo-Marxist analysis comes from Immanuel Wallerstein (1974; 1979; 1983). His starting point is the concept of 'world system'. World systems need not physically include the whole world; they are unified areas characterized by particular economic and political structures. The concept thus ties economics and politics together: a world system is characterized by a certain economic and a certain political structure with the one depending on the other. In human history, there have been two basic varieties of world systems: world-empires and world-economies. In world-empires, such as the Roman empire, political and economic control is concentrated in a unified centre. World-economies, in contrast, are tied together economically in a single division of labour, but politically, authority is decentralized, residing in multiple polities, in a system of states. Wallerstein's key focus is the analysis of the modern world-economy, characterized by capitalism.

The capitalist world-economy was established in 'the long 16th century' (1450–1640). It was based on an international division of labour that covered Europe first, but soon expanded to the Western hemisphere and later to other parts of the world as well. Within this division of labour, a process of specialization took place; this happened in a somewhat accidental way first; for a number of reasons Northwest Europe was in a better position to diversify its agriculture and to connect it with industrial advance in textiles and shipping. So the capitalist world-economy is built on a hierarchy of core areas, peripheral areas, and semi-peripheral areas. The core areas contain the advanced and complex economic activities (mass market industries and sophisticated agriculture). Furthermore, these activities are controlled by an indigenous bourgeoisie. Peripheral areas are at the bottom of the hierarchy; they produce staple goods such as grain, wood, sugar, etc. They often employ slavery or coerced labour; what little industrial activity that exists is mostly under the external control of capitalists from core countries. Semi-peripheral areas are economically mixed; they are a middle layer between the upper stratum of core countries and the lower stratum of peripheral countries.

A basic mechanism of the capitalist world-economy is unequal exchange. Economic surplus is transferred from the periphery to the core. Surplus is appropriated from low-wage, low-profit producers in the periphery to high-wage, high-profit producers in the core. This transfer is further accentuated by the emergence of strong state machineries in the core and weak state machineries in the periphery. Strong states can enforce unequal exchange on weak ones. Thus capitalism 'involves not only appropriation of surplus value by an owner from a laborer, but an appropriation of surplus of the whole world-economy by core areas. And this was as true in the stae of agricultural capitalism as uit is in the stage of industrial capitalism' (Wallerstein 1979: 18).

In the process of unequal exchange, tensions are created in the system. The semi-periphery has an important function in this regard. It provides an element of political stability, because the core countries are not facing a unified opposition; the semi-periphery acts as a buffer or shock absorber. At the same time, the world-economy is not entirely static; any single area of the system may change place from periphery to semi-periphery, from semi-periphery to core, and vice versa. Furthermore, the types of commodities involved in core and peripheral economic activities respectively are subject to dynamic change. Technological advance means that the concrete content of what is 'advanced economic activity' always changes. At one point it was textiles; in a later phase it was industrial machinery; today, it is information- and bio-technology together with financial and other services. But Wallerstein emphasizes that the capitalist system as such does not change: it remains a hierarchy of core, semi-periphery and periphery, characterized by unequal exchange.

Wallerstein sees the end of the Cold War and the destruction of the Soviet bloc as a consequence of the development of the capitalist world-economy. However, the long term prospect is the demise of the capitalist system, because the contradictions of that system are now unleashed on a world scale. Success, not failure, is the real threat to global capitalism; when the possibilities for expansion are all used up, the never ending quest for more profit will lead to new crises in the world capitalist economy which sooner or later will spell its transformation.

There are some similarities between Wallerstein's world systems analysis of capitalism and Waltz's neorealist analysis of the international system. Both focus on the system rather than on the single units or countries; what happens to countries very much depends on their position in the system. Both see the system as a hierarchy with strong states in the top and weak states in the bottom. But from here the differences take over: Waltz's focus is on relative political-military power in a condition of anarchy; Wallerstein's focus is first and foremost economic power and capability which is then connected with political power. Wallerstein analyses the historical development of capitalism since the sixteenth century, putting economics first and politics second. Waltz analyzes the international balance of power in the twentieth century, putting power politics first and economics second. The reader is encouraged to speculate about the advantages and drawbacks of each theory.

It is clear that the contributions by Wallerstein and Cox add a number of nuances to Marxist analysis. In the present context, however, we need to focus on the main thrust of the Marxist approach as compared to liberalism and mercantilism. This basic Marxist view can be summarized as follows: the economy is a site of exploitation and inequality between social classes, especially the bourgeoisie and the proletariat. Politics is to a large extent determined by the socio-economic context. The dominant economic class is also dominant politically. That means that in capitalist economies the bourgeoisie will be the ruling class. Global capitalist development is uneven and bound to produce crises and contradictions, both between states and between social classes. Marxist IPE thus concerns the history of global capitalist expansion, the struggles between classes and states to which it has given rise around the world, and how a revolutionary transformation of that world might come about.

Box 6.10 Marxism summarized

Relationship between economics and politics:	Economics decisive
Main actors/units of analysis:	Classes
The nature of economic relations:	Conflictual; zero-sum
Economic goals:	Class interests

Developed from Hettne (1996: 66)

Conclusion

In an overall summary of this chapter, it is helpful to summarize the three classical theories by combining the information in Boxes 6.3, 6.5, and 6.10. That information is contained in Box 6.11.

In the next chapter we shall introduce the main debates to which the principal IPE theories have given rise to convey an impression of the kind of questions and issues which are currently being discussed in IPE.

Box 6.11 **Three theories of IPE**

	MERCANTILISM	ECONOMIC LIBERALISM	MARXISM
Relationship between economics and politics:	Politics decisive	Economics autonomous	Economics decisive
Main actors/units of analysis:	States	Individuals	Classes
The nature of economic relations:	Conflictual, zero-sum game	Cooperative, positive-sum game	Conflictual
Economic goals:	State power	Maximum individual well-being	Class interests

KEY POINTS

- The relationship between politics and economics, between states and markets, is the subject matter of International Political Economy, IPE. There are three main theories of IPE: mercantilism, economic liberalism, and Marxism.

- Mercantilism posits the economy as subordinate to politics. Economic activity is seen in the larger context of increasing state power: the national interest rules over the marketplace. Wealth and power are complementary, not competing goals, but excessive economic dependence on other states should be avoided. When economic and security interests clash, security interests have priority.

- Economic liberals argue that the market economy is an autonomous sphere of society, operating according to its own economic laws. Economic exchange is a positive-sum game and the market will tend to maximize benefits for individuals, households, and companies. The economy is a sphere of cooperation for mutual benefit, among states as well as among individuals.

- In the Marxist approach the economy is a site of exploitation and inequality between social classes, especially the bourgeoisie and the proletariat. Politics is to a large extent determined by the socio-economic context. The dominant economic class is also dominant politically. IPE concerns the history of global capitalist expansion and the struggles between classes and states to which it has given rise. Capitalist development is uneven and bound to produce new crisis and contradictions, both between states and between social classes.

QUESTIONS

● What is IPE and why is it important?

● Give the core arguments made by the three main theories of IPE: mercantilism, economic liberalism, and Marxism. Which theory, if any, is the better one? Why?

● Politics is in control of economics, say mercantilists. Economics is the basis for everything else, including politics, say Marxists. How should we settle this dispute?

● Economic liberals argue that economic exchange is a positive-sum game. In the Marxist approach the economy is a site of exploitation and inequality. Who is right?

● Do security interests always have priority of economic matters, as mercantilists claim?

● Compare Waltz and Wallerstein. Who has the best theory?

 For additional material and resources see the companion web site at:
www.oup.co.uk/best.textbooks/politics/jacksonsorensen2e/

GUIDE TO FURTHER READING

Cox, R. W. (1987). *Production, Power and World Order: Social Forces in the Making of History*. New York: Columbia University Press.

Gilpin, R. (2001). *Global Political Economy. Understanding the International Economic Order*. Princeton: Princeton University Press.

Frieden, J. and **Lake, D. A.** (eds.) (2000). *International Political Economy: Perspectives on Global Power and Wealth*. New York: St. Martin's.

Polanyi, K. (1957). *The Great Transformation: The Political and Economic Origins of Our Time*. New York: Farrar Rinehart.

Schwartz, H. (2000). *States versus Markets. The Emergence of a Global Economy*, 2nd edn., London: Macmillan.

Strange, S. (1988). *States and Markets. An Introduction to International Political Economy*. London: Pinter.

WEB LINKS

http://csf.colorado.edu/ipe/
The IPENet home page provides a wide range of links to other sites on IPE as well as electronic archives and information about discussion groups.

http://www.westga.edu/~cscott/history/mercan.html
Carole E. Scott's essay 'Mercantilism in Practice and the (Resulting?) American Revolution' provides information about Mercantilism in the 17th and 18th centuries. Hosted by the State University of West Georgia.

http://www.mysunrise.ch/users/dbesomi/Links/links-1.htm
Daniele Besomi provides a wide range of links to web sites on Economic Liberalism.

http://www.marxists.org/
Comprehensive online archive of the works of several Marxist writers, including Karl Marx and Friedrich Engels. The site, hosted by the Marxists Internet Archive, also provides an account of Marxist history as well as an encyclopaedia of Marxism.

International Political Economy: Contemporary Debates

SUMMARY

This chapter presents three important IPE debates. They concern: (1) the exact relationship between politics and economics; (2) development and underdevelopment in the Third World; and (3) the nature and extent of economic globalization. The last part of the chapter presents recent developments in theorizing on IPE. We emphasize that there is a growing concern about issues of wealth and poverty in many countries. For this reason, the IPE research agenda is of increasing importance.

The Debate on US Hegemonic Stability

The most important debate stemming from mercantilism concerns the need for a strong state to create a smoothly functioning liberal international economy. A hegemon, a dominant military and economic power, is necessary for the creation and full development of a liberal world market economy, because in the absence of such a power, liberal rules cannot be enforced around the world. That, in its simplest form, is the theory of hegemonic stability which is indebted to mercantilist thinking about politics being in charge of economics. But hegemonic stability theory is not exclusively mercantilist. There is also a liberal element: the dominant power does not merely manipulate international economic relations for its own sake; it creates an open world economy based on free trade which is to the benefit of all participating states and not only the hegemon. The version of the theory we present here was first set forth by Charles Kindleberger (1973) and then further developed by Robert Gilpin (1987).

Why is the theory of hegemonic stability important? Because if it is true, we must expect international markets to be dependent on the existence of a liberal dominant power. In the absence of such a hegemon, an open world economy will be much more difficult to sustain. There is a risk that economic relations will deteriorate into nationalistic, self-interested, protectionist competition, as it did during the world economic crisis of the 1930s, when countries pursued national policies the effect of which was 'beggar your neighbor.' The United States was already the largest economic power, but America was not willing to take on the hegemonic responsibility of creating and maintaining a liberal world economic order. That willingness emerged only after World War II which put an end to American isolationism.

The war elevated the United States to a position of nearly unrivaled world leadership. A majority of American politicians recognized that the United States had to take on a responsibility for creating a liberal world market economy after the war. With Europe and Japan in ruins and Britain exhausted, there was no other post-war power to perform that global capitalist role. In short, for a liberal economic world order to come into being, the mere capability of a dominant power is not enough; there must also be a willingness to take on the task. And finally, there must be a commitment to sustain a liberal order once it has been created: to support it not only in good times when the world economy is expanding but also in bad times when it is in recession and participating states may be tempted to beggar their neighbors.

What kind of power resources are necessary for a hegemon to perform its role? The question is not an easy one to answer, because it involves the complex issue of the fungibility of power. A power resource is fungible if it can be used across several issue areas. For example, military force is not only useful on the battlefield;

it can also be used as a lever in other areas of foreign policy. The United States has employed its military power to provide security to Western Europe against the Soviet threat. That situation has given the United States influence in Europe in other areas, such as trade policies. The provision of military security thus paves the way for leverage in economic areas. In the IR debate about these issues the claim has been made that the fungibility of military power is decreasing (Nye 1990). We cannot pursue that debate here. It is sufficient to say that a dominant state needs a number of different power resources to perform the role of hegemon. In addition to military power, according to Keohane (1984: 32) it requires control over four sets of world economic resources: raw materials, capital, markets, and the hegemon's competitive advantage in the production of goods that can command a very high value.

Why is a hegemon required in order to create and maintain a liberal world economy? Might we not expect that smaller, less powerful states will also be interested in a liberal world economy because that is to the benefit of all? Why would they not cooperate to sustain such an economy? What is the use, then, for a dominant liberal power? According to the theory of hegemonic stability, the need for a hegemon has to do with the nature of the goods which it provides. A liberal world economy is a so-called public or collective good, that is, a good or a service which, once supplied, creates benefits for everybody. Public goods are charac terized by nonexcludability; others can not be denied access to them. The air that we breathe is an example of such a good. A lighthouse is another example of a public good, so is a road or a sidewalk.[1] The elements of a liberal world economy, such as a currency system for international payments, or the possibility to trade in a free market, are examples of public goods. Once created, they are there for the benefit of all.

The problem with public goods is underprovision and what the economists call 'free riding': i.e. making use of the goods without paying for them. Why should anyone sustain the cost to provide such a good in the first place if it is there to be used at no cost, once it is supplied? Existing public goods invite free riding. That is where the hegemon comes in: such a dominant power is needed to provide those goods and to deal with problems created by free riders, for example by penalizing them. Why would the hegemon do that? Because it has a huge stake in the system.

There are two major historical examples of liberal hegemons: Great Britain during the late nineteenth and the early twentieth century; and the United States after World War II. Britain was a global trading power and imperial power and, as such, had a profound interest in maintaining an open world economy based on free trade. Britain lost its position of hegemony in the early twentieth century when other powers began to rival and surpass it: particularly Germany and the

---

[1] Yet we know that some roads are closed off, unless you pay a toll; still, many roads are public goods. For further discussion on the difficulties with the distinction see, for example, Hardin (1982).

United States. After World War II, the United States took the lead in setting up new institutions of a reformed liberal world economy: the IMF, the World Bank, the General Agreement on Tariffs and Trade (the GATT, now replaced by the World Trade Organization, the WTO), and the Organization for Economic Cooperation and Development (the OECD). The system was called the Bretton Woods system, named after the small town in the US where the agreement was made in 1947.

It was clearly in the United States' own interest to restore the liberal world economy based on new institutions which it could largely control. As the world's dominant industrial power, an open world economy was of great benefit to the US because it gave America better access to foreign markets. Helping in the rebuilding of Western Europe and Japan was also important for American security reasons in its Cold War struggle with the Soviet Union. The United States was not interested in an unstable world, susceptible to Soviet influence, because that would be a threat to United States' political and economic interests. However, it can be argued that there was also an altruistic element in the American effort. The Marshall plan helped post-war reconstruction underway. The US accepted unequal treatment by her partners; Japan was allowed to maintain a limited access to its domestic market; Western Europe was allowed to continue its policies of subsidy and protectionism in agriculture.

By the late 1950s or early 1960s the economies of Western Europe and Japan had been rebuilt. The huge US economic lead was disappearing; Japan and Western Europe were catching up economically. There was a growing deficit in the American balance of payments. By the 1970s the US started running trade deficits for the first time in the post-war era. US policies became more oriented toward national interests. Instead of sustaining the post-1945 liberal world economy, the US adopted protectionist measures to support her own economy. America began to act as a 'predatory hegemon' (Jonn Conybeare, quoted from Gilpin 1987). In other words, the US became more concerned about its own national interests, began to lose sight of its role as the defender of an open world economy, and perhaps even started to exploit its power position. It was a new era characterized by 'increasing protectionism, monetary instability, and economic crisis' (Gilpin 1987: 351). With the relative decline of the United States, however, there was no longer a clearly dominant power to sustain the liberal world economy. Box 7.1 summarizes the theory of hegemonic stability using the United States as an example.

The line of reasoning summarized in the box has been subject to much debate within IPE. There are several observers that accept the general notion of the need for a hegemon to establish a liberal world economy. But they dispute the idea that US economic power has declined substantially (Strange 1987; Russett 1985; Nye 1990). They make two arguments; first, the United States remains very strong in traditional fungible power resources (military, economy, technology, territory). There has been a relative decline in the economic and technological areas, but that

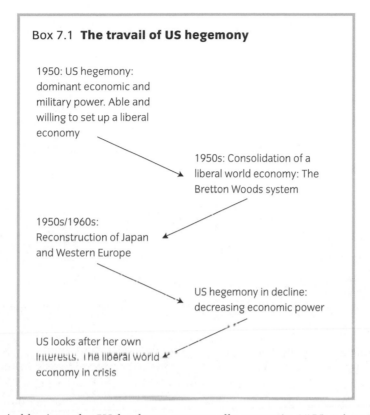

Box 7.1 **The travail of US hegemony**

1950: US hegemony: dominant economic and military power. Able and willing to set up a liberal economy

1950s: Consolidation of a liberal world economy: The Bretton Woods system

1950s/1960s: Reconstruction of Japan and Western Europe

US hegemony in decline: decreasing economic power

US looks after her own interests. The liberal world economy in crisis

was inevitable since the US lead was unnaturally strong in 1950, when Western Europe and Japan still had to rebuild. The US continues to lead the world in areas of high technology innovation and competition. Second, the ways in which the US position is calculated makes a difference. Susan Strange argues that it is misleading to focus on the territorial economy within United States borders. 'What matters is the share of world output—of primary products, minerals and food and manufactured goods and services—that is under the direction of the executives of US companies' (Strange 1987: 5). That share still puts the US in the lead because of the massive amounts of US foreign investment abroad. Furthermore, as indicated the US is especially strong in the most advanced, information-rich industries which now count more in terms of economic power than industrial capacity. And finally, the US also remains strong in non-material power resources, such as 'popular culture' with universal appeal: e.g., movies, television, Internet websites, etc. The American lifestyle is attractive to people in many countries around the world. Liberal values in line with American ideology also permeate international institutions such as the IMF and the WTO. That gives the United States a substantial amount of 'soft power' or 'co-optive power,': i.e., the ability 'to structure a situation so that other nations develop preferences or define their interests in ways consistent with one's own nation' (Nye 1990: 191).

Box 7.2 **Power resources of major countries**

SOURCE OF POWER	USA	RUSSIA	EUROPE	JAPAN	CHINA
Tangible:					
Basic resources	strong	strong	strong	*medium*	strong
Military	strong	*medium*	*medium*	*weak*	*medium*
Economic	strong	*medium*	strong	strong	*medium*
Science/technology	strong	*weak*	strong	strong	*weak*
Intangible:					
National cohesion	strong	*medium*	*weak*	strong	strong
Universalistic culture	strong	*medium*	strong	*medium*	*medium*
International institutions	strong	*medium*	strong	*medium*	*medium*

Modified from Nye (1990: 174)

If we accept these arguments, we are led to the conclusion that US hegemony is still very much in place. Why then the tendencies towards crisis in the liberal world economy? Susan Strange has claimed that the United States has made a number of 'managerial decisions of dubious wisdom that accounts quite adequately for financial and monetary disorder' (Strange 1988: 12). In other words, power is not the problem; the problem is about the United States getting her act together and assuming responsibility for the liberal world economy (for a similar line of reasoning, see Nye 1990). More recently, such criticism has also been voiced against the republican administration of George W. Bush: the US remains the world's supreme power but does not fill the role of enlightened leadership. Instead, US policy is more narrowly focused on satisfying domestic interest groups.

Another IPE debate concerns the issue of the need for a hegemon to run a liberal world economy in the first place. Robert Keohane has argued that hegemonic power helped establish international cooperation in such areas as finance, trade, and oil. When US power declined, however, cooperation did not break down, as the theory of hegemonic stability would expect. Keohane concludes that hegemonic power may have been important for the initial establishment of co-operation. But once the necessary international institutions are set up, they have a staying power of their own, they operate on their own, and they are able to promote further cooperation even in the circumstances of hegemonic decline. In other words, we should 'recognize the continuing impact of international regimes on the ability of countries with shared interests to cooperate' (Keohane 1984: 216).

Yet another objection against the theory of hegemonic stability concerns its one-sided emphasis on the leading power, the hegemon. The theory downplays the positive role of smaller powers in the establishment of a liberal world economy. Even the strongest hegemon can accomplish only so much on its own. It calls for the cooperative efforts of other states. Hegemonic stability theory tends to view smaller powers as egoistic free riders. In fact they have contributed greatly to the setting up of a liberal world economy by assisting in the establishment of liberal international regimes. Furthermore, US hegemony was always less altruistic than the theory leads us to believe. During the Cold War the United States had a vital security interest in tying Western Europe and Japan to the liberal camp. The liberal economic order set up by the US was not so much the pro- vision of a public good as it was in the best interest of the US herself (for these arguments see, for example, Gadzey 1994). Of course, that is not to deny that Western Europe was a major beneficiary of the American security guarantee during the Cold War.

Finally, the Marxist position recognizes the importance of hegemony, but con- nects it to long cycles of economic growth. For Marxists, US hegemony was a specific phase of capitalist expansion in the post-war era. This phase came to an end around 1970 because the preconditions that sustained the long upswing— especially the availability of cheap and skilled labor in Western Europe and Japan—were no longer present. Japan and Western Europe caught up eco- nomically (Wallerstein 1984; Amin 1975). US producers were thus squeezed by increasing and intensifying international competition. Robert Cox agrees that the economic decline of the US presents problems for a stable world order. But he follows the Italian Marxist Antonio Gramsci by emphasizing the ideological dimension of hegemony. A stable hegemonic order is based on a shared set of values and understandings derived 'from the ways of doing and thinking of the dominant social strata of the dominant state.' (Cox 1996: 517) In other words, US hegemony was not only based on material power but also on values: i.e. a model of society that other countries found attractive and wanted to emulate.

Marxists also point to the elements of inequality and hierarchy inherent in US hegemony. The liberal world economy under US leadership was never truly global. The Third World had a marginal position and the Soviet Bloc did not participate. Many Marxists see US hegemony as a vehicle for control over weaker states by the bourgeoisies of the US and other leading Western countries in ways that were to the economic and political benefit of the West (e.g. Frank 1980). On this view, the liberal world economy is a misnomer for economic and political control of the world by a Western capitalist elite for its own benefit.

What can we learn from these discussions about the larger debate concerning the relationship between politics and economics? First, while mercantilism is correct in pointing to the need for a political framework as a foundation for economic activity, that does not mean that there is a one-way relationship in which politics is in control of economics. The economic sphere has a dynamic of its own and unequal economic development between states reshuffles the basis for political power. There is a logic of politics and a logic of economics which influence each other, but economics is not entirely controlled by politics and vice versa. This relationship is summarized in Box 7.3.

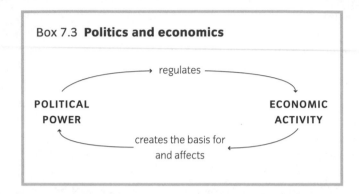

Box 7.3 **Politics and economics**

Second, the relative decline of the US has not meant a breakdown of the liberal world economy. The end of the twentieth century can hardly be described as a phase of severe international economic crisis, at least seen from the perspective of the industrialized West which has witnessed far greater crises in the past. In other words, political regulation of the world economy is possible without a highly dominant hegemon; the current regulation appears to rest on the cooperative efforts of the United States, Western Europe, and Japan. Should that cooperation break down severely, we might expect the rise of a more regionalized world. But the chances of that are not very great. Finally, the policies of a leading power may be altruistic in the sense that it accepts responsibility for international tasks which others cannot look after, but there will almost always be an important element of self-interest involved. There is a benign as well as a malign aspect of hegemony. The issue of which aspect shall dominate cannot be decided beforehand; it must depend on an analysis of each concrete case.

In conclusion, one cannot say that politics is in full control of economics, as mercantilists will have us believe; but it is true that political regulation creates the framework for economic activity. Nor can it be said that economics determines politics, as many Marxists claim; but it is true that economic dynamics affect and influence political power. The liberal claim that the market economy is an autonomous sphere of society is misleading; but it is true that once political regulation has created a market economy, that economy has a dynamic of its own. There is a complex relationship between politics and economics as shown in Box 7.4.

Liberalism, Marxism, and mercantilism have each revealed an important aspect of the political-economic relationship. They also disclose distinct shortcomings: they cannot stand alone. We need elements of each theory in order to investigate the complex relationship between politics and economics.

Box 7.4 **Politics and economics in theories of IPE**

	TRUE CLAIM	FALSE CLAIM
Mercantilism	Political regulation creates a framework for economic activity	Politics in full control of economics
Marxism	Economics affects and influences politics	Economics determines politics
Liberalism	The market has an economic dynamic of its own	The market is an autonomous sphere of society

Development and Underdevelopment in the Third World

The most important debate triggered by Marxism concerns development and underdevelopment in the Third World. The Marxist approach to IPE has concentrated on the issue of development and underdevelopment in the Third World (Asia, Africa, and Latin America). The Marxists were reacting to economic liberal ideas so it is best that we begin with the liberal view of development problems.

However, a few preliminary remarks about the development issue itself may be useful. Questions about development problems in the Third World were hardly ever asked before the 1950s. When they were asked it was in terms of colonial development, because most Third World countries were colonies controlled by European states. The development of colonies was an imperial issue but not strictly an international issue. Decolonization, beginning in the 1950s, marked the introduction of development research on a larger, international scale. 'New' states in Africa and Asia became members of the UN and raised their voices about the need to focus on development. The Cold War confrontation between East and West meant that each side was interested in cultivating closer links with the developing world to the disadvantage of the other side.

It was economic liberals who spearheaded development research in the West. Their various contributions were given the label 'modernization theory.' The basic idea was that Third World countries should be expected to follow the same developmental path taken earlier by the developed countries in the West: a progressive journey from a traditional, pre-industrial, agrarian society towards a modern, industrial, mass-consumption society. Development meant overcoming barriers of pre-industrial production, backward institutions, and parochial value systems which impeded the process of growth and modernization. Many economic liberals take note of a dualism in Third World countries, i.e. a traditional sector still rooted in the countryside and an emerging modern sector concentrated in the cities. The two sectors exist in relative isolation from each other. The only significant linkage is that the traditional sector functions as a reservoir of labor for the modern sector. This spread of development dynamics from the modern sector to the traditional sector is a core problem in getting economic development underway (Lewis 1970).

The theoretical endeavors among economic liberals, or modernization theorists as they are often called in the development debate, concern identification of the full range of impediments to modernization as well as all factors that promote modernization. Economic liberals underscore the need for an open economy, free of political interference, to help generate the large amounts of investment that is required to foster sustained economic growth and development (Lal 1983). A famous modernization theory by W. W. Rostow (1960; 1978) specifically stressed that the 'take-off,' the crucial push in moving from traditional towards modern, is characterized by a marked increase in modern sector investment, to a minimum of ten percent of the gross national product. Another critical element concerns the relationship of Third World countries to the world market. Close market relations with the developed countries is seen to have a positive developmental effect on Third World economies. Foreign trade is viewed as a road to market expansion and further growth of the modern sector. Foreign direct investment in the Third World by transnational corporations (TNCs) brings in much needed modern technology and production skills. The economic liberal theory can be summarized as shown in Box 7.5.

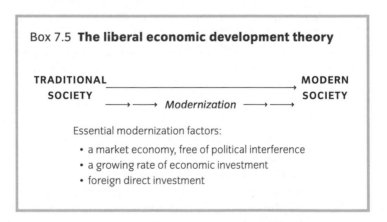

Box 7.5 **The liberal economic development theory**

TRADITIONAL ─────────────────────────→ MODERN
SOCIETY   ──→ ──→ *Modernization* ──→ ──→ SOCIETY

Essential modernization factors:
- a market economy, free of political interference
- a growing rate of economic investment
- foreign direct investment

The liberal understanding of development was subjected to increasing criticism during the 1960s and 1970s. That was partly in reaction to the lack of progress in many Third World countries at that time. While growth rates in the developed world reached unprecedented highs in the post-war decades, many Third World countries had difficulties in getting economic development underway. Their economies refused to 'take off.' That naturally led to increasing dissatisfaction with modernization theory.

The most radical critique of economic liberals came from neo-Marxist under-development theory which is also known under the name of 'dependency theory.' It draws on classical Marxist analysis. But it is different from classical Marxism in a basic respect. Unlike Marx, dependency theorists do not expect capitalist development to take root and unfold in the Third World in the same way that capitalism first took place in Western Europe and North America. And unlike Soviet Marxism, dependency theorists do not support a Soviet model with its centralized and highly authoritarian system. Instead, they argue in favor of a socialist model which is more decentralized and democratic. Their main aim, however, is not so much the formulation of alternative development models to those of capitalism or economic liberalism. Rather, it is to critique the dependency form that capitalist development is seen to take in the Third World (for general overviews, see Kay 1989; Hettne 1995). In short, dependency theory is an attack on late capitalism. It is an effort to provide the theoretical tools by which Third World countries can defend themselves against globalizing capitalism.

We saw earlier that for economic liberals 'traditional society' was the place where all countries started their process of development and modernization. Dependency theory rejects that view. The starting point for dependency theory is not tradition; it is underdevelopment. Underdevelopment is not a condition which once characterized all countries. It is a process within the framework of the global capitalist system to which Third World countries have been subjected: they have been underdeveloped as an intentional by-product of the development of the West. Underdevelopment is the process by which capitalist forces expand to sub-due and impoverish the Third World. Earlier forms of society in the Third World may have been undeveloped; but underdevelopment begins only with the arrival of global capitalism. That is, global capitalism in one single process generates development and wealth (in the industrialized world) and underdevelopment and poverty (in the Third World).

Under such adverse global conditions, how can development be brought to the Third World? Radical dependency theorists, such as Andre Gunder Frank (1969; 1977) and Samir Amin (1976; 1990) do not hesitate to argue that Third World countries have to cut off, or at least severely limit, their ties to the capitalist world market. Through reliance on their own strength, as well as mutual cooperation, real economic development becomes possible, outside the reach of capitalist world market exploitation. Moderate dependency theorists, such as Fernando Henrique Cardoso (Cardoso & Faletto 1979), are less severe in their critique of the capitalist world market. They argue that some development in the Third World is possible even given the ties of external dependence on the capitalist West. We can summarize the radical dependency view as shown in Box 7.6 (see also Evers & Wogau 1973).

Box 7.6 Dependency theory of underdevelopment

1. Underdevelopment is caused by factors external to the poor countries. Third World countries are dominated by foreign interests originating in the developed West.

2. Underdevelopment is not a phase of 'traditional society' experienced by all countries. Both development and underdevelopment are results of a single process of global capitalist development.

3. Underdevelopment is due to external, primarily economic, forces; these forces result in crippled and distorted societal structures inside Third World countries.

4. To overcome underdevelopment a delinking from external dominance is required.

Radical dependency theory came under fire during the 1970s and went into decline. A number of countries in South East Asia, most notably the 'Four Tigers' (South Korea, Taiwan, Singapore, and Hong Kong) experienced rapid economic growth combined with world market integration. That was a blow to dependency theory's prediction of stagnation and misery and seemed to support liberal modernization theory. Furthermore, dependency theory severely downplayed domestic factors in their analyses, such as the role of the state and domestic social forces. To some extent, the world systems analysis by Wallerstein set forth earlier has an answer to such critiques. Wallerstein builds on ideas from dependency theory about unequal exchange and underdevelopment in the periphery. But in his view some countries, such as the 'Four Tigers', may well move ahead; other countries will simply move in the opposite direction and overall, hierarchy and unequal exchange continues to characterize the capitalist world-economy. Furthermore, Wallerstein would protest against labelling his analysis as economistic; economics and politics affect each other in a dialectical interaction.

In any case, the 1980s saw a strong revival of economic liberal ideas in development thinking. Ronald Reagan's presidency in the US and Margaret Thatcher's administration in the UK both promoted liberal policies which emphasized the role of free market forces and the downsizing of state bureaucracies and state regulations. Third World countries were encouraged to pursue similar policies (Toye 1987).

Yet the late 1980s and early 1990s have also seen the return of ideas based on mercantilist thinking. Mercantilism has not set forth a brief and clear statement about Third World development comparable to the ones formulated by economic liberals and dependency theorists. But there is a broad and diverse mercantilist tradition in development which has gained new strength in recent years. The mercantilist view of development strikes a balance between economic liberal and dependency views. Whereas economic liberals argue in favor of world market integration in order to promote development, and dependency theorists argue for

Box 7.7 **Development or underdevelopment in Sub-Saharan Africa?**

PROGRESS	DEPRIVATION

HEALTH

• Between 1960 and 1993 life expectancy at birth increased from 40 to 51 years.	• There is only one doctor for every 18,000 people, compared with 6,000 in the developing world as a whole and 390 in the industrial countries.
• In the past decade the proportion of the population with access to safe water nearly doubled—from 25% to 43%.	• More than ten million people are infected with HIV, two-thirds of all those infected in the world.

EDUCATION

• During the past two decades adult literacy more than doubled—from 27% to 55%	• Only about half the entrants to grade 1 finish grade 5.
• Between 1960 and 1991 the net enrolment ratio at the primary level increased from 25% to 50%, and at the secondary level from 13% to 38%.	• At the primary and secondary levels more than 80 million boys and girls are still out of school.

INCOME AND POVERTY

• Over the period 1980–92 five countries—Botswana, Cape Verde, Lesotho, Mauritius and Swaziland—had an annual GDP growth rate of more than 5%.	• About 170 million people (nearly a third of the region's population) do not get enough to eat.
	• During the past three decades the ratio of military to social spending increased, from 27% in 1960 to 43% in 1991.

CHILDREN

• Over the past three decades the infant mortality rate dropped from 167 per thousand live births to 97.	• About 23 million children in the region are malnourished, and 16% of babies are underweight.

Sources: The World Bank (1997; 2000); UNDP (1996)

* Total population in Sub-Saharan Africa (1999): 642 million
* GNP per capita (1999): US$ 500

delinking, mercantilists suggest a middle road. Already in the 1950s Raul Prebisch (1950) and Gunnar Myrdal (1957) argued against free trade based on comparative advantage. The economic benefits which liberals said would accrue to the South according to the theory of comparative advantage were not forthcoming. Basically, that was owing to a secular decline in the terms of trade for the South's traditional exports.[2] In other words, those export commodities lost much of their previous value on world markets whereas industrial and increasingly high technology imports still cost the same or even more. Therefore, it was necessary to actively promote industrialization in the South, even if such industry may be comparatively high-cost in the initial phase. If liberal comparative advantage can be criticized, so can dependency ideas about delinking. Hettne (1995) goes through four cases of 'experiments with delinking' from the 1970s, namely Tanzania, Ghana, Jamaica, and Nicaragua, and finds a lack of success in every case, due to a combination of external destabilization and internal resistance to which should be added wholly unrealistic state economic plans and policies.

Modern mercantilists thus suggest a compromise between the extremes of economic autonomy and full integration into the global capitalist economy. It can be argued that the economic development success of East Asian countries and also Japan is precisely due to their pursuit of a successful mercantilist strategy (Amsden 1989; Toye 1987). A second core area of development where the mercantilists strike a balance concerns the market and the state. Economic liberals argue that free market forces and a minimal role for the state is best for the promotion of economic development. Mercantilists reply that there may be serious flaws in the alleged efficiency of the market (Weiss 1988: 177). Furthermore, there is no firm support in economic theory for maintaining that state intervention is by definition counterproductive. The fact that some interventions are flawed does not constitute a case against intervention per se (Toye 1987: Ch. 4). South Korea and Taiwan's development achievements have been based on states actively working towards building desired structures of production (Wade 1985; Ludde-Neurath 1985).

Yet mercantilists recognize that excessive state intervention can involve 'bureaucratic failures' (White 1984: 101) and they do not support the dependency view where there is no significant role at all for market forces. If too much is left to market forces, there is the danger of market failure: for example, monopolies may be created in some areas so that there is no competition among producers anymore; or there may be negative side-effects due to unregulated production, such as pollution. Yet if too much is left to state regulation, the result may be bureaucratic failures, that is 'red tape' problems of high cost and inefficiency. The actual balance between state and market will vary across societies and within the same society over time (White 1984). The recent years of prolonged economic crisis in Japan is an indication that after many years of successful growth the

---

[2] 'Terms of trade' is the ratio of export and import prices. When Third World countries get less for their raw material exports and have to pay more for import of industrialized goods, their terms of trade deteriorate.

political and bureaucratic establishment is unable or unwilling—because there are vested political and economic interests in the current system—to devise new strategies for viable economic development.

Another example of the mercantilist middle road in development thinking concerns the role of transnational corporations (TNCs). Economic liberals often see TNCs as 'engines of growth,' bringing progress and prosperity to the South; dependency theory, in contrast, frequently see TNCs as 'the devil incorporated' (Streeten 1979). Mercantilists note that TNCs have the potential for benefiting Third World development, but only under certain conditions. In weak states with undeveloped local economies, TNCs will totally dominate the host country and that is not helpful for the strengthening of local industry; the TNCs will be local monopolists. In stronger states with some local industry, TNC investment can assist in upgrading local undertakings technologically and otherwise, and thus significantly assist in developing the host economy (Sørensen 1983; Nixson 1988). In other words, TNCs will not bring economic development to the South on their own; there has to be a counterweight in the form of local industry and a host government strong enough to oversee TNC activity. We can summarize the modern mercantilist view of development as shown in Box 7.8.

Box 7.8 **Modern mercantilism**

1. Strike a balance between national autonomy and international integration, i.e. between incorporation into the world market and self reliance.

2. Strike a balance between state and market, i.e. between free market forces and state regulation.

3. Foreign direct investment by TNCs can be a strong modernization factor, but only pro- vided that TNCs are counterbalanced by local industry and host government supervision.

Modern mercantilism in many ways appears to offer a sensible strategy for economic development. Yet it is not without weaknesses. To follow the path advocated by modern mercantilists, the states of the South need a fairly high political-administrative capacity; otherwise they will not be able to undertake sophisticated state interventions and regulations of the economy. Even if there are a number of states with such developmental strength in East Asia and elsewhere, it is clear that the majority of states in the South are not very strong (Sørensen 1993b; Evans 1989). For example, in Sub-Saharan Africa corrupt and self-interested state elites are part of the development problem rather than part of the solution. Under such circumstances, there is little hope of success for the modern mercantilist strategy. Indeed, mercantilist policies might even lead to greater problems by creating conditions in which corruption can flourish.

It ought to be clear from this brief introduction that the problems concerning development and underdevelopment in the Third World continue to provoke debate among scholars who hold different theoretical positions. The popularity of the main positions has waxed and waned yet the development problem remains in place; some 800 million people do not get enough food, and about 500 million are chronically malnourished (UNDP 1996: 20). Economic liberals are right in claiming that a free market economy can be a powerful force promoting growth and modernization; but it is not true that an unregulated market will more or less automatically lead to optimum development for individuals and states in the long run. Dependency theorists have a point when they emphasize how relations of dependence shape and impact development in the Third World. But they are wrong in claiming that integration in the world market must lead to under-development and that developed, Western countries are no more than imperialist exploiters. Modern mercantilism appears to strike a sensible middle road between state and market, between autonomy and integration. But mercantilists tend to rely too much on prudent maneuvering by Third World states many of which are quite weak and are led by self-serving and often highly corrupt elites.

In sum and not surprisingly, each of the main theoretical positions has insights concerning the development problem; and each has blind spots, as shown in Box 7.9.

In recent years the debate on development has grown more complex. It almost had to happen, for two reasons. First, the major theories discussed above claim relevance for development problems everywhere, that is, they are general theories. But there are specific problems in many regions and countries, due to particular historical experiences and variation in local conditions. Africa south of Sahara, South Asia, East Asia, Latin America, and Eastern Europe are examples of regions with very dissimilar historical trajectories of development and very different local conditions. And even within these regions there is great variation. Current development thinking (for overviews see Martinussen 1997 and Nederveen Pieterse 2000) is much more aware of such differences. Consequently, development thinking is becoming increasingly complex: issues and recommenda-tions cannot always travel from one region, or even from a sub-region, to other places.

Second, the whole debate about development has been opened up in the sense that many different voices participate: grassroot organizations, NGOs, peasant movements, political parties, governments, international institutions, the develop-ment research community, and so on. These participants make up different stake-holders in the process of development. Therefore, they often have different views about what the important issues are and what should be done about them.

One result of this increased complexity is a renewed debate about the concept of development itself. We saw earlier how liberal thinking conceived of development in terms of acquiring the characteristics of modern, capitalist countries: when less developed countries get economic growth and modernization, they develop. That

Box 7.9 **The development problem in theories of IPE**

	TRUE CLAIM	FALSE CLAIM
Liberalism	A free market economy promotes growth and development	An unregulated market will lead to the best result for individuals and states
Dependency theory	Dependence shapes Third World development	Integration in the world market must lead to underdevelopment
Modern mercantilism	Development benefits from a sensible mix of state and market, autonomy and integration	Governments are always able to regulate the economy in an optimum fashion

view was promoted in the UN system in the 1950s and 1960s, because there was a need to identify those countries that were eligible for development aid. That group was simply defined in terms of not having achieved much in terms of economic growth per capita.

Dependency theory and mercantilist theory never disputed this liberal concept of development. Where they differ is in the strategies for achieving these results. So there is a mainstream concept of development that focuses on growth and modernization. In recent years this mainstream concept has become somewhat more nuanced. Development is not merely growth—it is distribution and welfare; and development is not merely satisfaction of material needs—it is also democracy, participation, freedom, and self-realization. But the core of the concept remains in place: modernization and growth.

There was always a critique of this mainstream concept of development. In recent years it has grown stronger. The critics are not a unified group. Some are directly anti-development; they reject the whole idea of development as progress. In this view, living conditions should be decided by local, autonomous communities steering their own course (cf. Sachs 1992). Many other critics favour some form of alternative development (Hettne 1995). Their visions vary, but there are also some common traits: a sceptical view of modernity and industrialization; a favourable attitude towards traditional values and practices in pre-industrial society; anti-materialism; and an embrace of ultra-democratic values involving a high degree of popular participation and control.

Liberal modernization theory is ready to accept that modernity is somewhat more complex than 'emulating the West'; therefore modernization is a much less uniform transformation than originally believed. It can move in different directions. There may also be aspects of 'tradition' worth preserving in a process of development. In the 1980s the World Bank and the IMF were convinced that 'more market and less state' was the appropriate road to development; today these institutions are less neoliberal. They accept a significant role for the state and they also emphasize the need for democratic accountability and the involvement of civil society in development.

Other international institutions, such as the UNDP, emphasize the need for a broad process of human development, making ordinary people better off, in contrast to a mere quest for economic growth. The construction of a Human Development Index (based on measures of life expectancy at birth; adult literacy rate; years of schooling; and real GDP per capita) has drawn attention to other aspects of the development process. The UNDP annual Human Development Report examines female–male gaps, child nutrition, health profiles, rural–urban gaps, and North–South gaps (UNDP 2002).

Critics continue to question the mainstream view of development. A new critique has been provided by discourse analysis (Escobar 1995). The mainstream view is seen as a dominant discourse which defines 'the truth' about development in a certain way and thereby also becomes an instrument of power because it defines what is common sense about development and thereby excludes alternative interpretations. Discourse analysis wants to unmask the dominant 'common sense' in order to make way for alternative ways of thinking about development.

These remarks are meant to indicate that we have only touched the tip of the iceberg of the large and complex development issue; development has to do with much more than IPE. It also involves all the different disciplines that deal with human and social affairs. The three main theoretical positions discussed above will nevertheless continue to influence our thinking about development problems.

. . . .

Economic Globalization and a Changing Role for States

Economic liberals have sparked a number of debates on various issues. We have chosen to concentrate on the issue of change in the context of economic globalization. The phenomenon of globalization has received a great deal of attention from IPE. Globalization is the spread and intensification of economic, social, and cultural relations across international borders. This means that globalization is almost everything; it can have to do with economics, politics, technology, communication, etc. Such a concept of globalization is very difficult to theorize; in social science one cannot have a theory about 'everything', because different aspects of reality have to be analyzed in different ways. So in order to move on, it is helpful to 'unpack' the concept, that is, to look at different major aspects of globalization. Because this is a chapter on IPE, we shall concentrate on the economic aspect of globalization, but it should be remembered that this is only one, albeit very important, aspect of globalization. It is related to interdependence, which was discussed in Chapter 4.

A growing level of economic interconnection between two national economies, for example in the form of more external trade or foreign investment, is one aspect of economic globalization. We might call it 'intensified interdependence'. But there is an additional aspect which signifies a shift towards a truly global economic system. Intensified economic interdependence involves more of the same in the sense that economic intercourse between national economies increases. True economic globalization, however, involves a qualitative shift towards a world economy that is no longer based on autonomous national economies; rather, it is based on a consolidated global marketplace for production, distribution, and consumption. In this latter case, the single global economy 'dominates' the numerous national economies contained within it (Hirst and Thompson 1992: 199). Some scholars call this process 'deep integration' in contrast to intensified interdependence which can be seen as 'shallow integration'. Deep integration is first and foremost organized by TNCs. They increasingly organize the production of goods and services on a global scale. The various segments of production, from development and design, over manufacture and assembly, are each placed in locations that offer the best conditions for that particular segment in terms of labour cost, input availability, proximity of markets, etc. At the same time, TNC set up networks with local firms that act as suppliers and subcontractors.

Box 7.10 Two aspects of economic globalization

	'More of the same'	***INDICATOR:* GLOBAL EXPORTS** (as % of GDP)	
		1990:	1999:
Economic globalization		19%	27%
	'Qualitative shift'	***INDICATOR:* INTRAFIRM TRADE** (as % of total US trade, 1994)	
		Exports:	Imports:
		36.3%	42.7%

Source: UNDP (2001)

Globalization is pushed by several factors; the most important is technological change which is driven by relentless economic competition between firms. The measures taken by states (e.g. trade and finance liberalization) are also important catalysts. The three main theoretical approaches to IPE are in agreement that economic globalization is taking place. But they disagree about the actual content of the process (shallow or deep integration); they also disagree about the consequences of economic globalization for states. Many economic liberals have an optimistic view of economic globalization. One example is the famous American economist Milton Friedman who celebrates the fact that it is now 'possible to produce a product anywhere, using resources from anywhere, by a company located anywhere, to be sold anywhere' (Friedman 1993). That is because states no longer interfere with production and consumption the way they used to. According to John Naisbitt (1994), such a world offers tremendous economic opportunities: the possibilities for economic advance are 'far greater than at any time in human history' not only for companies and institutions but also for individuals and families (1994: 59). A number of economic liberals share this optimistic view (e.g. Reich 1992; Ohmae 1993).

Globalization also means that the component parts of the world become smaller and far more numerous. Small is beautiful not only in the economic sphere but also in the political sphere. This process has profound consequences for the state. In a unified global economy, small, flexible economic players can grow increasingly powerful as national economies become obsolete. As globalization progresses, says Naisbitt, people become more and more conscious of their 'tribal' identities (e.g., language and culture), and that is driving the formation of an increasing number of smaller countries. Naisbitt foresees a thousand—maybe even two thousand—countries by sometime in the twenty-first century. That would entail the decline and fall of the nation state as we have known it for the past several centuries.

The idea that the Westphalian nation state is becoming too small for some things and too big for other things in an era of globalization resonates with many economic liberals (e.g. Zacher 1992). They argue that the nation state is pressured 'from above' in the sense that globalization creates cross-border activities which states are no longer able to control on their own—such as global economic transactions and environmental problems. And the nation state is also pressured 'from below': there is a trend towards ever stronger identification with the local community where people live their daily lives. The economic liberal view of economic globalization and its consequences can be summarized as shown in Box 7.11.

Box 7.11 Economic liberals' view of globalization

1. Economic globalization means a qualitative shift towards a global economic system

2. Economic globalization will bring increased prosperity to individuals, families, and companies

3. The nation state loses power and influence as it is pressed from above and from below

Mercantilists have not formulated a view of globalization that can rival the economic liberal analysis in scope and ambition. But there is what could be termed a mercantilist position in the globalization debate. That position is highly critical of the economic liberal analysis, both as regards the content of economic globalization and as regards the supposed consequences for the nation state. Mercantilists remain unconvinced that a qualitative shift towards a global economic system has taken place. In other words they do not believe there is a phenomenon called 'globalization'. Instead, they see economic globalization as 'more of the same', that is, a process of intensified interdependence between national economies. Furthermore, they argue that trade and investment flows between countries were at a very high level before World War I. In other words, there is little news in the fact of economic interdependence (Thompson and Krasner 1989). Mercantilists also reject the claim made by many economic liberals (see Reich 1992: 301–17) that corporations have lost their national identity in pursuit of their ambition to become truly global economic players. Instead, mercantilists argue, states and their national corporations remain 'closely linked' in spite of the noteworthy increase in world trade and investment flows since the end of World War II (Kapstein 1993: 502).

Box 7.12 **Selected top 100 TNCs, ranked by transnationality index,[1] 1995**

CORPORATION	ECONOMY	INDUSTRY	TRANSNATIONALITY INDEX
Nestlé SA	Switzerland	Food	94.0
Electrolux AB	Sweden	Electronics	88.3
Shell, Royal Dutch	United Kingdom/ Netherlands	Oil, gas, coal and related services	73.0
Bayer AG	Germany	Chemicals	69.3
Sony Corporation	Japan	Electronics	59.1
IBM	United States	Computers	54.9
Honda Motor Co., Ltd.	Japan	Automotive	52.6
Transnationalization index, top 100 world TNCs			**51.0**
Daewoo Corporation	Korea (Rep.)	Diversified	47.7
GTE Corporation	United States	Telecommunication	14.9

[1] The 'transnationality index' is calculated from the average ratios of foreign assets to total assets, foreign sales to total sales, and foreign employment to total employment

Based on United Nations (1997b)

Mercantilists thus reject the idea that nation states are being pressured and are somehow losing out in the process of economic globalization. They say liberals fail to take into account the increased capacity of nation states to respond to the challenges of economic globalization. The technological developments that foster globalization have also helped increase the state's capacity for regulation and surveillance. States are stronger than ever in their capacity to extract economic surplus, such as taxes from their citizens. Their ability to control and regulate all kinds of activities in society has also increased dramatically. The long-term trend is towards more, not less state autonomy. 'Economic development has made it generally easier for states to finance their activities . . . from internal sources rather than international borrowing' (Krasner 1993: 314). And lastly, the sovereign state remains the preferred form of political organization around the world. No serious competitor has emerged. We can summarize the realist-mercantilist view of economic globalization as shown in Box 7.13.

Box 7.13 **The realist-mercantilist view of globalization**

1. Economic globalization is 'more of the same', i.e. intensified economic interdependence; nothing much new in that

2. Corporations do not lose their national identities because they are global payers. They remain tied to their home countries

3. The nation state is not threatened by globalization. The state's capacity for regulation and surveillance has increased rather than decreased

---

The neo-Marxist view of economic globalization differs from that of both economic liberalism and mercantilism. We shall concentrate on the neo-Marxist contribution of Robert Cox which contains both aspects introduced above; economic globalization involves both intensified interdependence and a qualitative shift towards a global economy. According to Cox, there is a new global economy that exists alongside that classical capitalist world economy, but the tendency is that the former 'incrementally supersedes' the latter (Cox 1994: 48). Cox finds that in the process of economic globalization nation states have lost substantial power over the economy. However, the continued process of economic globalization requires the political framework provided by nation states; in particular, it requires 'the military-territorial power of an enforcer' (Cox 1994: 54). The United States has assumed that role. But America is beset by a contradiction between decreasing economic strength and increasing projection of military power on a world scale. Being the world's 'policeman' requires a strong economic base but that is diminishing under the pressures of economic globalization. The macro-regions (headed by the USA in America, by Japan in East Asia, and by the European Union in Europe) are the new political-economic frameworks of capital accumulation. Yet the macro-regions continue to be part of the larger, global economic system, as the global effects of the 1998 economic crisis in Asia amply demonstrated.

Robert Cox and other neo-Marxists thus stress the uneven, hierarchical nature of economic globalization. The global economy is characterized by dependence rather than interdependence. Economic power is increasingly concentrated in the leading industrialized countries, including the United States, Japan, and the states of Western Europe. That means that economic globalization will not benefit the impoverished masses of the Third World. Nor will it improve the living standards of the poor in the highly industrialized countries. For that situation to change, social forces from below, such as workers and students, will have to be successful in their struggle to reclaim political control over the economic forces of globalization (Cox 1994). In short, globalization is a form of capitalism, and as such it perpetuates capitalist class domination and the exploitation of poor people around the world. We can summarize the neo-Marxist view of economic globalization as set forth by Robert Cox as shown in Box 7.14.

Box 7.14 **The neo-Marxist view of globalization**

1. Economic globalization is both 'intensified interdependence' and the creation of a global economy

2. Nation states remain important regulators of globalization, but they are losing power over the economy. In response, they form macro-regions

3. Economic globalization is an uneven, hierarchical process, where economic power is increasingly concentrated in leading industrialized countries

---

The debate on economic globalization is not easily settled because each of the three theoretical positions outlined above can point to some empirical evidence which supports their views. It is true, as economic liberals claim, that globalization has the potential of bringing increased prosperity to individuals and companies; but it is also true, as emphasized by neo-Marxists, that current processes of globalization are uneven and may have little to offer large groups of underprivileged people. Economic liberals are perhaps right in claiming that globalization is a challenge to the nation state; but it is equally true, as stressed by mercantilists, that states remain strong players and that they have proven themselves able to adapt to many new challenges. Neo-Marxists correctly emphasize that 'intensified interdependence' and the creation of a global economy are simultaneously present. On that issue, however, economic liberals and mercantilists are too one-sided—they emphasize either one or the other aspect of globalization. In sum,

Box 7.15 **Economic globalization and theories of IPE**

	TRUE CLAIM	FALSE CLAIM
Economic liberalism	Economic globalization has the potential of bringing increased prosperity to all. Economic globalization challenges the state	Economic globalization benefits everybody. Economic globalization spells the demise of the state
Realist mercantilists	States adapt to challenges of economic globalization. States remain strong players	States are in full control of economic globalization. Economic globalization is merely more interdependence
Neo-Marxism	Economic globalization is an uneven, hierarchical process	Economic globalization benefits only a tiny minority

we can, again, find useful insights in each of the theoretical positions, but also weak components in each (see Box 7.15).

There is no doubt about the existence of sharp inequalities in today's world. At the turn of the twenty-first century, the richest 20 per cent of the world's population had:

- 86% of world GDP—the bottom fifth had 1%.

- 82% of world export markets—the bottom fifth had 1%.

- 68% of foreign direct investment—the bottom fifth had 1%.

- 74% of world telephone lines—the bottom fifth had 1½%.

- 93.3% of all Internet users—the bottom fifth had 0.2% (UNDP 1999:3).

It is important to understand that the poorest countries—and people—are in difficulty not because of economic surplus being taken from them by the rich. Rather it is because they are marginalized participants in the process of economic globalization. Their markets are not attractive to foreign investors because people's purchasing power is low; political institutions are inefficient and corrupt so there is a lack of stability and political order. Less than two per cent of total FDI goes to Sub-Saharan Africa.

There is a clear relationship between measures of inequality and progress in terms of industrialization. When industrialization began in earnest in Western Europe in the nineteenth century, the gap between the richest and the poorest fifth in the world was not very large; it stood at 3 to 1 in 1820. Today, the gap is much more dramatic:

1820	3 to 1
1870	7 to 1
1913	11 to 1
1960	30 to 1
1990	60 to 1
1997	74 to 1 (UNDP 1999:3).

Ironically, the poorest countries are not excluded from the global economic system. They are integrated in the sense that much of what they produce is agricultural goods or raw materials for export. As much as 30 per cent of Sub-Saharan Africa's GDP goes to export. But demand for what they have to offer has been stagnant; so have prices. And upgrading to more advanced products has proved difficult because of domestic political and economic conditions. At the same time, restricted access to global markets for Africa's agricultural products has added to the problem.

Inequality exists not merely between rich and poor at the global level. It tends to be growing between groups within the OECD countries themselves. Groups in these countries with less or no education above basic schooling and groups in agriculture and traditional industrial sectors tend to lose out in the process of economic globalization. The better educated in the advanced sectors of the economy stand to win. The OECD countries have seen big increases in inequality since the 1980s. This is especially true for the United States, the United Kingdom, and Sweden.

Against this background, the process of economic globalization has led to the formation of new social movements in many parts of the world. Manuel Castells has analyzed what he calls 'resistance identity', 'generated by those actors that are in positions/conditions devalued and/or stigmatized by the logic of domination' (Castells 1998: 8). It includes a large number of different movements, based on religious fundamentalism, nationalism, ethnic identity, and territorial identity (urban movements and local communities). His case studies include the Zapatistas in Mexico; the American militia; and the Japanese cult *Aum Shinrikyo*.

Economic globalization has also led to the formation of transnational resistance movements. The best know is probably the ATTAC (Association for the Taxation of Financial Transactions for the Aid of Citizens). The movement has set forth four core demands aimed at countering the inequalities of globalization: (a) taxation of cross-border currency speculation; (b) writing off the international debt of poor countries; (c) outlawing tax havens; and (d) more democratic control of large pension funds.

The growth of such movements demonstrate that economic globalization is much more than anonymous transactions across borders: it involves political struggle about the extent to which economic transfers should be put under political control and how the benefits from globalization should be distributed among countries and groups of people. This struggle also involves taking a stance in the debate between the three classical approaches to IPE discussed above. Note, for example, how there are elements of all three in the ATTAC movement: (a) a liberal element: there are potential benefits from globalization that all countries can get to share; (b) a mercantilist element: countries have the right to protect themselves against the negative consequences of globalization; (c) a Marxist element: there is hierarchy and exploitation involved in globalization and measures need to be taken to distribute the benefits in a more just and even manner. An important part of the globalization struggle concerns the extent to which the process of globalization should take place in a primarily liberal, a primarily mercantilist, or a primarily Marxist framework.

The debate on economic globalization obviously will be highly influenced by the course of future events and developments. Will the world become more regionalized? How will the benefits of globalization be distributed between countries and other groups or classes of people? What level of regulatory control will nation states have over the process? We have to wait for more history to occur before we can answer such questions. But it is important to pose them. And that is what IPE theorists who study globalization are contributing to our understanding of world politics.

. . . .

Recent Theoretical Developments in IPE

This previous chapter presented the three classical theories of IPE: mercantilism, economic liberalism, and Marxism. They are theories in the very broad sense of sets of assumptions and values from which the field of IPE can be interrogated. They are also macro-theories, with specific views of the relationship between politics and economics and the major institutions connected with politics and economics, namely states and markets.

Economic liberalism appears to be the approach with most success in practice. So-called 'free market' economies have been highly successful; state-led economies have not. This has certainly helped increase the confidence of economic liberals in the validity of their views. Over the last few decades, the theoretical views (often called 'neoclassical economics') of professional economists have dominated, not merely in the study of economic matters, but also in the general field of IPE and indeed also in other areas of political and social science.

The reason for this is not so much the content of ecomic macro-theory of liberalism which we have discussed above. It has to do with the micro-theory supported by economists. Neoclassical economics present a simple model of individuals and their basic behavior. That model—called rational choice theory—is relevant, so the economists claim, not merely for economics, but for every other sphere of human behavior. Many scholars believe that it is a valid claim. It is appropriate, therefore, to briefly discuss rational choice theory here.

As indicated, rational choice begins with individuals. Whatever happens in the social world, including in international relations, can be explained by individual choices. What a state or any other organization does can be explained by choices made by individuals as well. This view is called methodological individualism. Furthermore, individual actors are rational and self-interested. They want to make themselves better off. This is true for everybody; not merely for sellers and buyers in economic markets, but also for bureaucrats and politicians. Finally, when individuals act in a rational and self-interested way, the overall result or outcome for states or systems will be the best possible. Just as 'the invisible hand' in liberal economics leads from individual greed to the best possible economic result for all, so the individual actions by bureaucrats and politicians lead to the best possible outcome. So if we want to understand what governments do, our first priority must be to understand the preferences, that is the goals, of public officials. They will be looking for private benefits: re-election, promotion, prestige, and so on. Once we understand how these preferences condition their behaviour, we are in a position to understand how state policies are affected. That is a basic claim of rational choice theory (Nunn 1996).

Neoclassical economists have gone one step further in their claim for the relevance of their analytical tools. Not merely their view of individual behavior—the rational choice theory sketched above—but also a number of other key concepts from economic theory, such as marginal utility, optimization, and equilibrium are relevant for a more general study of human affairs including international relations. Amongst other things, this leads in the direction of using game theory and theories of strategic interaction as analytical frameworks (Carlson 2002).

Methodological individualism has been used in other ways as well. New institutional theory—which also goes under the name of 'New Economics of Organization' starts with the rational and self-interested individual actor. But in contrast to neoclassical economic analysis, institutions are not neglected. They play an independent role for outcomes and so they should, according to new institutional theory, be made a centerpiece of analysis (Spruyt 2002). New institutionalism is the analysis of how institutions affect individual behavior and policy outcomes. An electoral system is an example of an institution; different electoral systems lead to different behaviour of parties and candidates (Lijphart 1994). In IPE, a major research area for this type of analysis is how international institutions affect cooperation and conflict between states (see Chapter 4). Another research area concerns the processes which lead to the creation and preservation of international institutions; that points towards the debate about hegemony and hegemonic stability introduced earlier in this chapter.

Neo-Marxist and other critical theories have reacted against the entry of methods and theories from neoclassical economics into IPE. They especially argue against the basic idea that individuals are always rational and self-seeking and that they always know what they want, namely to be better off. Rational cost–benefit analysis has limitations in explaining much individual behaviour. Given the cost of going to the polls why would anyone vote when there are no visible benefits (one single vote cannot really affect the outcome of the election)? Why would anyone engage in the altruistic behaviour of helping others in need when there are no tangible benefits for oneself? Furthermore, individuals don't always know beforehand what they really want. Their preferences—what they want—are created in a process of interaction with others. Consequently, what happens in human affairs including IPE is decided in a much more open-ended and not so precisely predictable process of human interaction (Palan 2002). This view creates its own challenge for the critics, namely how to combine such analysis with other critical insights about the larger development prospects of capitalism and the role of class conflict.

In sum, much recent theorizing in IPE has been inspired by neoclassical economics and its methodological individualism. It is quite clear that neoclassical economics has an important role to play in IPE. Furthermore, the focus on individuals and their behaviour has helped other theories think about how they themselves look at individuals; in other words, methodological individualism helps sharpen the micro-theoretical foundations for theorizing in IPE.

At the same time, the neoclassical view does not really consider the larger socio-political setting within which individual behaviour plays out. It is exactly this larger setting which is the subject of the classical macro-theories of IPE discussed earlier, mercantilism, liberalism, and Marxism. While neoclassical micro-theory might yield important insights, it cannot replace the classical macro-theories (for a similar view, see Gilpin 2001). We need the classical theories in order to understand the complex interplay between economics and politics.

Conclusion: The Future of IPE

The issues of wealth and poverty raised by IPE are of increasing importance in world politics. The traditional focus of IR is on war and peace. But the danger of war between states, particularly great power war, appears to be in decline for reasons discussed elsewhere in this book. Violent conflict nowadays takes place mainly inside states, especially inside weak states. And that violence is bound up with problems of development and underdevelopment, one of the core issues in IPE. In other words, even when we look at the traditional core issue of IR, that of armed conflict between states, IPE is of increasing importance. IPE also addresses the issue of sovereign statehood: the national economy is a crucially important resource base for the nation state. When national economies are being integrated into a global economy in the course of economic globalization, the basis of modern statehood might be expected to change in significant ways. As indicated above, that raises new problems concerning the relationship of states and markets and the ability of states to control and regulate the process of economic globalization. IPE opens up several new research agendas, some of which move away from IR as traditionally understood. Such themes as 'international business,' 'micro and macro economics,' 'economic geography,' 'international finance and banking,' and 'economic history' are all part of IPE. Such research paths are a good reminder that IR involves a host of other issues studied by additional subdisciplines of the vast area of social science.

We have only been able to introduce the main theoretical approaches in IPE and to sketch the research agenda of a very large research territory. What we call 'economic liberalism' is a discipline in its own right, comprising the study of micro and macro economics. Marxism is a vast theoretical edifice, rather like a medieval castle, with many different ramparts, quarters, and schools. We have only been able to introduce a few of them. The literature on hegemonic stability, development and underdevelopment in the Third World, and economic globalization has grown to immense proportions with a large number of different contributions. However, we do believe that we have singled out the most important theories and the most important debates. We have also argued in favor of drawing on elements of all three classical theories of IPE. No single theory can stand alone; it needs to be combined with insights from the others. Only in that way can we expect to develop a comprehensive and well-founded IPE.

KEY POINTS

- The most important debate inspired by mercantilism concerns the need for a strong state to create a smoothly functioning liberal international economy; that is the debate on hegemonic stability. The most important debate triggered by Marxism concerns development and underdevelopment in the Third World. Finally, economic liberals have sparked a number of debates on various issues; one significant controversy is the issue of economic globalization.

- The issues of wealth and poverty raised by IPE are of increasing importance in world politics. The traditional focus of IR is on war and peace; but the danger of war between states appears to be in decline. Violent conflict nowadays takes place mainly inside states, especially inside weak states. And that violence is intimately bound up with problems of development and underdevelopment, one of the core issues in IPE. In other words, even when we look the traditional core issue or IR, that of armed conflict, problems addressed by IPE are of increasing importance.

- IPE also raises the problems of development and change of sovereign statehood in a very direct manner. The national economy is a crucially important resource basis for the nation state. When national economies are in a process of being integrated into a global economy in the context of economic globalization, the whole basis for modern statehood changes in a critical way.

- The theoretical views of professional economists have recently dominated IPE. Neoclassical economics present a simple model of individuals and their basic behaviour. That model—called rational choice theory—is relevant, so the economist's claim, for all spheres of human behaviour. Neo-Marxist and other critical theories argue against the idea that individuals are always rational and self-seeking. And rational choice theory fails to sufficiently consider the larger context within which individual behaviour plays out. The critics thus claim that the classical theories of IPE are still very much needed.

. . . .

QUESTIONS

- Should we support the claim that a hegemon is needed in order to create a liberal world economy?

- Is the United States currently an altruistic or a 'predatory' hegemon?

- What is 'soft power' and which countries have it?

- Define the development problem in the Third World and discuss how it should be analyzed; which theory is most helpful?

- Can the development problem be solved?

- What is economic globalization? What are the benefits and drawbacks of economic globalization? What are the implications for sovereign statehood?

- Think of one or two research projects based on IPE theory.

. . . .

For additional material and resources see the companion web site at:
www.oup.co.uk/best.textbooks/politics/jacksonsorensen2e/

GUIDE TO FURTHER READING

Martinussen, J. (1997). *State, Society and Market: A Guide to Competing Theories of Development*. New York: St. Martin's.

Nye, Joseph S. Jr. (1990). *Bound to Lead. The Changing Nature of American Power*. New York: Basic Books.

Palan, R. (ed.) (2002). *Global Political Economy. Contemporary Theories*. London: Routledge.

Rodrik, D. (1997). *Has Globalization Gone Too Far?* Washington D.C.: Institute for International Economics.

Scholte, J. A. (2000). *Globalization—a critical introduction*. London: Macmillan.

Stubbs, R. and **Underhill, G. R. D.** (1999). *Political Economy and the Changing Global Order*. Oxford: Oxford University Press.

Weiss, L. (1998). *The Myth of the Powerless State*. New York: Cornell University Press.

WEB LINKS

http://www.afsc.org/nero/pesp/ushegem.htm
Joseph Gerson explores 'The Age of U.S. Hegemony'. Hosted by American Friends Service Committee.

http://w3.acdi-cida.gc.ca/virtual.nsf
'The Virtual Library of International Development' is a Collection of links to international development resources. Hosted by the Canadian Development Agencies.

http://www.undp.org/
'UNDP is the UN's global development network, advocating for change and connecting countries to knowledge, experience and resources to help people build a better life. We are on the ground in 166 countries, working with them on their own solutions to global and national development challenges'. The home page of the UNDP.

http://www.emory.edu/SOC/globalization/
Information about Globalization Theory as well as links to related web resources.

8 Methodological Debates: Classical Versus Positivist Approaches

SUMMARY

Some of the most important IR questions are methodological in nature. Self-consciousness about concepts and terminology was first emphasized in the 1950s and 1960s by the behavioral movement in political science. IR scholars, particularly American scholars, began to apply social scientific or 'positivist' methods to international relations. That prompted a reaction on the part of defenders of traditional or 'classical' approaches which emphasized history, philosophy, and law. Several other social science-inspired methodologies were later adopted, such as structural analysis. Methodological issues involved in the study of foreign policy also captured the attention of IR scholars. Positivist methodologies, in turn, provoked several post-positivist approaches including critical theory, post-modernism, constructivism, and normative theory. These latter approaches are discussed in the next chapter.

Methodological debates

In most academic disciplines, including IR, there are two fundamental kinds of controversies. One kind involves debates over substantive issues: i.e. questions of fact. Examples of substantive questions include the following: What were the leading causes of World War I? Does democracy foster peace? Does globalization hinder or help Third World development? The other kind of academic controversy involves debates over methodological issues: i.e. conceptual and philosophical questions that are involved in the way that we carry out our research. Examples of methodological issues include the following: Can IR be studied using objective scientific methods? How plausible are the main assumptions concerning the nature of political reality upon which neorealism is based? Should we accept the realist view of human nature as basically competitive or the liberal view of human nature as basically cooperative? It is also important to notice that substantive questions—including those noted above—also embody conceptual issues: What is 'war'? What are 'causes'? What constitutes 'democracy' or 'peace'? What do we mean by 'globalization' or 'development'? So methodological issues are lurking in almost everything that IR scholars study.

Methodological controversies are an indication that IR has become more of an academic discipline. Such issues became prominent in IR in the second half of the twentieth century during which time IR became well-established in most universities. In the first half of the century IR was still a subject more than a discipline to which non-academic commentators contributed as much or more than academics. The idealist liberalism of the 1920s involved many leading writers who were not academics or were not based in university departments (see Chapter 2). Many of these commentators were politically active—i.e. they were engaged in making and publishing their arguments about problems of war and peace, freedom and progress, and the like, in the (somewhat naïve) hope that they would be acted upon by political leaders and other foreign policy-makers. They were writing and publishing on those problems in an effort to help bring about a better world. They were not writing about them in order to better understand the world. They thought they already understood it perfectly well. The realist reaction to liberal idealism was not basically concerned about methodology either. The realists were preoccupied with correcting what they believed were the fundamental errors and dangers of the idealists and their ideas. The first great debate in IR between the liberal idealists and the realists was about substantive questions of war and peace.

Methodological issues became prominent in connection with the 'behavioral revolution' in American political science which occurred in the 1950s and 1960s. As indicated in Chapter 2, the second great debate between the behavioralists and the traditionalists concerned methodological issues. The behavioralists wanted to place IR on a foundation of 'scientific' analysis. Their arguments were particularly influential in the United States where by far the largest number of IR scholars live. The traditionalists became a minority. During most of the Cold War the methodology associated with neorealism prevailed in IR. The new attitude to methodology later came to be known as 'positivism'—i.e. the belief that IR scholarship is an objective inquiry that is concerned with uncovering verifiable facts or regularities of world politics and is based on valid scientific research techniques. Positivist methodology was not controversial for most IR scholars at that time.

Since the end of the Cold War, however, methodological issues have returned to centre stage in a debate between positivist and post-positivist methodologies. The IR theory most strongly attacked by post-positivists is the neorealism of Kenneth Waltz, in part because of its perceived dominance in the discipline, and in part because of its perceived methodological weaknesses. Post-positivists find that those weaknesses are closely related to the positivism on which Waltz's theory is based. Post-positivists have thus opened up new and complex questions about IR methodology.

The Behavioral Revolution

In discussing any methodological approach to IR it is important to consider it on its own terms as well as those of its critics. That applies no less to the methodology of behavioralism than to any other methodology. As indicated, beginning in the 1950s and 1960s many political scientists became persuaded by the methodology of behavioralism. What is the behavioral persuasion in political science? Fundamentally it is a scholarly conviction that there can be a cumulative science of IR of increasing sophistication, precision, parsimony, and predictive and explanatory power. Behavioralists believe in the unity of science: that social science is not fundamentally different from natural science; that the same analytical methods—including quantitative methods—can be applied in both areas. The behavioralists also believe in interdisciplinary studies among the social sciences.

Political behavioralists thus seek to apply scientific attitudes and methods to the interdisciplinary study of politics. That leads them to hold conceptions of political life which are amenable to scientific research. They ask: how should we look at politics in order to study it scientifically? The answer: focus on human behavior as it involves politics and government. According to Heinz Eulau (1963: 21), one of the leading advocates of the approach, 'behavioralism investigates acts, attitudes, preferences, and expectations of people in political contexts'. The key elements of the approach are: the individual person is the basic unit of analysis; politics is seen as only one aspect of the behavior of people; and political behavior is to be examined at different levels of analysis, including the social level, the cultural level, and the personal level. A core focus of the study of political behavior is the roles of people in social structures. The central social structure is the political system.

The behavioral approach does not reject the analysis of groups or organizations or states. It only rejects any conception of these entities as more than structures of roles occupied by individual people. To speak of 'the state' is to employ a metaphor rather than to speak accurately and empirically. 'Groups, organizations, or nations have no independent status apart from the conduct of the individuals who are related by behaving towards each other in certain ways . . . institutions do not and cannot exist physically apart from the persons who inhabit them' (Eulau 1963: 14–15). However, some political behavioralists do employ nation states as units of analysis. David Easton (1971: 136–41) adopted that perspective in order to conceptualize the domestic political process. Morton Kaplan (1964) adopted a similar perspective in developing a systemic theory of IR. States were conceptualized as political systems (Easton 1961: 137): centers of political decision-making in which governments carried out decisions or policies (outputs) in response to demands and supports (inputs). Another way of putting that was to say that politics was about 'who gets what, when, how' (Lasswell 1958). The 'who' could be groups including states as well as individuals.

The behavioral approach seeks to transform political science into a true social science by emulating the scientific ideals of the natural sciences. The aim is to collect data which can lead to scientific explanation. That requires scientific methodology and a scientific attitude on the part of the researcher. Then it becomes possible to provide empirical explanations of political behavior: to determine 'why people behave politically as they do, and why, as a result, political processes and systems function as they do' (Eulau 1963: 25). The scientific study of political behavior requires rigorous research designs, precise methods of analysis, reliable instruments of analysis, suitable criteria of validation, and so forth, all of which are necessary to produce a reliable body of verifiable empirical propositions—i.e. empirical theory—about politics. 'Theory' is not a static body of knowledge; rather, it is a 'tool on the road to knowledge' in the same way that 'facts are not knowledge but only the raw materials' that have to be transformed via 'theorizing activity' into propositions that can be 'tested in the process of empirical research'.

Advocates of the behavioral approach emphasize the correct scientific attitude of mind. The tenets of the behavioral approach were summarized by David Easton, one of its leading advocates (see Box 8.1). Easton (1971: 129–41) attempted to supply a model or analytical framework of a political system which could be employed to frame hypotheses and carry out empirical research into political behavior. The state was the locus of political decision-making for society. Politics was a ceaseless interactive process of inputs > decisions > outputs > feedback > inputs, etc. That process could be studied empirically and objectively.

Easton was not concerned with the problem of applying his version of the behavioral approach to international relations. But 'systems theory' was further

---

Box 8.1 **Easton's political behavior tenets and credo**

1. Regularities: There are discoverable uniformities in political behavior . . . [which] can be expressed in generalizations or theories with explanatory and predictive value.
2. Verification: The validity of such generalizations must be tested empirically.
3. Techniques: Rigorous means are necessary to analyze political behavior.
4. Quantification: Measurement and quantification are necessary for precision.
5. Values: Ethical evaluation and empirical explanation should be kept analytically separate.
6. Systematization: Theory and research are intertwined elements of a coherent body of knowledge.
7. Pure Science: Explanation of political behavior logically precedes its application in public policy.
8. Integration: Political science theory and research is closely tied to other social sciences.

D. Easton (1965). *A Framework for Political Analysis.* Englewood-Cliffs, N.J.: Prentice-Hall, 7

---

developed by scholars who were interested in applying the behavioral approach to international relations. One prominent early example was the 'systems analysis' of Morton Kaplan. Kaplan (1964: 21–53) employed his systems theory to distinguish different kinds of international system which he conceptualized as a system of states: the 'balance of power' system; the loose bipolar system; the tight bipolar system; the universal international system; the hierarchical international system; and the Unit Veto International System. The various international systems are characterized by different patterns of behavior according to Kaplan. Box 8.2 summarizes how Kaplan thinks that states act in a 'balance of power' system.

Box 8.2 **Kaplan's balance of power system**

1. Act to increase capabilities but negotiate rather than fight.
2. Fight rather than pass up an opportunity to increase capabilities.
3. Stop fighting rather than eliminate an essential national actor.
4. Act to oppose any coalition or single actor which tends to assume a position of predominance with respect to the rest of the system.
5. Act to constrain actors who subscribe to supranational organizing principles.
6. Permit defeated or constrained essential national actors to re-enter the system as acceptable role partners . . . Treat all essential actors as acceptable role partners.

M. Kaplan (1964). *System and Process in International Politics.* New York: Wiley, 21–53

These actions of states lead to certain patterns of alignment in the system which the theory can predict.

If state behavior does not arise as expected that would have to be investigated and explained further, and if it were more than merely an isolated exception the theory might have to be revised accordingly. In that way empirical research would promote the refinement and improvement of empirical theory. Kaplan (1964: 25) raises the question: was there any time in the history of the 'balance of power' system 'during which the fluctuations in alignments did not shift as the theory predicts?' If there are instances of that happening then 'some other factors must be located to account for the pattern'.

In other words, other variables may have intervened to bring that about. Then it becomes an important research question to investigate and hopefully discover what these intervening variables are and to revise the systems theory accordingly. What we have in this example, and what we find in the behavioral approach to IR and political science more generally, is a specification of independent variables, dependent variables, and intervening variables all of which are involved in explaining domestic and international politics.

Kaplan's systems analysis of IR proved to be flawed in a number of ways. It did not satisfy very well and in some respects not at all Kenneth Waltz's test for empirical theories outlined in Box 8.6 below. Perhaps the most obvious difficulty is: the rules are both descriptive (empirical) and prescriptive (normative). They indicate not only how state actors in the 'balance of power system' are predicted to behave but also how they ought to behave. But if they do behave in that way there is no need to tell them that that is how they ought to behave. Prescriptions are intended to get people to act in ways that otherwise they might not and perhaps would not act. David Hume, a leading 18th century empiricist philosopher famously said 'one cannot derive an ought from an is'. In other words, a fact is not a norm and to confuse facts and norms is a fatal error. The propositions of Box 8.2 display that confusion. Kaplan's 'balance of power' system probably received its most severe criticism from Waltz (1979: 50–9) who found it does not provide a satisfactory empirical theory of IR.

As a summary of the discussion so far it is useful to introduce a few preliminary criticisms of the political behavioralists. Heinz Eulau (1963: 111) claimed that the behavioral persuasion in politics 'aspires to the status of science' and he remarked: 'I take it for granted that a science of politics is both possible and desirable'. Taking that for granted is a controversial issue because it cannot be taken for granted; the validity of that claim must be demonstrated. Most political scientists who sympathize with political behavioralism now recognize that. As a result the philosophy of science which seeks to clarify the grounds for justifying such claims has become far more important in IR. Eulau also claimed that behavioral science develops slowly piece by piece: 'An empirical science is built by the slow, modest, and piecemeal cumulation of theory, methods and data . . . [it is] a gradual "expansion of knowledge"' (Eulau 1963: 116). That can be questioned on the behavioralists' own empirical grounds. The most one can say is: it remains to be seen whether such an expansion of knowledge will be achieved in political science, including IR.

David Easton (1961: 137) provides a parsimonious 'formula' for a systems analysis of political life: inputs > political process > outputs. The problem with that concept is: human beings rarely conform very well to simple models of their behavior. They usually disagree, often profoundly, about what is expected or required of them. The model makes reference to 'values' but they are often highly contested. Some of the most fundamental political disagreements and conflicts concern values. Easton's model largely overlooks political disagreement, discord, conflict. And it provides no insight or guidance for resolving disputes or managing conflict.

Finally, Morton Kaplan (1964: 3) acknowledges the reality of historical change in international relations which behavioral research must come to grips with. But he is convinced that history is a 'laboratory' and that the variables that cause change can be brought within a scientific framework of analysis. Unfortunately, historical change is extremely difficult to pin down, explain, and predict even with only rudimentary precision. How many political scientists correctly predicted the end of the Cold War and its outcome? Are such skeptical observations merely limitations on the scientific enterprise at the present time, an indication that there is still some distance to travel, or are they a fatal blow to the enterprise? That question has not been answered to everybody's satisfaction.

The logic, language, and ethos of empirical analysis that the behavioralists introduced into political science in the 1950s and 1960s have become widespread since that time. Behavioralism rests upon an assumption that there is an external or 'real' world of international relations which operates in accordance with its own objective regularities or patterns that can be detected and explained in terms of empirical models and theories. For academics who are seeking objective knowledge, that is a very appealing assumption to work with. It probably enhanced the self-esteem and perhaps also the status of political science and IR—especially in the United States where scientific culture is deeper than anywhere else. Since the 1950s this academic orientation has come to be known as positivism. Today, as a result of the behavioral revolution, a large number of IR scholars, particularly in the United States, are positivists. But like any other methodology, positivism is open to criticism and it never was universally followed by IR scholars, even in the United States.

The Classical Approach Strikes Back

The first important reaction to the behavioral revolution in IR was that of the traditional or 'classical' approach that the behavioralists initially targeted as the main obstacle to creating a truly scientific discipline of political inquiry. The most articulate and sophisticated defender of the classical approach is Hedley Bull (1969; 1972; 1975). This section examines his most important arguments in defense of that approach.

Unlike behavioralism and its positivist successors and some of their post-positivist critics, the classical approach to IR does not have an explicit methodology. It does not frame hypotheses and test them. It does not employ a formal apparatus of research: i.e. models, statistical techniques, analytical tools, etc. It does not gather and organize data. Instead, it has an attitude to scholarship and to some extent an ethic of scholarship. It rejects the view that there can be one correct or valid scientific analysis of international politics. It is restrained about the empirical knowledge that IR scholars can reasonably expect to develop from their research programs. It is skeptical that there can be a cumulative science of IR of increasing sophistication, precision, parsimony, and predictive and explanatory power. Instead, it sees theories as limited by history (time) and culture (space).

The classical approach takes the view that sound scholarship is a matter of experience in the practice or vocation of scholarship: i.e., observing, reading, inquiring, reflecting, and writing about international relations. Good IR scholarship is not a matter of technical training in correct methods or models or statistical techniques. It is a matter of immersing oneself in the subject by becoming a careful, thoughtful, and critical observer of world politics, both contemporary and historical. The classical approach places a premium on an inquiring mind: i.e. curiosity, discernment, judgment, etc. For Hedley Bull the activity of research basically involves thinking an important topic under investigation through to some conclusions, however preliminary. 'Thinking is also research' was one of his favorite sayings (Holbraad 1990: 193). He dealt with big topics: international security, international order, international justice. One could deal just as well with small topics. But whether a topic is big or small the most important thing in carrying out research is not scientific methodology; it is knowledge of substance and particularly historical knowledge.

The principal elements of traditional scholarly activity are: identifying and ordering the central questions, clarifying the relevant concepts, drawing appropriate distinctions, investigating the historical evidence, and formulating a coherent argument that can comprehend it satisfactorily. The goal is to grasp or understand the substantive topic under study on its own terms. Foreign policies, for example, are intrinsically intelligible activities. They possess inherent meaning. They are not merely data that are waiting for explanation by a scientific observer. Historical, or legal or moral problems of world politics cannot be translated into the terms of science without misunderstanding them. The traditional approach operates with what has subsequently come to be known as an interpretive or reflectivist attitude to scholarship. That can be distinguished from the explanatory approach of behavioralists and other positivists. This distinction is examined at the end of the next chapter.

IR is a complex humanistic field of study. According to Bull (1969), it is not a single discipline; rather, it is interdisciplinary and draws heavily on three well-established disciplines: history, political theory or philosophy, and international law. History is important because it is the only academic way to grasp the particular characteristics of states: all states are distinctive; no two states are the same even though they may share some important characteristics. Because states have distinctive histories and are located in particular places there are definite limits in our ability to generalize about state systems. History is not only the starting point for the study of international relations but it is also the necessary companion and corrective to IR theory because it is a reminder of the limits of empirical generalization in world politics.

The traditional approach is philosophical and is especially concerned with moral questions which it believes cannot be separated from political questions or legal questions: it calls for a disinterested and detached examination of the moral foundations of international politics and international law. An instance of the classical approach in this regard is evident in a typical International Society question: what is the basic ethic of the NATO treaty? The answer is evident from the key Article 5 of the treaty: the obligation of mutual military assistance of all members of the alliance. International law is important because it is a comprehensive body of historical and contemporary knowledge of the basic rules and norms of Westphalian international society. To overlook international law is to leave out a basic dimension of international relations. Box 8.3 sums up the basic differences between the behavioral and the traditional, or classical, approach.

The central characteristic of the traditional approach, according to Bull (1969), is the exercise of scholarly discernment and judgment in considering historical,

---

Box 8.3 The traditional and the behavioral approach

The Traditional Approach: The approach to theorizing which derives from philosophy, history and law, and that is characterized above all by explicit reliance upon the exercise of judgment and by the assumption that if we confine ourselves to strict standards of verification there is very little that can be said of international relations, that general propositions about this subject must therefore derive from a scientifically imperfect process of perception and intuition, and that these general propositions cannot be accorded more than the tentative and inconclusive status appropriate to their doubtful origin.

The Behavioralist Approach: A concern with explanatory rather than normative theory; a concern with recurring patterns rather than the single case; a concern with operational concepts that have measurable empirical reference rather than reified concepts; a concern with the conceptual frameworks; a concern for the techniques of precise data gathering, measurement and presentation.

Quoted from Richard B. Finnegan (1972). 'International Relations: The Disputed
Search for Method,' *Review of Politics*, 34: 42, 52

legal, or philosophical questions of IR. The exercise of scholarly judgment can be informed by reading history and sharpened by thinking about philosophical problems of international relations. But it is rooted in 'everyday assumptions', observation, and common sense (Richardson 1990: 162). General propositions about international relations 'must derive from a scientifically imperfect process of perception or intuition' and can have only a 'tentative and inconclusive status' (Bull 1969: 20).

Classical scholars are skeptics about knowledge. They call attention to the limitations of IR. They see it is an imperfect field of study which can sometimes come up with partial answers to a question but cannot give definitive answers. There cannot be definitive answers to complex historical, legal or philosophical questions of international relations. The traditionalists are critical of overstatement and overconfidence in IR scholarship. This classical view is captured in a famous book by Herbert Butterfield (1973: 51), who was both a leading historian and a member of the 'English School' of IR: 'The historian like every other specialist is quick to over-step the bounds of his subject and elicit from history more than history can really give; and he is forever tempted to bring his stories to a conclusiveness and his judgments to a finality that are not warranted by either the materials or the processes of his research'. This skepticism about the truth claims of IR anticipates a similar post-positivist attitude discussed in the next chapter.

The classical approach emphasizes scholarly disinterestedness and detachment. It is the attitude of scholars who are committed to academic learning rather than technical or scientific expertise. For Bull (1972) the 'detached' or 'disinterested' attitude is not the same as a 'value free' approach. 'There is, of course, no such thing as a "value-free" inquiry into international relations or any other social subject' (Bull 1972: 256). By political detachment Bull means being aware of one's moral and political premises, being frank about them, and holding them firmly in check. Box 8.4 contains Bull's own words on academic study.

It is important to emphasize that the classical approach is not the same as the approach of the interwar liberal idealists (see Chapter 2). Hedley Bull rejected

---

Box 8.4 **Bull on the traditional approach**

The tradition of detached and disinterested study of politics is, I believe, a very delicate plant. It exists at all in relatively few countries, and even in these it has a precarious existence. Its survival depends on a form of commitment that is not political, but intellectual and academic: a commitment to inquiry as a distinct human activity, with its own morality and its own hierarchy of priorities . . .

H. Bull (1975). 'New Directions in the Theory of International Relations,' *International Studies*, 14: 284

liberal idealism because it was a political and ideological approach that displayed a lot of dogmatism and naïveté. It was attempting to change the world in favor of its own political values. It was not attempting to understand the world, to make sense of the world, to make world politics more intelligible and to place IR on a more academic foundation. It was not prepared to scrutinize its own values. Although Bull did not live to see the rise of critical theory and other forms of post-positivism in IR (discussed below), the clear implication is that he would also strenuously disagree with critical theorists who believe that IR theory is intrinsically political whether or not the theorist realizes it or acknowledges it, and that scholarship is a legitimate political engagement. Hedley Bull would probably see critical theorists as born-again idealists wanting to create a better world without making a sufficiently clear-headed and non-subjective analysis of the existing conditions of international relations.

The classical approach has come in for considerable criticism. The reason why Bull originally jumped to its defense was owing to strenuous criticism from the political behavioralists. They criticized the 'traditionalists' on several grounds: for engaging in historicism rather than empiricism (Easton 1971: 234–65); for providing idiographic (descriptive and particularistic) studies rather than nomothetic (explanatory and generalizing) studies; for being satisfied with ivory tower theory that is never tested against reality; for 'the comfortable assumption that theory is the same thing as knowledge' rather than merely being a tool. But there are some similarities too. Both approaches shared a dislike of ideology masquerading as scholarship. Although the behavioralists were ambitious in their scientific aims and goals, they also emphasized careful and scrupulous analysis based on clear concepts which avoid ideological bias.

Contrary to a widely held impression, the behavioralists were not totally critical of the classical approach. According to Eulau (1963: 9–10) it is a 'mistake' to see the behavioral persuasion as 'a revolt against the classical tradition'. Rather, it is 'a continuation of the classical tradition' because it 'represents an attempt, by modern modes of analysis, to fulfill the quest for political knowledge begun by the classical political theorists'. Eulau (1963: 32) finally adds: 'the behavioral persuasion is a continuation of the classical tradition . . . I believe the classical writers would have used . . . [behavioral technology] had it been available to them'.

In sum, there are points of difference and points of agreement between behavioralists and traditionalists. If, on the one hand, we stress the points of difference, we get a profound contrast between behavioralism and traditionalism. The two approaches can be seen to hold categorically different conceptions of the world (ontology) and fundamentally different ideas of the best way to gain knowledge of the world (epistemology). On the other hand, if we stress the points of agreement, the two approaches are 'different ends of a continuum of scholarship rather than completely different games . . . Each type of effort can inform and enrich the other and can as well act as a check on the excesses endemic in each approach' (Finnegan 1972: 64). When the battle rages, the contenders tend to draw up their positions very sharply, emphasizing points of difference. When the smoke clears, more moderate voices on both sides often emphasize areas of agreement. As we shall see, the methodological debate in IR illustrates both positions.

Positivist Methodology in IR

Positivism is an important methodology in IR. A lot of research is being done using methodologies based on positivist principles. Journals such as *International Studies Quarterly*, *Journal of Conflict Resolution*, and *American Political Science Review* publish many articles based on positivist methodology. There are several versions of positivism; we cannot discuss all of them. The conception of positivism presented here is that of 'moderate positivism' (Nicholson 1996).

Positivist methodology in political science, including IR, is a legacy of behavioralism: it employs most behavioralist assumptions and attitudes although usually in a more sophisticated way. It views the social and political world, including the international world, as having regularities and patterns that can be explained if the correct methodology is properly applied. It is based on the same assumption of the unity of all the sciences including the social sciences. It argues that observation and experience are keys to constructing and judging scientific theories. It holds that there can be an objective knowledge of the world—or at least 'a great deal of inter-subjective agreement' (Nicholson 1996: 131). It emphasizes the centrality of empirical propositions: i.e. the reasons for accepting hypotheses are evident from careful observation of reality. 'We observe events and on the basis of these observations hope to predict the consequences of actions carried out now or in the future' (Nicholson 1996: 132).

The leading philosophy of science criteria for a good scientific (positivist) theory are summarized in Box 8.5 which is based on Vasquez (1995: 230). According to that conception, IR theories should consist of empirical propositions that are logically related and can be tested against evidence so that 'the theory as a whole is confirmed or refuted by observations' of data (Nicholson 1996: 132).

The theory is precise: positivist theories are limited and specific. The theory is non-relativist: it holds everywhere that the specified conditions (independent variables) obtain. The kernel of positivism is its epistemology which asserts that scholars can make generalizations about the social world, including international relations, which are verifiable. That is based on empirical theories whose propositions are (or are striving to be) related in a logical way: 'some propositions imply other propositions' (Nicholson 1996: 129). The theory is consistent with well-established knowledge in related fields of inquiry. That recollects the behavioralist

---

Box 8.5 **Seven criteria of a good empirical theory**

1. Accurate and limited.

2. Non-relativist (universal).

3. Verifiable or falsifiable.

4. Powerful in its explanations.

5. Amenable to improvement.

6. Consistent with well-established knowledge.

7. Parsimonious.

Source: Vasquez (1995: 230)

---

unity of the natural and social sciences. Finally, its basic propositions are parsimonious: they are capable of statement in a spare and lucid fashion; the simplest theory is often the best.

Positivist approaches do not usually present themselves by waving a flag called 'positivism'. So how can we tell if a theory is scientific in positivist terms? According to Kenneth Waltz (1979: 13) whether or not an IR theory is an empirical theory—i.e. positivist—can be determined by a test involving the questions raised in Box 8.6. The test gives an indication of the most important conditions that theories in IR should be able to meet to count as scientific or empirical.

Waltz recognizes that the steps in Box 8.6 are rigorous and 'laboratory-like'; therefore, they may be difficult to carry out in practice. For example, it may be difficult to eliminate non-relevant, perturbing variables in carrying out the test;

Box 8.6 **Is that an empirical theory?**

1. State the theory being tested.

2. Infer hypotheses from it.

3. Subject the hypotheses to experimental or observational tests.

4. In taking steps two and three, use the definitions of terms found in the theory being tested.

5. Eliminate or control perturbing variables not included in the theory under test.

6. Devise a number of distinct and demanding tests.

7. If a test is not passed, ask whether the theory flunks completely, needs repair and restatement, or requires a narrowing of the scope of its explanatory claims.

Source: Waltz (1979: 13)

---

after all, the real world is not a laboratory where variables can be excluded. As a second-best procedure, Waltz suggests a less rigorous procedure, summarized in Box 8.7.

Box 8.7 **A less rigorous test of theory**

Simply negotiate the seven steps [Box 8.6] . . . in ways appropriate to the theory at hand. Ask what the theory leads one to expect rather than fixing arbitrarily on expectations that one's data and methods can cope with. Check expectations against one's (often historical) observations before trying for precise refinements and using elaborate methods.

Source: Waltz (1979: 16)

Kaplan's systems theory outlined above was not only criticized by Waltz but it also inspired Waltz (1979) to furnish a theory of international politics of his own that could meet the test of Box 8.6: Waltzian neorealism. The substance of neorealism was reviewed in Chapter 3. Waltz constructs his theory in such a way that if we can accept its assumptions, concepts and logic certain expectations and predictions follow about behavior and outcomes in international politics. For example, it can be predicted from the theory that states 'will engage in balancing behavior' and that such behavior has 'a strong tendency towards balance in the system' (Waltz 1979: 128). It can be predicted, further, that 'bi-polar systems' have a stronger tendency towards stability and order than 'multi-polar systems'. According to Waltz's structural theory, it is not that states are motivated to create and preserve order among themselves; the independent variable is not behavioral: it is not a consequence of foreign policy. Rather, it is structural: the structure of international anarchy produces that effect. That is, the structure of anarchy pushes states towards acting in certain ways that can be predicted by structural theory.

Neorealism and positivism are often equated in IR. But that equation is too narrow: positivism is broader than neorealism. According to Nicholson (1996*b*), there are basically two general research programs of contemporary positivism in IR: (1) a program of quantitative research, one important strand of which is associated with peace research; and (2) a program of rational choice analysis, such as game theory. Because positivists are seeking to establish verifiable empirical generalizations and ultimately to build empirical theory, they are inclined toward quantification, including the use of mathematical models. 'Quantification comes into play when one is trying to test theories' (Nicholson 1996*b*: 136). A program of quantitative research involves explanatory analysis. The criteria and test outlined in Boxes 8.5 and 8.6 are applicable to theories based on quantitative research. A program of rational choice analysis raises instrumental questions which belong to policy analysis as discussed in the next section.

Policy Analysis

The dictionary defines 'policy' as: 'prudence or wisdom in the management of affairs'; 'a definite course or method of action selected from among alternatives and in light of given conditions to guide and determine present and future decisions'. Policy is intimately connected with government administration: it defines the goals and directs the activities of governments and more specifically of government agencies. Policy, in that key meaning, is part of the rational management and conduct of government. Governments are involved in the management of the affairs of countries and policies can be understood as maps or guides for government actions. Policies identify goals and lay out courses of action of government agencies and their personnel. Foreign policies define the goals and activities of governments and particularly of foreign ministries in their relations with other countries. Some of those personnel, the ones in leading positions—such as presidents, prime ministers, foreign ministers, finance ministers, etc.—can be referred to as policy-makers. Other personnel carry out or implement policy.

The concept of policy assumes that governments define their goals and choose the methods and courses of action for reaching those goals. Policy analysis, which focuses on decision and choice, is fundamentally different from structural analysis. Policy analysis is a means–end way of thinking about goals and actions of government; it is an instrumental concept. Instrumental questions are not the same as explanatory questions. The latter ask for a correct account of an event or episode (a dependent variable) in terms of its causes or conditions (an independent variable). The former ask for the best method or course of action for reaching a target or destination. Instrumental analysis involves thinking of the best available choice or course—e.g. giving correct advice or good advice—so as to make things happen according to one's interests or wishes or desires. Instrumental analysis is an integral element of making and studying policy, including foreign policy. It involves calculating the decisions and actions that will most likely enable one to reach a goal. In that sense, it is Machiavellian. The methodology for policy analysis is basically the same as that for policy-making. It puts the IR scholar into the mind-set of the foreign policy-maker. It therefore reduces the distance between the theorist who is involved in thinking about foreign policy and the policy-maker or practitioner who is involved in framing and carrying out foreign policy.

Foreign policies consist of aims and measures that are intended to guide government decisions and actions with regard to external affairs, particularly its relations with foreign countries. Managing those foreign relations calls for carefully considered policies that are adapted to the foreign interests and concerns—i.e. goals—of the government. Foreign policy analysis may or may not involve thinking about what those interests and concerns ought to be. But it must involve thinking about the best means or measures for defending those interests and addressing those concerns. Policy analysis can thus involve giving advice or making criticisms which are addressed to the intelligence or wisdom of the policy under consideration. At that point policy analysis becomes not only instrumental but also prescriptive: it seeks and claims to know the correct course of action that will best enable a government to achieve its foreign policy goals.

Traditional foreign policy analysis involves being informed about a government's external policies: knowing their history, the interests and concerns that drive the policies, and the ways of defending and addressing those interests and concerns. That includes knowing the results and consequences of past foreign policy decisions and actions. It also involves an ability to recognize the circumstances under which a government must operate in carrying out its foreign policy. One very crucial circumstance is knowledge of the foreign policy intentions of foreign powers with whom one must deal. It involves, as well, the exercise of judgment and common sense in detecting the practical courses of action available to the government for carrying out its foreign policies. That 'feel' for what is possible is usually derived from experience. It could be said, in that regard, that satisfactory foreign policy understanding is best achieved by direct knowledge of a government's foreign affairs: e.g. by serving in a foreign ministry. The next best thing would involve trying to put oneself into the mindset of such an official: trying to grasp the circumstances of such a person, trying to understand the reasons such an official arrived at a decision, and trying to ascertain its consequences, both good and bad (Collingwood 1946: 282–3). In short, traditional policy analysis is a matter of gaining insight into the activity of foreign policy-making, either from experience or by careful scrutiny of past and present foreign policies.

There is a form of policy analysis, however, which does not depend upon experience or insight into the situation of policy-makers. Rational choice analysis in IR originated in the early 1960's in the work of Schelling (1960), Boulding (1962), and Rapaport (1974). Rational choice is a scientific version of instrumental reasoning which applies a formal type of analysis aimed at determining the most 'rational' or efficient means for achieving a pre-determined goal. (A mathematical version of rational choice is called game theory, which aims to deduce certain outcomes from given choices or options based on particular sets of information.) Rational choice is goal-directed choice in which the options are clearly defined and definitely limited but information is imperfect or incomplete. It seeks to provide empirical theories of how actors can be predicted to behave in their relations with other actors with whom they are dealing—international actors in the case of IR. It also seeks to indicate the optimal choice that decision-makers should take. It offers models for answering the question: with that information what would be the best decision to move towards one's goal? Michael Nicholson (1996b: 157) suggests that a better term for this approach is 'goal-directed theories'.

Rational choice analysis is derived from economics where it was first applied in the social sciences with considerable success. In IR, rational choice theory, including game theory, was applied most successfully in strategic studies during the Cold War when the United States and the Soviet Union were locked in a struggle involving weapons of mass destruction, including nuclear armed, long-range missiles (Schelling 1960). In strategic studies rational choice involves the use of limited military power for national security; in economics it involves the use of scarce economic resources for profits and wealth.

Rational choice places the analyst in a position of technical knowledge or expertise: the theory is intended to give the analyst a more precise grasp of the choices facing the policy-makers; the analyst becomes an expert—somebody who has technical knowledge or 'expertise'. The rational choice theorist who is consulted is in effect leading the policy-maker and the policy-making process—rather than merely trying to follow it by getting an insight into the policy-maker's mind and situation, as is the case in traditional foreign policy analysis by diplomatic historians. That elevates the analyst to a position of greater importance, for it makes the policymaker dependent on the analyst's technical expertise. That position of expertise which rational choice analysis is claimed to provide obviously appeals to many IR theorists.

This clarifies the point where positivism and policy come into contact. Positivists are apt to say: 'if we desire to control our relation to the world rather than be controlled by forces that we do not understand, then it is necessary to accept some version of positivism as a basis for a rational public policy, including foreign policy'. Contrary to a widely-held belief positivism does not ignore prescription. That is particularly the case in IR which involves the study of war and peace, wealth and poverty, and similar fundamental value questions about which positivists are as concerned as anybody else. It is precisely that concern about basic values that 'makes it all the more important that we have rigorous criteria for distinguishing between what is the case in the world and what we want to be the case. The temptations to self-deceit are so strong that an exceptional concern with the methodological criteria for determining what is and what is not the case is required' (Nicolson 1996a: 141). Positivists believe that scientific studies are and must be value-neutral in themselves. But that does not mean that they cannot or should not be put to use in the service of values. Just as nuclear scientists and rocket scientists can put their scientific knowledge to the service of a country's national defense, so, presumably, strategic theorists (Schelling 1960) can put their game theoretic knowledge to the service of a state's security.

The technical knowledge which rational choice claims to provide is not immune to criticism. The main criticism usually runs as follows. How can analysts be sure that the real choices facing the policy-makers are the ones that their model indicates? How can they be sure that the policy-makers involved are as rational as they are assumed to be? How can they take account of subjective elements in foreign policy behavior? In other words, is it really possible to find a form of technical knowledge that can take the place of and perhaps even prove superior to the insights of an experienced policy-maker? A more balanced view is the following: rational choice thinking can perhaps supplement the insights of experienced policy-makers and that can be of genuine instrumental value to the policy-making process, in foreign policy no less than other policy spheres. According to that view, policy analysis should try to combine traditional methods with those based on rational choice. But that still leaves open the fundamental problem: what should policy-makers decide when their experience and instincts contradict the course of action defined by rational choice analysis?

Conclusion

Many scholars are skeptical that international relations really lend themselves to strictly scientific inquiry. They take issue with Waltz's claim that the complex world of international relations can be squeezed into a few law-like statements about the structure of the international system and the balance of power. They would also be very concerned if rational choice theory were a basis of foreign policy because important subjective questions that call for judgment and interpretation are left out of account.

Such critics, who include the classical scholars, believe that the study of international relations requires a humanistic kind of knowledge which emphasizes judgment, interpretation, history, philosophy, and law. Other critics say that positivism is handicapped as a research methodology because it cannot come to terms with the complex and contradictory nature of human beings. There are two different ways of approaching this debate. One is to see the positions as completely incompatible, 'like two ships passing in the night'. The other is to view them as different versions of what is basically the same project of gathering insight into the complex world of international relations. As we shall see in the next chapter, many post-positivists take the first view, emphasizing confrontation instead of cooperation. But there are also examples of a moderate and middle position.

KEY POINTS

- Some of the most important IR questions are methodological in nature. Such issues became prominent with the 'behavioral revolution' in the 1950s and 1960s. Since the end of the Cold War, methodological issues have returned to center stage in a debate between positivist and post-positivist methodologies.

- The behavioralist approach: A concern with explanatory rather than normative theory; a concern with recurring patterns rather than the single case; a concern with operational concepts that have measurable empirical reference rather than reified concepts; a concern with conceptual frameworks; a concern with techniques of precise data gathering, measurement, and presentation.

- The traditional, or classical, approach: A skeptical approach that derives from philosophy, history, and law, and is characterized by explicit reliance upon the exercise of discernment and judgment. Knowledge of any human subject is derived from a scientifically imperfect process of perception and intuition; generalizations about international relations are, at best, always tentative, temporary, and incomplete.

- Policy Analysis: An approach that also is divided between traditional and scientific forms of analysis. Traditional policy analysts—e.g. diplomatic historians—try to get inside the minds of policy-makers by looking at historical experience or construing the intentions of current foreign policies. Positivists try to formulate models that explicitly identify rational choices that could be applied in foreign policy-making.

QUESTIONS

- Pick a concrete issue, such as for example the distribution of power in the world at the end of the Cold War. What are the differences between a behavioralist and a traditional approach to that issue?

- What is the methodological difference between scientifically explaining an international phenomenon and historically interpreting an international event or episode?

- Compare the IR methodologies of Kaplan and Waltz. Which is more satisfactory?

- How does the traditional approach compare to the rational choice approach to foreign policy analysis? Is one better than the other? Can these two approaches to policy analysis be combined? How?

 For additional material and resources see the companion web site at:
www.oup.co.uk/best.textbooks/politics/jacksonsorensen2e/

GUIDE TO FURTHER READING

Brown, C., Nardin, T., and **Rengger, N.** (2002). 'Introduction,' in C. Brown, T. Nardin, and N. Rengger (eds.), *International Relations in Political Thought*. Cambridge: Cambridge University Press.

Bull, H. (1969). 'International Theory: the Case for a Classical Approach,' in K. Knorr and J. Rosenau (eds.), *Contending Approaches to International Politics*. Princeton: Princeton University Press.

Kaplan, M. (1964). *System and Process in International Politics*. New York: Wiley.

Nicholson, M. (1996a). 'The continued significance of positivism?' in S. Smith, K. Booth, and M. Zalevski (1996). *International Theory: Positivism and Beyond*. Cambridge: Cambridge University Press, 128–49.

Nicholson, M. (1996b). *Causes and Consequences in International Relations*. London: Pinter.

WEB LINKS

http://www.utm.edu/research/iep/l/logpos.htm
Thorough introduction to logical positivism. Hosted by the University of Tennessee at Martin.

http://www.valt.helsinki.fi/vol/projects/behavior.htm
Information about the origins and ideas of behavioralism. Hosted by the University of Helsinki.

http://www.usip.org/
Home page of the United States Institute of Peace provides links to publications and other web resources related to peace research.

http://assets.cambridge.org/0521808707/sample/0521808707WS.pdf
A chapter from the book *Historical Sociology of International Relations* (Cambridge University Press). Here, John M. Hobson focuses on the possibilities of bringing historical sociology back into international relations.

9 Methodological Debates: Post-Positivist Approaches

SUMMARY

Positivist methodologies in IR provoked post-positivist reactions including critical theory, postmodernism, constructivism, and normative theory. Post-positivism also is a broad church. All these methodological approaches are elaborate and complicated and each one displays internal disagreements among its advocates. We can only touch on the basics of each. The chapter concludes with a discussion of a fundamental division between IR scholars who think that objective methods can be used to give scientific explanations of international relations and IR scholars who think that is impossible and that the most that IR scholarship can achieve is knowledgeable interpretations of international relations.

. . . .

Critical Theory

This methodological approach is mainly a development of Marxist thought and could be described as neo-Marxism. It was developed by a small group of German scholars many of whom were living in exile in the United States. They were known collectively as 'the Frankfurt School'. In IR critical theory is closely linked to Marxist IPE (see Chapter 6). Two leading IR critical theorists are Robert Cox (1981; 1996) and Andrew Linklater (1990; 1996). Critical theorists reject three basic postulates of positivism: an objective external reality; the subject/object distinction; and value-free social science. According to critical theorists, there is no world politics or global economics which operates in accordance with immutable social laws. The social world is a construction of time and place: the international system is a specific construction of the most powerful states. Everything that is social, including international relations, is changeable and thus historical. Since world politics are constructed rather than discovered, there is no fundamental distinction between subject (the analyst) and object (the focus of analysis).

For critical theorists knowledge is not and cannot be neutral either morally or politically or ideologically. All knowledge reflects the interests of the observer. Knowledge is always biased because it is produced from the social perspective of the analyst. Knowledge thus discloses an inclination—conscious or unconscious—toward certain interests, values, groups, parties, classes, nations, etc. All IR theories are biased too. Robert Cox (1981) expressed that view in a frequently quoted remark: 'Theory is always for someone and for some purpose'. Cox draws a distinction between positivist or 'problem-solving' knowledge and critical or 'emancipatory' knowledge. Problem-solving knowledge is conservative: it seeks to know that which exists at present. It is biased towards the international *status quo* which is based on inequality of power and excludes many people. It cannot lead to knowledge of human progress and emancipation which is the knowledge that critical theorists seek to provide. According to Robert Cox (1996) critical theory contains an element of historical utopianism.

Box 9.1 **Robert Cox on critical theory as historical utopianism**

Critical theory allows for a normative choice in favor of a social and political order different from the prevailing order, but it limits the range of choice to alternative orders which are feasible transformations of the existing world . . . Critical theory thus contains an element of utopianism in the sense that it can represent a coherent picture of an alternative order, but its utopianism is constrained by its comprehension of historical processes. It must reject improbable alternatives just as it rejects the permanency of the existing order.

Robert Cox (1996). *Approaches to World Order*. Cambridge: Cambridge University Press, 90

Critical theory is not confined to an examination of states and the state system but focuses more widely on power and domination in the world generally. Critical theorists seek knowledge for a political purpose: to liberate humanity from the 'oppressive' structures of world politics and world economics which are controlled by hegemonic powers, particularly the capitalist United States. They seek to unmask the global domination of the rich North over the poor South. Critical theorists in this regard are almost indistinguishable from Marxists IPE scholars. Their orientation toward progressive change and their desire to use theory to help bring about such change is also reminiscent of Idealism. Critical theorists are openly political: they advocate and promote their progressive (usually socialist) Ideology of emancipation believing that conservative scholars and liberal scholars are defending and promoting their political values. Critical theorists thus believe that theoretical debates are basically political debates. Like the inter-war idealists, critical theorists are trying to bring about the social and political revolution that their ideology proclaims. The difference is: critical theorists reject the possibility of academic detachment and objectivity, whereas the idealists were blissfully unaware of it.

Their view of knowledge as inherently political separates critical theorists from behavioralists, from those positivists who disdain using scientific knowledge for political purposes, and from classical theorists. According to critical theorists, IR scholars cannot be detached from the subject matter they are studying because they are connected with it in many subtle and some not so subtle ways. They are part of the human world they are studying. They are involved in that world. Whether they realize it or not social scientists and social science are instruments of power. Critical theorists seek to identify the political interests that different IR theories and theorists serve. But even more than that: they seek to use their knowledge to advance what they believe is the ultimate end of all knowledge: the great goal of human emancipation from global social structures which until now have privileged a relatively small minority of the world's population at the expense of the majority. Critical IR theory can thus be understood as explicitly and avowedly revolutionary: it seeks to overthrow the existing world political and economic system.

The main problem with this outlook is the problem it poses for academic independence and the integrity of scholarly and scientific research. If 'theory is always for someone and for some purpose' how can anyone decide whether it is a good theory in purely academic terms? The value of any theory would be based on political values: does it promote my political or ideological beliefs? It would not be based on academic values: does it shed light on the world, increase our rational knowledge of it, and ultimately demystify it? If IR theory is really political rather than scientific or scholarly there is no neutral way to decide which theory is the best academically. If that is so there can be no truly academic disagreements and controversies. Academic debates would really be political debates in disguise. But if IR theories and all other social science theories really are political how can we justify them as academic subjects? Why should critical theory or any IR theory be taken as a statement of knowledge if it is really a statement of politics? If theory is always an expression of political interests rather than academic curiosity, political science is neither science nor scholarship: it is politics. All of that may of course be true. But if it is true it is hard to justify IR scholarship (including this book) in purely academic terms.

A moderate version of critical theory is: no knowledge is completely value-free but even when that is the case there is a difference between pure partisan politics and intellectual understanding and scientific knowledge sought by progressive IR theorists. That academic enterprise does not take place in complete isolation from or ignorance of politics, but it does attempt to come up with systematic and detached analysis. Robert Cox's work is an example of how critical theorists struggle with finding their place between these views. While he is a political advocate for radical change, he is also the author of scholarly works that are widely recognized in the academic study of IR.

....

Postmodernism

Postmodernism is a social theory that originated among a group of post-war French philosophers who rejected the philosophy of existentialism which was prevalent in France in the late 1940s and early 1950s. Postmodernism did not enter IR until the 1980s, however. A leading postmodern theorist in IR is Richard Ashley (1996). Like critical theorists, postmodernists seek to make scholars aware of their conceptual prisons (Vasquez 1995). The most important conceptual prison is that of modernity itself and the whole idea that modernization leads to progress and a better life for all (for this idea, see Chapter 4). Postmodernists cast doubt on the modern belief that there can be objective knowledge of social phenomena. They are critical of classical liberals who believe in 'enlightenment': e.g. Kant. They are also critical of contemporary positivists who believe in 'science': e.g. Waltz. Both Kant and Waltz are wedded to a belief in the advancement of human knowledge which postmodernists regard as erroneous and unfounded. Postmodernists see neorealism as the epitome of intellectual error and academic arrogance. Neorealism is the prime example of an intellectual prison that postmodernists see themselves breaking out of.

Postmodern IR theorists reject the notion of objective truth. They dispute the idea that there is or can be an ever-expanding knowledge of the human world. Such beliefs are intellectual illusions—i.e. they are subjective beliefs, like a religious faith. The neorealists may think that they have found the truth about IR, but they are mistaken. Postmodernists pour cold water on the belief that knowledge can expand and improve, thus giving humans increasing mastery over not only the natural world but also the social world including the international system. They are deeply skeptical of the idea that institutions can be fashioned that are fair and just for all of humankind: men and women everywhere. They debunk the notion of universal human progress.

Postmodernism has been defined as 'incredulity towards metanarratives' (Lyotard 1984: xxiv). Metanarratives are accounts such as neorealism or neo-liberalism that claim to have discovered the truth about the social world. Post-modernists consider such claims to be far-fetched and lacking in credibility. The great theoretical constructions of IR such as realism or liberalism are houses of cards that will fall down with the first breeze of deconstructive criticism. Postmodernists argue, for example, that neorealist claims about the unchanging anarchical structure of international politics cannot be sustained because there are no independent and impartial grounds for judging them. There are no such grounds because social science is not neutral; rather, it is historical, it is cultural, it is political and therefore biased. Every theory, including neorealism, decides for itself what counts as 'facts.' There is no neutral or impartial or independent standpoint to decide between rival empirical claims. Empirical theory is myth. In other words, there is no objective reality; everything involving human beings is subjective. Knowledge and power are intimately related; knowledge is not at all 'immune from the workings of power' (Smith 1997: 181); see Box 9.2.

Box 9.2 **Postmodernist view of knowledge and power**

All power requires knowledge and all knowledge relies on and reinforces existing power relations. Thus there is no such thing as 'truth', existing outside of power. To paraphrase Foucault, how can history have a truth if truth has a history? Truth is not something external to social settings, but is instead part of them . . . Postmodern international theorists have used this insight to examine the 'truths' of international relations to see how the concepts and knowledge-claims that dominate the discipline in fact are highly contingent on specific power relations.

Smith (1997: 181)

Postmodernists are deconstructivists who speak of theories as 'narratives' or 'metanarratives'. Narratives or metanarratives are always constructed by a theorist and they are thus always contaminated by his or her standpoint and prejudices. They can thus be deconstructed: i.e. taken apart to disclose their arbitrary elements and biased intentions. The main target of postmodernist deconstruction in IR is neorealism. Here is a theory which claims that only a few elements of information about sovereign states in an anarchical international system can tell us most of the big and important things we need to know about international relations. And the theory even claims to validly explain international politics 'through all the centuries we can contemplate' (Waltz 1995: 75).

Postmodernist critiques of neorealism target the anarchical structure and ahistorical bias of the theory (Ashley 1986: 289; Walker 1993: 123). The theory is ahistorical and that in turn leads to a form of reification in which historically produced social structures are presented as unchangeable constraints given by nature. Emphasis is on 'continuity and repetition' (Walker 1995: 309). Individual actors are 'reduced in the last analysis to mere objects who must participate in reproducing the whole or . . . fall by the wayside of history' (Ashley 1986: 291). It follows that neorealism has big difficulties in confronting change in international relations. This discloses a poverty of theoretical imagination. Any thought about alternative futures remains frozen between the stark alternatives of either domestic sovereign statehood and international anarchy or the (unlikely) abolition of sovereign statehood and the creation of world government.

What is the contribution of postmodernist IR methodology? One benefit is the deflation of academic egos and conceits: scholars typically claim too much for their theories. Neorealism is a good example of that: it does not really live up to its billing; it provides less knowledge of IR than it claims to provide. Another benefit is the skepticism that postmodernism attaches to the notion of universal truths that are said to be valid for all times and places. That is typical of realism and also of much liberal idealism. Pouring cold water on academic or scientific pretensions can be a good thing.

But there is also a negative side. Why should we accept the analysis of the postmodernists if theory is always biased in some way? Why should the deconstruction be believed any more than the original construction? If every account of the social world is arbitrary and biased, then postmodernism cannot be spared: its critique can be turned upon itself. Postmodernist Richard Ashley says there is no 'positionality'—i.e. there are no stable platforms or certitudes—upon which social speech, writing, and action can be based. Yet, ironically, what makes postmodernism intelligible, including the work of Ashley, is its conformity to the basic conventions of intellectual and academic inquiry which are the foundations of all knowledge, including social knowledge. His own writing conforms to the conventions of English grammar and vocabulary, and no doubt he lives his own life as we live our lives within the compass of interpersonal standards of time, space, etc., which are marked and measured by calendars, clocks, miles, kilometers, etc. There are similar conventions of international law, politics, and economics. These measures and standards are some of the most fundamental elements of the modern world.

A more worrying problem is that postmodernism can deteriorate into nihilism—i.e. negativism for its own sake. Criticism can be made merely for the sake of criticism. Narratives can be taken apart with nothing to take their place. Ultimately, postmodernists can become estranged from the social and political world that they seek to understand. A world exclusively of contingency and chance (Ashley 1996), rather than choice and reason, may cease to be either intelligible or meaningful. In short, there is something about postmodernism which may appeal to nihilists. But nihilism cannot provide any foundations of knowledge because it rejects the possibility and the value of knowledge.

There is a moderate postmodernism that is premised on the notion that our ideas and theories about the world always contain elements of both subjectivity and objectivity. The subjective element is tied to our adherence to different values and concepts and the inescapable fact that each and every one of us looks out upon the world from his or her own personal standpoint. The objective element is tied to the fact that we can actually agree about very substantial insights about what the real world is like. We speak the same language. We calculate in the same units of weights and measures. All that is solid does not melt into air. At the core of this middle ground is the notion of intersubjectively transmissible knowledge (Brecht 1963: 113–16). Such knowledge is bound by standards of documentation and clarity of exposition; put differently, such knowledge is compelled to demonstrate that it is not the result of wishful thinking, guesswork or fantasy; it must contain more than purely subjective valuations. Moderate postmodernism approaches the position of the constructivists, which is based on the concept of intersubjectivity.

. . . .

Constructivism

The focus of constructivism is on human awareness or consciousness and its place in world affairs. Constructivists, like critical theorists and postmodernists, argue that there is no external, objective social reality as such. The social and political world is not a physical entity or material object that is outside human consciousness. The international system is not something 'out there' like the solar system. It does not exist on its own. It exists only as inter-subjective awareness among people. It is a human invention or creation not of a physical or material kind but of a purely intellectual and ideational kind. It is a set of ideas, a body of thought, a system of norms, which has been arranged by certain people at a particular time and place. If the thoughts and ideas that enter into the existence of international relations change, then the system itself will change as well. That is because the system consists in thought and ideas. The inter-subjective character of international relations lends itself to study by methods which are 'scientific' in the historical and sociological sense, although not in the strictly positivist meaning of the word. Constructivism, in that sense, is a rejection of positivist IR theory. But it is not a rejection of 'social' science as such.

Constructivism is sometimes regarded as a new approach. But it is in fact an old methodology that can be traced back at least to the eighteenth-century writings of the Italian philosopher Giambattista Vico (Pompa 1982). According to Vico, the natural world is made by God, but the historical world is made by Man (Pompa 1982: 26). History is not some kind of unfolding or evolving process that is external to human affairs. Men and women make their own history. They also make states which are historical constructs. States are artificial creations and the state system is artificial too. That, too, is an old idea in the history of political thought. Leading IR constructivist theorists include Peter Katzenstein (1996), Friedrich Kratochwil (1989), Nicholas Onuf (1989), and Alexander Wendt (1992). We shall address three aspects of the constructivist approach to IR: its philosophical assumptions, its research emphases, and its response to positivism, particularly neorealism.

Constructivism is an approach to IR that postulates the following: (i) Human relations, including international relations, consist essentially of thoughts and ideas and not of material conditions or forces. (ii) The core ideational element upon which constructivists focus are intersubjective beliefs (ideas, conceptions, assumptions, etc.) that are widely shared among people. (iii) Those shared beliefs compose and express the interests and identities of people: e.g. the way people conceive of themselves in their relations with others. (iv) Constructivists focus on the ways those relations are formed and expressed: e.g. by means of collective social institutions, such as state sovereignty, 'which have no material reality but exist only because people collectively believe they exist and act accordingly' (Finnemore and Sikkink 2001: 392). Each of these elements of constructivist philosophy can be amplified.

Human relations, including international relations, consist of thought and ideas and not essentially of material conditions or forces. This is the philosophical idealist element of constructivism which contrasts with the materialist philosophy of most social science positivism. According to constructivist philosophy, the social world is not a given: it is not something 'out there' that exists independent of the thoughts and ideas of the people involved in it. It is not an external reality whose laws can be discovered by scientific research and explained by scientific theory as behavioralists and positivists argue. The social and political world is not part of nature. There are no natural laws of society or economics or politics. History is not an evolving external process that is independent of human thought and ideas. That means that sociology or economics or political science or the study of history cannot be objective 'sciences' in the strict positivist sense of the word.

Everything involved in the social world of men and women is made by them. The fact that they made it is what makes it intelligible to them. The social world is a world of human consciousness: of thoughts and beliefs, of ideas and concepts, of languages and discourses, of signs, signals, and understandings among human beings, especially groups of human beings, such as states and nations. The social world is an inter-subjective domain: it is meaningful to the people who made it and live in it, and who understand it precisely because they made it and they are at home in it. The social world is in part constructed of physical entities. But it is the ideas and beliefs behind those entities which are most important: what those entities signify in the minds of people. The international system of security and defense, for example, consists of territories, populations, weapons, and other physical assets. But it is the ideas and understandings according to which those assets are conceived, organized, and used—e.g. in alliances, armed forces, etc.— that is most important. The physical element is there. But that element is secondary to the intellectual element which infuses it, plans it, organizes it, and guides it. The thought that is involved in international security is more important, far more important, than the physical assets that are involved because those assets have no meaning without the intellectual component: they are mere things in themselves.

Box 9.3 Wendt's constructivist conception of social structures

Social structures have three elements: shared knowledge, material resources, and practices. First, social structures are defined, in part, by shared understandings, expectations, or knowledge. These constitute the actors in a situation and the nature of their relationships, whether cooperative or conflictual. A *security dilemma*, for example, is a social structure composed of intersubjective understandings in which states are so distrustful that they make worst-case assumptions about each other's intentions, and as a result define their interests in self-help terms. A *security community* is a different social structure, one composed of shared knowledge in which states trust one another to resolve disputes without war. This dependence of social structure on ideas is the sense in which constructivism has as idealist (or 'idea-ist') view of structure.

Wendt (1992: 73)

The core ideational element upon which constructivists focus is inter-subjective beliefs (and ideas, conceptions, and assumptions) that are widely shared among people. In IR such beliefs include a group of people's notion of themselves as a nation or nationality, their conception of their country as a state, their notion of their state as independent or sovereign, their idea of themselves as different from other peoples in cultural or religious or historical terms, their sense of their history and traditions, their political convictions and prejudices and ideologies, their political institutions, and much else. These beliefs must be widely shared to matter. The existential reality of a nation is marked by evidence of a widely held belief among a population that they collectively compose a national community with its own distinctive identity. If such beliefs are only held by a few people they cannot claim to be sufficiently general to be of real social and political significance. For example, in many parts of Eastern Europe before the nineteenth century only small circles of intellectuals had a sense of national identity: e.g. being Serbian or Croatian or Romanian or Bulgarian, etc. The spread of that idea among the general population in the nineteenth century, along with the spread of education and literacy, was the process by which such nations were created. Nations, nationalisms, and national identities are social constructions of time and place.

As the foregoing implies, it is not only the sharing of beliefs and ideas but also the limits to such sharing that is important. Inter-subjectivity only goes so far. Shared beliefs constitute and express the interests and identities of certain people: the way that a group of people conceive of themselves and think of themselves in their relations with other groups of people who are deemed to be in some significant ways different from themselves. What it means to be an American, a citizen of a sovereign nation that is Christian and specifically Protestant in origin, an English-speaking nation, a nation based on a republican and liberal ideology, with a distinctive immigrant tradition, and a strong positive inclination to support capitalism and to reject statism and big government—that is not what it means to be a Mexican or a Russian or even a Briton. In short, national identities are constituted by distinctive inter-subjective beliefs which only extend a certain distance in space and time and no farther. While identities can overlap they are at some point incommensurate. If Americans decided to impose their core beliefs on Mexicans they would discover and probably encounter an intellectual resistance and rejection based on counterpart but significantly different Mexican beliefs.

Constructivists focus not only on differences among people and the ways that people institutionalize and regulate their differences but also on the ways that people manage to create and sustain social, economic, and political relations in spite of their social differences. Different groups of people have managed to do that by means of sovereignty, human rights, international commerce, international organizations, nongovernmental organizations, and various other social institutions. At base, these joint arrangements are expressions or applications of ideas and beliefs that different peoples around the world hold in common and through which they are able to relate to each other and deal with each other—at least up to a point. None of that elaborate ideational framework exists on its own. All of it belongs to a world of inter-subjectivity. It has not always existed in the past. It will not always exist in the future. It is a product of human intellect at a certain period of world history. It is specifically historical.

Constructivism is an empirical approach to the study of international relations which displays some distinctive research interests and approaches. If the social and political world consists, at base, of shared beliefs, how does that affect the way we should account for important international events and episodes? Constructivists, as a rule, cannot subscribe to positivist conceptions of causality. That is because the positivists do not probe the inter-subjective content of events and episodes. For example, the well-known billiard ball image of international relations is rejected by constructivists because it fails to reveal the thoughts, ideas, beliefs, etc. of the actors involved in international conflicts. Constructivists want to probe the inside of the billiard balls to arrive at a deeper understanding of such conflicts.

Conflict, for constructivists, is understood not as a collision between forces or entities (i.e. states conceived as units) but rather as a disagreement or dispute or misunderstanding or lack of communication or some other intellectual discord or dissonance between conscious agents. Conflict is always a conflict of minds and wills of the parties involved. To correctly understand such conflict calls for an inquiry into the discourses at play in the event. That would disclose the sources and depth of the dispute and its intellectual obstacles and possibilities of resolution—in other words the sentiments and beliefs and ideas by which it is organized and expressed. A constructivist research program into an international conflict might be compared to the task of a diplomat assigned to investigate an international dispute with the aim of finding some common ground of agreement upon which a resolution of it could be based. If the diplomat fails in his efforts to mediate perhaps his autobiography may later give an account, his account, of the reasons why: the unrealistic demands, the lack of trust or good will, the obstinacy of the parties, etc. In short, the ideational basis of the dispute will be revealed and the 'causes' of it will be seen in the correct light: i.e. as inter-subjective discord.

In other words, constructivists are among those scholars who see research as a matter of interpretation more than explanation. They are skeptical of the possibilities of having a neutral stance towards research, which will result in objective knowledge that can be expanded as research findings accumulate. Some constructivists are more skeptical about objective knowledge than others. Constructivists who lean towards postmodernism are likely to be more skeptical, and those who lean towards a social science research agenda are less skeptical of objective knowledge. Some constructivists, perhaps those who formerly were positivist social scientists, speak of 'mechanisms and processes of social construction' (Finnemore and Sikkink 2001: 403). The language of 'mechanisms' and 'processes' inclines scholars to view the international world as an external reality that can be explained by knowing its own social forces and laws. Other constructivists who emphasize discourse and communication are inclined to understand the business of research as that of entering into the world of the people under study, scrutinizing their reasoning and language, exposing their assumptions and beliefs and showing how that conditions and shapes their behavior.

Some examples of the constructivist approach to social research include the following (drawn from Katzenstein 1996). In the study of national security, for example, constructivists pay careful attention to the influence and effects, we might say the conditioning, of culture and identity on security policies and actions. In the study of deterrence, they pay careful attention to the role of norms, particularly 'prohibitionary norms' and taboos that condition the limited use of nuclear and chemical weapons. In the study of armed intervention, they pay careful attention to normative and institutional arrangements that encourage and inhibit, permit and prohibit, such international actions. As a rule, constructivists are not satisfied with the explanations of neorealists that tend to disregard such conditioning elements and focus, instead, on military power or material interests alone. Constructivists say that international relations are more complex, and they pay particular attention to the cultural-institutional-normative aspects of that greater complexity. All those factors that capture the attention of constructivist researchers noted above—i.e. culture, identity, norms, institutions—are instances of an inter-subjective world that is created rather than an objective world that is discovered.

In an oft-repeated phrase, Alexander Wendt (1992) captured the core of IR constructivism in the following remark: 'anarchy is what states make of it'. His work is distinctive in specifically arguing, at great length, against the positivist theory of neorealism and particularly that of Kenneth Waltz. There is no objective international world apart from the practices and institutions that states arrange among themselves. In making that statement Wendt argues that anarchy is not some kind of external given which dictates a logic of analysis based on neorealism. Here Wendt is disagreeing fundamentally with the central thesis of neorealism: 'Self-help and power politics are institutions, not essential features of anarchy' (Wendt 1992: 395). That means that there is no inevitable 'security dilemma' between sovereign states because any situation that states find themselves in is a situation that they themselves have created. They are not prisoners of the anarchical structure of the state system. Not only is there no state system independent of the practices of states, but there also are no states independent of the rules by which states recognize each other. States construct one another in their relations and in so doing they also construct the international anarchy that defines their relations. In short, the political world, including international relations, is created and constituted entirely by people. Nothing social exists outside of that human activity or independent of it.

There are some important implications that follow from constructivist IR methodology. If 'anarchy is what states make of it' there is nothing inevitable or unchangable about world politics. Nothing is given or certain. Everything is inter-subjective and thus uncertain. Everything is in flux. The existing system is a creation of states and if states change their conceptions of who they are, what their interests are, what they want, etc. then the situation will change accordingly because the situation is nothing more or less than what they decide and do. States could decide, for example, to reduce their sovereignty or even to give up their sovereignty. If that happened there would no longer be an international anarchy as we know it. Instead, there would be a brave new, non-anarchical world—perhaps one in which states were subordinate to a world government. Perhaps they would construct a world in which they were all subject to 'the common good' (Onuf 1995). That would be a world beyond sovereignty and in some fundamental respects beyond modernity too. Moreover, if everything is uncertain and in flux it would be impossible to predict what international relations will be like tomorrow. Among other things, that means that a predictive and explanatory social science of IR could not be achieved.

That is not a conclusion that many constructivists are satisfied with. They see themselves as involved in the ambitious project of building a social science of IR. They do not see themselves as accepting the more modest goals of a humanistic IR comparable to that espoused by the classical approach. So constructivists usually want to remain within the behavioural revolution while not accepting the notion of an external, objective reality. What they accept is an inter-subjective reality: i.e. the claim that between human agents, including those agents who act on behalf of states, there can be mutual understanding, shared ideas, joint practices, and common rules that acquire a social standing that is independent of any of those agents. Collectively the rules and practices constitute an inter-subjective political reality. A social science of IR can be built upon the constructivist analysis of that inter-subjective reality. That is the goal of most constructivists.

The distance between constructivism and positivism in that respect is not as great as it might seem. That is clear from the following remark of one of the most prominent behavioralists in political science: 'The meanings people give to their political behavior are critical data for scientific observation precisely because, from the standpoint of the behavioral persuasion, there is no "behavior as such" in a purely physical or mechanistic sense. Observation is a communicative act in which both the observer and observed are mutually implicated . . . The observer's questions and the observed's responses must be mutually meaningful' (Eulau 1963). Eulau is saying that the external world of human behaviour is a social world: a sphere of human communication. Social scientists can only access that world in the first instance by communicating with it and thus by understanding it. The observer's hypotheses and theories, however, are independent and objective. They occupy a separate scientific realm of explanation. The methodological problem with constructivism emerges at this point: it has a split personality. In emphasizing inter-subjectivity it is post-positivist, but in emphasizing scientific explanation it is positivist. This issue will be explored further in the concluding section of the chapter.

Normative Theory

Normative IR theory is not really post-positivist; it is pre-positivist. Indeed, it is both modern and pre-modern: it is part of the history of political thought and it can be traced back as far as European antiquity, for example in the writings of Thucydides. Three leading contemporary IR normative theorists are Chris Brown (1992), Mervyn Frost (1996), Terry Nardin (1983), and Brown, Nardin, and Rengger (2002). Chris Brown (1992: 3) defines the approach succinctly: 'by normative international relations theory is meant that body of work which addresses the moral dimension of international relations and the wider questions of meaning and interpretation generated by the discipline. At its most basic it addresses the ethical nature of the relations between communities/states'. International politics involves some of the most fundamental normative issues that human beings ever encounter in their lives: issues of order, of war and peace, of justice and injustice, of human rights, of intervention in state sovereignty, of environmental protection, and similar ethical questions of a fundamental kind.

In many respects, though not all respects, normative theory is synonymous with the classical approach, except that it reaches farther into political theory and moral philosophy and it draws heavily on recent developments in these fields. 'Normative theory' is really another name for the political theory or the moral philosophy of international relations.

Most positivist IR scholars draw a basic distinction between empirical theory and normative theory. They see the latter as exclusively *prescriptive*. In other words, (positivist) empirical theory is a theory of facts, of what actually happens, whereas normative theory is a theory of values, of an ideal world that does not exist as such. Most normative theorists would reject that distinction as misleading. As normative theorists see it, normative theory is both about facts and values. The 'facts' of normative theory are the rules, institutions, and practices which have normative content; for example, rules about the conduct of war, or about human rights. Normative theory is primarily concerned with giving a theoretical account of those normative rules, institutions, and practices. It seeks to make explicit the normative issues, conflicts, dilemmas involved in the conduct of foreign policy and other international activities. In other words, normative theory is empirical in its own way. Furthermore, normative theorists point out that so-called non-normative theories are also value-based. They merely fail to be explicit about their normative premises and values.

Normative theorists attempt to clarify the basic moral issues of international relations. One noteworthy attempt is that of Chris Brown (1992) who summarizes the main normative controversies of world politics in terms of two rival moral outlooks which are captured by the terms 'cosmopolitanism' and 'communitarianism' (these normative problems are also taken up by International Society theory, see Chapter 5). Cosmopolitanism is a normative doctrine which focuses on individual human beings and on the whole community of humankind as the basic right- and duty-bearing units of world politics. Communitarianism is a contrasting normative doctrine which focuses on political communities, particularly sovereign states, as the fundamental normative units of world politics whose rights, duties, and legitimate interests have priority over all other normative categories and agencies. For Brown, a big part of contemporary normative theory is concerned with assessing these rival moral doctrines. One of the tasks of normative theory is determining which of these two important doctrines has priority and which ought to have priority. The questions are complex: Which rights do states have? Should they be allowed to possess weapons of mass destruction which are a threat to mankind? Which rights do individuals have? Do individual rights come before state rights? Are individuals formed by states—i.e. subjects, citizens? There are no simple answers. Many theorists are content to live with the proposition that the normative conflict between cosmopolitanism and communitarianism cannot be resolved once and for all; it can merely be understood and hopefully managed in an enlightened fashion.

Brown presents what is perhaps the most widespread view of normative theory in IR at the present time. A less widespread but in some ways more fundamental attempt to interrogate the morality of individuals and the morality of political communities is set forth by Mervyn Frost (1996):

> ... normative theory should be directed in the first place to the question: What should I, as citizen (or we the government, or we the nation, or we the community of states) do? But finding an answer to this kind of question usually depends on finding an answer to a prior question which is quite different. This prior and more important question is about the ethical standing of the institutions within which we find ourselves (and the ethical standing of the institutions within which others find themselves).

According to Frost, if we find that states are more important than other institutions, we might conclude that in certain circumstances it is a duty of citizens to risk their lives to safeguard their state. The aim of normative theory is to sort out 'the ethical standing of institutions' in relation to each other (Frost 1996: 4).

A third approach to normative theory is linked to the international society school (see Chapter 5) and focuses on the ethics of international law (Nardin 1983) and the ethics of statecraft (Jackson 1995; 1996). This approach addresses questions such as the following: Which groups of people qualify for recognition as sovereign states? Are the international responsibilities of all states the same or do some states have special responsibilities? Are there any conceivable circumstances under which a sovereign state's right of self-defense could be legitimately infringed? Is there any valid normative basis for denying admission to the nuclear club? Is international society responsible for providing personal security or is that an exclusively domestic responsibility of sovereign states? Is international society responsible for governing independent countries whose governments have for all intents and purposes ceased to exist? Must 'ethnic cleansing' always be condemned? Does the goal of defending or developing democracy justify military intervention and occupation of a country? Can international society reasonably expect national leaders to put their own soldiers in danger to protect human rights in foreign countries? Is there any normative basis for justifying the use of force to change international boundaries? Are there any conceivable circumstances under which global environmental protection could justifiably interfere with state sovereignty?

This third approach attempts to *theorize* the normative *practices* of states and state leaders. It emphasizes that international ethics at its core concerns the moral choices of statespeople. Thus the answers to international normative questions, such as those listed above, are provided in the first instance by the practitioners involved. The main task of normative theory is to interrogate those answers with the aim of spelling out, clarifying, and scrutinizing the framework of justification disclosed by them. This approach emphasizes that international ethics, just like ethics in any other sphere of human activity, develops within the activity itself—in this case the activity of statecraft—and is adapted to the characteristics and limits of human conduct in that sphere. According to this third approach to normative theory, scholars must assess the conduct of statespeople by the standards which are generally accepted by those same statespeople. Otherwise theory not only misjudges practices and loses touch with reality but it also misunderstands and misrepresents the moral world in which state leaders must operate and must be judged.

Normative theory rejects positivism as a flawed methodology that cannot address what normative theorists consider to be the most fundamental issues of international relations: moral decisions and dilemmas. Yet normative theory also parts company with those post-positivists who repudiate the classical tradition of political theory and moral philosophy. However, that also means that normative theory, like constructivism, is exposed to attack from both sides: it is exposed to the positivist critique that it fails to explain anything in scientific terms; and it is exposed to the postmodernist critique that it is dealing in the myths, delusions, and deceptions of supposedly antiquated classical values. Normative theorists and constructivists share a common approach in focusing on inter-subjective ideas and beliefs. But most constructivists are hoping to create a proper social science whereas most normative theorists are content to preserve, transmit, and augment the classical political theory of international relations (Brown, Nardin, and Rengger 2002).

....

Explaining IR Versus Understanding IR

The basic methodological divide in IR concerns the nature of the social world (ontology) and the relation of our knowledge to that world (epistemology). The ontology issue is raised by the following question: is there an *objective* reality 'out there' or is the world one of experience only: i.e. a *subjective* creation of people (Oakeshott 1933)? The extreme objectivist position is purely naturalist and materialist; i.e. international relations is basically a thing, an object, out there. The extreme subjectivist position is purely idealist; i.e. international relations is basically an idea or concept that people share about how they should organize themselves and relate to each other politically: it is constituted exclusively by language, ideas, and concepts.

The epistemology issue is raised by the following question: in what way can we obtain knowledge about the world? At one extreme is the notion of scientifically *explaining* the world. The task is to build a valid social science on a foundation of verifiable empirical propositions. At the other extreme is the notion of *understanding* the world. This latter task is to comprehend and interpret the substantive topic under study. According to this view, historical, legal, or moral problems of world politics cannot be translated into the terms of science without misunderstanding them.

We have indicated several times above that there is both a 'confrontationist' and a 'cooperative' view of the ontological divide between objectivism and subjectivism and the epistemological divide between explaining and understanding. One extreme position is taken up by behaviouralists and some positivists who strive for scientific theory based on a view of the world as an objective reality. Another extreme position is taken up by postmodernists for whom reality is a subjective creation of people. As regards epistemology, some postmodernists find that a satisfactory interpretation of the social and political world is possible, but other postmodernists reject even that (see the remarks above, about a nihilistic tendency in postmodernism). According to some scholars, only the extreme positions are intellectually coherent. A choice has to be made between 'positivist' and 'post-positivist' methodology. The two cannot be combined, because they have 'mutually exclusive assumptions' (Smith 1997: 186) about the world of international relations.

However, other IR scholars strive to avoid the extreme positions in the methodological debate. They seek out a middle ground which avoids the stark choice between either objectivism or subjectivism, either pure explaining or pure understanding. The desire for the middle ground is contained already in Max Weber's (1964: 88) definition of 'sociology' as 'a science which attempts the *interpretive* understanding of social action in order thereby to arrive at a causal *explanations* of its course and effects'. Weber is saying that it is true that scholars must understand the world in order to carry out their research into social phenomena. He is also saying, however, that that does not prevent scholars from proceeding to frame hypotheses to test empirical theories that seek to explain social phenomena. On that view (Sørensen 1998), IR is not compelled to a cruel choice between extreme versions of positivism or post-positivism. It can proceed on a methodological middle ground between subjectivism and objectivism, and between explaining and understanding. In other words, there is not an insurmountable gulf between positivist and post-positivist methodological extremes. Instead of an 'either/or' it is a 'both/and': rather than having to choose between extremes on the two dimensions we have discussed (subjectivity versus objectivity and explaining versus understanding) it is a question of finding a place somewhere on the continuum between the extremes.

Box 9.4 gives an indication of the appropriate position of the different methodological approaches on the two dimensions. The question mark behind postmodernism reflects our doubts as regards the position of that approach on the explaining/understanding axis. Postmodernism is 'understanding' in its critique of established theories, but it also contains a nihilistic tendency, as noted above. That creates doubts as to where the approach belongs on this axis. Nihilism is neither explaining nor understanding but, rather, is a different category. Some

---

Box 9.4 **The methodological debate: a summary**

ONTOLOGY:
OBJECTIVIST

Behavioralism

Positivism

Critical
theory

EPISTEMOLOGY: ———————————————— UNDERSTANDING
EXPLAINING

Construc-   Classical theory
tivism   Normative theory

Postmodernism?

SUBJECTIVIST

---

methodological approaches—e.g. constructivism and critical theory as well as the classical and normative approaches—are oriented more towards the middle ground than the extremes. It is noteworthy that some of the major debates within the established theoretical traditions in IR concern precisely this issue of the proper combination. The issue is at the heart of debates between, e.g. classical realists and neorealists (see Chapter 3); between different currents of the International Society School (see Chapter 5); and between various schools within liberalism (see Chapter 4). This chapter has shown how the debate continues within and between the different post-positivist approaches. However we choose to view this question, there can be little doubt but that it is the most fundamental methodological issue in IR.

. . . .

KEY POINTS

- Post-positivist approaches include: critical theory; postmodernism; constructivism; and normative theory. Critical theory is a development of Marxist thought; it seeks to unmask the global domination of the rich North over the poor South. Critical theory views knowledge as inherently political; social scientists and social science are instruments of power.

- Postmodernism disputes the notions of reality, of truth, of the idea that there is or can be an ever-expanding knowledge of the human world. Narratives, including metanarratives, are always constructed by a theorist and they are thus always contaminated by his or her standpoint and prejudices. Narratives can thus be deconstructed: i.e. taken apart to disclose their arbitrary elements and biased intentions.

- Constructivists agree with positivists that we can accumulate valid knowledge about the world. But in contrast to positivists, constructivists emphasize the role of ideas, of shared knowledge of the social world. States construct one another in their relations and in so doing they also construct the international anarchy that defines their relations. Anarchy is not a natural condition; anarchy is what states make of it.

- Normative theory attempts to clarify the basic moral issues of international relations. The main normative outlooks are cosmopolitanism and communitarianism. The questions raised by these outlooks are complex, e.g.: Which rights do states have? Which rights do individuals have? Do individual rights come before state rights? International ethics also concern the moral choices of statespeople.

- The two basic methodological dimensions of IR are the nature of the social world (ontology) and the relation of our knowledge to that world (epistemology). The ontological dimension concerns the nature of social reality: is it an objective reality 'out there' or is it a subjective creation of people? The epistemological dimension concerns the ways in which we can obtain knowledge about the world. Can we scientifically explain it or must we instead interpretively understand it?

- There is a 'confrontationist' and a 'cooperative' view of the methodological divide. The confrontationist view sees an insurmountable gulf between positivist and post-positivist methodology. The cooperative view sees a middle ground between different approaches.

. . . .

QUESTIONS

- Summarize the main issues in the debate between positivists and post-positivists. Which side in the debate do you favor? Why?

- Identify at least two major post-positivist approaches. What are the most significant methodological similarities and differences between the approaches identified?

- What is the better way of looking at IR methodologies: as categorically different or as conceptually overlapping?

- Outline the methodological outlooks of the classical approach and normative theory. Are there any significant differences between them or are they basically the same approach?

For additional material and resources see the companion web site at:
www.oup.co.uk/best.textbooks/politics/jacksonsorensen2e/

GUIDE TO FURTHER READING

Brown, C., Nardin, T., and **Rengger, N.** (eds.) (2002). 'Introduction', *International Relations in Political Thought*. Cambridge: Cambridge University Press.

Nicholson, M. (1996). 'The continued significance of positivism?' in S. Smith, K. Booth, and M. Zalevski (1996). *International Theory: Positivism and Beyond*. Cambridge: Cambridge University Press, 128–49.

Smith, S. (1997). 'New Approaches to International Theory,' in J. Baylis and S. Smith (eds.), *The Globalization of World Politics*. Oxford: Oxford University Press, 165–90.

Smith, S., Booth, K., and **Zalewski, M.** (eds.) (1996). *International Theory: Positivism and Beyond*. Cambridge: Cambridge University Press.

Wendt, A. (1992), 'Anarchy is what states make of it,' *International Organization* 46: 394–419.

WEB LINKS

http://www.uta.edu/huma/illuminations/
Critical Theory web site for those interested in the Critical Theory project. A collection of articles, excerpts, and chapters from many contemporary writers, based on Frankfurt School thought. Additional submissions from graduate students and others, links to other web sites, and related sources.

http://www.ukc.ac.uk/politics/publications/journals/kentpapers/webb4.html
Keith Webb's thorough paper on postmodernist thought is entitled 'Preliminary Questions about Postmodernism'. Hosted by the University of Kent.

http://home.pi.be/~lazone/
Comprehensive collection of links to online papers related to constructivism as well as links to other constructivist web resources. Hosted by Planet Internet.

http://www.qub.ac.uk/ies/onlinepapers/poe13–01.pdf
Applies Normative Theory to an analysis of the legitimacy of the European Union. The paper is written by Richard Bellamy and Dario Castiglione and is hosted by Queen's University Belfast.

10 New Issues in IR

SUMMARY

The theoretical traditions we examined earlier focus on the classical issues of IR: war and peace, cooperation and conflict, wealth and poverty. After the Cold War, a number of new issues came to the fore which demand attention. This chapter discusses four of the most important of these issues: the environment; gender; sovereignty; and changes in statehood. These issues were evident earlier; but for several reasons they stand higher on the agenda today. The chapter discusses whether the new issues are merely additional items on an already crowded agenda, or whether they signal a more profound transformation of IR theory.

Introduction

There have always been dissident voices in IR; scholars unhappy with the traditional focus of the discipline have taken up alternative positions and approaches. Indeed, some scholars claim that they are out to transform the discipline altogether. Whether that is likely to happen will be discussed below. This chapter discusses four of the most important new issues raised by various critics of established approaches: the environment; gender; sovereignty; and changes in statehood involving new security challenges. We could have chosen other issues, but these are sufficient to illustrate how new ones can enter the discipline and change its theoretical focus.

A new issue in IR is a topic which is considered to be important in terms of both values and theory. Values come into the picture because the decision on what is important and what is not is always based on certain values. Theory comes in because arguing in favor of a new issue must derive from some theoretical idea that this issue is important for the study of IR. For these reasons 'new issues' often involve new approaches to IR.

The discussion of new issues will proceed in the following way. First, we shall examine what the issue is about in empirical terms. What are the problems raised and why are they claimed to be important? Second, we shall consider how the issue in question affects the traditional concerns of international relations: war and peace, wealth and poverty. Finally, we shall discuss the nature of the theoretical challenge that the issues present to IR. Can they be handled by traditional approaches or do they require the cultivation of new approaches and concepts?

Box 10.1 New issues in IR

1. Concrete content of issue: What is it we should study and why?

2. Consequences of issue for core problems in IR: War and peace, conflict and cooperation, wealth and poverty?

3. Nature of theoretical challenge: Does the issue demand new approaches and concepts or can it be covered by traditional approaches?

We shall start with the environment, then proceed to gender, sovereignty, and changes in statehood. The order of presentation is not an indication that one issue is more important than another. The introduction to new issues will necessarily have to be brief; the reader is urged to consult the guide to further reading at the end of the chapter for references to in-depth treatment of a particular issue.

The Environment

Environmental topics have appeared more and more frequently on the international agenda over the last three decades. An increasing number of people, at least in Western countries, believe that human economic and social activity is taking place in a way that threatens the environment. In the last fifty years, more people have been added to the world's population than in all previous millennia of human existence. A vastly increasing global population pursuing higher standards of living is a potential threat to the environment.

Food production is an example of that. World food supply has grown faster than the global population over the last forty years. But the supply is unevenly distributed; there is a huge food surplus in the developed countries in the West and substantial shortages in many poor countries. Where food is scarce, people will often over-exploit the land in order to squeeze out of it what they can; that can lead to deforestation and desertification. Where food is abundant there may still be environmental problems due to the use of pesticides, the depletion of scarce water resources, and the energy input required for high productivity agriculture.

Industrial mass production threatens the depletion of scarce resources of raw materials and energy. Local problems of environmental degradation have international ramifications. Air pollution does not stop at borders; acid rain from France, for example, threatens people, groundwater, fish in lakes, and forests not only in France but also in neighboring European countries. The production of CFC (chlorofluorocarbon) gases, used for refrigeration, air conditioning, solvents, and other industrial products, is a major threat to the ozone layer, the gaseous mantle which protects the earth from the ultraviolet rays of the sun. CFC interacts chemically with the ozone layer so as to deplete it. Carbon dioxide and other chemical compounds lock in heat close to the surface of the earth and thereby produce global warming, the so-called greenhouse effect. Global warming means severe air pollution and rising sea levels, a potential threat to perhaps half of the world's population which lives in coastal areas.

If international security and global economics are the two major traditional issue areas in world politics, some scholars now claim that the environment has emerged as the third major issue area (Porter and Brown 1996: 1). The United Nations created a Conference on the Human Environment which convened for the first time in Stockholm in 1972. The grand meeting in Rio in 1992, the occasion of the UN Conference on Environment and Development, was the first global environmental summit in world history.

How serious is the problem of environmental degradation? We do not know precisely, because any assessment will have to rest on uncertain estimates and a number of disputable assumptions about future developments. One side in this debate is taken up by 'modernists' who believe that continued improvement

---

Box 10.2 **The environment issue**

More than twice as many people inhabit the earth today as when the post-war era began. Indeed, more people have been added to the world's population in the past five decades than in all the previous millennia of human existence . . . Developing countries already have 78 per cent of the people in the world; as much as 94 per cent of the current increase is also taking place in these countries . . .

Evidence has accumulated of widespread ecological degradation resulting from human activity: soils losing fertility or being eroded, overgrazed grasslands, desertification, dwindling fisheries, disappearing species, shrinking forests, polluted air and water. These have been joined by the newer problems of climate change and ozone depletion.

The Commission on Global Governance (1995). *Our Global Neighbourhood*. New York: Oxford University Press, 25–29

---

in scientific knowledge and in our technological competence will enhance our capability to protect the environment. In other words, we shall continue to improve our skills and techniques of producing and consuming in environment-friendly ways. For example, emissions of CFC-gases are being cut down; industrial production requires less input of scarce raw materials than before; more food is grown in ecologically sustainable ways (see for example Simon and Kahn 1984; Lomborg 2001).

The other side in the debate is taken up by 'ecoradicals' who think that the ecosystem has a limited carrying capacity. Such a limit 'defines how large a species population can become before it overuses the resources available in the eco-system' (Hughes 1991: 410). 'Ecoradicals' believe that human societies on earth are moving dangerously closer to the limits of the planet's carrying capacity; they also think that there are no simple technological fixes that can take care of the problem. Therefore, many 'ecoradicals' call for strict population control and dramatic change in modern lifestyles towards a more environment-friendly, less consumption-oriented and waste-producing way of life (Hughes 1991: 409; see also *World Commission on Environment and Development*, 1987 [The Brundtland Report]).

Let us turn to the second question mentioned in Box 10.1; the consequences of the environment issue for the core problems in IR. In which ways can environment problems increase international conflict? A current example is the dispute over water resources in the Middle East. Water conflicts in the Middle East are not a new issue at all; they have been present in the area for a long time. The region is extremely arid and conflicts over water date back to the seventh century BC. Today this issue is part of the Arab–Israeli conflict. The relatively small Jordan river basin is shared by Syria, Lebanon, Israel, and Jordan; there are not many other sources of water. The Arab League attempted to divert the Jordan away from Israel

---

Box 10.3 **The environment issue: Main positions in the debate**

'MODERNISTS':

Environment is not a serious problem. Progress in knowledge and technology will enable us to protect the environment

'ECORADICALS':

Environment is a very serious problem. Drastic change of lifestyles plus population control to promote sustainable development is necessary

A modernist statement:

'More people and increased income produce problems in the short run. These problems present opportunity, and prompt the search for solutions. In a free society, solutions are eventually found, though many people fail along the way at cost to themselves. In the long run the new developments leave us better off than if the problems had not arisen'.

An ecoradical statement:

'[O]nly a thoroughgoing ecocentric Green political theory is capable of providing the kind of comprehensive framework we need to usher in a lasting resolution to the ecological crisis . . . an ecocentric polity would be one in which there is a democratic state legislature (which is part of a mutilevelled decision-making structure that makes it less powerful than the existing nation state and more responsive to the political determinations of local, regional, and international democratic decision-making bodies); a greater dispersal of political and economic power both within and between communities, a far more extensive range of macro-controls on market activity; and the flowering of an ecocentric emancipatory culture'.

Myers and Simon (1994: 65)

Eckersley (1992: 175, 185)

---

in the early 1960s; that was one of the major factors in the war between Israel and the Arabs in 1967 which Israel won. More than a third of Israel's current water supplies come from territories occupied since the 1967 war. If a permanent peace in the area is going to be built it will have to be based, at least in part, on a resolution of the conflict over water (Gleick 1993; Lowi 1993). Water in the Middle East is a clear example of how environmental scarcity can exacerbate inter-state conflict.

As some of the previous chapters indicate, the classical focus of IR is on international conflict, and particularly war between states. Some scholars argue, however, that the typical violent conflict stemming from environment problems is not inter-state, but intra-state—i.e. within countries. A research project led by Thomas Homer-Dixon argues that environmental scarcity involves persistent, low-intensity conflict that may not lead to dramatic confrontations, but can wear down governments (Homer-Dixon 1995: 178). For example, it can cause urban migration and unrest, decreased economic productivity; ethnic conflicts, etc. Homer-Dixon argues, in a more speculative vein, that 'countries experiencing chronic internal conflict because of environmental stress will probably either fragment or become more authoritarian. ... Authoritarian regimes may be inclined to launch attacks against other countries to divert popular attention from internal stresses' (1995: 179). Environmental scarcity demonstrates the connection between international conflict and domestic conflict and that is where environmentalist IR scholars focus their analysis.

But environmental problems can also put pressures on states to engage in greater international cooperation. The reason is that environmental degradation can be said to make up a special kind of 'threat' which is not a threat to states but to mankind as a whole. It is a threat to the 'global commons'—i.e. the oceans, the seas, the ozone layer, and the climate system, which are a life support system for mankind as a whole. Consequently, some IR scholars see a need for global cooperation in order to face that threat.

Environmental problems have in fact encouraged international cooperation in recent years. International regimes (see Chapter 4) have been set up in a number of specific areas to address various environment issues, including: acid rain; ozone depletion; whaling; toxic waste trade; Antarctic environment; global warming; biodiversity loss (see Porter, Brown, and Chasek 2000). The ozone regime is one of the more prominent examples of international cooperation on the environment. It contains an international agreement to cut back and eventually phase out the production of CFCs and thus aims to reverse the damage to the ozone layer which has occurred in recent decades. Several other regimes, by contrast, have been less promising because of the lack of sufficient commitment and tangible cooperation from participating countries (see Haas *et al.* 1993). In sum, the environment issue can involve international conflict over scarce resources, such as water, as well as international cooperation to preserve the global commons, such as the ozone regime. It is not possible to predict whether collaboration or discord will prevail because that depends on a number of different, unforeseen circumstances.

It remains to address the third item in Box 10.1: the nature of the theoretical challenge posed by the environment issue. Does the issue demand new

---

Box 10.4 **Environment, cooperation, and conflict**

Environment as a source of *inter-state* conflict: e.g. water in the Middle East

Environment as a source of *intra-state* conflict: e.g. soil erosion; population growth; migration

Environmental pollution and degradation as a *special hazard* requiring international cooperation: e.g. regimes to preserve the global commons approaches and concepts or can it be explained by traditional approaches? Many of the questions raised by the environment issue can be comfortably tackled by traditional approaches. For realists the environment issue is merely one more explainable source of conflict between states which can be added to an already long list. For liberals the environment adds one more issue, albeit a very important one, to the agenda of international cooperation and regime formation. For IPE scholars the environment can be accounted for as an aspect of the global economy. In short, the traditional approaches take us a long way in dealing with the environment issue.

However, some aspects of that issue sit uncomfortably with the traditional approaches. Domestic social and political conflict is one such aspect; the environment cuts across the dividing line between domestic politics and international politics in ways not taken sufficiently into account by the traditional approaches' focus on international relations (Hurrell 1995). IR environmentalist scholars argue that it is necessary to get beyond the traditional focus on states, because so many other actors are important when it comes to the environment: e.g., transnational corporations, NGOs, consumers, etc. Yet it is possible to argue, in reply, that liberals and IPE theorists are used to dealing with domestic conflict and with many different types of actors.

We made a distinction earlier between 'modernists' and 'ecoradicals'. It is the 'ecoradical' position which challenges traditional IR approaches. 'Ecoradicals' call for dramatic changes in lifestyles, including very significant changes in economic and political organization. They criticize arguments, such as the Brundtland Report, which call for environment protection within a framework of sustainable growth. 'Ecoradicals' find that this is 'not a call for abandoning the race, but for changing the running technique' (Sachs 1993: 10). For them, real sustainability means abandoning industrial mass production and reverting to some form of de-industrialized society (Lee 1993). Behind such extreme ideas lie a world view profoundly different from the 'modernist,' anthropocentric view that is dominant in Western secular thinking—i.e. that man is above nature. This point is also dominant in Christian thinking; i.e. in Genesis (see Box 10.5) man is commanded to master the natural environment. The corollary of this view is that man is allowed to exploit nature in pursuit of human destiny and development. The 'ecoradical' world view is very different; it puts equal value on man and nature as part of one single biosystem. On this view man has no right to exploit nature. Man has a duty to live in harmony with nature and to respect and sustain the overall ecological balance (Eckersly 1992; Goodin 1992).

'Ecoradicals' call for profound changes not only in economic but also in political organization. They argue that the state is more of a problem than a solution for environmental problems. The state is part of modern society and modern society is the cause of the environmental crisis (Carter 1993). But there is no agreement among 'ecoradicals' about the role of the state or what to put in place of the state. On the one hand, there is a recognition of the need for centralized, global political

---

Box 10.5 A Christian view

Then God said, 'Let us make man in our image, after our likeness; and let them have dominion over the fish of the sea, and over the birds of the air, and over the cattle, and over all the earth, and over every creeping thing that creeps upon the earth'.

Genesis, Book 1, Verse 26; extract from *The Oxford Annotated Bible* (1962)

---

control in order to facilitate overall management of the global ecosystem. On the other hand, there is a recognition that small, self-reliant, local communities are best suited to promote non-consumerist lifestyles in ecological balance with specific local conditions (Hurrell 1995; Paterson, 1996). It is clear that 'ecoradicals' repudiate the conventional view of international relations based on the state system. If we adopt the 'ecoradical' view, much traditional IR theory will have to be abandoned. International relations would take on a whole new meaning from the viewpoint of a global ecosystem mortally endangered by the arrogance of the human quest for modern living based on high levels of material well-being. If we adopt the 'modernist' view, most traditional IR-theory can be retained because it is well suited to deal with collaboration and discord including conflicts arising from the environment issue.

In short, the nature of the challenge to IR posed by the environment issue depends to a large degree on one's position in the environment debate. Depending on that position, the environment issue is either one additional item on an agenda which can comfortably be managed by traditional approaches, or it is a very special issue which requires us to reconstruct our entire way of thinking about international relations.

....

Gender

Gender issues have received increasing attention in many areas of the social sciences in recent decades. The starting point for introducing gender to IR is often the debate about basic inequalities between men and women and the consequences of such inequalities for world politics. For example, a recent book on global gender issues (Peterson and Runyan 1993; 1999) argues that compared to men, women are a disadvantaged group in the world. Women own about one per cent of the world's property and make up less than five per cent of the heads of state and cabinet ministers. Women put in about 60 per cent of all working hours, but they only take home 10 per cent of all income. Women also account for

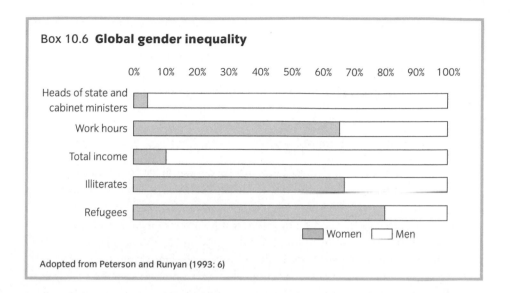

Box 10.6 **Global gender inequality**

Adopted from Peterson and Runyan (1993: 6)

60 per cent of all illiterates and about (together with their children) 80 per cent of all refugees.

Peterson and Runyan emphasize that these dramatic differences have nothing to do with objective differences between men and women. Very few educated Westerners would argue that men are naturally brighter, wiser, and better suited for high-paid jobs than women. They claim that the differences have to do with gender inequality. Gender 'refers to socially learned behaviour and expectations that distinguish between masculinity and femininity' (Peterson and Runyan 1993: 5). The argument is that we presently live in a gendered world in which values associated with 'masculinity' (e.g. rationality, activity, strength) are assigned higher value and status than values associated with 'femininity '(e.g. emotionality, passivity, weakness). This amounts to a gender hierarchy: a system of power in which men are privileged over women.

Peterson and Runyan go on to argue that most statistical and other indicators of development conceal the unequal position of women. Growth rates, the gross national product per capita, unemployment rates, etc. reveal little about the position of women. A gender-sensitive focus on world politics seeks to bring such gender inequalities into the open, to empirically demonstrate the subordinate positions of women and to explain how the working of the international political and economic system 'reproduces' an underprivileged position for women. For example, Peterson and Runyan point out that much work done by men is visible and paid while much work done by women is invisible and unpaid. Other studies suggest that economic development policies of 'structural adjustment' adopted by the IMF and the World Bank and changes in the international division of labour contribute to an increased 'feminization of poverty' (True 1996: 219). Low-paid, strenuous work in export processing zones in the developing world, sex-tourism, and migrant domestic labour are examples of how developments in the international economy involve the exploitation of women. Different forms of gender inequality and discrimination can be found in advanced industrial societies even after many decades of high rates of participation of women in the workforce.

Box 10.7 **Women and unpaid work**

Much work in society goes unrecognized and unvalued—work in the household and in the community. And most of it is done by women. *Human Development Report 1995* estimated that, in addition to the $23 trillion in recorded world output in 1993, household and community work accounts for another $16 trillion. And women contribute $11 trillion of this invisible output.

In most countries women do more work than men. In Japan women's work burden is about 7% higher than men's, in Austria 11% and in Italy 28% higher. Women in developing countries tend to carry an even larger share of the workload than those in industrial countries—on average about 13% higher than men's share, in rural areas 20% higher. In rural Kenya women do 35% more work than men. In some countries women's work burden is extreme. Indian women work 69 hours a week, while men work 59. Nepalese women work about 77 hours, men 56.

United Nations Development Programme (UNDP) (1996: 15–16)

Box 10.8 **Gender dichotomies**

Conquering nature, digging out her treasure and secrets . . . these are familiar and currently deadly refrains. The identification of nature as female is not an accident but a historical development that is visible in justifications by elites for territorial and intellectual expansion . . . The gendered dichotomies of culture–nature, subject–object, exploiter–exploited, agency–passivity, and leader–follower are reproduced in the process and justification of exploiting human mothers and 'mother nature'.

Peterson and Runyan (1993: 40)

Feminist IR scholars also argue that the way many conventional IR scholars approach the study of world politics discloses gendered thinking. According to radical feminists, the realist idea of security based on the military defence of states in an international anarchy is a masculinist way of thinking which conceals the continued existence of a gender hierarchy in world politics: i.e. protection from an outside threat is also protection of a domestic jurisdiction which insures a persisting subordination of women (Sylvester 1994).

In sum, a gender sensitive perspective on IR investigates the inferior position of women in the international political and economic system and analyses how our current ways of thinking about IR tend to disguise as well as to reproduce a gender hierarchy.

Let us turn to the second question in Box 10.1: what are the consequences of the gender issue for core problems in IR? Feminist IR scholars argue that war and peace, conflict and cooperation are gendered activities, and they believe that a research focus which reveals that fact will provide fresh insights. On the one hand, the military and indeed most activities connected with war and conflict and the conduct of foreign policy are conducted by men and take place in a universe dominated by male values. Nancy McGlen and Meredith Sarkess (1993) have studied the small group of women working close to the top in the US Departments of State and Defense. They point out that women are rarely 'insiders' in those institutions. Foreign policy and military policy is largely a male preserve.

On the other hand, women do play crucial roles in many activities related to war and conflict, and feminist IR scholars show that those roles can be revealed if we care to look for them. Women are there as diplomatic wives, as workers for defense contractors, as prostitutes serving military bases, as civilian victims of wars, and particularly as refugees (Enloe 1990). In other words, war is not an activity reserved for men or confined to men. Rather, war is a gendered activity with specific, frequently subordinate, positions for women. Yet the dominant ideology sees men as 'Just Warriors' and women as the 'Beautiful Souls' who are being protected (Ehlstain 1987). Feminist scholars argue that this ideology 'keeps women and men from questioning the essential purpose and the negative effects of war, militarization, and violence on their own and other's lives' (Peterson and Runyan 1993: 91).

According to some scholars, gender inequality is in itself a source of conflict. Population analysts argue that a high level of inequality between men and women, particularly inequality of masculine and feminine roles, leads to a faster rate of population growth. This is because there is 'a strong inverse correlation between the adult female literacy rate and the total fertility rate' (Kennedy 1993: 341). In other words, women in poverty without any education marry early, have little knowledge of contraceptives, and give birth to a large number of children. Paul Kennedy argues that the population explosion will perhaps be the biggest challenge in the coming century. Successfully confronting that challenge will require a change in gender roles, because 'a change in the status of women would significantly reduce population growth in the developing world' (Kennedy 1993: 342).

We saw in Chapter 2 that the academic discipline of IR was founded around the First World War for the purpose of promoting international peace and cooperation. Yet the discipline has not paid much attention to women's movements for peace and cooperation. Feminist scholars have tried to change that. For example, Amy

Swerdlow argues that the activities of the Women Strike for Peace (WSP) movement in the US in the early sixties persuaded President Kennedy of the urgent need for a nuclear arms control treaty with the Soviet Union (Swerdlow 1990). Cynthia Enloe argues that the withdrawal of Russian mothers' support for the Soviet army as a result of the war in Afghanistan contributed to the delegitimation of the Communist regime and so helped end the Cold War (Enloe 1994).

We turn now to the third question in Box 10.1, concerning the nature of the theoretical challenge posed by the gender issue. When we look at the gender debate, we can identify a number (see for example Steans 1998) of feminist theories that challenge mainstream IR in different ways. The three major theoretical approaches to gender are: liberal feminism; Marxist/Socialist feminism; and Radical feminism.

Liberal feminism has equal rights for men and women as its major concern. In Chapter 4 we emphasized that the core concern of liberalism is the freedom and happiness of individual human beings. Liberal feminists point out that basic liberal rights of life, liberty, and property have not been extended in equal measure to women. Mary Wollstonecraft wrote *Vindication of the Rights of Woman* in 1792, arguing that women should have the same access as men to economic opportunities and to education (see Steans 1998: 16–18). Contemporary liberal feminists want women to be more active in world politics, to eliminate unequal access to power and influence of men and women, and thus to achieve equal rights for men and women (Tong 1989; Eisenstein 1983, and Gatens 1989). Robert Keohane has argued in favor of an alliance between neoliberal republicanism and liberal feminism. He finds that such theory can help examine international relations 'from below'; i.e. from the standpoint of those that have been excluded from power. Furthermore, according to Keohane, such a theory of IR 'could help articulate an institutional vision of international relations—a network view, emphasizing how institutions could promote lateral co-operation among organized entities, states or otherwise' (Keohane 1989b: 248). Yet some feminist scholars are worried by the prospect of such an alliance; they fear that it would involve the subordination of a gender approach to an established mainstream theory which seeks to mould the gender view according to its own priorities (Zalewski 1993: 13–32).

Marxist feminism ascribes the inferior position of women to the economic, social, and political structures of the capitalist system. One of the earliest detailed analyses that posits that connection is *The Origins of the Family, Private Property and the State* by Friedrich Engels, close friend of Karl Marx, written in 1884. Engels noted how capitalism established a division between productive work in the factory and 'invisible' work in the private sphere, at home. Men took care of the productive, paid work in the factory while women were at home, taking care of the unpaid, 'invisible' work. This reduced women to second-class citizens. Marxist feminists note how women in the contemporary labor market are mostly in low paid, low-status jobs. They argue that the only road to equal treatment of women is an overthrow of the capitalist system (Barrett 1980; Tong 1989; Landry and Maclean 1993). Socialist feminism attempts to combine the insights of Marxist feminism with an analysis of patriarchy—i.e. a male-centered and male-dominated household. The oppression of women is seen to follow inevitably from the dual systems of capitalism and patriarchy (Mitchell 1977). Capitalism is the oppressive mode of production; patriarchy is the oppressive mode of reproduction (Steans 1998: 21). Marxist/Socialist feminism thus focuses on the ways in which capitalism and patriarchy places women in an underprivileged position. This focus can be connected with IPE-theory inspired by Marxism. From the analysis of economic exploitation based on class it is relatively easy to include gender (and race) in the inquiry.

In sum, we can find some common ground between liberal feminism and the liberal tradition in IR, and between Marxist/Socialist feminism and the Marxist tradition in IPE. The remaining feminist approach, radical feminism, rejects any such cooperation. Radical feminists want to develop a more genuine and independent feminist analysis that can entirely avoid subordinating gender to traditional IR agendas (Peterson and Runyan 1999; Daly 1979). Only then will it be possible to undertake the theoretical and practical steps necessary to fully develop a gender sensitive analysis of international relations. We cannot lay out and investigate such an analysis in the present context; we can only sketch the direction it is supposed to take (Peterson and Runyan 1999).

Core concepts of IR, such as violent conflict, security, power, and sovereignty would have to be redefined. For example, violent conflict is not only inter-national; it must include both domestic violence against women, and structural violence against women i.e. the oppression and hardship that women suffer from political and economic structures that subject them to unequal positions. Such aspects of violence demand a concept of security that is radically different from the traditional concept. New theories will be needed that locate gender hierarchies and the question of women's rights and status at the constitutive core. Most probably that will involve a significant downgrading of an autonomous discipline of IR. The gender focus will thus open IR up to a broader tradition of social theory concerned with studies of social power and human emancipation. Finally, gender studies in IR would encourage or even necessitate a methodological move away from the positivism that has been closely connected with neorealism and neo-liberalism, towards some of the post-positivist positions introduced in the previous chapter.

Sovereignty

Sovereignty is an international institution, meaning a set of rules that states play by. The rules constitute and regulate the external independence and the domestic authority of states. It is perhaps somewhat surprising to see 'sovereignty' listed among the new issues in IR. After all, from the beginning the discipline has had the analysis of relations among *sovereign* states as one of its central preoccupations. So what could possibly make sovereignty a 'new issue'? One answer is that the institution of sovereignty is developing and changing in ways not sufficiently foreseen by the traditional approaches. There has been a tendency for many IR scholars, especially realists, to consider sovereignty as a given which, once established, does not change. This assumption has probably never been strictly true. But today there is more reason to question it.

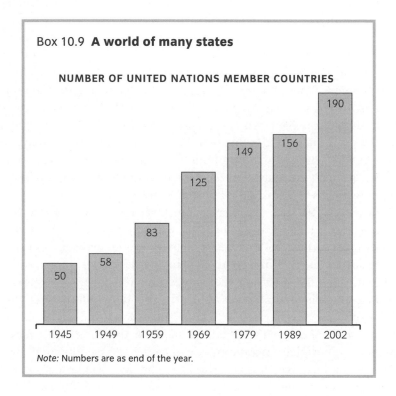

Box 10.9 **A world of many states**

NUMBER OF UNITED NATIONS MEMBER COUNTRIES

1945	1949	1959	1969	1979	1989	2002
50	58	83	125	149	156	190

Note: Numbers are as end of the year.

What are the changes that are sparking a new debate about sovereignty? Recall that sovereignty means that a state enjoys political independence from other states. The government has supreme authority to give and enforce the law within its territory. States are juridically equal under international law. In particular, 'No state or group of states has the right to intervene, directly or indirectly, for any reason whatever, in the internal or external affairs of any other state' (UN Declaration of Principles of International Law, 1970). In other words, sovereign governments have a right to control their own territory and to be independent of all other states. Many scholars still think of sovereignty in that way as a basic institution of international society (James 1986).

But a growing number of scholars consider this view to be outdated. These latter authors argue that sovereignty is increasingly challenged from several sides.

First, global market forces more easily penetrate borders and affect national economies in unprecedented ways. Environmental concerns; global communication systems; nuclear weapons; terrorism; the drug trade; all of that and much else are examples of activities and forces that reach across borders and call into question older notions of autonomous sovereign states in full control of their territories (Camilleri & Falk 1992; Lapidoth 1992; Elkins 1995).

Second, the development of norms concerning international protection of human rights and humanitarian law are seen to infringe sovereignty because they challenge the principle of non-intervention—i.e. the right of states to govern their citizens free from outside interference. Several UN General Secretaries have argued in favor of a move away from the norm of non-intervention. In 1991, Javier Perez de Cuellar stated that all nations had a responsibility to live up to the UN Charter requirements concerning human rights and democracy. Failure to do so, he indicated, could provoke UN intervention. In 1992, Boutros Boutros-Ghali claimed that 'the time of absolute and exclusive sovereignty . . . has passed. Its theory was never matched by reality' (quoted from Helman and Ratner 1992–3: 10).

Finally, there is the core area of warfare and control of the means of violence. On the one hand, states are no longer in exclusive control of the means of violence in their domestic jurisdiction. In the United States, for example, expenditures for private security forces are now more than double the amount spent on public police forces (*The Economist*, April 19–25, 1997: 21–23). That is of course legal. But if it was illegal it probably could not be entirely prevented. On the other hand, in weak states the order provided by the government may only extend to some parts but not to all parts of the country; in other areas, dissident groups often control significant territory.

In sum, if sovereignty means that governments must actually be in control within their own territory then there is reason to doubt the efficacy and extent of their sovereignty. Some authors think that these developments may even spell an 'end of sovereignty'—at least in the sense that state sovereignty tells us less and less about how states actually function and what type of constraints they really face (Camilleri & Falk 1992). Yet this observation fails to appreciate that sovereignty is an *institution* based on *norms* and there has rarely been a time when those norms have not been challenged or disobeyed by somebody. It must also be stressed that we continue to live in a world of sovereign states. There are no rival forms of political organization which seriously challenge state sovereignty. The sovereign state has out-competed a large number of rival forms of political organization since its first establishment in Europe three or four centuries ago (Tilly 1990). Sovereign statehood also remains very popular around the world. The number of sovereign states has increased more than threefold since 1945. Many ethno-political groups would like to form their own state; Kurds and Palestinians are only two well-known examples from a much larger number of cases (Gurr and Harff 1994).

Finally, new challenges to the state, such as an increasingly internationalized economy, must be seen in context of the state's increased capacities for response. States can exploit modern science and technology as much as anyone. They have been doing just that for centuries. Technological developments have enhanced the state's capacity for surplus extraction, regulation, and surveillance. Some scholars argue that the capacity of states to regulate and control their societies has increased over time rather than declined (Krasner 1993). In other words, even if there are challenges to sovereignty as noted above, in the past sovereignty has usually responded and remain a strong and prominent institution (see Box 10.10). We therefore find the 'end of sovereignty' thesis to be somewhat misleading. Sovereignty still remains a supremely important institution of world politics.

Box 10.10 **Sovereignty under pressure?**

CHALLENGES TO SOVEREIGNTY:

1. Global market forces; environmental concerns; global communication; nuclear weapons; terrorism; drug trade
2. Human rights and humanitarian law
3. Domestic monopoly of violence challenged: terrorism, etc.

ARE STATES THEN WEAKER?

Yes: They face new constraints on sovereignty.

No: They have increased capacities and no rivals exist.

Let us recall the second question in Box 10.1. What are the consequences of the foregoing challenges to sovereignty for core problems in IR? It is not possible to address all aspects of this question here. We shall investigate changes in the institution of sovereignty and the consequences of such changes for conflict and cooperation. Talking about change avoids two pitfalls; one is the static view of some traditional approaches (especially neorealism) where sovereignty remains a fixed given. Another is the 'endism' view in which all change is taken to mean the demise of sovereignty.

We shall argue that state sovereignty has become a more diversified institution over time as it has encompassed the entire world. Some changes in sovereignty have led to new forms of cooperation among the developed democracies in the North. Other changes have led to new forms of conflict in weak states in the South (Jackson 1990; Sørensen 1997). New forms of cooperation among sovereign states in the North have been pushed by economic globalization which makes it more difficult and costly for countries to control economic developments within their own borders. To resort to isolation—i.e. to shut off the country from outside influence (autarky)—is hardly a way out. In an increasingly interdependent world, isolation is not good for national welfare as demonstrated by North Korea and a few other countries. Globalization obliges advanced states to cooperate with others for mutual benefit; the industrialized democracies reap considerable welfare benefits from globalization. Closer cooperation means that states allow other states to participate in regulating certain mutually beneficial activities within their borders. Each cooperating state does that in return for a similar influence on other states. One scholar has argued that this means sovereignty is becoming 'less a territorially defined barrier than a bargaining resource for a politics characterized by complex transnational networks' (Keohane 1995: 252).

Such forms of cooperation commonly take place among the developed OECD countries but it is the members of the European Union that have gone farthest in that direction. The EU has autonomous authority in certain agreed areas, which has consequences for the sovereignty of participating states. In some areas the EU is able to make binding rules for its members, e.g. matters concerning the Single Market. States involved in that form of concentrated cooperation can be called postmodern states. They are different from modern, Westphalian states in that sovereignty is no longer exclusively vested in the state.[1]

This intense form of cooperation is not anticipated by neorealist and neoliberal approaches. Relations between EU members are not characterized by anarchy and self-help as claimed by neorealists. There is an element of 'authority, administration, and law' in EU-relations, words that neorealists exclusively reserve for the analysis of domestic politics (Waltz 1979). EU cooperation has also gone further than the linkages foreseen by republican and interdependence liberalism. EU states are not merely liberal democracies that share common moral values; there is an integrated polity that exists beyond the sovereignty of member states. There is not merely economic interdependence; there is an integrated economic space which is no longer based on purely national economics. In such a context, the use of military force to solve conflicts is out of the question. The EU is a special kind of security and welfare community which is not a new state but is substantially more than standard forms of inter-state cooperation. The argument is summarized in Box 10.11.

We turn to the Third World to take a closer look at the sovereignty of its weak states and the distinctive patterns of conflict which that involves. These weak states originally were European colonies that achieved sovereignty as a result of decolonization. That process created a new type of 'quasi-states' in the international system which is unable to play by the full set of rules set up by the developed countries (Jackson 1990). Such states have fragile or ineffective

---

[1] Formally, states retain the freedom of choice: they can opt out of cooperation. But outside of a few special cases using that possibility would have disastrously negative consequences for the standard of living. See also Keohane (1995: 253).

Box 10.11 New forms of sovereignty and cooperation

Sovereignty changes due to more intense cooperation: Countries bargain about influence on each other's internal affairs.

EU members have taken this cooperation farthest. The EU can make binding rules for its members in some areas.

The EU is a special kind of tightly knit security and welfare community. Violent conflict among members is out of the question.

---

political institutions that can claim little or no legitimacy from the population. There is also usually a lack of national unity and most often the economy is poor and underdeveloped. As a consequence, such weak states are not able to stand on their own feet in the international system.

The traditional assumptions of sovereignty do not apply to such weak states. They need special, preferential treatment from the developed world, for example in the form of economic aid. For such states the international system is not one of anarchy and self-help—as argued by neorealists. It is rather a political order which supports the survival of weak states. These states are at best marginal players in the international system. They are often obliged to take what they can get from the richer and stronger countries.

In addition to being vulnerable and dependent externally, weak states have often been incapable of creating domestic order. In extreme cases this has led to a more or less complete breakdown of domestic order, i.e. 'failed states', such as Somalia, Rwanda, Liberia, and Sudan. That is the domestic background for humanitarian intervention: i.e. attempts by the UN to intervene in order to safeguard the population (Zartman 1995; Weiss and Collins 1996). In short, the external dependency and internal disorder of weak states has provoked some basic changes in the sovereignty game.

Box 10.12 Weak states and new forms of conflict

Sovereignty changes with decolonization: Weak states become independent but they are unable to take care of themselves.

The international system supports the survival of weak states. In regard to such states international order is often combined with domestic anarchy.

State failure may lead to humanitarian intervention. That challenges the sovereignty principle of non-intervention.

This brief discussion has by no means exhausted the issue. What we do hope to have demonstrated is that it is more accurate to speak of 'changes in sovereignty' than to speak of the 'end of sovereignty.' The changes taking place do not necessarily mean the demise of sovereignty but that does not make them any less important. What they do seem to indicate is important alterations in the nature of independent statehood—both by postmodern states in the North and by weak states in the South. We further explore some of the most important of these changes in the next section.

Let us recall the third question in Box 10.1. We believe that the analysis of sovereignty does not require wholly new approaches to IR. What it does call for is further development of existing approaches and abandonment of a view of sovereignty as a fixed and unchanging institution. The fact is: sovereignty is an historical and thus an evolving institution. Changes in the institution of sovereignty should be a high priority on the research agenda of IR. There are indications that this is happening. Neorealists have started investigating state sovereignty in a longer historical perspective as well as the concept itself (Krasner 1993; 1988; 1999). Neoliberals are examining how complex interdependence changes sovereignty (Keohane 1995). Scholars working from an International Society perspective are exploring the historical diversity of the institution of state sovereignty (Jackson 1999; Sørensen 1999). Several of the alternative approaches discussed in Chapter 9 also take an active interest in sovereignty (see for example Biersteker and Weber 1996).

....

Changes in Statehood and New Security Challenges

We emphasized in Chapter 1 that states are historical institutions and we briefly traced the development from city-states and empires to the Christian common-wealth of medieval Europe and finally to the modern state. The modern state, it was also argued in Chapter 1, is usually theorized as a valuable place. It provides, or seeks to provide security, freedom, order, justice and welfare for the popula-tion. Most conventional IR-theories, including realism, liberalism, and Inter-national Society, adopt this view of the state. That is to say, they asume states are valuable institutions. They are not overly concerned with what happens inside states, their *domestic* developments. Their attention is focused on the outside, on the *international* realm, the relations between states.

Many scholars think that this onesided focus on international relations of states is inadequate today (Sørensen 2001; Rosecrance 1999; Holsti 1996). That is because the 'modern state' concept fails to indicate how statehood has developed since the mid-twentieth century. Just as the institution of sovereignty has changed so has the substance of the state. And the changes have important implications for the international relations of states, including the way in which these states face problems of security, freedom, and welfare for the population. On this view, changes in statehood is a new issue of great importance; it challenges the conventional ways of theorizing about the international relations of states.

In order to trace how states have changed it is necessary to identify the basic features of the concept of the modern state as it existed in the mid-twentieth century. That creates a 'baseline model' against which recent developments can be characterized. What is the substance of the modern state—i.e. what is the content of actual, empirical statehood? We can think of it in terms of three different dimensions: the government; the nation; and the economy. The core characteristics of the modern state are set forth in Box 10.13.

Box 10.13 **The modern state**

Government   A centralized system of democratic rule, based on administrative, policing and military organizations, sanctioned by a legal order, claiming a monopoly of the legitimate use of force, within a defined territory.

Nationhood   A people within a territory making up a community of citizens (with political, social, and economic rights) and a community of sentiment (based on linguistic, cultural, and historical bonds). Nationhood involves a high level of cohesion that binds nation and state together.

Economy   A segregated and self-sustained national economy, that comprises the necessary sectors for its reproduction and growth. The major part of economic activity takes place within independent countries.

The concept of the modern state corresponds to the picture of the state in conventional theories of IR. The modern state is understood to be a valuable place that provides for the good life of its citizens, including their security, their freedom, and their welfare. The defense of the realm from external threat and the upholding of domestic order via police and courts provides for security. Freedom is achieved through democratic institutions and a political order based on civil and political rights and liberties. Welfare can be provided by the resources produced in the national economy.

To the extent that this is an accurate picture of current statehood, the conventional theories have no problems. They can proceed to focus on the international relations of states on the assumption that all is well on the domestic front: the modern state actually provides for the good life for its citizens. But states are historical institutions: they are open to change. The modern state emerged from a very long process of development that took place between the seventeenth and twentieth centuries. It came to full maturity in the developed world around the mid-twentieth century. Since then it has not stood still, of course. Changes in statehood continue to take place. Nobody can know where they will eventually lead. But it is possible to theorize about those changes. In this section we shall review the main elements of the theory that statehood is undergoing important change.

Some of those changes were discussed earlier. In Chapter 6, we reviewed arguments about how economic globalization was changing the economic basis of states. There are two economic globalization arguments; one is 'more of the same', meaning a higher level of economic intercourse across borders. The other is a 'qualitative shift' towards an integrated world economy. Both processes are taking place, but the latter is most important here. If it is valid, it means that transnational corporations increasingly organize production chains across borders, on a regional and global basis. Most of US manufacturing is now taking place outside of the United States, at foreign production sites that are linked to or integrated with US companies. Production by transnationals outside their home countries exceeds world trade. There is also a globalization trend in the financial sector; instead of purely national financial systems a globally integrated financial market is emerging. So according to the 'qualitative shift' argument we must conclude that the economies of the advanced states are no longer aptly described as 'segregated national economies'; the 'national' economy is part of a larger world economy which it is much more difficult for the single state—even if it is a large state—to control.

According to the theory of changing statehood, significant changes are also underway at the political level. In the section on sovereignty in this chapter, we noted the intense cooperation between the members of the EU; in some areas the EU can now make binding rules for its members. Such forms of supranational cooperation are beginning to emerge in other contexts as well, for example in the WTO. Increasingly, governance is changing away from its confinement to the context of national governments towards multilevel governance in several interlocked arenas overlapping each other. The participants are not merely governments and traditional international organizations, but also nongovernmental organizations and other nonstate actors. Some of that multilevel governance reflects a more intense conventional cooperation between independent states; and some of it reflects a more profound transformation towards supranational governance. To the degree that the latter is happening, modern statehood will be significantly changed.

What about nationhood, the national community? According to the theory of changing statehood, important changes are taking place here also. *Citizen rights* used to be exclusively granted by the state, but other organizations are now active in this area. In the UN-system, a set of universal *human* rights have been legally instituted. In some world regions, notably Europe, close cooperation has led to *common* rights for citizens of different countries. Citizens of the European Union enjoy some common rights in all member states, including right of employment and residence and political rights of voting in local and European elections.

In Scotland, Northern Italy, Quebec, Spain, and elsewhere movements for greater autonomy have emerged; some even seek secession from their respective states.

According to the theory of changing statehood, the community of sentiment appears to be undergoing transformation as well. There appear to be two major developments in different directions. One trend is towards a common civic identity for the Western political order, the core of which is political democracy, individual rights, and an economy based on the market and private property (Deudney and Ikenberry 1999). The other trend is towards fragmentation along ethnic, national, and religious fault lines which disclose a more narrow and exclusive conception of community (Castells 1998). These changes together would appear to indicate a significant transformation of the modern state. However, the changes are still underway and nobody can be sure where the present process of change is taking us. That is the reason for suggesting the label of 'the postmodern state'. As an ideal type, the postmodern state contains the following features:

Box 10.14 **The postmodern state**

Government   Multilevel governance in several interlocked arenas overlapping each other. Governance in context of supranational, international, transgovernmental and transnational relations

Nationhood   Supranational elements in nationhood, both with respect to the 'community of citizens' and the 'community of sentiment'. Collective loyalties increasingly projected away from the state.

Economy   'Deep integration': major part of economic activity is embedded in cross-border networks. The 'national' economy is much less self-sustained than it used to be.

This change in statehood is a challenge to conventional IR theory because the core problems of the discipline—war and peace, conflict and cooperation—play out in new and unexpected ways. A good example is the 'security dilemma'. Among modern states security must be obtained under conditions of anarchy: states co-exist in an international 'state of nature', 'having their weapons pointing, and their eyes fixed on one another' (Hobbes 1946: 101). A world of postmodern states would eliminate this traditional security dilemma. Postmodern states cooperate in far more intense ways. International anarchy is increasingly replaced by authority. Violent conflict is out of the question. These countries are liberal democracies; their level of cooperation through international institutions is very high; they are highly interdependent, both in economic and other areas. And they are developing a common civic identity.

But the changed situation also creates new challenges to postmodern states. The first challenge concerns the definition of 'security'. In the modern state, national security meant defence of the realm: of the national polity, of the national economy, of the nation. Postmodern states, however, are much more integrated with each other; the substance of state is not neatly confined within territorial borders. The economies are deeply integrated across borders; the national poli-titical systems are parts of a complex multilevel governance; collective identities are projected away from the nation and are no longer linked to the socio-political cohesion and thus to the strength of the state. Therefore, the standard way of protecting the state—by strengthening the 'hard shell' (Herz 1950) behind which the good life can be pursued—is no longer a feasible security strategy. And because postmodern statehood does not simply involve the amalgamation of states to larger units, the hard shell cannot be established at any higher level either. The objects of security therefore remain suspended in a space that is not easily territorially demarcated and confined. That is a challenge to all conventional security strategies, because they are predicated upon such demarcated and confined spaces as their objects of security.

A very significant and shocking instance of postmodern insecurity was the terrorist attack on New York and Washington on September 11, 2001. It clearly revealed the extreme vulnerability of open societies. There is a peculiar security dilemma here: how to create sufficient protection of open societies without shutting down or even reducing their openness. Openness requires freedom of movement, speech, organization, and behaviour in general, within constitutional limits. Sufficient protection, however, requires surveillance, undercover intelligence, control of the behaviour and movements of civilians, the citizens. This dilemma is not entirely new of course; it was present during the Cold War also. But it has become much more pertinent after September 11.

There is another important type of state in the present international system which challenges IR theory because it is neither modern nor postmodern: the weak states of the Third World. These states are unable to provide the political goods that we normally expect from states. There is a decided lack of security, freedom, welfare, justice, and order in these states. Most importantly, the state is frequently a significant source of threat to the population, instead of a source of protection and security. Therefore, the basic security problem in weak states is domestic violent conflict and in many cases the state itself is actively taking part in the conflict against large groups of the population. In Rwanda for example, the mass murder of an entire ethnic group of several hundred thousand people was organized by the state which was under the control of a rival ethnic group.

We cannot offer a detailed treatment of weak statehood (see Sørensen 2001 and Jackson 1990). The important point here is: both weak and postmodern states disclose security dilemmas that are markedly different from the classical security dilemma of modern statehood. So in order to understand the most important security challenges facing states, analysis of their external relations is not enough. It is also necessary to look inside states, at their domestic developments. 'Domestic' and 'international' are tied closely together and each significantly affects the other. In order to understand the most important security challenges in the present international system, the transformation of statehood will have to be incorporated in the analysis.

Let us recall the third question in Box 10.1: in what way do these insights challenge conventional IR-theories (for a comprehensive discussion, see Sørensen 2001)? The theory of changing statehood challenges the neorealist way of looking at security through the strengthening of the 'hard shell' of the state from external threat. The idea that 'domestic' and 'international' can be sharply separated, is also put into question by the dynamic interplay between 'domestic' and 'international' which lies behind the theory of changing statehood.

To sum up: the study of international relations has tended to insulate itself from the study of domestic politics. Traditional IR theory operates on the assumption that sovereign states promote the 'good life' for their citizens. Both postmodern states and weak states present a significant challenge to that view. They suggest that the conventional divorce between the 'international' and the 'domestic' in IR theory should be brought to an end.

. . . .

Conclusion

We have looked at four new issues in IR and discussed their implications for IR theory. The nature of the challenge to IR posed by these issues depends on one's valuation of what is actually at stake. Radical views demand radical solutions. A radical feminist analysis of IR will demand substantial changes of both core concepts and theories in IR. A radical view of the environment issue demands that we reconsider our whole way of thinking about IR.

These radical interpretations point away from traditional IR approaches, but the conceptual and theoretical directions taken are not at all the same. That brings us back to a point made in Chapter 2 about the three main factors which influence IR-thinking. The first is changes in the real world which keep throwing up new issues, such as those taken up in this chapter. The second is debates between IR scholars both within and between different traditions. Such debates help us come to a decision about the challenge posed by different issues and what the consequences will be for the discipline. The third element is the influence of other areas of scholarship, especially debates about methodology in a broad sense. We saw in Chapters 8 and 9 how reflections on methodologies help point IR in new directions.

The joint shaping of IR thinking by these three main factors is an ongoing process. There is no end station where scholars can sit back and proclaim that IR-thinking is finally developed to perfection. History does not stand still. Intellectual inquiry does not stop. There are always new issues to confront, new methods to apply, and new insights to discover. There are always new generations of scholars inquiring into them. Scholars are not architects working on buildings that will one day be finished. There is no one blueprint. There are several: some plans are abandoned, others are adopted. Scholars are more like travelers with different maps and open-ended tickets. A textbook such a this one is a sort of unfinished travelogue of IR. We know where the journey began and we know about the main stations visited so far. But we are less certain about where IR will go from here because old and new travelers will continue the debate about the best direction to take and the proper places to visit on the way. Some readers of this book might eventually take IR to destinations that we have never heard of.

. . . .

KEY POINTS

- A 'new issue' in IR is a topic which is considered to be important. The proponents often argue that the issue has received too little attention so far. New issues involve both values and theory.

- The environment problem is one of several important new issues. How serious is the problem of environmental degradation? 'Modernists' believe that continued improvement in human knowledge will enhance our ability to protect and safeguard the environment for future generations. 'Ecoradicals' think that there are no simple technological fixes that can take care of the problem. They want revolutionary changes toward environment-friendly lifestyles.

- Gender is another important new issue. A gender focus on world politics seeks to bring inequalities between men and women into the open, to demonstrate the subordinate positions of women, and to explain how the international political and economic system helps reproduce the underprivileged position of women. Radical feminists want to develop an autonomous feminist discipline that addresses the gender issue in a way which avoids subordinating it under traditional analytical agendas.

- Sovereignty is an international institution, meaning a set of rules that states play by. There is a renewed debate about sovereignty in IR. That is because of the challenges to sovereignty by a number of recent developments. It is probably more fruitful to analyse changes in sovereignty than to speak of the 'end of sovereignty'. Changes in sovereignty are connected with new forms of cooperation among the developed democracies in the North and new forms of conflict in weak states in the South. This calls for further development of existing approaches to IR rather than wholly new theories.

- The theory of changing statehood identifies two types of state different from the modern state: the postmodern state and the weak state of the Third World. Each of these types challenges the neorealist way of looking at security through the strengthening of the 'hard shell' of the state from external threat. The idea that 'domestic' and 'international' can be sharply separated, is also put into question by the dynamic interplay between 'domestic' and 'international' which lies behind the theory of changing statehood. Traditional IR theory operates on the assumption that sovereign states promote the 'good life' for their citizens. Both postmodern states and weak states present a significant challenge to that view. They suggest that the conventional divorce between the 'international' and the 'domestic' in IR theory should be brought to an end.

- The nature of the challenge to IR posed by the new issues depends on one's valuation of what is at stake. A radical view of the environment issue demands that we reconsider out whole way of thinking about IR. A radical feminist analysis of IR will demand wholesale changes of both core concepts and theories in IR. Many scholars who study the new issues are less radical and more prone to operate within existing traditions in IR.

....

QUESTIONS

- How serious is the problem of environmental degradation? What are the consequences for IR?

- Is gender inequality a relevant new issue in IR? Why or why not?

- What does it mean that sovereignty is an institution? Outline the important changes in the institution of sovereignty and discuss the consequences for patterns of conflict and cooperation.

- Outline the characteristics of the postmodern state. How does it challenge traditional thinking about IR?

- Should the 'international' and the 'domestic' always be studied together or should we prefer to uphold conventional IR theory's focus on the 'international'?

- Does the arrival of 'new issues' in IR mean that the discipline will have to be fundamentally changed and some or all of the established ways of thinking will have to be discarded? Why or why not?

....

 For additional material and resources see the companion web site at: www.oup.co.uk/best.textbooks/politics/jacksonsorensen2e/

GUIDE TO FURTHER READING

Cerny, P. G. (1990). *The Changing Architecture of Politics: Structure, Agency and the Future of the State*. London: Sage.

Diehl, P. F. and **Gleditsch, N. P.** (eds.) (2000). *Environmental Conflict. An Anthology*. Boulder: Westview Press.

Ehlstain, J. B. (1987). *Women and War*. New York: Basic Books.

Goodin, R. E. (1992). *Green Political Theory*. Cambridge: Polity Press.

Jackson, R. (1990). *Quasi-states: sovereignty, international relations and the Third World*. Cambridge: Cambridge University Press.

Jackson, R. (ed.) (1999). 'Sovereignty at the Millennium', *Political Studies*, Special Issue, 47/3.

Krasner, S. D. (1999). *Sovereignty. Organized Hypocrisy*. Princeton: Princeton University Press.

Lomborg, B. (2001). *The Sceptical Environmentalist*. Cambridge: Cambridge University Press.

Peterson, V. S. and **Runyan, A. S.** (1999). *Global Gender Issues* (2nd edn.). Boulder: Westview.

Porter, G., Brown, J., and **Chasek, P.** (2000). *Global Environmental Politics*. Boulder: Westview.

Sørensen, G. (2001). *Changes in Statehood. The Transformation of International Relations*. London & New York: Palgrave.

Steans, J. (1998). *Gender and International Relations* Cambridge: Polity.

WEB LINKS

http://www.deakin.edu.au/IRonline/links/themes/issues/enviro.html
Comprehensive collection of links to web resources on environmental issues, including links to the home pages of NGOs focusing on the environment. IR Online is hosted by Deakin University.

http://www.cddc.vt.edu/feminism/enin.html
'The Feminist Theory Website provides research materials and information for students, activists, and scholars interested in women's conditions and struggles around the world'.

http://www.globalpolicy.org/nations/sovereign/sover/index3.htm
Comprehensive collection of links on sovereignty, hosted by Global Policy Forum.

http://www.ippu.purdue.edu/failed_states/1999/papers/Nicholson.html
Michael Nicholson's paper on 'Globalization, Weak States and Failed States'. Hosted by Purdue University.

References

Adler, E., and **Barnett, M. N.** (1996). 'Governing Anarchy: A Research Agenda for the Study of Security Communities', *Ethics and International Affairs*, 10/1: 63–98.

Amin, S. (1975). 'Toward a Structural Crisis of World Capitalism', *Socialist Revolution*, 5/1: 1–25.

—— (1976). *Unequal Development*. Sussex: Harvester Press.

—— (1990). *Delinking. Towards a Polycentric World*. London: Zed.

Amsden, A. (1989). *Asia's Next Giant: South Korea and Late Industrialization*. New York: Oxford University Press.

Angell, N. (1909). *The Great Illusion*. London: Weidenfeld & Nicolson.

Ashley, R. K. (1986). 'The Poverty of Neorealism', in R. O. Keohane (1986: 255–301).

—— (1996). 'The Achievements of Post-Structuralism', in S. Smith *et al.* (1996: 240–53).

Axelrod, R. (1984). *The Evolution of Cooperation*. New York: Basic.

Baldwin, D. A. (ed.) (1993). *Neorealism and Neoliberalism: The Contemporary Debate*. New York: Columbia University Press.

Ball, C. (1998). 'Nattering NATO Negativism? Reasons Why Expansion May Be a Good Thing', *Review of International Studies*, 24 (Jan.): 43–68.

Barber, P. (1979). *Diplomacy: The World of the Honest Spy*. London: The British Library.

Barrett, M. (1980). *Women's Oppression Today: Problems in Marxist Feminist Analysis*. London: Verso.

Baun, M. J. (1996). *An Imperfect Union: The Maastricht Treaty and the New Politics of European Integration*. Boulder: Westview Press.

Beck, U. (1992). *Risk Society*. London: Sage.

Biersteker, T. J., and **Weber, C.** (eds.) (1996). *State Sovereignty as a Social Construct*. Cambridge: Cambridge University Press.

Birnie, P. (1992). 'International Environmental Law: Its Adequacy for Present and Future Needs', in A. Hurrell and B. Kingsbury (1992: 51–84).

Blumenthal, M. W. (Chief Executive Officer of the Unisys Company) (1988). 'The World Economy and Technological Change', *Foreign Affairs*, 66: 537–8.

Booth, K. (1991). 'Security and Emancipation', *Review of International Studies*, 17 (Oct.): 313–26.

—— (1995). 'Human Wrongs and International Relations', *International Affairs*, 71: 103–26.

Botcheva, L., and **Martin, L.** (2001). 'Institutional Effects on State Behaviour: Convergence and Divergence', *International Studies Quarterly*, 45/1:1–26.

Boulding, K. (1962). *Conflict and Defense: A General Theory*. New York: Harper & Row.

—— (1979). *Stable Peace*. Austin: University of Texas Press.

Brecht, A. (1963). *Man and His Government*. New York: Harcourt, Brace.

Bridges, R. *et al.* (eds.) (1969). *Nations and Empires*. London: Macmillan.

Brierly, J. L. (1938). *The Law of Nations*, 2nd edn. Oxford: Oxford University Press.

Brown, C. (1992). *International Relations Theory: New Normative Approaches*. New York: Harvester Press.

——(1997). *Understanding International Relations*. London: Macmillan.

Brown, C., Nardin, T., and Rengger, N. (eds.) (2002). *International Relations in Political Thought*. Cambridge: Cambridge University Press.

Brown, L. (1989). 'Reexamining the World Food Prospect', in L. Brown (ed.), *State of the World 1989*. Washington, DC: Worldwatch Institute, 41–58.

Brown, S. (1994). *The Causes and Prevention of War*, 2nd edn. New York: St. Martin's Press.

Brownlie, I. (1979). *Principles of Public International Law*, 3rd edn. Oxford: Clarendon Press.

Bull, H. (1969). 'International Theory: The Case for a Classical Approach', in K. Knorr and J. N. Rosenau (eds.), *Contending Approaches to International Politics*. Princeton: Princeton University Press, 20–38.

——(1972). 'International Relations as an Academic Pursuit', *Australian Outlook*, 26: 251–62.

——(1975). 'New Directions in the Theory of International Relations', *International Studies*, 14: 280–90.

——(1979). 'Recapturing the Just War for Political Theory', *World Politics*, 32: 590–9.

——(1984). 'The Great Irresponsibles? The United States, the Soviet Union, and World Order', in R. O. Matthews, A. G. Rubinoff, and J. C. Stein (eds.), *International Conflict and Conflict Management*. Scarborough: Prentice-Hall Canada.

——(1985). *Justice in International Relations* (The Hagey Lectures). Waterloo: University of Waterloo Press.

——(1990). 'The Importance of Grotius in the Study of International Relations', in H. Bull *et al.* (1990: 65–93).

——(1995). *The Anarchical Society: A Study of Order in World Politics*, 2nd edn. London: Macmillan.

——Kingsbury, B., and Roberts, A. (eds.) (1990). *Hugo Grotius and International Relations*. Oxford: Clarendon Press.

——and Watson, A. (eds.) (1984). *The Expansion of International Society*. Oxford: Clarendon Press.

Burton, J. (1972). *World Society*. Cambridge: Cambridge University Press.

Butterfield, H. (1953). *Christianity, Diplomacy and War*. London: Epworth.

——(1973). *The Whig Interpretation of History*. Harmondsworth: Penguin.

Buzan, B., Jones, C., and Little, R. (1993). *The Logic of Anarchy: Neorealism to Structural Realism*. New York: Columbia University Press.

Camilleri, J. A., and Falk, J. (1992). *The End of Sovereignty? The Politics of a Shrinking and Fragmenting World*. Aldershot: Elgar.

Caporaso, J. A. (1993). 'Global Political Economy', in A. W. Finifter (ed.), *Political Science: The State of the Discipline*, ii. Washington, DC: American Political Science Association, 451–83.

Cardoso, F. H. (1972). 'Notas sobre el estado actual de los estudios sobre dependencia', *Revista Latinamericana de Ciencias Sociales*, 4: 3–31.

——and **Faletto, E.** (1979). *Dependency and Development in Latin America*. Berkeley: University of California Press.

Carlson, L. J. (2002). 'Game theory: international trade, conflict and cooperation', in R. Palan (ed.), *Global Political Economy. Contemporary Theories*, London: Routledge, 117–30.

Carnoy, M. (1984). *The State and Political Theory*. Princeton: Princeton University Press.

Carr, E. H. (1964). *The Twenty Years' Crisis*. New York: Harper & Row.

Carter, A. (1993). 'Towards a Green Political Theory', in A. Dobson and P. Lucardie (eds.), *The Politics of Nature: Explorations in Green Political Theory*. London: Routledge.

Castells, M. (1998). *The Power of Identity*. Oxford: Basil Blackwell.

Cerny, P. G. (1993). 'Plurilateralism: Structural Differentiation and Functional Conflict in the Post-Cold War World Order', *Millennium: Journal of International Studies*, 22/1: 27–51.

Cipolla, C. M. (1977). 'Introduction', in C. M. Cipolla (ed.), *The Fontana Economic History of Europe*. Glasgow: Fontana/Collins, 7–8.

Clark, G. (1960). *Early Modern Europe: From about 1450 to about 1720*. Oxford: Oxford University Press.

Claude, I. (1971). *Swords into Ploughshares*, 4th edn. New York: Random House.

Coates, A.J. (1997). *The Ethics of War*. Manchester: Manchester University Press.

Cobden, R. (1903). *Political Writings*. 2 vols., London: Fisher Unwin.

Collingwood, R. G. (1946). *The Idea of History*. Oxford: Clarendon Press.

Commission on Global Governance (1995). *Our Global Neighbourhood*. New York: Oxford University Press.

Cooper, R. (1996). *The Post-Modern State and the World Order*. London: Demos.

Cox, R. (1981). 'Social Forces, States and World Orders', *Millennium*, 10: 126–55.

Cox, R. W. (1992). 'Towards a Post-Hegemonic Conceptualization of World Order: Reflections on the Relevancy of Ibn Khaldun', in J. N. Rosenau and E.-O. Czempiel (eds.), *Governance without Government: Order and Change in World Politics*. Cambridge: Cambridge University Press, 132–59.

——(1994). 'Global Restructuring: Making Sense of the Changing International Political Economy', in R. Stubbs and G. R. D. Underhill (eds.), *Political Economy and the Changing Global Order*. London: Macmillan, 45–60.

——with **Sinclair, T. J.** (1996). *Approaches to World Order*. Cambridge: Cambridge University Press.

Daly, M. (1979). *Gyn/Ecology: The Metaethics of Radical Feminism*. London: Women's Press.

Deudney, D. (1996). 'E Pluribus Unum: The Problem of Liberal Identity and Community in Pluralistic Security Community Theory', paper for ISA Annual Meeting, 17–21 Apr., San Diego.

Deutsch, K. W. *et al.* (1957). *Political Community and the North Atlantic Area*. Princeton: Princeton University Press.

Donnelly, J. (1992). 'Twentieth-Century Realism', in T. Nardin and D. Mapel (eds.) (1992: 85–111).

Dougherty, J. E., and **Pfaltzgraff, R. L.** (1971). *Contending Theories of International Relations*. New York: Lippincott.

Doyle, M. W. (1983). 'Kant, Liberal Legacies and Foreign Affairs', pts. 1 and 2, *Philosophy and Public Affairs*, 12/3: 205–35 and 12/4: 323–54.

—— (1986). 'Liberalism and World Politics', *American Political Science Review*, 80/4: 1151–69.

Dunn, J. (1984). *Locke*. Oxford: Oxford University Press.

Easton, D. (1961). 'An Approach to the Analysis of Political Systems', in S. S. Ulmer (ed.), *Introductory Readings in Political Behavior*. Chicago: Rand McNally, 136–57.

—— (1965). *A Framework for Political Analysis*. Englewood Cliffs: Prentice-Hall.

—— (1971). *The Political System*, 2nd edn. New York: Knopf.

Ebenstein, W. (1951). *Great Political Thinkers: Plato to the Present*. New York: Holt, Rinehart, Winston.

Eckersly, R. (1992). *Environmentalism and Political Theory: Towards an Ecocentric Approach*. London: UCL Press.

Economist (1997). 'Policing for Profit', 19–25 Apr., 21–3.

Eisenstein, H. (1983). *Contemporary Feminist Thought*. London: Hall.

Elkins, D. J. (1995). *Beyond Sovereignty: Territory and Political Economy in the Twenty-First Century*. Toronto: Toronto University Press.

Elshtain, J. B. (1987). *Women and War*. New York: Basic.

Enloe, C. (1990). *Bananas, Beaches, and Bases: Making Feminist Sense of International Relations*. Berkeley: University of California Press.

—— (1994). *The Morning After: Sexual Politics at the End of the Cold War*. Berkeley: University of California Press.

Escobar, A. (1995). *Encountering Development*. Princeton: Princeton University Press.

Eulau, H. (1963). *The Behavioral Persuasion in Politics*. New York: Random House.

Evans, G., and **Newnham, J.** (1992). *The Dictionary of World Politics*. London: Harvester Wheatsheaf.

Evans, P. B. (1989). 'Predatory, Developmental, and Other Apparatuses: A Comparative Political Economy Perspective on the Third World State', *Sociological Forum*, 4/4: 561–88.

Evers, T., and **Wogau, P. v.** (1973). ' "Dependencia": Lateinamerikanische Beiträge zur Theorie der Unterentwicklung', *Das Argument*, 79/4–6, 414–48.

Falk, R. (1985). 'A New Paradigm for International Legal Studies', in R. Falk, F. Kratochwil, and S. H. Mendlovitz (eds.), *International Law: A Contemporary Perspective*. Boulder: Westview Press.

Fallows, J. (1994). *Looking at the Sun*. New York: Pantheon.

Fann, K. T., and **Hodges, D. C.** (eds.) (1971). *Readings in US Imperialism*. Boston: Porter Sargent.

Fierke, K., and **K. E. Jørgensen** (2001) (eds.). *Constructing International Relations: The Next Generation*. London: M.E. Sharpe.

Finley, M. I. (1983). *Politics in the Ancient World*. New York: Cambridge University Press.

Finnegan, R. B. (1972). 'International Relations: The Disputed Search for Method', *Review of Politics*, 34: 40–66.

Finnemore, M., and K. Sikkink (2001). 'Taking Stock: The Constructivist Research Program in International Relations and Comparative Politics', *Annual Reviews of Political Science*, 4: 391–416.

Forde, S. (1992). 'Classical Realism', in T. Nardin and D. Mapel (eds.) (1992: 62–84).

Fortes, M., and Evans-Pritchard, E. E. (eds.) (1940). *African Political Systems*. London: Oxford University Press.

Frank, A. G. (1967). *Capitalism and Underdevelopment in Latin America*. New York: Monthly Review Press.

——(1969). *Latin America: Underdevelopment or Revolution?* New York: Monthly Review Press.

——(1971). 'On the Mechanisms of Imperialism: The Case of Brazil', in K. Fann and D. Hodges (eds.) (1971: 237–8).

——(1977). 'Dependence is Dead, Long Live Dependence and the Class Struggle: An Answer to Critics', *World Development*, 5/4: 355–70.

——(1980). *Crisis: In the World Economy*. London: Heinemann.

——(1997). *Freedom Review*, 28/1: 15.

Friedman, M. (1962). *Capitalism and Freedom*. Chicago: University of Chicago Press.

——(1993). 'Cooperation, Competition Go Hand in Hand', *Nikkei Weekly*, 31 May.

Frost, M. (1996). *Ethics in International Relations*. Cambridge. Cambridge University Press.

Fukuyama, F. (1989), 'The End of History?' *National Interest*, 16: 3–18.

——(1992). *The End of History and the Last Man*. New York: Avon.

Gaddis, J. (1987). *The Long Peace: Inquiries into the History of the Cold War*. New York: Oxford University Press.

Gadzey, A. T.-K. (1994). *The Political Economy of Power: Hegemony and Economic Liberalism*. New York: St. Martin's Press.

Gallie, W. B. (1978). *Philosophers of Peace and War: Kant, Clausewitz, Marx, Engels and Tolstoy*. Cambridge: Cambridge University Press.

Gatens, M. (1989). *Feminism and Philosophy: Perspectives on Equality and Difference*. London: Routledge.

Gilbert, M. (1995). *The First World War*. London: HarperCollins.

Gill, S. (1994). 'Knowledge, Politics, and Neo-Liberal Political Economy', in R. Stubbs and G. R. D. Underhill (eds.), *Political Economy and the Changing Global Order*. London: Macmillan, 75–89.

Gilpin, R. (1981). *War and Change in World Politics*. Cambridge: Cambridge University Press.

——(1984). 'The Richness of the Tradition of Political Realism', *International Organization*, 38/2 (Spring): 287–305.

——(1987). *The Political Economy of International Relations*. Princeton: Princeton University Press.

——(2001). *Global Political Economy. Understanding the International Economic Order*. Princeton: Princeton University Press.

Gleick, P. H. (1993). 'Water and Conflict: Fresh Water Resources and International Security', *International Security*, 18/1: 79–112.

Goldgeir, J., and McFaul, M. (1992). 'A Tale of Two Worlds: Core and Periphery in the Post-Cold War Era', *International Organization*, 46/1: 467–92.

Goldhagen, D. J. (1996). *Hitler's Willing Executioners: Ordinary Germans and the Holocaust*. New York: Knopf.

Gong, G. W. (1984). *The Standard of 'Civilization' in International Society*. Oxford: Clarendon Press.

Goodin, R. (1990). 'International Ethics and the Environment Crisis', *Ethics and International Affairs*, 4: 93–110.

—— (1992). *Green Political Theory*. Cambridge: Polity Press.

Grieco, J. M. (1977). 'Realist International Theory and the Study of World Politics', in M. W. Doyle and G. J. Ikenberry (eds.), *New Thinking in International Relations*. Boulder: Westview Press, 163–202.

—— (1993). 'Anarchy and the Limits of Cooperation: A Realist Critique of the Newest Liberal Institutionalism', in D. A. Baldwin (ed.) (1993: 116–43).

Gurr, T. R., and Harff, B. (1994). *Ethnic Conflict in World Politics*. Boulder: Westview Press.

Gutkind, P., and Wallerstein, I. (eds.) (1976). *The Political Economy of Contemporary Africa*. Beverly Hills: Sage.

Haas, E. B. (1958). *The Uniting of Europe: Political, Social and Economic Forces 1950–1957*. Stanford: Stanford University Press.

—— (1975). *The Obsolescence of Regional Integration Theory*. Berkeley: Institute of International Studies.

—— (1976). 'Turbulent Fields and the Theory of Regional Integration', *International Organization*, 30/2: 173–212.

Haas, P. M. *et al.* (eds.) (1993). *Institutions for the Earth*. Cambridge, MA: MIT Press.

Haftendorn, H., Keohane, R.O., and Wallander, C. (eds.) (1999). *Security Institutions Over Time and Space*. New York: Oxford University Press.

Halliday, F. (1994). *Rethinking International Relations*. Vancouver: UBC Press.

Hardin, D. (1982). *Collective Action*. Baltimore: Johns Hopkins University Press.

Helman, G. B., and Ratner, S. R. (1992–3). 'Saving Failed States', *Foreign Affairs*, 89: 3–21.

Herz, J. (1950). 'Idealist Internationalism and the Security Dilemma', *World Politics*, II/2: 157–81.

—— (1951). *Political Realism and Political Idealism*. Chicago: University of Chicago Press.

Hettne, B. (1995). *Development Theory and the Three Worlds*. Harlow: Longman.

—— (1996). *Internationella relationer*. Lund: Studentlitteratur.

Heurlin, B. (1996). *Verden 2000: Teorier og tendenser i international politik*. Copenhagen: Gyldendal.

Hirst, P., and Thompson, G. (1992). 'The Problem of "Globalization": International Economic Relations, National Economic Management and the Formation of Trading Blocs', *Economy and Society*, 21/4: 357–94.

Hobbes, T. (1946). *Leviathan*. Oxford: Blackwell.

Hoffmann, S. (1977). 'An American Social Science: International Relations', *Daedalus*, 106: 41–61.

—— (1990). 'International Society', in J. D. B. Miller and R. J. Vincent (eds.), *Order and Violence: Hedley Bull and International Relations*. Oxford: Clarendon Press, 13–17.

—— (1991). 'Ethics and Rules of the Game Between the Superpowers', in L. Henkin (ed.), *Right v. Might: International Law and the Use of Force*. New York: Council on Foreign Relations Press.

Holbraad, C. (1990). 'Hedley Bull and International Relations', in J. D. B. Miller and R. J. Vincent (eds.), *Order and Violence: Hedley Bull and International Relations*. Oxford: Clarendon Press, 186–204.

Hollis, M., and Smith, S. (1990). *Explaining and Understanding International Relations*. Oxford: Clarendon Press.

Holm, H.-H., and Sørensen, G. (eds.) (1995). *Whose World Order? Uneven Globalization and the End of the Cold War*. Boulder: Westview Press.

Holsti, K. J. (1988). *International Politics: A Framework for Analysis*. Englewood Cliffs: Prentice Hall.

—— (1991). *Peace and War: Armed Conflicts and International Order 1648–1989*. Cambridge: Cambridge University Press.

—— (1996). *The State, War, and the State of War*. Cambridge: Cambridge University Press.

Homer-Dixon, T. F. (1995). 'Environmental Scarcities and Violent Conflict', in S. M. Lynn-Jones and S. Miller (eds.), *Global Dangers: Changing Dimensions of International Security*. Cambridge, MA: MIT Press, 144–79.

Howard, M. (1976). *War in European History*. Oxford: Oxford University Press.

Hughes, B. B. (1991). *Continuity and Change in World Politics: The Clash of Perspectives*. Englewood Cliffs: Prentice Hall.

Hurrell, A. (1995). 'International Political Theory and the Global Environment', in K. Booth and S. Smith (eds.), *International Relations Today*. University Park: Pennsylvania State University Press, 129–53.

—— and Kingsbury, B. (eds.) (1992). *The International Politics of the Environment*. Oxford: Clarendon Press.

Jackson, R. (1990). *Quasi-States: Sovereignty, International Relations and the Third World*. Cambridge: Cambridge University Press.

—— (1992). 'Dialectical Justice in the Gulf War', *Review of International Studies*, 18: 335–54.

—— (1993). 'Armed Humanitarianism', *International Journal* 48 (Autumn): 579–606.

—— (1995). 'The Political Theory of International Society', in K. Booth and S. Smith (eds.), *International Relations Today*. University Park: Pennsylvania State University Press, 110–28.

—— (1996a). 'Can International Society be Green?', in R. Fawn and J. Larkins (eds.), *International Society after the Cold War*. London: Macmillan.

—— (1996b). 'Is There a Classical International Theory?' in S. Smith *et al.* (1996: 203–18).

—— (2000). *The Global Covenant: Human Conduct in a World of States*. Oxford: Oxford University Press.

James, A. (1986). *Sovereign Statehood: The Basis of International Society*. London: Allen & Unwin.

Jones, E. L. (1981). *The European Miracle: Environments, Economies and Geopolitics in the History of Europe and Asia*. Cambridge: Cambridge University Press.

Kacowicz, A. M. (1995). 'Pluralistic Security Communities in the Third World? The Intriguing Cases of South America and West Africa', paper for ISA Annual Meeting, 22–5 Feb., Chicago.

Kant, I. (1795). 'Perpetual Peace', repr. in H. Reiss (ed.), *Kant's Political Writing*. Cambridge: Cambridge University Press (1992), 93–131.

Kaplan, M. (1964). *System and Process in International Politics*. New York: Wiley.

Kapstein, E. B. (1993). 'Territoriality and Who is "US"?' *International Organization*, 47/3: 501–3.

Katzenstein, P. (1996) (ed.). *The Culture of National Security: Norms and Identity in World Politics*. New York: Columbia University Press.

Kay, C. (1989). *Latin American Theories of Development and Underdevelopment*. London: Routledge.

Kegley, C. W., Jr., and Wittkopf, E. R. (1991). *American Foreign Policy*, 4th edn. New York: St. Martin's Press.

Kennan, G. (1954). *Realities of American Foreign Policy*. Princeton: Princeton University Press.

Kennedy, P. (1993). *Preparing for the Twenty-First Century*. New York: Vintage.

Keohane, R. O. (1984). *After Hegemony: Cooperation and Discord in the World Political Economy*. Princeton: Princeton University Press.

——(ed.) (1986). *Neo-Realism and Its Critics*. New York: Columbia University Press.

——(1989a). *International Institutions and State Power: Essays in International Relations Theory*. Boulder: Westview Press.

——(1989b). 'International Relations Theory: Contributions of a Feminist Standpoint', *Millennium: Journal of International Studies*, 18/2: 245–55.

——(1993). 'Institutional Theory and the Realist Challenge after the Cold War', in D. A. Baldwin (ed.) (1993: 269–301).

——(1995). 'Hobbes's Dilemma and Institutional Change in World Politics: Sovereignty in International Society', in H.-H. Holm and G. Sørensen (1995: 165–87).

——and Hoffmann, S. (eds.) (1991). *The New European Community: Decisionmaking and Institutional Change*. Boulder: Westview Press.

——and Martin, L. L. (1995). 'The Promise of Institutionalist Theory', *International Security*, 20/1: 39–51.

——and Milner, H. V. (eds.) (1996). *Internationalization and Domestic Politics*. New York: Cambridge University Press.

Keohane, R. O., and Nye, J. S. (eds.) (1971). *Transnational Relations and World Politics*. Cambridge, MA: Harvard University Press.

—— ——(1975). 'International Interdependence and Integration', in F. Greenstein and N. Polsby (eds.), *Handbook of Political Science, viii: International Politics*. Reading, MA: Addison-Wesley, 363–414.

—— ——(1977). *Power and Interdependence: World Politics in Transition*. Boston: Little, Brown.

—— ——(1987). 'Power and Interdependence Revisited', *International Organization*, 41/4: 725–53.

—— —— (1993). 'Introduction: The End of the Cold War in Europe', in R. O. Keohane *et al.* (1993: 1–23).

—— ——and **Hoffmann, S.** (eds.) (1993). *After the Cold War: International Institutions and State Strategies in Europe, 1989–1991*. Cambridge, MA: Harvard University Press.

Keynes, J. M. (1963). *Essays in Persuasion*. New York: Norton.

Kindleberger, C. (1973). *The World in Depression, 1929–1939*. Berkeley: University of California Press.

Kissinger, H. (1994). *Diplomacy*. New York: Simon & Schuster.

Krasner, S. D. (ed.) (1983). *International Regimes*. Ithaca: Cornell University Press.

——(1988). 'Sovereignty: Institutional Perspective', *Comparative Political Studies*, 21: 66–94.

——(1993). 'Westphalia and All That', in J. Goldstein and R. O. Keohane (eds.), *Ideas and Foreign Policy: Beliefs, Institutional and Political Change*. Ithaca: Cornell University Press, 235–65.

Kratochwil, F. (1989). *Rules, Norms and Decisions*. Cambridge: Cambridge University Press.

Kuhn, T. S. (1970). *The Structure of Scientific Revolutions*. Chicago: University of Chicago Press.

Lake, D. (1992). 'Powerful Pacifists: Democratic States and War', *American Political Science Review*, 86/1: 24–37.

Lake, D. A. (2001). 'Beyond Anarchy. The Importance of Security Institutions', *International Security*, 26/1:129–60.

Lal, D. (1983). *The Poverty of 'Development Economics'*. London: Institute of Economic Affairs.

Landry, D., and Maclean, G. (1993). *Materialist Feminism*. Oxford: Blackwell.

Lapidoth, R. (1992). 'Sovereignty in Transition', *Journal of International Affairs*, 45/2: 325–47.

Lasswell, H. (1958). *Politics: Who Gets What, When, How*. New York: World Publishing.

Layne, C. (1994). 'Kant or Cant: The Myth of the Democratic Peace', *International Security*, 19/2: 5–49.

Lee, K. (1993). 'To De-Industrialize: Is It so Irrational?', in A. Dobson and P. Lucardie (eds.), *The Politics of Nature: Explorations in Green Political Theory*. London: Routledge.

Lenin, V. I. (1939). *Imperialism: The Highest Stage of Capitalism*. New York: International Publishers.

Levy, M. A., Young, O. R., and Zürn, M. (1995). 'The Study of International Regimes', *European Journal of International Relations*, 1/3: 267–330.

Lewis, W. A. (1970). *Theory of Economic Growth*. New York: Harper & Row.

Lijphart, A. (1994). *Electoral Systems and Party Systems*. Oxford: Oxford University Press.

Linklater, A. (1989). *Beyond Realism and Marxism*. New York: St. Martin's Press.

——(1990). *Beyond Realism and Marxism: Critical Theory and International Relations*. Basingstoke, UK: Macmillan.

——(1996). 'The Achievements of Critical Theory', in S. Smith *et al.* (1996: 279–98).

Lipson, C. (1984). 'International Cooperation in Economic and Security Affairs', *World Politics*, 37 (Oct.): 1–23.

List, F. (1966). *The National System of Political Economy*. New York: Kelley.

Little, R. (1996). 'The Growing Relevance of Pluralism?' in S. Smith *et al.* (1996: 66–86).

Lodge, J. (ed.) (1993). *The European Community and the Challenge of the Future*. New York: St. Martin's Press.

Lowi, M. R. (1993). 'Bridging the Divide: Transboundary Resource Disputes and the Case of West Bank Water', *International Security*, 18/1: 113–38.

Lucdde-Neurath, R. (1985). 'State Intervention and Export-Oriented Development in South Korea', in G. White and R. Wadc (eds.), *Developmental States in East Asia*. Brighton: IDS Research Reports No. 16, 62–126.

Lyotard, J.-F. (1984). *The Postmodern Condition: A Report on Knowledge*. Manchester: Manchester University Press.

McGlen, N., and Sarkess, M. (1993). *Women in Foreign Policy: The Insiders*. New York: Routledge.

McGwire, M. (1998). 'NATO expansion: "A Policy Error of Historic Importance"'. *Review of International Studies*, 24 (Jan.): 23–42.

Machiavelli, N. (1961). *The Prince*, trans. G. Bull. Harmondsworth: Penguin.

——(1984). *The Prince*, trans. P. Bondanella and M. Musa. New York: Oxford University Press.

Maoz, Z., and Russett, B. (1993). 'Normative and Structural Causes of Democratic Peace, 1946–86', *American Political Science Review*, 87/3: 624–38.

Martinussen, J. (1997). *State, Society and Market: A Guide to Competing Theories of Development*. New York: St. Martin's.

Marx, K., and Engels, F. (1955). *The Communist Manifesto*, ed. S. Beer. New York: Appleton-Century-Crofts.

Mayall, J. (1989). *Nationalism and International Society*. Cambridge: Cambridge University Press.

——(1996). *The New Interventionism: 1991–1994*. Cambridge: Cambridge University Press.

Mearsheimer, J. (1993). 'Back to the Future: Instability in Europe After the Cold War', in S. Lynn-Jones (ed.), *The Cold War and After: Prospects for Peace*. Cambridge, MA: MIT Press, 141–92.

——(1995*a*). 'A Realist Reply', *International Security*, 20/1: 82–93.

——(1995*b*). 'The False Promise of International Institutions', in M. E. Brown *et al.* (eds.), *The Perils of Anarchy: Contemporary Realism and International Security*. Cambridge, MA: MIT Press, 332–77.

Meinecke, F. (1957). *Machiavellism: The Doctrine of Raison d'Etat and Its Place in Modern History*. New Haven: Yale University Press.

Mill, J. S. (1963). 'A Few Words on Non-Intervention', in G. Himmelfarb (eds.), *Essays on Politics and Culture: John Stuart Mill*. New York: Anchor.

Milner, Helen (1991). 'The Assumption of Anarchy in international Relations Theory: A Critique', *Review of International Studies*, 17: 67–85.

Mitchell, J. (1977). *Women's Estate*. Harmondsworth: Penguin.

Mitrany, D. (1966). *A Working Peace System*, repr. with introd. by H. J. Morgenthau. Chicago: Quadrangle.

Moravcsik, A. (1991). 'Negotiating the Single European Act: National Interests and Conventional Statecraft in the European Community', *International Organization*, 45: 19–56.

—— (1997). 'Taking Preferences Seriously: A Liberal Theory of International Politics', *International Organization*, 51/4: 513–53.

Morgenthau, H. J. (1960). *Politics among Nations: The Struggle for Power and Peace*, 3rd edn. New York: Knopf.

—— (1965). *Scientific Man versus Power Politics*. Chicago: Phoenix Books.

—— (1985). *Politics Among Nations: The Struggle for Power and Peace*, 6th edn. New York: Knopf.

Mueller, J. (1990). *Retreat from Doomsday: The Obsolescence of Major War*. New York: Basic.

—— (1995). *Quiet Cataclysm: Reflections on the Recent Transformation of World Politics*. New York: HarperCollins.

Myers, N., and Simon, J. L. (1994). *Scarcity or Abundance? A Debate on the Environment*. New York: Norton.

Myrdal, G. (1957). *Economic Theory and Underdeveloped Regions*. London: Duckworth.

Naisbitt, J. (1994). *Global Paradox*. New York: Avon.

Nardin, T. (1983). *Law, Morality and the Relations of States*. Princeton: Princeton University Press.

—— and Mapel, D. (eds.) (1992). *Traditions of International Ethics*. Cambridge: Cambridge University Press

Navari, C. (1989). 'The Great Illusion Revisited. The International Theory of Norman Angell', *Review of International Studies*, 15: 341–58.

Nederveen Pieterse, J. (2000). 'Trends in development theory', in R. Palan (ed.), *Global Political Economy. Contemporary Theories*, London: Routledge, 197–215.

Neibuhr, R. (1932). *Moral Man and Immoral Society*. New York: Scribner's.

Nicholls, D. (1974). *Three Varieties of Pluralism*. London: Macmillan.

Nicholson, M. (1996). 'The Continued Significance of Positivism?', in S. Smith *et al.* (1996: 128–49).

Nixson, F. (1988). 'The Political Economy of Bargaining with Transnational Corporations: Some Preliminary Observations', *Manchester Papers on Development*, 4/3: 377–90.

Nunn, E. (1996). 'The Rational Choice Approach to IPE', in D. N. Balaam and M. Veseth, *Introduction to International Political Economy*, Upper Saddle River: Prentice Hall, 77–99.

Nye, J. S., Jr. (1988). 'Neorealism and Neoliberalism', *World Politics*, 40/2: 235–51.

—— (1990). *Bound to Lead: The Changing Nature of American Power*. New York: Basic.

—— (1993). *Understanding International Conflicts*. New York: HarperCollins.

Oakeshott, M. (1975). *Hobbes on Civil Association*. Oxford: Blackwell.

—— (1933). *Experience and its Modes*. Cambridge: Cambridge University Press.

OECD (Organization for the Economic Cooperation and Development) (1993). *Trade Policy Issues*. Paris: OECD.

Ohmae, K. (1993). 'The Rise of the Region State', *Foreign Affairs*, 72/2: 78–87.

Onuf, N. (1989). *A World of Our Making*. Columbia: University of South Carolina Press.

Onuf, N. (1995). 'Intervention for the Common Good', in G. Lyons and
M. Mastanduno (eds.), *Beyond Westphalia?* Baltimore: Johns Hopkins University
Press, 43–58.

Osiander, A. (1994). *The States System of Europe, 1640–1990*. Oxford: Clarendon
Press.

Oye, K. A. (ed.) (1986). *Cooperation Under Anarchy*. Princeton: Princeton University
Press.

Palan, R. (2002). 'New trends in global political economy', in R. Palan (ed.), *Global
Political Economy. Contemporary Theories*, London: Routledge, 1–19.

Parish, R., and Peceny, M. (2002). 'Kantian Liberalism and the Collective Defense of
Democracy in Latin America', *Journal of Peace Research*, 39/2:229–50.

Parry, J. H. (1966). *Europe and a Wider World: 1415–1715*, 3rd edn. London:
Hutchinson.

Paterson, M. (1996). 'Green Politics', in S. Burchill and A. Linklater (eds.), *Theories of
International Relations*. London: Macmillan, 252–75.

Peterson, M. J. (1992). 'Transnational Activity, International Society and World
Politics', *Millennium*, 21: 371–88.

Peterson, V. S., and Runyan, A. S. (1993). *Global Gender Issues*. Boulder: Westview
Press.

Plato (1974). *The Republic*. Indianapolis: Hackett.

Pollard, S. (1971). *The Idea of Progress: History and Society*. Harmondsworth: Penguin.

Pompa, L. (1982). *Vico: Selected Writings*. Cambridge: Cambridge University Press.

Porter, G., and Brown, J. W. (1996). *Global Environmental Politics*. Boulder: Westview
Press.

Prebisch, R. (1950). *The Economic Development of Latin America and Its Principal Problems*.
New York: United Nations.

Rapaport, A. (1960). *Fights, Games, Debates*. Ann Arbor: University of Michigan Press.

Reich, R. (1992). *The Work of Nations: Preparing Ourselves for 21st-Century Capitalism*.
New York: Vintage.

Ricardo, D. (1973). *The Principles of Political Economy and Taxation*. London: Dent.

Richardson, J. (1990). 'The Academic Study of International Relations', in
J. D. B. Miller and R. J. Vincent (eds.), *Order and Violence: Hedley Bull and
International Relations*. Oxford: Clarendon Press, 140–85.

Risse-Kappen, T. (ed.) (1995). *Bringing Transnational Relations Back In*. Cambridge:
Cambridge University Press.

Rittberger, Volker (ed.) (1993). *Regime Theory and International Relations*. Oxford:
Clarendon Press.

Rosecrance, R. (1986). *The Rise of the Trading State: Commerce and Conquest in the Modern
World*. New York: Basic.

——(1995). 'The Obsolescence of Territory', *New Perspectives Quarterly*, 12/1: 44–50.

——(1999). *The Rise of the Virtual State*. New York: Basic Books.

Rosenau, J. N. (1967). 'Games International Relations Scholars Play', *Journal of
International Affairs*, 21: 293–303.

——(1980). *The Study of Global Interdependence: Essays on the Transnationalisation of World
Affairs*. New York: Nichols.

—— (1990). *Turbulence in World Politics: A Theory of Change and Continuity*. Princeton: Princeton University Press.

—— (1992). 'Citizenship in a Changing Global Order', in J. N. Rosenau and E.-O. Czempiel (eds.), *Governance Without Government: Order and Change in World Politics*. Cambridge: Cambridge University Press, 272–94.

Rosenblum, N. L. (1978). *Bentham's Theory of the Modern State*. Cambridge, MA: Harvard University Press.

Rostow, W. W. (1960). *The Stages of Economic Growth: A Non-Communist Manifesto*. Cambridge: Cambridge University Press.

—— (1978). *The World Economy: History and Prospect*. Austin: University of Texas Press.

Rousseau, J.-J. (1964). 'Que l'état de guerre nait de l'état social', in *Œuvres Complètes, iii*. Paris: Pléiade.

Ruggie, J. G. (1998). *Constructing the World Polity: Essays on International Institutionalization*. London: Routledge.

Russett, B. M. (1985). 'The Mysterious Case of Vanishing Hegemony, or, Is Mark Twain Really Dead?' *International Organization*, 36/2: 207–34.

—— (1989). 'Democracy and Peace', in B. Russett *et al.* (eds.), *Choices in World Politics: Sovereignty and Interdependence*. New York: Freeman, 245–61.

—— (1993). *Grasping the Democratic Peace: Principles for a Post-Cold War World*. Princeton: Princeton University Press.

Sachs, W. (ed.) (1992). *The Development Dictonary*. London: Zed.

—— (ed.) (1993). *Global Ecology: A New Arena of Political Conflict*. London: Zed.

Samuelson, P. A. (1967). *Economics. An Introductory Analysis*, 7th edn. New York: McGraw Hill.

Schelling, T. (1960). *The Strategy of Conflict*. Cambridge, MA: Harvard University Press.

—— (1996). 'The Diplomacy of Violence', in R. Art and R. Jervis (eds.), *International Politics*, 4th edn. New York: HarperCollins, 168–82.

Schneider, G. (1995). 'Integration and Conflict: The Empirical Relevance of Security Communities', paper for 2nd Pan-European Conference on International Relations. 13–16 Sept., Paris.

Schweller, R. L. (1992). 'Domestic Structure and Preventive War: Are Democracies More Pacific?' *World Politics*, 44/2: 235–69.

Senghaas, D. (1989). 'The Development Problematic: A Macro-Micro Perspective', *Journal of Peace Research*, 26/1: 57–69.

Seragia, A. M. (ed.) (1992). *Euro-Politics: Institutions and Policymaking in the 'New' European Community*. Washington, DC: Brookings Institution.

Shaw, M. (1992). 'Global Society and Global Responsibility', *Millennium*, 21: 421–34.

Simon, J., and Kahn, H. (eds.) (1984). *The Resourceful Earth*. Oxford: Blackwell.

Singer, M., and Wildavsky, A. (1993). *The Real World Order: Zones of Peace, Zones of Turmoil*. Chatham, NJ: Chatham House.

Smith, M. J. (1992). 'Liberalism and International Reform', in T. Nardin and D. Mapel (eds.), (1992: 201–24).

Smith, S. (1995). 'The Self-Images of a Discipline', in K. Booth and S. Smith (eds.), *International Relations Theory Today*. University Park: Pennsylvania State University Press, 24–5.

—— (1997). 'New Approaches to International Theory', in J. Baylis and S. Smith (eds.), *The Globalization of World Politics*. Oxford: Oxford University Press, 165–90.

—— Booth, K., and Zalewski, M. (eds.) (1996). *International Theory: Positivism and Beyond*. Cambridge: Cambridge University Press.

Sørensen, G. (1983). *Transnational Corporations in Peripheral Societies: Contributions Towards Self-Centered Development?* Aalborg: Aalborg University Press.

—— (1992). 'Kant and Processes of Democratization: Consequences for Neorealist Thought', *Journal of Peace Research*, 29/4: 397–414.

—— (1993a). *Democracy and Democratization: Processes and Prospects in a Changing World*. Boulder: Westview Press.

—— (1993b). 'Democracy, Authoritarianism and State Strength', *European Journal of Development Research*, 5/1: 6–34.

—— (1997). 'International Conflict and Cooperation: Toward an Analysis of Contemporary Statehood', *Review of International Studies*, 23/3 (July): 253–69.

—— (1998). 'IR Theory After the Cold War', *Review of International Studies*, 24/5: 83–100.

—— (1999). 'Sovereignty: Change and Continuity in a Fundamental Institution', *Political Studies*, 47: 590–604.

—— (2001). *Changes in Statehood. The Transformation of International Relations*. London & New York: Palgrave.

Spegele, R. (1996). *Political Realism in International Theory*. Cambridge: Cambridge University Press.

Spero, J. E. (1985). *The Politics of International Economic Relations*. London: Allen & Unwin.

Spruyt, H. (2002). 'New institutionalism and international relations', in R. Palan (ed.), *Global Political Economy. Contemporary Theories*, London: Routledge, 130–43.

Steans, J. (1998). *Gender and International Relations. An Introduction*. Cambridge: Polity Press.

Stein, A. A. (1990). *Why Nations Cooperate: Circumstance and Choice in International Relations*. Ithaca: Cornell University Press.

Stoessinger, J. G. (1993). *Why Nations Go to War*. New York: St. Martin's Press.

Strange, S. (1970). 'International Economics and International Relations: A Case of Mutual Neglect', *International Affairs*, 46/2: 304–15.

—— (1987). 'The Persistent Myth of Lost Hegemony', *International Organization*, 41: 551–74.

—— (1988). *States and Markets: An Introduction to International Political Economy*. London: Pinter.

—— (1995). 'Theoretical Underpinnings: Conflicts between International Relations and International Political Economy', paper for the British International Studies Association Annual Meeting, Dec., Southampton.

Streeten, P. P. (1979). 'Multinationals Revisited', *Finance and Development*, 16/2: 39–43.

Stubbs, R., and **Underhill, G. R. D.** (1994). *Political Economy and the Changing Global Order*. London: Macmillan.

Swerdlow, A. (1990). 'Motherhood and the Subversion of the Military State: Women Strike for Peace Confronts the House Committee on Un-American Activities', in J.-B. Elshtain and S. Tobias (eds.) (1990), *Women, Militarism, and War: Essays in Politics, History, and Social Theory*. Savage, MD: Rowman & Littlefield.

Sylvester, C. (1994). *Feminist Theory and International Relations in a Postmodern Era*. Cambridge: Cambridge University Press.

Taylor, A. J. P. (1957). *The Trouble Makers: Dissent over Foreign Policy 1792–1939*. London: Panther.

Tetreault, M. A. (1992). 'Women and Revolution: A Framework for Analysis', in V. S. Peterson (ed.), *Gendered States: Feminist (Re) Visions of International Relations Theory*. Boulder: Lynne Rienner.

Thompson, J. E., and **Krasner, S. D.** (1989). 'Global Transactions and the Consolidation of Sovereignty', in E.-O. Czempiel and J. N. Rosenau (eds.), *Global Changes and Theoretical Challenges: Approaches to World Politics for the 1990s*. Lexington, MA: Lexington Books, 195–221.

Thompson, K. W. (1980). *Masters of International Thought: Major Twentieth-Century Theorists and the World Crisis*. Baton Rouge: Louisiana State University Press.

Thompson, W. R. (1996). 'Democracy and Peace: Putting the Cart Before the Horse?', *International Organization*, 50/1; 141–75.

Thucydides (1972). *History of the Peloponnesian War*, trans. R. Warner. London: Penguin.

—— (1980). *The Peloponnesian War*. Harmondsworth: Penguin.

Tilly, C. (1992). *Coercion, Capital and European States*. Oxford: Blackwell.

Tong, R. (1989). *Feminist Thought: A Comprehensive Introduction*. London: Unwin Hyman.

Toye, J. (1987). *Dilemmas of Development: Reflections on the Counterrevolution in Development Theory*. Oxford: Blackwell.

Tranholm-Mikkelsen, J. (1991). 'Neofunctionalism: Obstinate or Obsolete? A Reappraisal in Light of the New Dynamism of the EC', *Millennium*, 20: 1–22.

True, J. (1996). 'Feminism', in S. Burchill and A. Linklater (eds.), *Theories of International Relations*. London: Macmillan, 210–51.

Tucker, R. W. (1977). *The Inequality of Nations*. New York: Basic.

Underdal, A. (1992). 'The Concept of Regime "Effectiveness"', *Cooperation and Conflict*, 27/3: 227–40.

UN (United Nations), *Statistical Yearbook*, annual edns. New York: UN.

—— (1997a). *World Economic and Social Survey 1997*. New York: UN.

—— (1997b). *World Investment Report 1997*. New York: UN.

UNDP (United Nations Development Programme) (Annually). *Human Development Report*. New York: Oxford University Press.

—— (1996). *Human Development Report 1996*. New York: Oxford University Press.

UN General Assembly (1970). *Declaration on Principles of International Law*, Resolution 2625.

Vasquez, J. (1995). 'The Post-Positivist Debate', in K. Booth and S. Smith (eds.), *International Relations Theory Today*. Cambridge: Polity Press, 217–40.

——(1996). *Classics of International Relations*, 3rd edn. Upper Saddle River, NJ: Prentice-Hall.

Vincent, R. J. (1986). *Human Rights and International Relations*. Cambridge: Cambridge University Press.

——(1990). 'Grotius, Human Rights, and Intervention', in H. Bull *et al.* (1990: 241–56).

——and Wilson, P. (1993). 'Beyond Non-Intervention', in I. Forbes and M. Hoffmann (eds.), *Political Theory, International Relations, and the Ethics of Intervention*. London: Macmillan.

Viner, J. (1958). *The Long View and the Short: Studies in Economic Theory and Policy*. New York: Free Press.

Wade, R. (1985). 'State Intervention in Development: Neoclassical Theory and Taiwanese Practice', in G. White and R. Wade (eds.), *Developmental States in East Asia*. Brighton: IDS Research Reports No. 16: 23–62.

Walker, R. B. J. (1995). 'International Relations and the Concept of the Political', in K. Booth and S. Smith (eds.), *International Relations Theory Today*. University Park: Pennsylvania State University Press, 306–28.

Wallerstein, I. (1974). *The Modern World System, i*. New York: Academic Press.

——(1979). *The Capitalist World-Economy: Essays*. Cambridge: Cambridge University Press.

——(1983). *Historical Capitalism*. London: Verso.

——(1984). *The Politics of the World-Economy: The States, Movements, and Civilizations: Essays*. Cambridge: Cambridge University Press.

——(1991). *Unthinking Social Science. The Limits of Nineteenth-Century Paradigms*. Oxford: Polity Press.

Waltz, K. N. (1959). *Man, the State and War. A Theoretical Analysis*. New York: Columbia University Press.

——(1979). *Theory of International Politics*. New York: McGraw-Hill; Reading: Addison-Wesley.

——(1986). 'Reflections on "Theory of International Politics": A Response to My Critics', in R. O. Keohane (ed.), *Neorealism and Its Critics*. New York: Columbia University Press, 322–47.

——(1993). 'The Emerging Structure of International Politics', *International Security*, 18/2: 44–79.

Watson, A. (1982). *Diplomacy: The Dialogue between States*. London: Mcthuen.

——(1992). *The Evolution of International Society*. London: Routledge.

Webber, M. (1995). 'Changing Places in East Asia', in G. I. Clark and W.B. Kim (eds.), *Asian NIEs and the Global Economy*. Baltimore: Johns Hopkins University Press.

Weber, M. (1964). *The Theory of Social and Economic Organization*. New York: Free Press.

Weiss, John (1988). *Industry in Developing Countries: Theory, Policy and Evidence*. London: Croom Helm.

Weiss, T. G., and Collins, C. (1996). *Humanitarian Challenges and Intervention*. Boulder: Westview Press.

Weller, M. (ed.) (1993). *Iraq and Kuwait: The Hostilities and Their Aftermath*. Cambridge: Grotius Publications.

Welsh, J. M. (1995). *Edmund Burke and International Relations*. London: Macmillan.

Wendt, A. (1992), 'Anarchy Is What States Make of It', *International Organization*, 46: 394–419.

——(1995). 'Constructing International Politics', *International Security*, 20/1: 71–81.

——(1999). *Social Theory of International Politics*. Cambridge: Cambridge University Press.

Wheeler, N. (1996). 'Guardian Angel or Global Gangster: a Review of the Ethical Claims of International Society', *Political Studies*, 44: 123–35.

White, G. (1984). 'Developmental States and Socialist Industrialisation in the Third World', *Journal of Development Studies*, 21/1: 97–120.

Wight, M. (1966). 'Why is There No International Theory?' in H. Butterfield and M. Wight (eds.), *Diplomatic Investigations*. London: Allen & Unwin, 12–33.

——(1977). *Systems of States*. Leicester: Leicester University Press.

——(1986). *Power Politics*, 2nd edn. Harmondsworth: Penguin.

——(1987). 'An Anatomy of International Thought', *Review of International Studies*, 13: 221–7.

——(1991). *International Theory: The Three Traditions*, ed. G. Wight and B. Porter. Leicester: Leicester University Press.

World Bank (1994). *World Tables 1994*. Washington DC: World Bank.

——(1996). *World Development Report 1997*. New York: Oxford University Press.

World Commission on Environment and Development (1987). *Our Common Future* (The Brundtland Report). New York: Oxford University Press.

Young, O. R. (1986). 'International Regimes: Toward a New Theory of Institutions', *World Politics*, 39/1: 104–22.

——(1989). *International Cooperation. Building Regimes for Natural Resources and the Environment*. Ithaca: Cornell University Press.

Zacher, M. W. (1992). 'The Decaying Pillars of the Westphalian Temple', in J. N. Rosenau and E.-O. Czempiel (eds.), *Governance Without Government: Order and Change in World Politics*. Cambridge: Cambridge University Press, 58–102.

——and Matthew, R. A. (1995). 'Liberal International Theory: Common Threads, Divergent Strands', in C. W. Kegley, Jr., *Controversies in International Relations: Realism and the Neoliberal Challenge*. New York: St. Martin's Press, 107–50.

Zalewski, M. (1993). 'Feminist Standpoint Theory Meets International Relations Theory: A Feminist Version of David and Goliath?' *Fletcher Forum*, 17: 13–32.

Zartman, W. I. (1995). *Collapsed States: The Disintegration and Restoration of Legitimate Authority*. Boulder: Lynne Rienner.

Zürn, M. (1995). 'The Challenge of Globalization and Individualization: A View from Europe', in H.-H. Holm and G. Sørensen (eds.), *Whose World Order? Uneven Globalization and the End of the Cold War*. Boulder: Westview Press, 137–65.

Index

N